"Helena Allen has written what may be the definitive account of Liliuokalani's overthrow and her life before and after. . .(Allen) came to understand Liliuokalani both as a person and historical figure as well as anyone ever has."
Honolulu Advertiser

"Helena Allen has a respectfully cozy relationship with the later members of Hawaii's reigning family. She writes about them as a longtime friend might, one perhaps who had enjoyed their hospitality over the years and never quite paid it back. She can speak of them intimately, but only in a positive light."
Honolulu Star Bulletin

". . .This is certainly the definitive study of the courageous and valiant woman who reigned but briefly, as queen of the Hawaiian Islands.

To read this volume is to live history, to live alongside a gentle people, to see Hawaii through opened eyes. Truly this is a tribute to a great woman written by an author who cares about the people she has written about."
Redla   ly Facts

". . .a good job of showing t   rson torn between two worlds   nes. . . a worthwhile   es*

"Allen wri   netic to the 'best educate   a Christian queen by education and   ural preservationist by heritage. Deco   liuokalani's diaries at the Bishop Museum, exploring old documents and taking testimony from the queen's adopted daughter, Allen is not so much a revisionist as she is a payer of respects long due."
Los Angeles Times

THE BETRAYAL OF LILIUOKALANI

Last Queen of Hawaii
1838-1917

by
Helena G. Allen

E 'Onipa'a
I Ka 'Imi Na'auao

MUTUAL PUBLISHING
Honolulu, Hawaii

Printed in Australia by Australian Print Group

Cover design by Tamara Moan, Bechlen/Gonzalez Inc.

Cover photos Baker-Van Dyke Collection

*This book contains the complete text of the
original hardbound edition.*

Mutual Publishing
1127 11th Avenue, Mezz. B
Honolulu, Hawaii 96816
Ph: (808) 732-1709
Fax: (808) 734-094
Email: mutual@lava.net
Url: http://www.pete.com/mutual

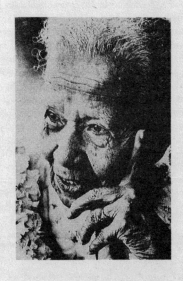

To the memory of
Lydia Kaohohiponiponiokalani Aholo
1878-1979
Hanai daughter of Queen Liliuokalani

Photograph of Lydia Aholo, 1978
Courtesy of *Star Bulletin*, Honolulu.

Contents

Illustrations

Acknowledgments

My special appreciation and thanks go to Clorinda Low Lucas for years of continued encouragement and support, and to Richard Kekuni Blaisdell. It is impossible for me to mention all the dedicated workers in repositories of Hawaii whose help has made the book possible, but I wish to thank Cynthia Timberlake and her excellent staff of the Bernice Pauahi Bishop Museum Library, especially Lynn Davis in photographs; Agnes Conrad and members of her staff of the Hawaiian State Archives, for help and encouragement; Henry J. Bartels for unfailing support at Iolani Palace; Thomas King, Susan Nance, Don Billam-Walker and Sen. Richard Lyman of the Liliuokalani Trust and the Hui Hanai; Mrs. John Burns, while her husband was governor, for a personal tour of Washington Place; Staff members of the Hawaiian Historical Society Library and the Hawaiian Mission Children's Society Library; Dr. E. G. Biggerstaff of the British Public Records Office in London; Dr. Larry Marshburn, Armacost Library, University of Redlands, Redlands, California; Phyllis Irshay and her staff of the A. K. Smiley Public Library, Redlands, California; members of the staff of Mills College Library, California; Oberlin College Records Department, Ohio; New England Historical and Genealogical Society Library, Boston; Howard Library, Harvard University; Boston Public Library (Rare Book Room), and Maine Historical Society, Portland, Maine.

My thanks go to persons who have graciously given me time for personal interviews: Inez Ashdown, Maui; Maude Wodehouse, Aala Akana, and Alii Noa, Hawaii; Virginia Dominis Koch, Oahu.

Special appreciation is given to those persons who generously shared their friendship, time, and private collections with me: Don and Leilehua (Berger) Billam-Walker, David M. Bray, Betty Dole Stodieck, Dr. S. Stillman Berry, Ruth Prosser McLain.

Individuals who have gone out of their way to be of special help are:

Nancy M. Tomlinson, Redlands, California, legal research; Mrs. Eric Cyrus Patch, Boston, genealogy; Dr. Joseph T. McKeon for reading the manuscript, and especially Paul M. Yockey for helpful critical evaluation.

Other technical advice and valuable services in translations, code breaking, research and general helpful suggestions in writing go to Dorothy Barrere, Prof. Alfons Korn, Dr. George Kerr, Edwin Bryan, Larry Kimura, Betty Tatar, Frances Knight, Fanny Burns, Don Britton, Robbie Sprague (Hawaii), and James Vickery (Maine).

Other important services were rendered by Dorothy Banker Turner, Lynn Fugle, Paul H. Letsch, Nancy Bel Weeks, Paul M. Kahn, John Stephenson, Sandra Knight, Richard L. Wilkerson and Dr. Frederick C. Gros for introducing me to Miss Lydia Aholo.

Special thanks to my editor, Robert A. Clark, for firmness coupled with patience. Of course, my appreciation to my husband, Dr. Paul F. Allen, and my son, Randall Kauhimakakaukalani Allen, for help in research, proofreading, and "putting up with me."

My very special thanks must go to my patient, persistent, encouraging friend and typist, Grace Hall Hollenbeck.

HELENA G. ALLEN
Redlands, California

Preface

Those readers with only passing acquaintance of the history and language of Hawaii oft-times find themselves tongue-tied and at a loss when confronted with words dominated by vowels. Differentiating between characters with similar names can become time-consuming and tedious work. It is therefore hoped that the following glossary of terms, place names and characters will help relieve that burden and provide a handy spring-board for the enjoyment of the story.

In preparing this biography, I was confronted with another interesting situation regarding the language. Much work relative to diacritical marks has been done by linguists and students of the language in the past several years—work which will no doubt prove to be of great value to scholars in the field.

During the time span of this biography (1838-1917) these marks had not yet been established. Even now there is some debate about their proper usage and placement. I have therefore chosen not to use them in the text of this work. However, for the benefit of those who will find these marks helpful in pronunciation, the following glossary includes them in the initial definition for each character, term or place.

Ali'i: chief
'Aumakua: household god
Hānai: "foster" child or parent
Haole: foreigner
Hapa-haole: half-Hawaiian/
   half-*haole*
Kahili: feather standard
Kahuna (pl. Kāhuna): priest
Kahu: servant
Kapu: forbidden
Kane: man (also a god)

Konohiki: overseer
Kuhina nui: premier
Lanai: shed, porch or booth
Lei: garland of flowers worn
   around the neck
Mana: authority, power, wisdom,
   might
Mahalo: thank you
Mo'i: king
Mo'i wahine: queen

PLACES

Haleakalā: home of Liliuokalani
with Bishops

Hamohamo: Waikiki

Hawai'i: the island chain

Kawaiaha'o Church: Missionary
Church

Kealohilani: Liliuokalani's home
at Waikiki

Muolaulani: Liliuokalani's home
in Palama district

Paoakalani: Liliuokalani's home
at Waikiki

PRINCIPAL CHARACTERS

Joseph Aea: father of Kaipo Aea

Kaheo Aea: mother of Kaipo Aea

Kaipo Aea: *hanai* son of
Liliuokalani

Lydia Aholo: *hanai* daughter of
Liliuokalani

Aikanaka: Liliuokalani's grandfather (mother's father)

John Aimoku: *hanai* son of Liliuokalani and blood son of John
Owen Dominis

Mary Purdy Lamiki Aimoku:
mother of John Aimoku

Prince Albert, "Prince of Hawaii":
son of Kamehameha IV

Auhea: Premier after Kinau,
mother of Lunalilo

Henry Berger: German Bandmaster

Prince Bill: see Lunalilo

Charles Reed Bishop: husband of
Bernice Pauahi

Archibald Cleghorn: husband of
Likelike

Juliette and Amos Starr Cooke:
teachers at Royal School

Sanford Ballard Dole: president
of Hawaiian Republic

John Owen Dominis: Liliuokalani's husband

Mary Lambert Jones Dominis:
mother-in-law of Liliuokalani

Walter Murray Gibson: Prime
Minister for King Kalakaua

Curtis P. Iaukea: friend and advisor to Liliuokalani in sanity
suit

John I'i: Hawaiian teacher

Ka'ahumanu: Kamehameha I's
favorite wife

Kaikai: Liliuokalani's nursemaid

Princess Ka'iulani: child of Likelike and Cleghorn

King (David) Kalākaua: Liliuokalani's brother, preceeding her
on throne

Queen Kalama: Kamehameha
III's wife

Jonah Kūhiō Kalaniana'ole:
nephew of Kapiolani

Lili'u Kamaka'eha: Liliuokalani's
name given at birth

Kameeiamoku: Liliuokalani's
grandfather (father's side)

Kamehameha I: unifier of
Hawaiian islands

Kamehameha II: son of first
Kamehameha and successor

Kamehameha III: second son of
first Kamehameha and King at
time of Liliuokalani's birth

Kamehameha IV: see Liholiho

Kamehameha V: see Lot

Kanaina: father of Lunalilo

Kapaʻakea: Liliuokalani's blood father

Queen Kapiʻolani: Kalakaua's wife

Prince David Kawānanakoa: nephew of Kapiolani

Keawe-a-Heulu: Liliuokalani's ancestor (mother's side)

Kekaulike: sister-in-law to Kalakaua

Keohokalole: Liliuokalani's blood mother

Keōpuōlani: Kamehameha I's sacred wife

Kīnau: Premier at time of Liliuokalani's birth

Konia: Liliuokalani's *hanai* mother

Leleiōhoku: brother of Liliuo-kalani

Liholiho: successor to Kameha-meha III as Kamehameha IV

Likelike: sister of Liliuokalani

Liliʻuokalani: last queen of Hawaii

Prince Lot: successor to and brother of Liholiho as Kamehameha V

Lunalilo (Prince Bill): successor as king to Kamehameha V

Prince Moses: student at Royal School

Nāhiʻenaʻena: daughter of Kamehameha I

Mary Purdy Pahau: grandmother of John Aimoku

Paki: Liliuokalani's *hanai* father

Lydia Paki: Liliuokalani's "Christian" name

Bernice Pauahi (Bishop): Liliuokalani's *hanai* sister

Princess Poomaikelani: sister-in-law to Kalakaua

Emma Rooke: student at Royal School, later Queen Emma

Princess Ruth: half-sister of Kamehameha IV and V

Lorrin Thurston: adversary of Liliuokalani

Princess Victoria: Liliuokalani's childhood friend (Kinau's child)

Introduction

Early in 1917, eight months before she died, Liliuokalani called Lydia K. Aholo, her *hanai* (foster) daughter, to her side. She exacted a promise from Lydia to tell her "true and complete story." "My story is a universal one," she said. "The same betrayal of all peoples can happen if 'they' do not understand."

These were words spoken by a sensitive, perceptive student of history, philosophy, religion, Hawaiian traditions and cultures, and one who had gained an intuitive insight into people of many races in her seventy-nine years. Liliuokalani lived during a little-known period of Hawaiian history, the period between "early Hawaii" and United-States-Government-Hawaii: The Hawaiian Monarchial Period.

In 1969, at the age of ninety-two, "Miss Lydia," as she was then known, chose me, a *haole*, or non-Hawaiian, to carry out the promise given a half-century before, saying, "For what other reason have I outlived all those who knew her, only to find you?" Miss Lydia had over the years been reluctant to speak in detail about her queen, and would never allow her brief interviews to be taped. However, she gave me, in a span of two years, over thirty hours of taped interviews, revealing some of the most intimate and personal experiences and thoughts of Liliuokalani. She also pressed on me another burden: "I trust you to tell the truth."

I must admit I did not, at the time, believe Miss Lydia's reminiscences to be completely accurate, because the story was so startlingly different and new from what was generally known about "Hawaii." I therefore began an in-depth research for documentation of activities, persons, times, and places. This project was both fascinating and frustrating, for it was the custom among the Hawaiian royal *alii* (high chiefs) to have all their papers destroyed immediately after their death. This problem was compounded in Liliuokalani's case by the wanton destruction of manuscripts, letters, papers, and diaries by members of the Provisional Government;

not only her own, but also those of her brother—the former king—
and even those of her husband. Tragically, all the remaining possessions
of the monarchy that could be found were later sold at auction after
the American annexation. Many valuable materials, even revealing "marked" newspaper clippings, were scattered across the United States and into
Europe, beyond the reach of the Hawaiian repositories.

Many writers of Liliuokalani have been misled by placing the emphasis of her life on the abrogation of the monarchy. The panorama of
her life shows her country was politically lost to other powers before
her birth—the final overthrow in 1893 was politically inevitable. She had
been betrayed not only by persons, but by the changing culture from
before her birth.

Liliuokalani's life dramatizes the Hawaiian story as lived by a high
born Hawaiian Chief, an *alii*, from 1838 to 1917. More important, it reveals the amazing elasticity of the human spirit, if endowed with the
Hawaiian *aloha*, to survive intact monumental historical, social, economic,
and political changes, while caught in the vortex of clashing cultures and
mores.

It was a special kind of Fate that selected Liliuokalani to be born of
the bodies of the Keawe line (Kalakaua and Liliuokalani dynasty), but
to be given in *hanai* to be reared by a Kamehameha heir; for had the
latter not happened, we would have no record of her whatsoever until
she was thirty-four. Only through studying the better documented lives
of the members of the Kamehameha line, do we get our glimpses of the
young Liliu. On the other hand, had she not been born of the Keawe
line, she would never have become a princess nor a queen, and we would
never have known her at all through history.

From being born on a pandanus-mat floor in a grass hut, she would
one day tread on Oriental rugs at home and abroad. From being wrapped
in tapa cloth, to being clad in fashionable Paris gowns of black velvet,
adorned with broaches, wearing pearl earrings, and diamond buckles on
her shoes; from dipping her fingers into wooden calabashes filled with *poi*
and drinking coconut milk from hulls, to using sterling silver forks for
pate-de-foie-gras on gold-plated china and drinking the best wines from
the finest crystals, she weathered radical cultural change in her private
and public life.

She was to become known for writing "Aloha Oe," but she was a
writer of over 200 songs—words and music. She was to be noted by

historians as the "dethroned queen of Hawaii," but to her people she was never "dethroned."

Hers was a life of outer drama and inner conflict. It was first and foremost a love story—not for a man, nor even for many men—but for mankind, specifically her beloved Hawaiian people; but she came to include members of all races in Hawaii, even those who had vilified her, dethroned her, impoverished her, desecrated her land, and nearly completed total genocide.

Through five ruling kings, a provisional government, a republic, and a territorial government, she lived through traumatic times which generated incest, doctrinal cruelty, sexual abandonment versus sexual repression, alcoholism, drug abuse, and terrorism; religious, educational, speech and press misuse were rampant. She saw values change from the intangibles of love of country, appreciation of nature, reverence to gods—or God— to tangibles of position, power, property, and money.

She was accused of sorcery, planning a political assassination, adultery, promiscuity, savagery, dealing in the occult, treason, and misprision. She was a victim of deceit, attempted murder, imprisonment, poverty, degradation, personal humiliation from pulpit and press, and above all, betrayal not only by her avowed enemies but by those closest to her, those whom she loved and trusted.

As a woman, she was excitingly female without being sensual, leading men in all walks of life to come to her aid, but often expecting more than she was able in her Victorian-upbringing to give. These experiences led to disappointment, heartbreak, blackmail, and once to great, fulfilling joy. She was a feminist, a musician, a woman in a matriarchal society—none of which were appreciated by the foreigners of her time.

All her life she was deeply concerned with religion. She could not correlate the many happenings in the world about her with the Christian doctrine as it had been taught her. She moved through the orthodox Protestant religions, Catholicism, Mormonism, Metaphysics and both Eastern and Western mysticism to a renewed interest in Christian-Kahunaism. At the end of her life she came to a synthesis of her own, which she felt was the basis of mysticism, hidden in all religions.

The purpose of this book is not to judge categorically either the actions of the queen or the opposition, but it is to show forth the betrayal of the rights of a country, its people, and its rulers, especially the betrayal of Hawaii's last queen, Liliuokalani. She was betrayed from the moment of her birth by the changing concept of *hanai;* she was betrayed by the lack of understanding of the Hawaiian *alii* at the Royal School. She was betrayed by cultural differences in her marriage. She was betrayed by her brother's ambivalence; by both *haole* and natives during the two years she was queen—by her cabinet, her friends, and members of her household. Even after the overthrow of her government, she continued to be betrayed in her personal life.

Miss Lydia Aholo, her *hanai* (foster) daughter, lived to be 101. On June 13, 1979, in a slight drifting rain, I stood at Miss Lydia's graveside, and listened to her nephew, Alfred Apaka, Senior, sing "Aloha Oe," the Queen's best-known composition. Then I heard a voice asking, "Is there a tiny rainbow for Miss Lydia?" Mrs. Laura Thompson, granddaughter of the ward of Sanford B. Dole, opponent of Liliuokalani, had turned to Mrs. Virginia Dominis Koch, Liliuokalani's adopted son's daughter. Reaching across time of dissension, these two women metaphorically joined hands in *aloha,* to look for the rainbow of promise and tribute to the death of an *alii.*

I looked, as they did, to the Nuuanu Valley, and there fast retreating into that unchanging, misty valley was a tiny shimmering rainbow, as fragile, as beautiful, as mysterious, and as full of promise as the Spirit of Aloha, and as elusive.

This story, inspired by Miss Lydia, has been thoroughly substantiated and documented, footnoted accordingly. It is the *untold* story of the betrayal of the Hawaiians and their last queen, Liliuokalani, from 1838-1917.

If I have achieved any of the true *aloha* in telling it, I owe it to my patient, kind, generous, and loving Hawaiian friends. If I have failed, it is my own failure.

HELENA G. ALLEN
Redlands, California

PART I
The Old Ways in Transition

Liliu Kamakaeha to Lydia Paki
1838-1848

CHAPTER 1

Hawaii Nei[1]

❧ 1 ❧

In 1838 Hawaii was eight islands united into one kingdom under one king—Kamehameha III—second son of Kamehameha the First and his sacred wife, Keopuolani.[2] Kamehameha III ruled a gentle, contented people of some 40,000 Hawaiians. At the time of his father, before *haole* or white foreigners' disease had begun to take its toll, the population had been 300,000. Through his father the islands had been united, wars had ceased—wars, in which the commoners and lesser chiefs had fought for the *moi*[3] (kings) of each island against each other. The wars had finally centered around the steady gain and final conquest of Kamehameha I in 1795, just seventeen years after Captain James Cook had discovered the Sandwich Islands, named for the Earl of Sandwich. War was over, and the commoner had returned to till the land of *alii* (high chiefs) to fish, to nap, when and where he wished, in a leisurely life in a leisurely climate of soft tradewinds, gentle rains, warm sunshine, fragrant flowers, and many-hued rainbows. It was a world in which the gods were exceedingly good.

Kamehameha I had, however, foreseen the inadequacy of his first son as a ruler. Although he allowed his son and heir the title of "Kamehameha II," he established the office *kuhina nui* (premier), thereby making provisions for his favorite and talented wife, Kaahumanu, to be the real power in the kingdom after his death in 1819. From earliest time, Hawaiian rulers, through genealogical descent from the gods and goddesses, had set a precedence for holding women in high esteem. Through Kaahumanu, Hawaii became a matriarchal society, with the peoples' love for their queen or *moi wahine* bordering on adulation.

It was Kaahumanu who was responsible for overthrowing the *kapu* (laws or taboos). The young Kamehameha II played only a small, puppet part. What began with Kaahumanu's personal wish for her own freedom from the restrictive *kapu* of having to eat separate from the men, and of other foods, such as bananas and roast pig, resulted in open rebellion against all the *kapu*.

When Kaahumanu persuaded Kamehameha II, with the help of Keopuolani, to sit between his two "mothers" at the men's long mahogany table at a feast held for foreigners and native chiefs, she had no idea of the chaos that would follow. The astonished guests, at first unbelievingly beheld the two *kapu* defiantly broken without retribution from the gods. Fire did not fall from heaven; the earth did not shake; the sea did not send out huge tidal waves; sudden death did not even come to the large, placid chiefess, who contentedly licked her fingers and reached for more roast pig.

Then pandemonium broke loose. There were no gods! Men and women mingled hysterically, sharing food and caresses. All the *kapu* must go! There were no gods! The *kahuna* (priests) were false teachers! They must die! The *kahuna* fled in a shower of stones, coconuts, and clubs. In the days that followed, the *heiau* (temples) were torn down, and general destruction prevailed.

Had a group of foreigners not been present at the feast, it is possible that the overthrow of all the *kapu* would not have been so complete. But the *haole* now saw total freedom for themselves—sexual, political, social—without realizing what would happen to the foundations of Hawaiian life. Many of the lesser chiefs joined them. Kaahumanu knew. The high chiefs knew. But the people were out of control with sudden freedom.

The *kapu* had been the guiding mores of the Hawaiian people, forming the essence of their economic, social, and religious life. They established the class structure and held it firm, keeping the *alii* apart from the *haole* and the commoners. The *kahuna* set the *kapu,* which established the moral standards, religious worship, healing processes provided by the gods and herbs, and the mystical right of prayer to a power greater than man.

Kaahumanu was wise enough to see what her personal desire had cost her people; she helped countless *kahuna,* including Kamehameha's own—Hewahewa—to escape. She also knew that although unpleasant yokes can be cast off in a day, century-old beliefs and customs do not yield so quickly. The Hawaiians would not easily lose their gods nor their way of life.

She wisely allowed the oppressive *kapu* to go, but she recognized a need for laws—which were to arrive in less than a year with the missionaries. In an uneasy vacuum Kaahumanu waited for she knew not what.

The missionaries sailed into a religious vacuum in 1820. The old gods were officially gone; Kaahumanu saw a way to provide new laws and fill the obvious need of the people for a "god."

The Hawaiian people, like many people who live close to nature, had always been spiritually oriented, mystically religious. They saw the gods in softly colored rainbow, in the calm and angry foamy sea, in the volcanic flame, in the shadowy trees, in the black lava rocks, in the *aumakua* or family gods,[4] and in themselves—for how else could there be life? Everywhere was life. So everywhere were the gods.

By 1838, the missionaries, despite the rapid building of church structures to take the place of *heiau,* had not yet made strong in-roads among the natives. Many of the natives had retreated into the valleys taking their household gods with them, as well as harboring their *kahuna.* The missionaries concentrated their work on the *alii,* especially the royal household; it was believed that where the chiefs went, the commoners would follow.

2

In the beautiful valleys where bananas, coconuts, breadfruit and other staples flourished in a mild climate of gentle rain and warm sunshine, the natives lived as retainers to their *alii*. Goods and services were their way of life. They served their *alii* in building his grass huts and his canoes and in providing transportation. The young *alii* was always accompanied by at least one *kahu* (servant), whether walking or riding a horse. And the *kahu* was responsible for his safety.

The retainers cultivated the land of the *alii* and provided him with worldly needs. In turn he gave them shelter in grass huts, quite adequate in a seasonless land of warmth and ease, where one could sleep out-of-doors the year round except during a drenching, but god-sent, rain. The commoners owned no land of their own, but unlike the serfs of Europe, they wanted none. Their life was good. In general the *alii* were generous and kind to their retainers. Why shouldn't they be? Chiefs had been chosen because all men need leaders.[5] And the leaders came from the best—chiefs who had proved themselves valiant in battle. To be successful in battle one had to be close to the gods, and, without doubt, god-descended. Had not Kamehameha the Great proved this by his remarkable lineage from the first gods, and had not Goddess Pele of volcanic vengeance helped him win his battles? And now in 1838 the Kamehameha dynasty reigned through his second son, Kamehameha III, whose only fault, many of the high chiefs thought, was listening to the foreigners. And if the chiefs thought so, then the people did also.

Kamehameha II was sadly remembered as a king who had listened too closely to the *haole*. His foreign-indoctrinated greed had resulted in a depletion of the forests of sandalwood, finally halted by a royal *kapu* delivered by Kaahumanu. Even sadder was his sailing from their midst to England, where he and his wife had died in 1824, far from home and his people.[6]

The people thought well of their *alii*, who expected royal treatment, but gave generously as well. No one hesitated to ask of the *alii* if his own need became acute. For an *alii* to have refused aid of any kind, would have been a breach in *aloha*, generosity in this sense, and the admittance that his *mana*, or power and spiritual wisdom, wasn't great.

The royal and high *alii* were far less demanding than the lesser chiefs, *konihiki* (overseers), whose ancestors were not gods, and who did not have the *aloha* and *mana* of the high chiefs. All men were not equal, and the further one fell from the god-descendants and *alii* ancestry, the less one had of *aloha* and *mana*.

These lesser chiefs could be harsh, cruel, and unjustly demanding, but any retainer who wished had a right to pick up his chicken, his pig, his women and children and move to the household of another *alii*, who had a kinder overseer. Therefore the highest *alii* had the most retainers, and, among them, often the laziest, for all retainers, like all men, were not equal.

❦ 3 ❦

In the back country the commoners lived with little change from the past except in their freedom from the oppressive *kapu* and wars. The native Hawaiian worshipped as he always had, offering prayers to his gods before every activity. A man had no right to take more from the land or sea than he needed for himself or those with whom he had trade. If greed overtook him and he took more than was required in order to sell for the new commodity, Spanish money, the gods would punish him, and it would take a *kahuna* to save his life.

The *kahuna* continued to play an important role: they were the spiritual guides who set social and economic, as well as moral and religious, standards. They chose and blessed the trees that were to be made into canoes. They were the healers—thus they held a power of life and death.

Both men and women completed their days with prayers of joy for the *aloha* of the gods. In the long somnolent evenings they gathered to tell the legends of their people—of great warriors and of the gods and goddesses, who had made possible this wonderful world of contentment. To the accompaniment of the beat of the gourd drum, they repeated the old *mele,* or chants, which held a poetic and reverent history that had been handed down from generation to generation for the education of their children.[7] They also composed their own chants of their *aumakua.* Each child was expected to remember every *aumakua* and every chant. The *mele* held not one, but numerous, meanings. The obvious one told of praise and glory of heroes and gods. The "hidden one," known to the elders, revealed the meaning of the parable; and the sacred one, interpreted only by the *kahuna,* disclosed its spiritual mysticism.

The women lived good lives. They sometimes helped the men in the taro patches, but as often the men did the cooking in the cook house. The women took the felted tapa, made from beaten mulberry leaves, gathered by their men, and created intricate designs that competed in originality, detail, and "story." They began to learn quilting from the missionaries, and the old tapa designs were transferred to the quilts.

On the long, warm, seasonless days, the women had another occupation. They spent many hours massaging the hands, feet, arms, legs and bodies of their children in order to make their bodies supple in the dream that one day a particular girl-child would be chosen to be the court hula dancer—the highest honor that could befall a commoner. Both male and female children could become court dancers, but the highest privilege was to be a solo-hula dancer for the king.

If chosen, the child received rigid special training from a hula-*kahuna.* Both sexes remained virgins throughout their training period, and the girls were sacred even from the royalty through their entire time as hula dancers. The hula was an expression and depiction of life and love for the Hawaiian; it was nature; it was the gods; it was man and woman; it was *life.*

There were not so many celebrations now as before the missionaries had come, but there were a few. The birth or death of a member of the royal family called the natives from afar. A conch shell blower, telling of such an event while standing on the shores of the sea, could be heard echoing into the far valleys. A royal death was still the greatest of occasions. From the time the royal one died to the burial two to three weeks later—while the spirit lay dormant before ascending to the gods above—

was a period of mourning. Although few in 1838, as in "ancient" times, cut off their hair or knocked out their teeth to show proper grief, nevertheless, the time of mourning gave vent to a magnificent display of unbridled emotion from continuous wailing and copious tears to excessive sexual freedom—a not unnatural transition of uncontrolled passion: comfort in grief.

Whether the native Hawaiian went forth to till his taro patch, fish in the sea, or roam the streets of Lahaina on the Island of Maui or Honolulu on Oahu, he went with a song on his lips and a flower in his hat—if he had a hat—or a lei of fragrant maile leaves or heavy scented blossoms about his neck. Song and flowers were as indigenous to the Hawaiian as the rain, the rainbow, the sea, the air, the misty mountains, the verdant growth, the ease with which the red soil produced plenty were native to Hawaii.

And wherever he went he said "Aloha" in meeting or in parting. "Aloha" was a recognition of life in another. If there was life there was *mana,* goodness and wisdom, and if there was goodness and wisdom there was a god-quality. One had to recognize the "god of life" in another before saying "Aloha," but this was easy. Life was everywhere—in the trees, the flowers, the ocean, the fish, the birds, the pili grass, the rainbow, the rock—in all the world was life—was god—was *aloha. Aloha* in its gaiety, joy, happiness, abundance. Because of *aloha,* one gave without thought of return; because of *aloha,* one had *mana. Aloha* had its own *mana.* It never left the giver but flowed freely and continuously between giver and receiver. "Aloha" could not be thoughtlessly or indiscriminately spoken, for it carried its own power. No Hawaiian could greet another with "Aloha" unless he felt it in his own heart. If he felt anger or hate in his heart he had to cleanse himself before he said "Aloha." Life had a tremendous spirituality in the paradise of the Pacific in 1838.

Honolulu, on Oahu, and Lahaina, on Maui, the main seaports, were not unlike hundreds of other western world seaports, except for the diversity of the people. Of the two, Lahaina was more placid, with luxurious growth of taro and banana patches and a misty rising background beyond which grew the scarlet lehua blossoms, sacred to the Goddess Pele of the distant volcanic crater of Haleakala.

But Honolulu was more striking, from its sentinel, Diamond Head, to the wide coconut groves of Waikiki and the broad plain beyond which was rapidly being filled with buildings. On the water front were stone quays, dockyards, and storehouses. As one moved inland among the native grass structures one could also see frame buildings of stores, as well as premature consulates, and the large wood-constructed Blonde Hotel—an active house of prostitution, owned by a high chief and later taken over by a man of the cloth.

Nearer Punch Bowl Hill, inland, the king had his Honolulu seat of government. Surrounded by a sturdy fence was a large compound of thatched buildings for eating, sleeping, and conducting government business, and smaller buildings housing royal retainers and innumerable others who had sought the excitement of town life. The royal guards, dressed in white and scarlet uniforms, paraded before the palace. The king himself appeared in a Windsor uniform when he was in residence, for the official capital was at Lahaina.

The seaport was a bustling place, filled with sailors seeking drink and women; the merchants, advertising their wares. The missionary women picked up their long black skirts and studiously looked away from the sailors, who called out to them, "Hey, Longnecks!" Color seeped up the long necks, tightly encased in high white, lace-edged collars, to suffuse the faces of the ladies. Yet they waited urgently, despite the insolence and humiliation that surrounded them, for letters from home with news as much as three to six months old. The men, in their black coats, high hats, and stern expressions, hid their desire for letters behind a haughty indifference and pretended to wait only for the unloading of supplies: barrels of flour, sugar, molasses, and an occasional special package sent from "home." The "rag barrels" from the Mission Society were becoming less frequent, but friends and relatives remembered their "brothers and sisters" in the savage Sandwich Islands[8] with material for a dress, a sun bonnet, a small personal memento such as a lock of hair, and surprisingly in the climate replete with flowers—bulbs.

The sailors jostled aside the curious natives, who were colorfully, if oddly, dressed in cast-off trousers, or merely a top hat, worn proudly with their loin cloths. Intermingling, but ignored, were the early-arrival Chinese, both men and women dressed in their tight black trousers reaching just above their ankles—and brown or black jackets.

The conch-shell blower notified the country people that a ship was in port. Many, still unfamiliar with ships, came to see it and its strangers, and to acquire some of the new drink—the rum, the wine, the gin, or the whisky—all of which excitingly loosened the inhibitions, as the old alcoholic, but soporific, *awa* root drink, did not.

Many of them, especially the young, intrigued by the new ways, decided to stay in the seaports. Both young and old, soon failing in the new competitive world of the *haole,* sought refuge among the *alii,* who housed and fed an enormous number of non-productive retainers. But such was *aloha* and the *mana* of the high chiefs, as well as of the king, the *moi.*

A new population of young girls was available to the sailors. These were, besides a few of the country-excitement-seeking native girls, primarily half-Hawaiian, those who had been left as seed-reminders of early *haole* visits and had now grown into young girlhood. The *alii* were strict about keeping their blood lines pure, except in rare instances when a *haole* had proved himself valuable to the king, as John Young and Isaac Davis had. They had been given Hawaiian *alii* wives.

Many, both chiefs and commoners, left on shore after the ship sailed, entered enthusiastically into church building; and churches, fashioned after New England models, sprang up with remarkable rapidity. Attendance at the church services—the sermon given in a peculiarly pronounced Hawaiian or an even stranger language, New England American—was surprisingly well attended by the natives. Women sat on the matted floor, while the men stood against the walls. The *alii* were accorded rough-hewn benches. All seemed to listen avidly to the condemnation of their sins and to a possible, but not probable, salvation from the new, vengeful Calvinistic God.

Even the missionaries questioned whether the crowds were due to religious repentance and fervor or a desire to see how the *alii* would be dressed. The *alii* never disappointed the people.

From the purple velvet suit trimmed in gold worn by the king, to the cloaks of multi-colored feathers, the multi-layered tapa skirts and trains, the feathered skirts lined with the brightest red, yellow or purple satin, the royalty gave both pageantry and flowers to an environment which banned both. The sanctuary was permeated by an almost overwhelming sweet fragrance from the flowers conspicuously adorning the *alii*—it was well worth going to church to see these magnificent people.

❧ 4 ❧

In 1838 Kamehameha III was king in his own right. Kamehameha II, his brother, had considered himself king in name only, as indeed he was. He had grown increasingly resentful of the matriarchal control of Kaahumanu and of the missionaries, and when his sacred mother, Keopuolani died, with the words, "I believe in Christ Jesus. The Hawaiian gods are false," the missionaries were overjoyed, and so was Kamehameha II—but for different reasons. It set him free to travel to England with his favorite wife-and-half-sister; he left his younger brother as his proclaimed heir. With his death in England, the second son of Kamehameha I, only thirteen, became Kamehameha III in 1825.

The new Kamehameha inherited many problems, not the least of which was his being in love with his own sister, Nahienaena. In the old traditional ways he would have married her, for she was closest in blood to his rank; but now the missionaries cried "Incest!" Kaahumanu, leaning toward Christianity, along with some of the other high chiefs, was against the marriage, but many of the other high chiefs were not.

Deprived of his marriage, but certainly not of the love of his sister, Kamehameha III began his rule with drunkenness, debauchery, card playing, and total disinterest in governmental procedures, leaving all government to Kaahumanu, as his brother had done.

When Kaahumanu died, as a professing Christian, the missionaries felt they had made a great step forward, but almost immediately after her death, Kamehameha III married his sister in the home of High Chief Paki. Nahienaena[9] had all her life rocked between the Christian missionaries at Lahaina and the incestuous love of her brother in Honolulu. Now she turned her back on the missionaries to go to her brother, but not for long. She was threatened with excommunication—eternal damnation— and so was prevailed upon to give up her brother-husband and marry another high chief, Leleiohoku, in a Christian ceremony. She did so, but when her child was about to be born, she was brought to the palace for the birth, and every indication was given that the child was Kamehameha's. Nahienaena never recovered from child-birth, and when she died, Kamehameha was terrified, for the missionaries told him that it was the "will of God," for they had sinned unforgivably.

On a premise all his own, Kamehameha decided that he would rectify the sin of his sister by marrying before she was buried, so that she would not be damned. While Nahienaena lay in state awaiting burial, Hiram Bingham, a missionary, performed the Christian wedding ceremony of Kamehameha III and High Chiefess Kalama.

Nahienaena had two funeral ceremonies: one in Honolulu following the Western traditions with the high chiefs marching in procession, and a small cart draped in black silk carrying her coffin, escorted by *kahili* bearers. The second service was held in Maui and much more to Hawaiian liking. A roadway had been cut through the kou groves, going from the sea to the mountains, surfaced in sand, grass, and over-laid with mats —like the royal highways of the ancient times. In a long cortege of high chiefs, Nahienaena's coffin was born to rest. The natives watched and wailed.

The Hawaiian kingdom was shaken. The chant "The chiefs joined together the earth will be eternal . . . while the chiefs join the earth abides"[10] trembled on the weak but far-carrying winds of the Old Hawaii across the waters to the eight islands. A royal marriage between brother and sister and the union of such a marriage would have great *mana,* such was the deep belief of the Hawaiians.

But now even the King feared before the new God and his emissaries. No longer were old customs to remain inviolate. Traditions of old were scattered on the wild hurricane winds of something new and strange and fearful.

Eighteen months later, in this twilight of Old Hawaii and the dawn of New Hawaii, the last queen of Hawaii, Liliuokalani, was born. She was to live in the fast fading light of one and the tenuous new light of the other that was to proceed to a new day, a new way of life. Before that new day would end, greater sadness than any of the past would afflict all the Hawaiians.

Kamehameha III moved his capital to Lahaina on Maui. He acknowledged fully that Kinau, his half-sister and wife of the governor of Oahu, was the new Premier, taking Kaahumanu's place. At Lahaina he established his government with a Council of High Chiefs who included his old friend, Paki; Paki's wife, Konia; and High Chiefess Keohokalole, the mother-to-be of Liliu Kamakaeha, later known as Liliuokalani.

Holding fast to one of the few remaining revered customs, Keohokalole promised her next-to-be-born child to High Chief Paki and High Chiefess Konia in *hanai*—one of the oldest and most beautiful customs among the Hawaiians. It involved the greatest of all gifts—one's own child—being given to a beloved friend. It was *aloha.* It was love in its highest sense. It also achieved greater *mana* for the child and cemented relationships among the high chiefs.

The Infant Alii

❧ 1 ❧

On September 2, 1838,[1] Liliu Kamakaeha, later to be known as Queen Liliuokalani, was born in a high chief's compound, for her mother, Keohokalole, through her father, Aikanaka, came from high chiefly descent. Liliu's father, Kapaakea, was of a lesser line, but also traced his ancestry to chiefly warriors.

His grass-thatched compound, at the foot of Punch Bowl Hill, was not unlike the king's except it had no sturdy fence around it. There were the similar grass structures for eating, cooking, sleeping, and sheltering numerous retainers. In the largest of these huts Keohokalole awaited the birth of her third child.[2]

She was attended by other high chiefesses, her women retainers, a midwife, and a *kahuna*. The chiefesses sat at a small table playing cards, fanning themselves, smoking short pipes and making use of the small gourds, containing a few blades of grass—spittoons.

Outside the hot sun shone mercilessly down and there seemed to be no cooling shower in sight to give respite from the heat. But more important, the heavens were not signalling the birth of a great *alii* with thunder, lightning, and heavy rain. Indeed it was an inauspicious day for the birth of an *alii*, especially one who was to be *hanai* to the granddaughter of Kamehameha I.

The men lounged under the trees, on grassy mounds of straw, finding comfort in their pipes and poi. Keohokalole's family were court chanters and composers of *mele*, so now they heralded the birth of the about-to-be born child by tracing the family genealogy and telling of the great deeds of their ancestors.[3]

Some of the men listened diffidently, but two were especially attentive. One, her father, High Chief Kapaakea, lounging against a soft mound of straw was strangely stirred by the chanters who linked the child's genealogical descent with his great-grandfather, Kameeiamoku. The latter was honored in the chant as one of the high chiefs who in 1790 had joined Keawe-a-Heulu in aiding Kamehameha the Great. It was recorded that he had also been instrumental in bringing Kamehameha two valuable foreign seamen and advisors, Isaac Davis and John Young.

The second listener was the more important. He stood apart from the other chiefs, the retainers, and the chanters. This was High Chief Aikanaka. Tall and straight, as became a Hawaiian *alii*, he stood under a hau tree, also listening. He heard with pride the exploits of *Keawe-a-Heulu*.

Both men felt that many years had passed—actually only forty-three— since Kamehameha the Great had declared himself *moi*, king, of United Hawaii. Now the royal dynasty of the Kamehameha line was firmly established. Kamehameha's last heir to the throne, Kamehameha III, had no children of his own, but had been given in *hanai* his half-sister's three children, who would be his heirs. And these children and grandchildren would go on for many years, peacefully ruling Hawaii.

At the moment the two men were proud and content as high chiefs. The genealogical recitation pleased them, for it told also of the Tradition of Creation, of their god-descent, and of their *mana*—their strength and wisdom.

The changes Aikanaka had seen in the years since Captain Cook had arrived were great. There were now small coffee and sugar plantations, churches, a printing machine, which not only printed Bibles and missionary tracts, but a newspaper, with unusual markings that were words. When he *heard* them, however, they were strangely different from the spoken language he knew.[4] Aikanaka himself could not read nor write; therefore, the missionaries had not allowed him to be a Christian.[5] He did not regret this. In fact, it rather pleased him that now the chanters had not included in the chant deeds of his aunt by marriage, Kapiolani, a Christian who had defied the goddess Pele by picking the sacred berries that grew near the volcano and hurling them defiantly into the vast maw. Aikanaka was not sure that Kapiolani had been too wise. Although nothing had happened to her *then*—well, the gods could be waiting.

The missionaries had made much of her "bravery." Aikanaka held his own counsel. Why were so many of his people dying if the gods were satisfied with the new ways and with a new God?

Inside the windowless grass hut, the air was filled with the heavy odor of human birth, pain, perspiration, and of old and new flesh. The heat of

KAPAAKEA
Father of Liliuokalani
Courtesy, H.L. Chase:
Bishop Museum.

KEOHOKALOLE
Mother of Liliuokalani

the day pressed down even more oppressively upon the woman lying on the many-layered pandanus mats which lay on the smooth pebbled floor. The women retainers walled the room, their long, loose tent-like garments clinging to their sweat drenched bodies closing out any breeze that might have come into the room through the woven structure.

Suddenly, the midwife moved with the *kahuna,* for the large chiefess had cried out. The child was born quickly, and the *kahuna* blessed it immediately and almost surreptitiously, for *kahuna* were not yet welcome where missionaries might appear at any moment.

Suddenly there was a cry from outside, echoing the cry of the child within, and the women moved quickly and gratefully through the single door of the windowless grass hut. A few drops of rain had fallen from the cloudless sky leaving pock marks on the hard red soil. But in the ever-misty Nuuanu Valley a rainbow spanned the dim green hillsides, dropping almost into the ground.

"Alii Alii! That is the sign of our *alii!"* the men cried out.

Within a few hours the child was to be wrapped in soft felted tapa of beaten bark from the mulberry trees to be taken to Konia and Paki by a high chiefess who had witnessed the birth, so there would be no question that this child was one worthy of *hanai* to the granddaughter of Kamehameha the Great.

But first Kinau, as the highest ranking chiefess of the land, the half-sister of the king and wife of the Governor of Oahu, according to custom, was immediately informed of the birth, as she had the prerogative of naming the new born child. The name was to be given in accord with the old method of dating a child's birth, after an important event in the local regent's life occurring at that time, or an important anniversary.

Kinau was petulantly concerned about her eyes which had developed an infection. She had been surrounded for days by high chiefs and chiefesses, as well as missionaries, who had administered various remedies, none of which had been effective. To Kinau her distress seemed an important event, one that was to be remembered. Consequently, when the news came that Keohokalole and Kapaakea's child had been born, and was to be *hanai* and heir to Paki and Konia, the premier dated the child's birth by her own affliction: naming her, Liliu (smarting) Kamakaeha (the sore eye).

The full name given Liliuokalani at birth was Liliu (smarting) Loloku (tearful) Walania (a burning pain) Kamakaeha (the sore eye).

The name *Liliuokalani,* by which she was to be known in history, was "given" her by her brother David Kalakaua after he, as "elected" king, named her heir apparent in 1877—a name which she said in 1891 was "no name at all."[6]

❧ 2 ❧

Konia welcomed the infant Liliu with complete *hanai.* She was her child and heir. Konia's natural child, Bernice Pauahi, had been given in *hanai* to Kinau. Kinau's own children were *hanai* to the king. These children were about to be placed in the High Chiefs' School, a boarding school under the supervision of Juliette and Amos Starr Cooke, missionary teachers.[7]

Hanai had a changing concept that would plague Liliuokalani all her life. The missionaries did not understand either the *aloha* or the social value of *hanai.* To them, parents simply did *not* give their children away. Among the high chiefs, a child was socially advanced to a higher position by *hanai.* The parents not only gave the child in *aloha* to a close relative[8] or a friend, but also to better the child's station in life. This further cemented the relationship among the chiefs, as well.

Thus, as Kinau's children had become heir of the king, and Bernice Kinau's heir to the other Kamehameha lands, Liliu would be the heir of Konia, as her *hanai* child, and an heir of the Kamehameha line, although not by birth.[9]

Missionary laws and customs, however, were to decree it otherwise.

❧ 3 ❧

Liliu spent her first two years in the Old Hawaiian way of an *alii* child. Konia took the tiny infant, and cradled her against her ample breasts. Although she was of small stature, she was inclined to stoutness. She placed Liliu in the care of Kaikai, an inferior chiefess and one of her retainers who had recently given birth to a child of her own. True to her native character of *aloha,* Kaikai took the infant, Liliu, to her own breast and heart.[10]

Konia had the baby brought to her daily to fondle and to love. To express her special love and complete relationship of *hanai* she wrote Liliu a name song.[11]

Konia, combining what she considered the best of the old and the new, took an old chant and gave it new words, a method that was not uncommon, adding the suffix *lani* to Liliu, thus recognizing her of high birth.

O Liliu-lani

Profuse bloom glowing as a delight
And lei for Kamakaeha,
For Kamakaeha the lei of the forest goddesses,
The ladies with baskets of flowers.

Wear a lei, O Liliulani
Wear a lei, O Liliulani

Pluck *kamani* flowers to link with ti flowers
As a lei to adorn the lady
Beloved by the forest glens
And the buds in the mountain greenery.

Kaala* wears a lei of rain and showers
Pouring down on Hale-auau,**
Rainbow mist that is a lei on pili grass
Where *nene* grass grows close *kupukupu* ferns.

Wearing a lei of *hala* fruit of Kekele†
Hala of Malailua that sweethearts dream of
Swaying freely amid *Kawelu* grasses
Kamakahala flower leis of Waahila‡ rain.

Thus, Konia "gave," in her song, a legacy to Liliu beyond property as the westerner conceived of it. She gave Liliu the flowers, fruits, the leaves of the trees and vines; she gave her rain; the riches, the verdure, the beauty of Nuuanu Valley; the showers from the mountain tops to the lowest valleys. A royal princess could have no higher heritage; but it could never be hers entirely, for it was shared by all, from "forest goddesses" to the "being" of a rainbow lei for *pili* grass.

Konia held considerable power in the twilight of the Hawaiian matriarchal society. She was well thought of by both Hawaiians and missionaries. Completely self-contained, as a high chiefess, a member of the king's council, a Kamehameha descendant, she had a quiet power and influence in the Court and at the High Chiefs' School, as well as among the natives who held her in high esteem. She was one of the few

---

* Kaala (Mount Kaalala in Oahu)
** Hale-auau (gulch at Waialua)
† Kekele (below Nuuanu Pali)
‡ Waahila (rain at Manoa and Nuuanu)

Abner Paki

Konia
Hanai parents of Liliuokalani

high chiefesses who had been allowed to join the church without being subject to a probationary period. She had been baptized "Laura," after Laura Fish Judd, the missionary doctor's wife.

Konia's husband, Paki, was of lesser chiefly genealogy, but also of the king's council. Paki's past showed him to be a restless, ambitious, and sometimes contentious person. Several years before, he had joined with his then mistress, Liliha, the widow of the controversial governor of Oahu and owner of the notorious Blonde Hotel, Boki, to attempt to defy Kamehameha III. The attempt was abortive to say the least. Kaahumanu scotched the scheme with her little finger, Liliha retreated to her father, and Paki returned to Konia, but not before having had confiscated, by Kaahumanu, considerable lands in Maui which he claimed had been given him by Kamehameha I.

A smouldering resentment lay in Paki against any authority that did not satisfy his particular desires. He had made an attempt to regain Kamehameha III's confidence and friendship by persuading him, when he decided to marry his sister, Nahienaena, to have the ceremony in Paki's home. Here he showed his rebellion against the cry of "Incest" of the missionaries.

Finding himself again on the wrong side when Kamehameha III succumbed to the wishes of the missionaries and married Kalama, Paki swung, with a new desire for approbation, to the missionary side by opposing *hanai*. In 1835 he began making arrangements to have "proper papers" drawn up to have Bernice returned to him as his daughter. However, as Bernice was *hanai* to the highest chiefess of the land, Kinau, and the Governor of Oahu—no one paid any attention to him.

Konia was content with Liliu.

❧ 4 ❧

Liliu was baptized at the same time as Victoria, last child of Kinau, by Levi Chamberlain. Liliu was given her "Christian" name of "Lydia." Officially, she became Lydia Paki, registered as "adopted daughter of Paki and Konia."[12] Paki, who was well aware of the difference between Hawaiian *hanai* and western "adoption," let the matter stand. No "official" papers were drawn up even for adoption, and Lydia was to fall first from *hanai* to adoption, then to "foster daughter."

Konia was unaware of the havoc the use of new *haole* words would later bring to her *hanai* child. She proved her ignorance of the matter, of which Paki was fully cognizant, by six months later taking Liliu in old

Hawaiian fashion to the new premier, Auhea,[13] the half-sister and successor of the late Kinau, to be made a member of the royal family along with Victoria by the custom of *aikane*.

Auhea, whose lineage was unquestionable, took Liliu and Victoria, placed them against her breast simultaneously and declared they were now *aikane*, sisters, fed of the same breasts. What was Victoria's was to be Lydia's.[14]

Thus, unbeknownst to Lydia, only two years old, she became a pawn in the hands of missionary-Americans and the Hawaiian royal *alii* in their intricate game of political chess, based on genealogy and the changing concept of *hanai*.

✘ 5 ✘

When Lydia was three, Paki decided that she should attend the High Chiefs' School along with other *alii* children. Juliette Cooke was at her wits end when Lydia arrived. She had just been told, with complete adamancy, that she *had* to "take" two-year old Victoria, whose mother (Kinau) had just died. Juliette also had her own children all under the age of seven, as well as her infant, Charles.

"I cannot take another infant," she wrote desperately in her Journal.[15] Fortunately for her, Paki had expressed some reservations about Lydia entering the school, as she spoke "only native," and would be a bad influence on Victoria. Victoria was a princess and Lydia was only a high chiefess, Paki had pointed out, contradicting the vitality of old *hanai*. For the first time in public life, Lydia was refused the place of a royal *alii*. She, however, returned happily with her *kahu*, Kaikai, to live her early childhood in Hawaiian fashion.

Konia and Paki had differing points of view on the missionaries. Konia recognized the value of knowledge in books, and the practicality the white ministers had brought. The lands were beginning to produce more goods; the missionaries were trying to protect the Hawaiians from the ravages of the whaling crews and their diseases. Paki, on the other hand, saw the missionaries as negative influences. Yet he had shrewd sagacity in holding to what was his, and a diplomatic attitude toward all.

He was a giant among giants—six-feet-six-inches tall, exceeding 300 pounds, well-formed and of Herculean strength. Liliu heard the story that he had held Bernice as an infant in his cupped hands. She hoped he had also held her; but she doubted it. She heard and gloried in his legendary strength of once having stopped a pair of horses that bolted with his carriage. Ignoring the reins, he had jumped from the carriage and thrown "himself across the plunging animals and held them by main force, as he might hold a pair of unruly dogs," the story went.

His prowess on the surfboard, his strength and general appearance made him conspicuous among the chiefs and early won him the admiration of the boy-king Kamehameha III, whom he had once befriended, and who, now in his twenty-sixth year, had chosen Paki as one of his advisers, along with Konia and Keohokalole, Liliuokalani's blood mother. Paki fascinated Liliu.

She experienced an ambivalence toward this man, as he vacillated from being her father to not accepting her fully. She adored him, yet feared him; her heart ached for his acceptance and she would have crept on her knees for his total love. On the other hand her resentment and jealousy flared against his "injustices."

Liliuokalani was a happy child, a child of the land. She saw the gods and spirits in the trees, in the sky, in the clouds. Contentedly, under the careful, but often sleepy eye of Kaikai, who kept her from playing with the "common children" of the retainers, she developed from infancy to three years of age. A contemplative child, as her later life was to show, she quietly strung flower and shell leis. Liliu loved music and songs, and Kaikai often entertained her. She eagerly clapped her small hands and wriggled her body to sounds unheard by a *haole* listener. She came by her love of music naturally.

Kaikai had transferred all her affection to Liliu from her other children, who had either died or been given to other inferior chiefs to cement relationships there, as in higher levels. She had accepted the custom, as all did, without question, regret, or loss, especially as she had never been troubled in her births by marriage. She devoted her days and nights to the baby. Only once was she remiss.

Given to drowsiness, to which the warm days were so conducive, she slept soundly while Liliu was napping, only to be awakened by a child's wild scream that could belong only to Liliu.

Liliu lay in vocal agony on the ground not far from her. She had fallen from someplace. But from where? Kaikai had put her to sleep in her own hut on the pandanus mats on the floor. But she was now outside. Then Kaikai saw the movement of the empty morning-glory vine swing —and she knew. Liliu had disobeyed her, and now she lay on the hard, red ground, one leg unnaturally curled under her.

Kaikai swept the howling child into her arms, holding her until there were just gulping sobs that would not disturb Konia in the large house. Carefully she felt all the parts of the child's body and discovered that it was by touching the leg that caused her to emit the loudest of all screams.

Kaikai was terrified. She called on all the gods, the new God too, in case He had any interest in a non-church-admitted Kaikai. If she went to Konia, a doctor would be called, she knew. But if a missionary doctor came he would condemn her to hell. And a hell-condemned Kaikai could very well be banished from the household of Konia. She *would* be banished. There was no doubt. No, she could not go to Konia.

No doctor. She weighed her faith in a doctor's healing powers against his social-political influence and decided to send a runner for a *kahuna*. The priest came quickly. He agreed with Kaikai that no *haole* must be told of this matter, for this child, he had heard, had been born under a royal sign and the gods were caring for her.

He bound the leg tightly with pandanus and ti leaves over a precious sandalwood splint. He chanted melodiously of the great heritage of the child, of the care the gods gave to such a one. Whether it was the assurance of her protection, or the bandaging, that was the more efficacious, neither the *kahuna* nor Kaikai knew, but blessed silence fell as the child ceased to cry. A soporific herbal drink extended the peace throughout the day and night, as Liliu slept.

Konia and Paki accepted the bound leg with no questions. They were both aware that these were times when the less they knew of what had already transpired, the better.

When the leg was finally unbound, Kaikai was horrified to discover that the knee would not bend properly. When she tried to force it, cries of anguish from Liliu stopped her. The *kahuna* was again secretly summoned.

He would pray to Kane, yes. But perhaps Kaikai should also tell the child nightly of the strange coincidence between herself and the Moon Goddess, Hina. Thereby, she would see that she was royal and close to the gods. To Kaikai the *kahuna* spoke of the "evil spirit" that must be in one who had had such a serious accident; but Kaikai, deeply desirous of having the matter settled, insisted the "evil" was disobedience in not napping when she should have. Unfortunately, the highly sensitive and impressionable Liliu sensed that she had done wrong.

For many nights Liliu listened to one of the legends of Hina.[16] Once Hina had been Goddess of the Sea, but being betrayed by men of the

Land, had allowed her moon to escape out of her secret calabash in the Sea, and in trying to rescue it via the lunar rainbow injured her ankle.

"And to this day she is slightly lame," Kaikai told Liliu.

The child listened intently. True, it made her a goddess, and, in a lesser perceptive child, she could have played Hina, limping and rejoicing in her false status; but Liliu had a frighteningly practical streak in her, even then. She preferred being Kaahumanu to Hina. Kaahumanu had not lost her moon through betrayal, but had ruled with Kamehameha the Great as his Favorite Wife. She had been regent during the "reign" of both Kamehameha's sons (II and III) until her death in 1832, only six years before Liliu was born. This was the great matriarch—the great queen, the one to be like.

Liliu determined there and then she would not be lame all her life, as a mark of having done something wrong. "Doing wrong," especially "to the people," however variously defined, was the greatest "sin" among the *alii;* the second was inhospitality.[17] *She would never do anything wrong again.* Like Kaahumanu she would win the love and respect of both her òwn people and the foreigners in the land; she would walk without a limp. And she certainly wouldn't let *her* moon escape through the betrayal of men. The *kahuna* of 1893 said the whole incident was prophetic, for, they said, she had been betrayed by men to lose her land.[18]

Kaikai watched her fearfully, but each day she walked less and less with a limp. Although the leg remained somewhat stiff all her life, few actually knew it.[19] Perhaps if anyone then had watched her determination, only John Ii[20] would have sensed that the difference between greatness and mediocrity is that greatness overcomes its defects and mediocrity capitalizes on them.

❧ 7 ❧

Liliu's first two years were spent overcoming her limp, experiencing the gentleness of Kaikai and Konia, and being happy that she was not at the High Chief's School with Bernice. Juliette Cook was also content with her absence. However, circumstances beyond her, or Juliette's, control came into play.

As early as 1827 Catholic priests had come to Hawaii. Neither the persecutions nor the threats against them had prevented their perseverance. Both Kaahumanu and Kinau were their bitter enemies. Having accepted one new religion of which they were zealous converts, they were not about to accept another. Further encouraged by the missionaries that the Catholics reverted to "paganism" with their idols, they ordered their expulsion. However, the Catholic influence was growing, especially among the lesser chiefs, who found the Catholic pomp and ceremony, as well as their icons, an easier bridge between their old beliefs and the new.

To the dismay of the missionaries by 1837, the Catholic influence was growing rapidly in Honolulu. The missionaries appealed to Kamehameha III and Premier Kinau to forbid these "heretics" from landing on Hawaiian soil.

On December 18, 1837, at Lahaina, the King issued "An Ordinance Rejecting the Catholic Religion." The ordinance not only forbad the religion from being taught, it prevented the vessels carrying priests from landing. France, traditionally a defender of the Catholic faith, also saw this as an economic threat. Thereupon, Captain Laplace was ordered by the French to make it clear to Hawaii that it would be unwise to "incur the wrath" of France. If necessary, he was to "use force for complete reparation" and not "quit those places [Tahiti and Hawaii] until he had left in all minds a solid and lasting impression."[21]

Laplace demanded that the persecution of Catholics cease, Catholic worship be declared free and open, a site for a church provided, and $20,000 in reparation be paid. He further demanded that French wines and brandies "be not prohibited" and a favorable duty set—or there would be immediate war with France.

Kamehameha III signed the treaty and paid the $20,000. The missionaries were furious, for not only had the Catholics been allowed in, but the non-liquor law was scuttled, and with it, temperance laws. Yet, they knew that Kamehameha III could not have done otherwise.

As a result of this turmoil, Juliette Cooke wrote on July 28, 1841, that they "were expecting Lydia," not yet three years old, because "we must save her from the Catholics—after all, she will some day be a high chief."

So despite Paki's fears of Lydia's adverse influence upon Victoria, on April 4, 1842, tall, stout Kaikai placed the nearly four-year-old Lydia on her broad shoulders and carried her to Amos Starr Cooke's School. Lydia was not about to dismount from her safe position, and letting out a yell, clung tenaciously to Kaikai.

Juliette Cooke was particularly harassed on this day with the thought of one more strange little brown creature whom she was determined, with her husband, Amos Starr Cooke, to educate at all costs. She approached the huge Hawaiian Kaikai and the equally formidable looking child. Juliette walked unswervingly toward them, pushing back strands of loose black hair that defied the bun on the top of her head. The strands escaped across her moist cheeks, as she sweltered in the tight long-sleeved blouse, long black skirt, high-laced shoes, and proper but uncomfortable undergarments—all unsuited for the climate.

"Come," she said to the child, who replied with a whooping yell. Here was a child who spoke only Hawaiian, a further obstacle for Juliette to overcome. This peculiar language was a living nightmare for the missionary teachers as well as for the preachers. Although seeming simple enough, when used by a *haole* teacher, the slightest difference in vocal inflection would send the sturdy little bodies shaking, like coconut trees in a high wind, with suppressed—and sometimes not quite suppressed— laughter.

The Hawaiians had no written language, and the missionaries, incapable of dealing with the "vocalic chaos," decided to "give" the Hawaiians an alphabet to be used in writing. The best the New England ear could differentiate was the five vowels of the soft "Italian" sound and seven consonants—*h, k, l, m, n, p,* and *w.* "The glottal stop, that Polynesian shibboleth,. was acknowledged but not denoted," according to historian Edward Joesting.

The result was neither Hawaiian as a Hawaiian knew it, nor an accurately translated English language; it was instead a new language.[22]

As the high chiefs did not cooperate—partly through disinterest and partly through the inability of the missionaries being able to reach them[23] —the language was drawn from the lower classes.

Thus, in 1841 Mrs. Cooke stood, determined but unhappy, before Kaikai and the now quietly but continuously weeping child. Kaikai placed the child on the ground, loosened her tightly clasped hands from around her huge legs and spoke gently and musically to her. Yet Lydia "cried so desperately for her *kahu,*" whom the Cookes very naturally discouraged having around "spoiling the children," "telling wild tales" and destroying the Cookes' discipline, that Lydia was sent home for the second time.

Konia then interceded, as she had with Lydia's brother, David Kalakaua, and on May 23, 1842, Lydia Paki, "foster child of Konia and Paki" and "foster sister of Bernice Pauahi"[24] entered the Royal School.

CHAPTER 3

The Royal School

❧ 1 ❧

The building blocks of Liliuokalani's national and personal life were fashioned between the years of 1843-1848.

She was more often an observer than an actor in her early days at the school, being one of the youngest. There was much for a child to observe, and all of it difficult to sort out in any proper way.

The High Chiefs' Children's School (often shortened to High Chiefs' School), the boarding school for the royal children and those of the highest chiefs, was a long frame two-story building with a large dining room, separate sleeping quarters for the children and for the Cooke family. There was also the New England parlor, furnished with home-made and treasured furniture sent from home, but much brought from China. It resembled nothing Hawaiian in its appearance nor its atmosphere.

It stood near the palace, near Beretania Street, on ground that Kamehameha III had given the Cookes for the school.

For the children it became their "compound"—their household—and as in the old way of *hanai*, the children united. Eight of these children, who were to come prominently into history, regarded each other as "brothers and sisters." Although not all were related by blood, they were to remain close to the "royal-family," and court-allied.

In 1843 when Lydia Paki, became an established pupil, the children's ages ranged from five to fifteen. The oldest children were the King's *hanai* sons—Moses, fifteen; Lot, thirteen; and Liholiho, twelve—Bernice Pauahi[1] was also twelve. Lunalilo, the child of Auhea (premier) and a lesser chief, Kanaina, was next in age, being eight. Emma Rooke[2] and David Kalakaua, Liliu's blood brother, were both seven. The last two children who were to play their parts upon the stage of history were Victoria and Lydia, both five years old.

Lydia, labeled by the Cookes as the "foster sister of Bernice," developed the feeling that she was somehow "wrong"—that she fell short of Bernice, who became her measuring stick. Over and over, she heard about "our darling princess," Bernice, for Bernice was the Cookes' favorite.

Bernice, being the oldest of the *alii* girls, and having a disposition of docility and malleability, quickly learned the "things a gentlewoman should know" from Juliette. She was "hostess" with Juliette when the high chiefs or important foreign visitors came; she read aloud to Juliette, whose eyesight was rapidly failing as a result of an accident. But most important she was the only student allowed to go into the Cookes' "tabu" (meaning taboo) yard to play with Charles, whom she dubbed her "little red robin,"[3] because of a red garment he frequently wore.

Only once did Lydia enter the "tabu" yard. She wrote in her book that the children were often sent to bed hungry, although the Cookes themselves were proud of their midday table, frequently noting "the menu" in their letters and journals: "fried fresh pork, boiled kalo and sweet potatoes, boiled rice dessert and a bowl of poi."[4]

On Sundays two meals a day were served, and after an "abundant midday repast," supper was a thick slice of bread covered with molasses. Though adequate for a thrifty-minded and slim-bodied New Englander, it left a grumbling hollowness in the chubby Hawaiian children.

Liliuokalani reminisced[5] that by rubbing two sticks together the children lighted small fires to cook roots, that they gathered in and about the School. Partly to stave off hunger and partly for sheer excitement, after the Cookes had gone to bed, the silent *menehunes*[6] or goblins stole through the still moonlit night, casting elongated ghostly shadows, to gather these roots, roast them over small fires or eat them raw.

One night Lydia was chosen to climb over the "tabu" fence to get some of the choice table vegetables from the garden. In her eagerness and with a heart pounding for joy and excitement, she unfortunately chose some of Mrs. Cooke's precious tulip bulbs.

The next day was the first, and only time, Lydia saw Juliette Cooke cry. Huge gulping sobs racked the thin body as Mrs. Cooke hid her face in her handkerchief. Lydia was horrified. Hawaiian tears flowed easily, quickly, and were grief-and-sadness cleansing. But the missionaries adhered to the principle that expression of emotion of any kind was a sin. Intuitively, the Hawaiian children sensed this. What was now happening was something horrible beyond belief: Mrs. Cooke was doing the unforgivable. Mrs. Cooke, who had never shed a public tear for illness or even the death of her own child, now sobbed on uncontrollably for the loss of this small vestige of home. It was a terrifying sight—and Lydia felt it was her fault. *What had she done?*

Juliette uttered muffled words of "my home," "my land." *"Gone."* There was great emptiness of soul and spirit in *"Gone."*[7] Lydia, a sensitive child, responded by becoming violently ill. She was not sure *what* she had done that was so wrong, but she was sure it was irredeemably terrible. Her illness she associated again, as with her fall from the swing, with "disobedience," "sin." All her life she was to make this association, to the degree of being impatient with illness in herself and in another, especially in her husband. Worse, with the impatience, came also a paralyzing guilt and fearful demand of *what had she done wrong?*

Juliette decided that Lydia needed more attention from the "Little Princess, Lydia's foster sister," to have a good example set for her. But Juliette was not sure how to achieve this goal. Then the answer came unexpectedly. Bernice had been taught by Juliette to play the piano, and Lydia had shown an inordinate amount of curiosity regarding the treasured piano. She had also shown a fine ability to carry a tune and an eagerness to memorize hymns, as most of the children did.

One rainy day, Lydia was caught in the parlor, fingering the keys of the piano. Juliette seized the idea as a solution of "controlling Lydia," by asking Bernice to spend an hour a day teaching Lydia to play the piano. It was the happiest hour of the day for Lydia, and Bernice seemed quite content with it, too. The only thing Lydia would have preferred more would have been two hours, but Juliette's days were strictly structured.

By the age of seven, Lydia and Victoria spent their school days in six hours of being taught by John Ii[8]—reading, writing, English grammar, arithmetic, spelling; one hour, they were restricted to their rooms for study; one hour, was spent in the parlor to "Read miscellaneous writings, revealing the character of people in every land and the way royalty lives in those lands."[9]

In later years Liliuokalani's summary recollection of the school was that she did not like it. Although she had some kindly memories of Juliette Cooke, she had none of the stern Amos Starr Cooke. To the end of her life, she could hear his severe condemnation of the older children who had engaged in "infraction of the rules"—usually sexual.

Before she understood what was happening between the young high chiefs and "Emma, Jane, and Abigail," she knew something terrible was going on and a fear of "sexual misbehaving," whatever that was, overcame her, with a dire foreboding. Juliette, who strongly believed that at least the two youngest chiefesses, Victoria and Lydia, could be saved from the horrors of sex, took the two aside and explained the "tabu" word in such a Victorian fashion of *"Don't. It is evil,"* that it was later to bring disaster to Victoria and grief to Lydia.

While the other children deliciously savored the forbidden fruits of known and unknown sex, Lydia grew to shun the very thought and refused to think about it at all.

✖ 2 ✖

Except for Bernice, Lunalilo was the only pupil whom the Cookes considered having "real parents." Auhea had been reached early by the missionaries to "keep her child." She had been thoroughly lectured on the "sins" of *hanai* and the virtues of motherhood, which she now took very seriously.

Auhea shared her motherly generosity with her two *aikane* children, Victoria and Lydia, by frequently inviting them to her home, a large stone house on the palace grounds. Lydia long cherished these visits, far beyond any memories of going "home" to Paki and Konia.

Lydia also envied the fortunate Lunalilo whose mother came to stroke his brow, sit by him, and care for him in his illness in contrast to the careful but brusque attendance of the Cookes. Konia was the only "mother" Lydia knew, but she seldom came to the School, for Bernice was an ideal pupil. The Cookes considered Konia only as Bernice's mother. Keohokalole and Kapaakea, Lydia's own parents, had moved to Lahaina, so it was Konia who inquired about her and David Kalakaua, but only inquired, never indulged, as Auhea did.

Auhea was the only one who could—or would—break through the stern gates of the High Chiefs' School. The children strained at their leashes, but received little support from the chiefs, as they had been placed in *hanai* to the Cookes. As with the food so with the discipline—for or against—the chiefs left the matter with the Cookes.

All the *alii* children were undisciplined and spoiled. Permissiveness was the keynote of the children's rearing among the high chiefs. The sudden change to unduly strict discipline of the Cookes left its scars on the children to become evident for the next fifty years, when they were in governmental power in Hawaii, and leave a serious weakness in the country's leadership.

Gerrit P. Judd was to say later that Liholiho, as Kamehameha IV, was not so much anti-American as anti-missionary. "He hated everything missionary . . . having had to be obedient . . . having had to attend innumerable religious and church services, nearly every day of the week."[10]

Lunalilo, because of being envied, as well as being several years younger than the King's *hanai* children, was unpopular with the older *alii* children and seldom included in their games or secrets except when his *kahu* came, bringing not only the sweets but wonderful "gossip."[11] What the Cookes called "gossip" was Hawaiian lore full of tales of a *kahuna* who had prayed someone to death, of another who had caught an evil spirit "like an egg in the air and squeezed the yolk . . . until the yellow substance . . . ran down his arm . . ." Then the evil spirit was dead. There was always an *aumakua* who had appeared to warn the Hawaiians against the *haole;* a ghost that appeared with tidings of evil or had prevented a *kahu* from passing over a piece of sacred ground. Yes, indeed the gods of old still lived in Hawaii through the *kahu* and children's delight in the unknown, mysterious, ghostly—the thrill of the supernatural. All the preaching and hymn singing could not remove these instilled beliefs of the young *alii*.

On a bright summer day Lunalilo brought both *haole* and Hawaiian to a startling standstill, and set Lydia's heart pounding for her first love. Whether Lunalilo knew he needed to perform an act of valor to win his place among Moses, Lot, and Liholiho is uncertain, but he did. One Saturday afternoon, when both commoners and *haole* crowded around the High Chiefs' School to see the "royal" children at play, Lunalilo's *kahu* brought him an unbroken horse at his request. Lunalilo flamboyantly declared he could ride the animal. The Hawaiians, both boys and girls, were superb riders from early youth, but an unbroken horse was a challenge, even to them.

While the children watched, with anticipation of delightful and frightening disaster, awe, and skepticism, Lunalilo mounted the beautiful prancing animal. A moment later, the horse bolted toward the beach, with Lunalilo clinging precariously amidst the shouts of encouragement.

Suddenly Lunalilo was thrown violently, but unhurt, to the ground. As he came striding back, to the awed onlookers, his father, having watched his son's feat, ordered the *kahu* to be put to death immediately, for the life of the *alii* was the responsibility of the *kahu*. The terrified *kahu* tried to disappear in the crowd, but they held him.

Lunalilo continued to walk with chiefly strides to his father's side.

Placing his hand upon his father's arm, he declared magnificently that not only should the life of the *kahu* be spared, but he, Lunalilo, would "liberate" him. He no longer needed to be a *kahu*—he was a free man, by Lunalilo's decree.

The *haole* cheered the "young liberator;" the children were impressed; the high chiefs, puzzled.

The missionaries nodded their approval of democracy at work, and Lydia fell in love with the young *alii,* four years her senior. Lunalilo was lauded by all, and the incident was to be remembered and repeated far and wide some twenty-five years later when Lunalilo became a "candidate" for kingship.[12]

❧ 3 ❧

In 1846 the High Chiefs' School became a government school and was renamed the "Royal School." At this time it was opened to day students, among whom was John Owen Dominis, later to be Lydia's husband.[13] Although the Cookes had to put up with much from the high chiefs' children, they could make short shrift of the *haole* day students. John was soon expelled, amidst fiery protestations from his mother.

Shortly thereafter, the Cookes, feeling more secure now that the School was government sponsored, with Rev. Richard Armstrong as the School Commissioner, decided they had had enough of Moses, even though he was the King's oldest *hanai* son and heir to the throne. Moses was frequently taken by the sailors on drunken brawls and promiscuous adventures, tales of which he related in secret, but also in vivid detail, to the other *alii* children. The Cookes punished him by having him write compositions of repentance for his evil deeds. Moses had a facile pen and a quick mind. His compositions were masterpieces of repentance, which could have brought tears to more sentimental readers than Amos Starr Cooke. Moses turned his no small poetical and musical talents to a hell-condemnatory song about the evils of rum,[14] truly worthy of the best revivalist, and the Cookes felt it could well be sung by the whole class as a daily reminder. The repentant, condemning words against rum and the graphic terrible fate that befell those who fell into its evil grip was incongruously set to the music of a modified drinking song, easily recognized by those who frequented the saloon. One evening, when returning from an errand, Amos Starr Cooke was rooted to the ground in the midst of his quick stride, before an open-doored saloon on Hotel Street. There he heard Moses' "rum song" being drunkenly and approvingly sung by the occupants of the saloon. For the first time the tune overrode the words; and Amos Starr Cooke *knew*.

His face burned with humiliation at the cruel and deliberate ridicule. Upon returning to the School, he peremptorily dismissed Moses. The situation might have passed without repercussions from the other children, had not Moses unfortunately been caught in the measles epidemic, and died a few weeks later at the palace. The children were shaken, as were the Cookes.

The young *alii* of the school were told they could go to the dead Moses for a "silent aloha." It was a remarkable concession for the Cookes, for measles was highly contagious and a deadly disease to the Hawaiians. Silent, the children were not. The wailing reached an ear-splitting crescendo and "some were sent home for the infraction." Many of the young chiefs linked the death of Moses with the disciplinary action of the Cookes and held them responsible for the loss of their high chief, the next heir to the throne. So strong was the feeling that Dr. Judd decided to take the next two older *hanai* sons and heirs of the King, Princes Liholiho and Lot, to Europe and the United States.

Lydia was doubly disturbed because in the epidemic her younger sister,[15] who had been given in *hanai* to the king and queen, also died. As the epidemic swept across the city, mass burials were made the day after the deaths. No doubt from the *haole* point of view it was the best method of holding the dreaded disease in check, but for the Hawaiians it was another cultural shock. No lying in state was allowed; no wailing was permitted, though *alii* in the country, the last edict was ignored. The forbidden wailing could be heard echoing through the valleys and volleying against the mountain slopes, as if nature herself objected to the *haole* command. The *alii* of the Royal School were well aware of what was happening and how *their* gods of nature were reacting.

✵ 4 ✵

The Cookes made one concession to celebrations—birthdays. They did not celebrate Christmas, as it was a holy day to be untouched by material self-satisfaction. Not until 1860 was Christmas "officially" celebrated in Hawaii.

Birthdays, however, the Cookes acknowledged meticulously. Often only a special fruitcake was the "celebration," but other times a small birthday party was given. Lydia, newly arrived at the school, was deeply impressed by a grand party for Bernice Pauahi's twelfth birthday on

December 19, 1843. She inquired immediately when *her* birthday was to be. The Cookes replied it would be on September 2nd, news that meant her birthday was almost a year away—a seeming eternity.

But the time passed quickly, and, when September came, Lydia was content with her small fruitcake.

It was her ninth birthday which she never forgot. Rapid changes were taking place in the Royal School and in 1847 Jane Loeau was to be married at the school to *haole* John Jasper. The high chiefs in general were strongly opposed to a high chiefess marrying a *haole,* but with Jane there was no protest. First, Jane was not of highest chiefly descent, and secondly, she was pregnant with Kamehameha III's child. Certainly this situation was unknown to the Cookes, but just as certainly known both to the king and Jasper.[16]

The marriage, although simple, was an occasion of feasting for the *alii* children, as the king had provided the "table." All the children attended the ceremony, and it was here that Bernice Pauahi met Charles Reed Bishop, whom she was later to marry. Everyone was excited throughout the entire day, and exhausted by evening, when the Cookes served their "thick slice of bread and molasses" to the children and gratefully sent them to bed. All were satisfied, for the feast had been bountiful—all, that is, except Lydia. She had a hunger that had not been met. The date was September 2, 1847, her ninth birthday, and no one remembered.[17]

This time Lydia did not give way to tears. She furiously stamped her small foot and declared with "stubborn, haughty, queenly authority" that some day no one would *dare* forget her birthday. It was the first time that the Cookes noticed Lydia's temper, but remembered it again in 1891.

❧ 5 ❧

The children of the Royal School, were taught two different ideologies, and often what appeared to be diametrically opposite "facts." One was taught at the school—the other at home, where the children went for vacations and holidays. While at home, they came under the influence of the *kahu* and the native chiefs who were being instructed, outside of a school, by the "educated" students from Lahainaluna High School in Maui. Most important were the native historians, David Malo and Samuel Kamakau.[18] These two had been taught by William Richards and other missionary teachers, and served as Hawaiian resource persons for the missionary teachers. The two young students were willing to write of "ancient Hawaiian customs and practices," as they had been handed down to them by oral tradition. But they were non-judgmental. As the missionaries gained more information, recorded it, edited it, judged it, and condemned the "savage" and "pagan" customs and practices, the two young chiefs also took on a judgment value of what the missionary teachers taught.

David Malo early warned Kinau that the "Big fish were coming up out of the sea to eat the little fish, unless they (the Hawaiians) changed their ways." This warning was incorrectly interpreted to mean, "become more *haole*"; what Malo meant was to listen less to the missionaries, for he wrote later, of them and others, that no early foreigner had been endowed with the wisdom to understand and preserve or build upon the culture of the Hawaiians. "First they came sightless, then blinded by self-righteousness, and lastly eyes open to self interest."[19]

At the school Lydia and her classmates were learning of Kamehameha III's great progress toward a Constitutional Monarchy, of which neither the American advisers nor the Hawaiian king and his royal council had any clear concept. Many of the "learned" chiefs were opposing the movement on the argument that the Hawaiians were not ready for such freedom. It would bring about the loss of the country, they prophesied.

The children of the school recited dutifully the Declaration of Rights, written in 1839: "God had made of one blood all nations of men to dwell on the face of the earth in unity and blessedness. God has bestowed certain rights alike on all men, all chiefs, and all people of all lands," only partially understanding their meaning or applicability to their society.

The students were given long hours of study of the first constitution the Hawaiians ever had.[20] They had no understanding of "the transfer of power . . ." *from* the high chiefs *to* an elected legislature—elected for the first time by the commoner. They merely memorized the words.

The greatest of Constitutional Rights was for the protection "to the persons of all people, together with their land, their building lots, and all their property, and nothing whatsoever shall be taken away from an individual, except by express provisions of the laws."

The Hawaiian *alii,* who knew the commoner had no land, building lots, nor property of his own, found the Right non-applicable; the commoner who had no desire for land, building lots, or property, ignored the Right completely. The *haole* who wanted land, building lots, and property, thought the Right a great forward step into democracy; but they were not willing to accept the "law of the government," relative to land claims. They saw hundreds of ways to gain land from the "lazy kanaka" (a slang term used by the *haole* for the Hawaiian native commoner), and make it profitable; some worked from an altruistic purpose for Hawaii, but most for themselves. Hawaii was unique in allowing non-citizens to take an active part in the government, both to vote and hold office.

In order to give the commoner the land he didn't want, Kamehameha III was prevailed upon through missionary advisers to institute the Land Reform movement. Out of it came the Great Mahele, hailed by the teachers of the Royal School as the "greatest of Kamehameha's contributions." The chiefs, always dutiful to their king, divided their land with him; *then* the lands were divided into three parts: the king's land; the high chiefs' land, as recorded in the Book. The land then became available to the commoners. The king divided his newly-apportioned one-third share into two parts: one for the use of the government and one for his own personal use.

The royal children, Moses, who was then still alive, Lot, Liholiho, and Victoria would be heirs to the Kamehameha lands of Kamehameha III, called the "crown lands," as distinct from government lands. Whoever held the "crown" was heir to the "government lands" as well. Other high chiefs' children's parents laid claim to their new divisions: Kanaina claimed his portion for Lunalilo, and High Chief Aikanaka claimed his lands for his daughter Keohokalole and another chief, a son. Bernice was to be heir to Konia and Paki's lands, known both as "Pauahi lands and Kamehameha lands." In old *hanai* Lydia would have been heir to these lands as well as those of Aikanaka, but new legal-historical-*hanai*-adoption systems were to finally leave her heir only to Aikanaka's lands, through Keohokalole, and then only after David Kalakaua had disposed of most of those.

The Hawaiians were already at the mercy of the foreign element in their society, politically, economically, and culturally as the old *kapu* became obsolete under the guidance of the *haole*.

❦ 6 ❧

In 1843, amidst the confusing events that were beginning to separate the chiefs from their king, and all the Hawaiian *alii* from the missionaries and other *haole*, came a national calamity. Like all national calamities, it tended to pull the differing groups together.

George Paulet, an ambitious Englishman, decided that the Islands should belong to England. He had seen the vulnerability of the Islands to the guns of any nation in the dispute with France. Paulet's *coup* had

been building for sometime through the British consul, Captain Richard
Charlton. It was aided by the fact that Hawaii, through the influence of
Rev. William Richards, who had become "Chaplain, Teacher, and Trans-
lator of the King" in 1838, had begun to send foreign envoys abroad in
hopes of receiving some assurance of protection for their independence.[21]

The threats to Hawaii's independence never came from the government of a foreign country, but always from the foreign element within
Hawaii itself. So in 1843 through three men—Charlton, Alexander Simpson, and Captain Paulet—Hawaii fell under the British flag. Charlton,
the British Consul, who had always believed that the islands should belong to the British, passed on his personal invectives, clothed in words
of "unfair treatment to British subjects and property," to Alexander
Simpson, a resident. Charlton *personally* appointed Simpson British Consul in his place so that he would be free to go to England to prevent the
Hawaiian envoys from gaining British protection. Simpson was refused
acceptance as consul by the king. With his personal vanity now badly
injured, he became infected with Charlton's unfounded accusations; he
called on the British navy for "protection of British property and persons."

Captain Lord George Paulet was sent by Admiral Richard Thomas,
to whom the news came officially, to investigate the problem.

Paulet, also a personally ambitious man of few principles, was met
in Hawaii by the angry Simpson; together they quickly recognized the
vulnerable position of the king and the country.

Remembering the Frenchman, Laplace, and his successful demands,
Paulet went further; he demanded "complete restitution" under the
threats of "coercive action." Kamehameha III was not sure what "complete restitution" was, inasmuch as no details of the controversy had been
clearly spelled out. He *did* know, however, that the guns aimed at Honolulu signified "coercive action."

The restitution amounted primarily to giving Charlton some disputed
property he claimed he owned, acknowledging Simpson as Consul, and
settling a case between Henry Skinner (an Englishman) and American
John Dominis, father of John Owen Dominis, in "fairness to the British".[22] However, the matter was settled to give Dominis the land on
which he built Washington Place, later Liliuokalani's home and now
the Governor's Mansion.

The king quickly acquiesced; so easily, that Paulet made further un-
warranted demands of land indemnity for "unfair treatment of British
subjects," of over $200,000. The king appealed for help from the French

Consul, who refused, as France at the time was having its own problems with Tahiti. Kamehameha also appealed to his good friend and adviser, Dr. G.P. Judd, a missionary who had entered the king's service. Judd also refused, not believing that Simpson and Paulet were serious in their demands and threats.[23]

Kamehameha III's rule had been thrust upon him amidst his own personal problems of incest with and the untimely death of his beloved sister, Nahienaena. The resulting doubts and confusion regarding his Christian conversion and allegiance to the old ways, and his fear of the missionary hell left him hopelessly reliant on the advice of his American missionary advisers. They gave him counsel that would have been good in America, but which included little understanding of the background or disposition of the Hawaiian people.

Now neither the French nor the Americans would help him with either material aid or prayers. Kamehameha, mentally and physically exhausted, and hopelessly confused, simply said in essence "Let them take the country."[24] It was not the first time he had tried to relieve himself of his onerous burden.[25]

The British frigate *Carysfort* offered asylum to its subjects as did the U.S.S. *Boston* for the Americans, in case of war. Juliette Cooke, expressing the opinion of most of the foreigners, wrote wearily and prophetically ". . . made no effort to get away, [in answer to the *Boston's* offer of 'refuge' to the Cookes and the children of the High Chiefs' School], knowing the king and the chiefs would offer no resistance, but comply as they had heretofore to whatever was demanded of them at the mouth of the cannon, however unjust such demand might be." After Kamehameha's verbal relinquishment of the islands, Paulet demanded a "formal cession."

The children of the High Chiefs' School marched, two by two, to Honolulu's crumbling fort to see the Hawaiian flag lowered and the British Standard raised. It was a subdued crowd that watched in silence.

The children heard Kamehameha speak the historic words:

> Hear ye! I make known to you that I am in perplexity by reason of difficulties into which I have been brought without cause; therefore, I have given away the life of the land, hear ye! But my rule over you, my people, and your privileges will continue, for I have hope that the life of the land will be restored when my conduct is justified.

These were indeed noble words. Typically Hawaiian, the Highest

KAMEHAMEHA III

Chief took the blame, assured his people of his "continuing care," and expressed hope. They were words for Hawaiian ears, not Westerners', as time was to prove.

Juliette Cooke revealed the frame of mind of the Hawaiians, as seen in the king and the premier, whom she visited shortly thereafter, and found them ". . . eating and jolly. How little they realize their degradation, brought upon them by their yielding up everything to others." After Mrs. Cooke had talked with them, they seemed "downcast."

The children caught the "spirit" of revolt, and played at retaliation, as the Hawaiians were to continue to do until they lost their country. They held "indignation meetings"; Lot, to the delight of the children, called the British officers "lobster backs"; "[they] glared at them with scorn whenever [they] met on the street."

Further, "Moses put up the American flag, but Mr. Cooke [wisely] took it down."[26] Interestingly, none of the *alii* children objected that Moses did not put up the Hawaiian flag, but the American.

It became immediately evident that Paulet had no intentions of allowing Kamehameha to have any "rule" over his people nor allow their "privileges to continue." He recruited a native regiment, calling it the Queen's Own (reference to Queen Victoria), and began a heavy taxation system. It was then that Dr. Judd moved into action by joining the king in withholding records of lands, resulting in endless legal upsets, refusing to grant monies so that the regiments and others could not be paid, and lastly working secretly at night in the Royal Mausoleum using, not inappropriately, Kaahumanu's coffin as a desk, to reach the envoys enroute to England.

The envoys reached Great Britain and notified an "unamused queen." Admiral Sir Richard Thomas also received word of Paulet's action. Thomas sailed for Honolulu, from the west coast of South America. He arrived on July 26, 1843, six months after Paulet's "take-over."

Thomas made short order of Paulet; he conferred with Paulet, Judd, and the king; drew up "articles of parity for British subjects," similar to those of the French, and "restored" the islands.

On July 31, 1843, a wildly cheering crowd gathered on the plains east of Honolulu, waving and shouting as the king appeared with his royal guards. The children of the High Chiefs' School stood at attention while the Hawaiian flag was again raised, and cannons were fired at the fort, on the plains, in the harbor, and at Punchbowl. It was a day of wild rejoicing.

In the afternoon Kamehameha III went in a solemn procession with his chiefs to Kawaiahao Church to speak the words that were to become the motto of Hawaii: *"Ua mau ke ea o ka aina i ka pono"*—"The life of the land is perpetuated in righteousness." The High Chiefs' School children, sitting in the front row of straight-backed pews, would find much to contemplate in these often ambiguously interpreted words as the years passed. A ten-day celebration of Restoration Day followed, and was annually observed.

The last of the Restoration Day celebrations came in 1847. The missionary element in the government were thereafter to declare the celebrations "too expensive." Lydia, now nine, took a more active part, riding in the "royal carriage" with Victoria. She carried a furled flag, which, to the annoyance of the Cookes, she continually unfurled and waved at the crowd.

The older children rode horseback, leading the parade, with the state carriage of the king and queen, following. A thousand special riders, five abreast, horses and riders alike wearing gay ribbons and flowers, were followed by 2500 regular horsemen. This colorful procession arrived at the Nuuanu picnic ground in a pouring rain, with spirits undampened. The delighted native crowds gathered under two open *lanai*, or covered pavilions, thatched with ti leaves and thickly carpeted with rushes, from where they threw flowers into the passing carriages.

It was to be the last of such Hawaiian festivities, and although no one knew it at the time, it was a worthy farewell to another old custom.

Lydia long treasured the memory of John Ii, a trustee and teacher at the School, who on this day began the ancient games. Standing tall and muscular in a dark broadcloth suit and a brilliant yellow cape, he came to salute the children before he stepped into the arena. In the tradition of ancient warriors he stood alone, unarmed, opposed to twenty spearsmen each of whom endeavored to hit him. "Dextrously catching the first spear, he successfully parried all the rest, aimed with furious force at all parts of his body. With the lithe grace of a dancer, he tossed the spears back at his opponents, driving them one by one, from the field." Even the *haole,* from under their frame structure, cheered wildly and "applauded thunderously."[27]

When the games were over, Lydia went with the other children to the "Long House" where the chiefs and king sat on the floor at the far end of the mats and ate with the people, the natives, while the foreigners dined on linen covered tables in a frame shelter. It was *alii aloha* and the strange democracy that could not be defined by western terms, nor understood, for each "commoner" later returned with marvelous equanimity to his own station in life, after dining with the king.

Sophia Cracroft best described this situation in a letter of June 24, 1861,

> . . . (the masses) are always pleased to see honour paid their chiefs. And yet there is no very great *outward* respect shewn to those of highest rank by the lower classes. This is because of the fixed and positive distinction between them, which can neither be enhanced or diminished by outward circumstances. There is not the smallest approach to a sense of equality, and all the essentials of supremacy lie behind a familiarity of manner, which is very remarkable.[28]

❧ 7 ❧

Two more school memories, curiously intertwined, were to become a part of Lydia's childhood. The first caused her poignant remembered pain, and both were to contribute to her ambivalent feeling toward Paki, which later extended into a shifting between an abandoned trust and faith and a reluctant suspicion toward all men who were to come into her life.

The first of these experiences came at the beginning of her school days, and the last, at the end. Lydia was only five-and-a-half when she heard that the Cookes were planning an excursion for the children to visit the capital at Lahaina, where the king was in residence, Paki and Konia were attending the council, and where her own parents lived. It was a tribute to the staunch New England couple that all fourteen children—all under fifteen years of age—were to go on the trip.

On Friday evening, the wriggling, delighted young bodies were placed aboard a sailing vessel with "ten sailors and ten rowers." It was not a night for sleep, so it was to the relief of the Cookes when they arrived two hours before daylight.

Out of the morning darkness, over the black surf, a war canoe came to meet them. A shiver of delight passed through both the Cookes and the children, a shiver not unmixed with atavistic wonder, of the distant, yet not so distant, past.

Lydia strained against the railing of the vessel to see more clearly the mountainous silhouetted figure in the prow of the double-canoe. She pointed a chubby finger and was about to cry out in joy at seeing her father, Paki, when the bird-sound strangled in her throat. For at that moment the Cookes hurried Bernice forward, calling out that *her* father, the High Chief Paki, was there to greet them. Not Lydia's father, Bernice's. Yet was it not Lydia who was *hanai* to Paki?

Lydia slithered back into the refuge of the schooner and into the inner self that children have—as impenetrable as a turtle's shell to the adult, but much more fragile for the child. It became a shell she retained for refuge nearly all her life, when far greater disappointments came to her.

When the vessel beached, the children tumbled out. It took a great deal of restraint on the part of the Cookes to get them into a proper wavering line to greet the king and the premier in a befitting manner. The missionaries had no royalist's attitudes of curtsying, but they did demand a group of well-behaved children who spoke in a well-mannered way to their elders—be they kings, parents, or foreign visitors.[29]

After the formality, Paki caught up both Lydia and Victoria and placed them, one on each shoulder. Lydia's uncertain heart fluttered; and then a huge grin split her no longer troubled face. Her childlike resiliency was at work—as it would be throughout her life, often to her detriment.

Each child was given a calabash of cool water in which to bathe and in which each splashed happily. The children were then towel-dried and dressed by a *kahu*.

Lydia's usual healthy appetite quickly returned as she sat down at the long table covered with a white linen damask cloth, set with knives, forks, spoons, castors, teacups, and saucers, to the Cookes' satisfaction. After a gratifyingly brief prayer of thanksgiving by Amos Starr Cooke, the children began to gorge themselves on a breakfast of roast pig, fried fish, stewed birds, and an abundance of fruit.

The king with the premier presided at one end of the table, the Cookes at the other. Behind each guest stood two lesser chiefs; one fanned the guests with the *kahili,* while the other poured tea. Thus the old and the new stood side-by-side in the world of change.

The afternoon was spent in enjoying the glories of nature, of the rolling, white surfed ocean, the palms silhouetted against the brilliant blue sky like sentinels set to guard the royal children. Lydia entwined flower leis in the hair of her girl schoolmates, swam in the surf, and her total joy was restored when Paki, the champion surf-board rider, placed her on his shoulders and took her skimming over the great swells. So the day ended with mixed emotions.[30]

Lydia's second experience in the changing culture, and more significant in her ever-changing status, came about just before the Cookes left the Royal School.

The Cookes delayed leaving until they could see their "dear little princess" fulfilled in her desire to marry Charles Reed Bishop, who had come to Hawaii in 1846 with his friend, William Lee. Both had stopped off on their way to Oregon for economic reasons and decided to stay. Charles had entered the mercantile businesss, and Lee had gone into law practice.

Unlike Jane Loeau's marriage, this time a full scale opposition developed to the marriage of so important an *alii* as Bernice to a *haole*. Paki peremptori.y forbade the marriage; the king forbade the marriage; the council forbade the marriage. From birth, it was said, Bernice had been betrothed to Prince Lot. It was he she was to marry—to be queen some day.

Bernice proved to be her father's daughter, and, with or without permission, she intended to marry the young *haole,* ten years her senior. This was no easy decision for Bernice, for the Hawaiian children had a deep devotion to their parents and profound respect for their wishes.[31]

Bernice, however, had strong support on her side in the Cookes. The Cookes had a romantic streak in them, for all their cold exterior, and also a strong prejudice in favor of the *haole* marriage. Juliette sided with Bernice against Konia and Governor Paki (Paki was then Governor of Oahu) in their "wish for Bernice to become engaged to Lot without seeing him, without saying he loves her."[32]

Bernice took things into her own delicate but firm hands: she wrote Lot she would agree to her parents' wishes but knew he did not love her nor she him; she then wrote more strongly to her parents that she'd "sooner be buried than marry Lot." Lot somehow saw this letter—by design or mistake—and "exonerated her from promises made in youth," and hoped she would marry one more worthy of her; he himself was "unworthy."

After a turbulent affair in which she almost lost Charles to the California lure of gold, they were finally reconciled. As Paki and Konia refused to have anything to do with the marriage or wedding, the Cookes agreed to have the wedding at the Royal School. It was a simple ceremony with seventeen-year-old Bernice in white muslin and only a wreath of jessamine in her shiny black hair. Although all the children of the Royal

School attended the wedding, including Lot, Bernice's only attendant was ten-year-old Lydia.

Paki and Konia did not attend, and Paki announced that now he had only one child—Lydia Paki.

The old patterns were shifting. The Cookes decided to close the School and go into business—Castle and Cooke. Dr. Judd left for Europe taking the two young princes, Lot and Liholiho, with him to "show them how other people live." And Lydia Paki became the "only daughter and heir" of Paki and Konia.

PART II
Joining of the Old and the New

❧ ❧

High Chiefess Lydia Paki
or the
Honorable Liliu Kamakaeha

1848-1862

CHAPTER 1

The Young Alii of the Royal School

❧ 1 ❧

To be a young *alii* in Hawaii from 1848 to 1854 was to be an anachronism in Hawaiian history. Eight of the young *alii* of the Royal School (Moses had died in 1848) found themselves in an anomalous situation. They were the elite of the Hawaiians, but not of Hawaii. The missionary descendants, who had inter-married with the fast-rising-to-wealth commercial class, many of whom were also missionary descendants, were the elite in a new but highly elitist society. The *alii* were of the royalty—of the ruling class—but they did not rule. Although they held the throne and legislative seats, they had little power; they were subtly, but inexorably directed toward the American democracy. Hawaii was their country in name only. The language was English; the religion was Calvinistic-Congregational-Presbyterian; the commercial exchange was American money.

The true reins of government were not in the hands of the Hawaiian *alii*, but in those of the foreigners, primarily the Americans: in the teaching corps, in the pulpit, in the press, and in what was to become all-powerful—the economy.

The eight closely related young *alii* had been separated after the Royal School was closed by the Cookes in 1848. But it was almost immediately reopened under the principalship of Edward G. Beckwith, with his two younger brothers as teachers. Dr. Judd had taken the two throne-aligned princes to Europe and America. Bernice had been married to Charles Reed Bishop. Victoria divided her time between the Island of Hawaii with her elder half-sister, Princess Ruth,[1] and the palace with her *hanai* parents, the king and queen. Lunalilo lived with Kanaina, his father, after his mother's death in 1845. There he came under the influence of Lorenzo Lyons, who not only worked with him in translations of Hawaiian songs, but also introduced him to his life-long love—Shakespeare. Emma Rooke,

David Kalakaua, and Liliu had returned to their *hanai* parents to continue their education through tutors and other schooling.

Liliu lived at Haleakala, or the House of Fire, in Honolulu, with Konia and Paki, the home Paki had said he had built for Bernice, had she not married Charles Bishop. The breach between Paki and his daughter lasted only a short time. After Paki sent a huge ornate mirror to the small Bishop home in Nuuanu Valley, the reconciliation was complete and the Bishops moved to another home, owned by Paki, on Alakea Street. Charles' starched white collar would not allow him, however, to live at Haleakala as long as Paki was alive.

In their new home, aided by Paki's money, Bernice began to live as a young princess should; meanwhile Liliu loved Haleakala beyond and above all places. She was a sentimentalist; she loved her home; her birthplace; her roots.

From the wide upstairs veranda of Haleakala, across the well-manicured grass and through the trimmed shrubs and shading trees, Liliu could view a new Honolulu, drastically changed over the ten years just passed. The grounds of Haleakala were extensive, and the estate bore the name of "Little Egypt." The interior was filled with ornate furniture, heavy silver services, the best in glass and dinner ware, and expensive vases and other decorative pieces, imported from half-way around the world, as were most of the furnishings in the *haole* and *alii* homes. But at Haleakala there was also a collection of "Hawaiian antiquity," which Liliu loved best. The *kahili*, tapa, necklaces of dogs' teeth, feathered capes—all these were Hawaii.

Her own birthplace of thatched houses was gone. Already many luxurious buildings, taking the place of the simple missionary houses, were spreading toward the base of Punch Bowl Hill among the sweeping coconut groves that lined the streets.

Honolulu was still a seaport and carried the atmosphere of raucous immorality. The *hapa-haole* (Hawaiian of mixed blood and mixed culture) had passed out of the amorality of the early Hawaiians, through the superimposed morality of the missionaries, and had come out immoral, a natural transition among people without innate discipline.

Paki had been removed from his war canoe and his feet placed on the less firm ground of agriculture-business. Like all the high chiefs, he was notoriously poor at business ventures, but with the help of his son-in-law, he was doing exceedingly well. He replaced, at Bishop's suggestion, the Hawaiian *konohiki* (overseer) with *haole* overseers, and thus his land prospered. Konia however, retained her "old ways," and instilled these further into Liliu.

Former retainers, now "owners of land," displaced from the land in the confusion of Kamehameha III's Land Reform Movement, came daily to ask for aid from Konia, in the old fashion of *aloha* and *mana,* that flowed from the high chiefs.

When the Great Mahele and Land Reform Movement took place, the boundary lines at best were sketchy and ownership to the commoner (and to many *alii*) totally incomprehensible. A Hawaiian "owning a piece of land" "from the large rock *ewa* [to the west] to the hou tree *mauka* [inland]" often found, after an unseasonal rain and wind, both the rock and the hou tree gone. When his cow wandered across the non-existent line to graze peaceably on the pili grass of the *haole* neighbors, the *haole* neighbor shot the cow for trespassing.

The native confused, disturbed, cowless, "sold" his land to the *haole* for a dinner pig, never expecting for a moment he could not return that evening to his thatched hut to sleep and eat with his family. But that evening his family was gone—had been driven off the land, for he had "sold" it. Countless of these homeless refugees straggled into the grounds of Haleakala, and Konia accepted them as "retainers."

The one socio-economic part of life the native understood best was giving service. This was *aloha*. One gave goods when one had goods, but when one didn't, one could always give service and in turn receive *mana,* care. The *alii* were still their source of supply. The gods of old indeed stocked the world with abundance, but it often reached the commoner only through the *alii,* who were closer to the gods and therefore had much *mana* and *aloha*.

The new money-medium of exchange was totally foreign to the Hawaiian's concepts of service. It seemed to dam the free flow. When one offered goods or services one should not receive a coin that was then to be further exchanged for its exact amount. That exchange limited the worth of the service, the worth of the coin, the worth of *aloha*.

It was difficult to teach accounting to those who had never accounted for anything, and no one made any great effort to do so. It was easier to go to an old *alii,* like Konia, who understood. This was the new Hawaii in which the young *alii* lived.

2

Liliu, to her delight, was to go on to day school. She would be taught the new accounting, but like the other Hawaiians, she never comprehended the intrinsic value of money or land or goods.

She was sent to the Beckwith School (Royal School) in 1848, and there she developed almost immediately a school-girl crush on the youngest of the Beckwith brothers, Maurice. It embarrassed him greatly and he tried to discourage the amorous fervor with scholastics. It was an unfortunate defensive weapon, for Liliu was not only studious, but also quick-minded, curious, and fascinated by languages, myths, tradition, history, and codes. Liliu was to carry her interest in codes through to the end of her life, when in her latter years she wrote her diary entries in two different numerical codes.

Maurice, like his brothers, was a Classicist. He was less aggressive, less pedantic, and certainly less Calvinistically oriented than his brothers. To his delicate fingertips he was a scholar and teacher, but he was no administrator; as a result he held a lesser pedagogical position in the Honolulu schools.[2]

His greatest love was Greek, and in Greek his young, embarrassing student found a new language written in "code," telling of traditions and legends that she could relate to her own background. She made an easy transition in time, and developed a quick empathy with the Greek gods and legends.

Greek was everything Liliu, the student, wanted, and Maurice was everything she thought a teacher should be until she later met Susan Tolman Mills, founder of Mills College in Oakland, California, whom she characterized as a "true educator."[3]

Maurice was slight, fair-haired, a little scholarly stooped, and soft spoken, and had a burning desire to impart knowledge. Liliu was both an enigma and a fascination to him. Her mind challenged him, and he sensed something of the insecurity that changing *hanai* was giving her, for he wrote of her years later that she was "more a child of history than of parentage . . . she often did not know where she belonged among the royalty."[4]

Liliu did not spend all her time in the classroom activities, either at the day school nor at Haleakala, where Maurice tutored her. The two young princes returned from their trip and began "holding court" in their own homes and on their vessels. All of this resulted for Liliu in exciting sea trips to the outer islands, entertainment extended to the young *alii* by the natives, who, as of old, still laid out their tables of hospitality and abundance; moonlit horseback rides over the pali; surfing and swimming in the ever-welcoming Pacific. Evenings were spent in dancing and singing; music was the heart and soul of the Hawaiian, *alii* or commoner.[5]

But there was something new added to the evenings: political discussions.

❧ 3 ❧

Both Lot and Liholiho had returned from abroad, rebellious against the Americans. In England the young princes had been treated with deference, cordiality, and respect. If there was a touch of condescension that Victorian England had against the "lesser races" of its empire, it was not shown to the young princes. They were well content with their acceptance on the Continent, and especially in England.

America was a contrasting disappointment to them. At best, they had been treated diffidently by the government. Their interviews with governmental officials had been brusque, and when an effort toward entertaining them had been made, it seemed to have been extended half-heartedly and reluctantly.

The final stamp of insult came in Philadelphia. For the first time Lot and Liholiho had had their place in society challenged because of their color. They had been removed from a pullman car because they were "niggers." Dr. Judd, after explaining who they were, had them "reinstated," but the affront still remained. By such discourtesies, resulting from ignorance, the respect of nations can rise or fall. The United States' fell.

These two princes—Lot and Liholiho—both of the same parents, upbringing, schooling, visiting the same foreign countries under the tutelage of the same person, Dr. Judd, returned to Hawaii with completely different attitudes toward themselves, their country, and foreign nations.

Liholiho, bright, witty, intense, and satirical, returned as a young would-be-Britisher, determined to make Hawaii as British as possible. England! That was the country; the people to emulate! Ah, yes, one had only to remember Thomas the Great.

America seemed like a rebellious child who had run away from home and selfishly saw its new world as its own toy to do with what it wished at the expense of those who "owned" it first. And those who wandered from this strange new "motherland" decided that wherever they went the land was theirs—not for their country's glory, but for themselves. They had no *aloha*. "Every man for himself!" that was their motto.

Lot saw a more realistic picture than his brother. Hawaii was *Hawaii Nei.* It was Hawaii for Hawaiians. English, German, French, Chinese, Americans, especially Americans—all were the intruders. Hawaii should be brought back to the Hawaiians, for the Hawaiians, and by the Hawaiians.

While Liholiho was quick, energetic, impetuous and British-oriented, Lot was taciturn, indomitable, plodding, and thoroughly Hawaiian. Both, however, were deeply concerned over their *hanai* father's attitudes; for Kamehameha III was so exhausted by his turbulent reign and "squabbling foreigners," he was again ready to take the line of least resistance and offer Hawaii to the United States through the "peaceful annexationists," led by American Commissioner Luther Severance.

It never seemed to occur to Kamehameha III that annexing Hawaii to any other country would mean the end of the monarchy. He seemed to believe that "protection" would come as *aloha,* as from the *alii* to the commoner.

Since 1843, when George Brown had been appointed Hawaiian Commissioner,[6] there had been a continuous official movement in favor of "peaceful annexation" of Hawaii to the United States. When Brown was recalled for "undue interference" in the Hawaiian government, Anthony TenEyck took his place and rented a suite of rooms from the then-widowed Mrs. Mary Dominis in her newly completed home. He declared the home "the American consulate," calling it "Washington Place." Ten-Eyck went a step further and had Kamehameha III publicly and officially authorize the name—"to be known so forever afterward."

He thus proclaimed, albeit subtly, that there would "always be a piece of American soil in Hawaii."[7]

⚓ 4 ⚓

Liliu's amorous and unrequited enchantment with the scholarly Maurice was short lived, and she found herself emerging into her early teens in the strange position changing *hanai* had placed her; growing up among royalty, but not being royal.

She was deeply devoted to Konia as her "only mother." After Paki's death on June 13, 1855, Bernice and Charles came to live at Haleakala, but it was quite evident that now Konia and Liliu lived with *them.* It was the Bishops' home; Paki had willed it to Bernice.

All her early life Liliu had remained somewhat in the shadow of Bernice, but now it was becoming more evident. Everyone who came

BERNICE PAUAHI AND LYDIA PAKI
An ambrotype, circa 1859
Courtesy, Bishop Museum, Harold W. Kent Collection.

into contact with the two tended to draw a comparison: Bernice was "beautiful," and Liliu was "plain."[8] An interesting small ambrotype[9] shows the two girls side-by-side and the likeness between the two is so striking it would be difficult to say which one was "plain" and which one, "beautiful." Liliu accepted her place in the shadow of Bernice, and wrote of her "good as she was beautiful." She also accepted her as her "guardian" and mentor—until "Prince Bill" came on the scene.

"Prince Bill" was Lunalilo, having taken his "democratic" name of "Prince Bill" from his Christian name of William. "Prince Bill" suited him. He was vibrant, eager, enthusiastic toward life, in a word, joyous; his greatest love was music and Shakespeare. Astride his horse, he rode through the streets of Honolulu, greeting everyone, *haole* and Hawaiian alike, *alii* or commoner.

"My kingdom for a horse!" was his favorite Shakespearian cry. And quite appropriately, for he had no kingdom and he loved his horse! Whether Prince Bill was aware of it or not, the cry reminded the *haole* fondly of the time he *freed* his *kahu*.

He was well-liked by all. The *haole*, particularly found him enchanting. He could tease the British unmercifully and still be their friend. One evening at a gathering in a British home he sang a parody on "God Save the Queen," angering his host to the point of fisticuffs. Then Prince Bill threw his arms about the Englishman and cried: "I'm as good an Englishman as you are! All a joke—only teasing." With not altogether sober tears both men then joined in a lusty singing of "God Save the Queen," as it should be sung—and all was well.

An evening later Lunalilo could be found at the Judd home, singing with the sweetest piety "Home Sweet Home"[10]—all in deference to the United States, Americans, and all they stood for.

Among the Hawaiians he excited a fervor of love that responded to his carefree attitude, his warm-hearted *aloha* for all, and his delightful poetry of sparkling waters, fragrant flowers, many-hued rainbows—always with a meaning especially for the Hawaiians, the Hawaiians of the sacred *mele* and *hula*. Even Shakespeare, as recited by Lunalilo, had a musical rapport with the old "sonorous Hawaiian," that Lorenzo Lyons helped him keep alive. It is not surprising he attracted the attention of two of the young *alii* ladies: Liliu and Princess Victoria.

No two young women could have been more different than Liliu and Victoria. Both had been active in playing the organ and leading the choir in Kawaiahao Church, but while Liliu returned to the missionary-instilled respectability of the Bishop household, Victoria returned to her non-Christian, *kahuna*-empowered half-sister, Princess Ruth. After Kamehameha III's death, she went to live with Queen Dowager Kalama. Neither Ruth nor Kalama spoke English; they were completely Hawaiian in their outlook and attitudes. Victoria found herself pulled among missionary restrictions, old Hawaiian freedom, and new *hapa-haole* immorality. Liliu, on the other hand, found herself "under the control of the Bishops," against which her free nature rebelled, and also fettered by the indoctrination of the missionary Cookes' teachings. No other member of the Royal School took early missionary Christianity as seriously as Liliuokalani did, nor stayed with its principles as long.

Liliu was told of the correctness of marrying a *haole,* and her first *haole* suitor was Gorham Gilman,[11] who after his early rescue by Konia and Paki, had landed nicely on his feet as a respectable merchant. Liliu was not interested in this rather unattractive man, who was setting himself up as a commentator and authority of Hawaiian life and ways. Gilman, however, was fairly easily disposed of; Liliu reminded Bernice that her own marriage had been a rebellious one against the high chiefs and her own father, and that she had married "for love." Liliu did not intend to marry by "arrangement" either, but for love. Bernice acquiesced easily. Liliu was still only fifteen; yet she had the care of Konia. It was a good arrangement for the time being, as Bernice saw it.

Victoria, however, fell madly and completely in love with a handsome, debonair, auctioneer, Julian Monsarrat. Julian was married and had three children, but he found Victoria desirable, and a flagrant affair began. Victoria wavered between her early moral teachings and her love for Monsarrat.

Thus stood the beginning of the romantic life of Liliu, and her soon-to-be rival, Victoria, at the time of Kamehameha III's death in 1854.

5

On December 15, 1854, Kamehameha III died. *The Polynesian* (January 13, 1855) stated:

> The age of Kamehameha III was that of progress and liberty—of schools and of civilization. He gave us a Constitution and fixed laws; he secured the people the title to their lands, and removed the last chain of oppression. He gave them a voice in councils and the mak-

ing of the laws by which they are governed. He was a great national benefactor, and has left the impress of his mild and amiable disposition on the age for which he was born.

Thus he was characterized for history.

But the young *alii,* close to his life, knew of a far different man.

They knew the troubled, confused, tired king. And before his death, the two princes, along with John Ii and Abner Paki, had fought vigorously in the Privy Council against American annexation. With the aid of British Consul Miller and French Consul Perin, they had called to Kamehameha's attention the "evils of slavery, race prejudice, hatred of aristocracy, crime and corruption, vigilantes and lynch laws," which they said were all a part of the United States political climate.

Liliu was caught up in the adamancy of Paki. Nightly, she heard of anti-Americanism. From the princes her unformed beliefs were guided further, and Liliu was beginning to develop a strong feeling against annexation. She was, however, moving toward Prince Lot's side of "Hawaii for Hawaiians," rather than Liholiho's pro-British stance.

The constant bickering between the British and the Americans in Hawaii resulted in Dr. Judd's removal from office and his being replaced as an influence by R.C. Wyllie, a Scotsman of British leanings.

Liholiho had been "chosen" at birth to succeed Kamehameha III, although he was younger than Lot. On April 7, 1853, however, Kamehameha III said he "felt death approaching," and reaffirmed the choice by officially proclaiming Liholiho his successor. In February of 1854, Kamehameha III, despite the Hawaiian *alii* protests, began trying to open doors for French, English, and American protectorates. As late as one week before he died he proclaimed: that he had accepted " . . . the aid offered in support of his sovereignty by representatives of the United States, Great Britain and France." A month later the United States Commissioner (successor of TenEyck), Luther Severance, protested that the United States had *not* joined Great Britain and France in a permanent protectorate, giving the impression that the United States was interested only in annexation.

Liholiho was determined to put an end to these annexation threats, and his first act as king was to "discontinue all protectorate talks."

But before Liholiho could don the tattered garment of King, there was the burial of his *hanai* father to be considered. The young ruler decreed that there would be a death-watch, a lying in state, for two weeks for the old king, during which time the people could pay their respects to a king they felt had saved their country from the French and the British, and who had also lived and understood the old ways. The Hawaiians wept for their "little king."[12]

It was the first royal death-watch in which Liliu took an active part. The king's body lay in state for two weeks at the coral palace with appointed *alii* standing watch, day and night, with guards and *kahili* bearers changing continuously throughout the time.

"The natives followed the ancient custom of mourning. For several days they wailed, and this wild rhythmical noise, eerie and piercing, continued to the beat of hula drums throughout the nights," wrote Judd. This was in direct defiance against the forbidden wailing at the death of Kinau. But the missionaries were no longer "in authority," in this regard, and wailing was permitted by the young *alii*.

The day of the funeral was delayed from January 6, 1855, to January 10, because the heavy rains (an omen that a great king had died) made the streets impassable. On the day of the funeral the streets were spread with grass and rushes so that the funeral procession could pass more easily. The Hawaiian cavalry, infantry, and artillery, all draped in black were followed by the band with muffled drums. The black charger of the late king was led before the funeral procession, its trappings empty to emphasize the loss. *Kahili* bearers, wearing red and yellow feather capes, accompanied the coffin. Yet it was a subdued funeral procession from times past.

The story was told around Honolulu that in order to pay for Kamehameha III's funeral—an expensive affair—the burden of collecting money was placed with American W.C. Parke, Marshal of the Kingdom. Parke, at that time, was living with his wife (nee Annie Severance), the daughter of the American Commissioner, at Washington Place. It was said that the Marshal went about Honolulu paying the bills to the various merchants from a wheelbarrow loaded with coins—American coins.

There was a grim warning in these rumors. What had happened to the Royal treasury? Why were the bills so high? Where was *aloha*? And why was all the coinage American?

Liholiho, apparently did not stop to consider the significance of those questions and began to govern a country that was becoming largely American. The spirit was still Hawaiian—fragile, but Hawaiian.

But Liholiho sought to make it British, as the young *alii* passed into a new era of royalty.

LIHOLIHO
(Kamehameha IV)

QUEEN EMMA

CHAPTER 2

Romance in the Royal Court

❧ 1 ❧

The reign of Liholiho, now Kamehameha IV, was to be peacefully unpolitical, in his opinion. He felt he had destroyed the "annexation movement" with his proclamation of "all talks of a protectorate to cease forever." He had merely sent it underground, but he was aided by a period of prosperity. Agriculture was coming into its own, small plantations were beginning to develop, trade was favorable, and the people were delighted with their charismatic young king.

Politically, the king chose primarily men of British origin to replace Americans. He retained William Lee, a close friend of Charles Reed Bishop, and Elisha Allen, a distant relative of Bishop's. The amiable, non-imperialistic new American Commissioner, David Gregg, did much to quiet the fears of the country. He and his attractive wife, "one of the most beautiful women in Hawaii," became a close friend of the king.

As Judd had written, Kamehameha IV was not so much anti-American as he was anti-missionary. It was not for the reason Judd gave —"excessive missionary training"—but because many former missionaries and their descendants had been behind the "peaceful annexation movement," during the previous reign.

Liliu found herself again caught in the midst of a newly emerging royal order, as the young king began to seek a wife.

Liholiho had been attracted to Emma Rooke from their Royal School days. It was not surprising the attraction had grown, for now among all the young *alii* she was exceedingly desirable. She was a dark-haired, Caucasian-featured beauty. She had been well brought up, having been privately tutored after her Royal School days—not only in academics but in social behavior. Emma was the perfect young *alii* to be Kamehameha IV's wife—especially as they loved each other. They were the romantic royal couple suitable to the Hawaiians as well as to the *haole*—

even to those of anti-royalist sentiments, whose ambivalence toward royalty became painfully evident during this period.

The old chiefs however, were not convinced that love was enough for such an important union. The age-old belief still existed that the highest chiefs and chiefesses should marry to bring forth the most *mana* for the country. The high chiefs held a council, and Kapaakea, Liliu's blood father, brought to the attention of the group that Liliu Kamakaeha, the descendant of Keawe-a-Heulu, was of higher lineage than Emma, whose blood was mingled with *haole* (John Young). Even more important, Liliu was the *hanai* daughter of Paki and Konia, a direct descendant of Kamehameha the Great. She was truly the next in both chiefly descent and *hanai* rank to Liholiho—except for his sister, Victoria. But that relationship brought up incest.

Together with Paki, Kapaakea had a message sent to Kamehameha IV that he should consider that "there is no other chief equal to you in birth and rank but the adopted daughter of Paki."[1]

Kamehameha IV was extremely annoyed, and the Kamehameha temper was no small one in Liholiho, as was later to be seen. Now it merely rumbled beneath the surface. He declared adamantly he would marry whom he pleased and made his announcement, publicly and officially, January, 1855, that he would marry Emma Rooke, *hanai* daughter of T. C. B. Rooke and Grace Young. The date was set for the same month.

One week after the announcement, Moana Loa erupted and began sending its lava flow toward Hilo.

"Pele is opposed to the marriage!" the natives cried, and the chiefs agreed, especially Paki and Kapaakea. Even Liholiho became uncertain. He said he would "postpone his decision," for the time being. The old and the new were still warring in the young king.

On June 13, 1855, Paki died and left all his property to his "only child, Bernice." The old *hanai* was broken, and Kapaakea stood on the shifting sands of time and custom. Liliu had been dropped from her *hanai* position, not even declared the "adopted" or "foster" child of Paki. These terms, it must be remembered, were not understood among the Hawaiians. An even more ambiguous word was to come in later—"ward."

In March, nine months later, in 1856, Moana Loa also ceased her protest, and the lava flow stopped five miles from Hilo. Kamehameha IV gave a sigh of relief, and in May, 1856, the young king read a formal announcement to the privy council: that "consulting the obligations which the Almighty conferred upon [him] as King, and in due regard to the perpetuity of the Hawaiian sovereignty and to the good of the people," he resolved to marry Emma Rooke.

❧ 2 ❧

The wedding was one to excite all Hawaii. It was the first royal wedding. It was also to be the last. It was a far cry from the secret ceremony of Kamehameha III's marriage to Nahienaena at Paki's home, or his later expeditiously simple missionary ceremony with Kalama.

Liliu, with Victoria, was to be a principal bridesmaid, which spoke for Liliu's social position and the lack of resentment on all sides. She was as excited, joyous, anticipatory, as any eighteen-year old bridesmaid would be, to take a prominent position in the wedding party of the most prestigious marriage ever to be held in Hawaii.

An exciting deviation from custom, more pleasing to the Hawaiians than to the American *haole*, was that the wedding ceremony would neither be Old Hawaiian nor missionary. True to his love of Britain, Kamehameha IV requested an Anglican service. As there was no Anglican churchman in Hawaii in 1856, a nod of appreciation must be given to Rev. Richard Armstrong, a missionary who rose admirably to the occasion and agreed to read "the vows according to the ceremony of the Church of England."

The day was declared a holiday—all offices and most stores were closed; flags of all countries represented in Hawaii waved, and people thronged the streets, awaiting the royal wedding party.

> Three thousand guests of native Hawaiians, *haole*, chiefs and foreign dignitaries, who filled the church to capacity, waited inside the stone edifice, festooned with maile and other greenery hanging from the ceiling and the galleries and entwined about the columns, the air heavy with the scent of flowers. They waited in breathless stillness for the bride to walk down the aisle.
>
> At eleven-thirty the bride entered the church. Walking with her *hanai* father, Dr. Rooke, Emma was dressed in a wedding gown of the richest white embroidered silk selected at Stewart's in Broadway, New York, which with an elegantly wrought bridal veil and a head dress of white roses and orange blossoms, gave her the appearance and beauty to which Parisian art could have added but little.

The twenty-year old bride was then joined by a handsome uniformed twenty-two-year old king who was accompanied by the Governor of Oahu, his blood father. The couple met at "an altar covered with rich figured silk with gold trimmings." There the two knelt on a rich carpet before Dr. Armstrong, who read the vows in both English and Hawaiian.

"All foreign dignitaries and guests were graciously received," at the magnificent reception at the palace that evening. Liliuokalani in later years wryly commented that she had never known a *haole* to refuse a royal invitation, and where pleasures were to be offered by the Hawaiians, "the missionaries apparently made no distinction between royalists and themselves."

Dancing continued throughout the night. Lunalilo (Prince Bill), also in the wedding party, danced with Liliu, the graceful young bridesmaid, who had now completely conquered her slight limp. It may have been the first time he came to realize she was a grown-up young lady. Julius Palmer[2] later wrote of her that, while on the dance floor, she "looked as if she were in love with every man she danced."

❧ 3 ❧

There is nothing like a beautiful wedding to inspire romance, especially in the young unmarried woman. It aroused in nearly every young girl present, a sense of being in love—if only being in love with love. Many misalliances are brought about by a beautiful wedding.

As for Liliu, she was ripe for falling in love, and Prince Bill was close at hand—both as a prince and as an attractive young man. Lunalilo, "Prince Bill," stood six-foot one, slender, of good features and dark complexion. Later he was to be called "one of the most handsome men in the kingdom."

He was, however, in a curious genealogical position. As the cousin of the young king, he had a close relationship, but he was not a Kamehameha. His mother was the niece, step-daughter and one of the wives of Kamehameha I, bearing him no children, but having her child by a second husband of lesser chiefly descent, Kanaina. Prince Bill later drew himself away from all Kamehameha contacts, saying that they had always "slighted" him and his mother. Yet at this time he was "selected" by the king to marry Victoria.

This arranged marriage had many ramifications. Victoria's love for Julian Monsarrat was no secret, but the gossip surrounding the affair was not yet scurrilous. Prince Lot, it was said, threatened Julian with banishment, forbad him to enter the palace grounds, and even threatened his life.[3] Lot deeply loved his sister Victoria; in many ways they were much alike. They had the same brooding quality that was mistaken for

sullenness. There was a heaviness about them both mentally and physically.

It seemed best now, however, in the king's eyes that Victoria should
make as nearly a royal alliance as possible, and it was also remembered
that Prince Bill, although currently involved with a Maui princess, had
been "betroth" to Victoria when they were both children, their mothers
having been sisters.

Prince Bill was not overly impressed with the arrangement and was
somewhat distant toward Victoria. Victoria, to avoid possible rejection
by Prince Bill, as well as to please her brother by disentangling herself
from Julian, chose another high chief, David Kalakaua, Liliu's brother.

During the recent waiting period of Kamehameha IV to announce
his engagement to Emma, the lineage of Liliu had been carefully studied,
and David's as well. He had not been found wanting and rose on the
ladder of high chiefs. He had been given government appointments and
been made a member of a privy council. Kalakaua in the mid-1800's was
in good chiefly standing.

He was a handsome, largely self-educated but knowledgeable, quick-
witted and shrewd young man of immeasurable charm and personality,
qualities he never lost.

Victoria now wrote David a note asking him to set the date, for they
were, indeed, engaged.[4] Now that brothers and sisters of biological parentage had become more important than *hanai*, David, having grown
closer to his sister, showed the note to Liliu, who was delighted. It set
her Prince Bill free. It appears she accepted the engagement with more
hope than either of the two parties concerned did.

Prince Bill had become aware of Liliu, and she seemed to have attracted him more than Victoria did. They both shared the common interest of
music. She had written the music to Kamehameha III's "The Forest is
for Love Making" as a remembrance of Nahienaena. It contained mystical symbols of life and nature dear to the Hawaiians and known to
both Liliu and the king.

Liliu's clear young voice was so impressive that Prince Bill certainly
became aware of her in the many musical sessions the *alii* held. Her
piquant charm and good looks, that were to become evident later, were
beginning to emerge from the shade cast by Bernice.

At this time Konia's health had begun to fail, and Liliu, as her affec-
tionate *hanai* daughter, accompanied her on a trip to the healthful climate
of Kona on the Island of Hawaii. There Liliu met for the first time her

own sister Likelike, then a ten-year-old child. In her *Story* she commented that Kona was "dull" in comparison with the court activities of Honolulu. An invitation to a ball to be given by Prince Bill in Honolulu provided a welcome diversion. Konia agreed to go to Lahaina, Maui, to be with Liliu's own parents while Liliu returned to Honolulu with a retinue of five "ladies of high chiefly descent," and numerous retainers, who served them.

Liliu had double excitement in going to Honolulu. Besides the ball, Kalakaua was to announce his engagement to Victoria. However, both were to have startling disappointments.

Upon her arrival, David reported he had not heard from Victoria since he had set the date for their marriage. He assumed that the engagement had been broken. Apparently Kalakaua was not too eager to pursue the young lady, and it is possible he was already interested in Kapiolani, at the time married to High Chief Ben Namakeha and Queen Emma's highest lady-in-waiting.

But there was still Prince Bill's ball, and Liliu attended with her brother and their combined retinues. The dancing in the elaborately decorated hall was interrupted at will with spontaneous singing. It was a festive affair and one to gladden the heart of young Liliu.

Then in the midst of the festivities, Victoria, with a vast retinue of over a hundred men and women, arrived. The music and dancing stopped and Victoria imperiously made her way across a rapidly clearing floor to her host, Prince Bill. Taking his arm, she called for silence. She then publicly announced her engagement of long standing, indeed from birth, to Prince Bill. The crowd cheered, for few knew Kalakaua's supposed engagement or of Liliu's love for the prince.

A badly shaken and hurt Liliu decided she must return to Konia at Lahaina, Maui. The next day as she and her attendants boarded a crowded schooner belonging to Prince Bill, he offered Liliu and her party his own cabin space, which he had cleared of "oranges . . . his wearing apparel, boots, and other belongings" for her convenience. Then before the witnesses aboard, he asked Liliu to marry him. Standing on the vessel, looking back to the Honolulu to which she had arrived with such anticipation, Liliu showed the person she was later to become. She reminded the prince of his duty, his engagement to Victoria; he dismissed the previous night's announcement with a flick of his graceful, white laced wrist. Turning to an old Hawaiian priest, he stated he wanted to show

VICTORIA KAMAMALU

his true love by having the priest marry them at once, before the witnesses present.

The enamored teenager and the missionary-trained young woman struggled in Liliu, and the latter won. She chose to tell him in her quiet voice that she would, indeed, take the matter under consideration, and write to him at Kona where he was to go to join his father.

After some days of troubled emotions, Liliu's romanticism won out, and she wrote a letter from Lahaina accepting his proposal. With a fluttering heart, she sent it by messenger to be placed on the vessel then in the harbor, the *Kamamalu*—which unfortunately belonged to Victoria. Prince Bill never received her letter.

He did, however, receive a letter from Victoria, reminding him of *their* engagement, which she intended for him to keep. He decided to return to Honolulu, where Victoria was at the time living with her own father, the Governor of Oahu, but stopped first at Lahaina to see Liliu. He told her he had never received her letter and assumed that she did not wish to marry him. Liliu protested, taken by his romantic persistence. Thus, there at the old capital city of Hawaii, under a starlit sky, beside a softly murmuring surf, Liliu and Prince Bill became engaged. A very happy and excited Liliu wrote her brother, "It is so joyous. I am so glad . . ."[5]

Victoria, on the other hand, did not seem to care. She was back in Honolulu near Julian Monsarrat. The way seemed clear for Prince Bill and Liliu. But other elements soon came into play.

Konia died June 2, 1857, and Liliu came "more and more under the charge of Mr. and Mrs. Bishop." There followed a period of angry words, bitter quarrels, and furious tears between Bernice and Liliu. She wrote several times to Kalakaua that she "had words" with Bernice and Charles Bishop, the latter to whom she referred to as merely "B." But she was dependent on the Bishops' support, and because of shifting *hanai,* she was not heir to any of Paki or Konia's lands. Her own mother and father were still alive, and no inheritance from her grandfather, Aikanaka, had come to her.

She must have argued her case for Prince Bill somewhat successfully, because finally the Bishops assented to consult Kamehameha IV, who replied "if [she] were [his] daughter [he] should not approve it, but if each wanted to marry, [he] would not oppose it . . ."[6] It was a short-lived victory.

Victoria had lost Julian Monsarrat through his return to his wife.

Thoroughly confused about sex, morality, her place in the old and new Hawaii, Victoria turned to alcohol and began swinging back and forth between the old and the new ways. Rumors were beginning to circulate about her return to the old ways of kahunaism and sorcery, as well as her obvious alcoholic proclivities.

She was replaced at Kawaiahao Church by Liliu as leader of the choir, and more importantly, was also replaced by Liliu in the royal court. Liliu now held "the highest rank of an unmarried woman in the land."[7]

The effect upon Liliu was profound. The old unreasonable terror that she must somehow have been at fault—that *she* had done something wrong—assailed her. She retreated into her shell, and refused to marry Prince Bill.

She became a constant attendant to Queen Emma and placed herself in the background.

Prince Bill, spoiled as a child, pampered as a young prince, disliked and distrusted by the Kamehamehas, responded to his failures with drunkenness, gambling, and wastrel living. Even his father became concerned, and put Prince Bill's monies under the guardianship of Charles Bishop, who doled out an always insufficient allowance, causing the young prince to go dangerously into debt.

As the romance between Prince Bill and Liliu came to its tragic end, Bernice carried a burden of guilt for her role in preventing what would undoubtedly have been a disasterous marriage. She began looking for a more agreeable suitor for her *hanai* sister, and found him in John Owen Dominis, whose relatives had become curiously entwined with those of Charles Bishop.

John's father was an Italian sea captain who had married Mary Lambert Jones of New York and Boston in 1821.[8] They had three children before sailing to Hawaii to settle and live in the house which would be known as Washington Place. Of the three children, only John moved to Hawaii. His two sisters were left in New England to "be educated properly." Before 1848 both girls had died, and the Captain was lost at sea. Mrs. Dominis thereafter took in "guests" at her home to help pay expenses.

John was sent to the Royal School, but only briefly. While there he became friends with young Lot, and upon the Prince's return from abroad, he became Lot's private secretary, after having held a few minor governmental appointments. He thus joined the inner circle of young *alii*.

Though she had had contact with John since childhood, Liliu's first recollection of him was vague—so vague that when she wrote her memoirs forty years later, she forgot his attendance at the Royal School, and remembered only a "curious urchin" who had peered over the walls at the royal children.

Bernice reminded her of the many gatherings they had both attended —the royal wedding party, the many social engagements that followed, and especially a beautiful ball given by the Chinese,[9] during which he had been most attentive to Liliu.

Remembering these times Liliu was willing to listen to Bernice's talk about John Owen Dominis. She also remembered another meeting, which had proved him extraordinarily gallant. It also made her begin to suspect he had physical courage beyond that of Prince Bill's.

It was during a horseback riding party of Kamehameha IV's in 1856: "The king was returning from Moanalua with a large escort", she wrote in her *Story,* "a cavalcade of perhaps two hundred riders of both sexes. Amongst these was General J. O. Dominis, then a young man [he was twenty-five] on the staff of Prince Lot. He was riding by my side when an awkward horseman forced his horse between us, and in the confusion Mr. Dominis was thrown from his horse and his leg broken.[10] He gained the saddle, however, and insisted on accompanying me to my home, where he dismounted and helped me from my horse." A gallant and romantic gesture to a young nineteen-year-old girl! But one for which his mother never forgave *her,* for it later led to his bouts with rheumatism.

If he caught Liliuokalani's attention, as he certainly did, he also caught the Bishops'. Here was the perfect husband for Liliu. Charles Reed Bishop continued to praise him throughout his life; and Bernice was acquiescent.

Another factor was on the side of this union. In 1859, R. C. Wyllie, Kamehameha's and Emma's most trusted adviser and friend, had taken ill. He was removed from his home, Rosebank, to Washington Place, there to be cared for by a nurse under Mrs. Dominis' administrations. Wyllie was so excited about the possible romance that he misinformed Lady Franklin that Lydia Paki wanted "to marry an Englishman." Lady Franklin and Sophia Cracroft were both delighted, saying they "couldn't blame her." What a shock it would have been to them had they known that it was John Dominis, the American, of Washington Place!

CHAPTER 3

Problems in the Royal Household

❧ 1 ❧

Before she could reach a decision regarding John Owen Dominis, Liliu became directly involved in the problems of the new royal household and the establishment of Queen's Hospital.

As early as 1855 Kamehameha IV had attempted to solve the greatest and fastest growing problem of the Hawaiian people: "the decrease of our population." Grim evidence was everywhere to be seen in abandoned villages, untilled fields, crowded cemeteries. Only 70,000 now remained of the 300,000 in Kamehameha I's time.

In his opening speech to the legislature, Kamehameha IV had recommended that public hospitals for the Hawaiians be established, but for the next four years only small appropriations were made. There were hospital facilities provided by foreign governments for foreign seamen and some private hospitals for foreign residents, but nothing for the Hawaiian population, especially the poor. Queen Emma finally appealed to Dr. Charles F. Guillou, her personal physician, who stated publicly that "the only means of prolonging the existence of the Hawaiian race is by bringing them . . . medical aid."

In 1859 the legislature passed a law permitting the organization and incorporation of Queen's Hospital and provided that "when the corporation reached the amount of $5,000 the Minister of Interior, Prince Lot, with the consent of the king, might convey to it government lands of equal value in which case, the government should have a proportional voice in the management of the corporation."

Prince Lot noted that while no *haole* were required to contribute to the hospital in monies nor land, yet they, while in legislative power, had the right of management. The King apparently saw nothing disproportionate in the law, and an early breach opened between Prince Lot and Kamehameha IV.

As the $5,000 had to be raised outside of "the government" appropriations, the burden of doing so fell upon the king and queen. In 1859, after her romance with Prince Bill and before her arrangement with Dominis, Liliu threw herself full-heartedly into the project of raising money.

In a dramatic procedure she joined the king and queen in walking from door to door in Honolulu, to business houses and private homes, soliciting monies for the hospital. Coins poured in regardless of the forboding *haole* voice that the native Hawaiians would not use the facility because they preferred their *kahuna*. Even the country folk offered a pig, a basket of vegetables or fruits, or even a cherished coconut.

Liliu took the lead in organizing the first public benefits to be given by royalty, and gained the later praise, from Emma: "She is a good woman. She did more than I ever did."[1]

Fourteen-thousand dollars was collected, enough to begin a temporary hospital building, and shortly a sum was raised sufficient to build a two-story hospital of stone, capable of accommodating 100 patients. The hospital, in Hawaiian *aloha*, was open to foreigners as well as Hawaiians.

There immediately arose again the question whether the Hawaiians would "forsake their *kahuna* practices and use the foreigners' methods." Dr. William Hillebrand, physician of the hospital, reported "Their faith in the old kahunas has not been demolished yet, but faith in the foreign kahunas seem to have been sensibly increased . . ." The hospital also came under adverse criticism by the foreigners because prostitutes were treated for venereal diseases, a practice they felt merely encouraged "looseness." The Hawaiians were quite aware that the decrease in population was due in large part from venereal diseases brought in by foreigners. To them, the source did not matter, only the cure.

❧ 2 ❧

Queen Emma went into labor of childbirth on May 20, 1858. Present at her bedside was an anxious Liliu, as well as Madame Namakeha, Emma's close friend and lady-in-waiting, and Emma's doctor. Tension was ramrod stiff, for all were aware of the danger of stillborn babies, so frequent now in Hawaii. At ten minutes past six in the evening, Queen Emma gave birth to a son, and the rejoicing throughout the islands was great. Not since the time of Kamehameha the First had a "royal" queen[2] given birth to a child. Now there was an heir!

Such a day! One always to be cherished! But it held a heartache for Liliu, whose arms longed to take the tiny infant. Madame Namakeha preceeded her. It was she who was given the highest honor, now that *hanai* was gone, of being "nursemaid and constant attendant" to the young prince.

The following day Albert (named after England's Prince Albert) Edward Kauikeaouli Leiopapa a Kamehameha, with the approval of the Privy Council, was given the title of "His Royal Highness Prince of Hawaii." The day was declared a holiday; flags were flown; places of business were closed. The parade of well-wishers, foreign and Hawaiian, seemed unending.

During the entire first year of the infant's life, various groups came to pay homage and present gifts. The Prince was touted as "the representative of two distinct races:" the British and Hawaiian, as Emma was part British as well as *hanai* to a British doctor. But nearly all part-Hawaiian foreigners claimed a place through bringing gifts and honoring the young prince, and during the first year he was much on display.

The first anniversary of the Prince was properly and gloriously celebrated. A child's first birthday (later known as the one-year-old luau) was one of the most important events in the child's life. The baby had survived the first crucial year.

The first anniversary was proclaimed a public holiday. It was a "lovely day, a proper day for a national jubilee." Love for the little Prince and "joy in the prospect of a brilliant future was evidenced by all." Bishop Maigret held a Mass in the Catholic Church.

Liliu, although still a devoted member of the Kawaiahao Church, was remarkably tolerant toward other religions and partook with pleasure in her first Mass. Later she joined in her favorite activity—that of entertaining the children. A reception for all the school children was held at the palace, and they were "received" by the infant prince with Queen Emma, Madame Namakeha, and Liliu attending him and greeting the children.

The afternoon witnessed a regatta, the first ever attempted in Honolulu, and in the evening there was a grand reception and a ball at the palace.

Liliu continued to travel in the royal party to the outer islands, and she records in her *Story* that while the king and queen were on one of these trips, news was received that "Baby" had become ill. Emma was frantic, and Liliu's first dislike of the king becomes evident in her saying that he refused to allow his wife to go immediately to her child, "lest she reach him before he did."[3]

Fortunately, news was received that the young prince had recovered before there was opportunity for either party to prepare to leave, or for the quarrel to go further.

❧ 3 ❧

It was on one of the royal tours to Maui and Hawaii that a scandal broke over the royal household that could easily have shaken the Islands. The fact that it didn't gives one of the clearest pictures of the place the monarchy held in 1858.

The king shot, with intent to kill, his secretary, Henry Neilson. There are many accounts of the shooting in biographies, histories, and letters of the period, among which are Neilson's own letters. Succinctly, but reservedly, Kuykendall gives the essentials:

> While the royal party was on Maui, or even earlier, the king's mind had been poisoned against Neilson by some means—idle or malicious gossip—and he was led to believe that his secretary had abused his confidence; the queen's name had been somehow involved in the reports that came to the king's ear. For days the king brooded over this matter and it appears that he finally decided—deliberately—what action he would take. He then spent a day and part of two nights on a small vessel at sea, drinking heavily, then came on shore, sought out Neilson, and shot him with a pistol at close range. Luckily, the wound, though very serious was not immediately fatal.

Liliuokalani's account reveals best her reaction after the fact, and shows her developing royalist attitudes. Her terse account reads:

> There were causes which were apparent to any of our people for something very like righteous anger on the part of the king. His Majesty was trying to make us each and all happy; yet even during moments of relaxation, undue familiarity, absence of etiquette, rudeness or any other form which implied or suggested disrespect of royalty in any manner whatsoever, would never be tolerated by any one of the native chiefs of the Hawaiian people. To allow such a breach of good manners to pass unnoticed would be looked upon by his own retainers as belittling him, and they would be the first to demand the punishment of the offender.

What Liliuokalani with Victorian delicacy refers to as "undue familiarity" was considered by others as somewhat more intimate: Emma's flirtations.

There is no reason to believe that Emma was unfaithful to her husband. Neilson denied all—a chivalrous, and wise action. Whatever had been the direct cause, Kamehameha saw it through a red alcoholic fog, and *did* fire his gun point blank at Neilson. Neilson received the chest wound that was not "immediately fatal."

Horrified after the fact at what he had done, Kamehameha IV gave all attention to Neilson he could, and offered to abdicate in favor of his infant son.

A most revealing point regarding the position of the monarchy was that no one made the slightest move to accept this abdication. Liliu took the view, supported by Prince Lot, and most natives, that "the right [of the King] of life and death was unchallenged; . . . the whole people owed its national life to the throne".[4]

A question does arise: Why did the *haole* population not protest? What about the "power-hungry missionaries" of whom later accounts have been written? Here was a perfect opportunity to seize the government through a baby. But no one moved to do so. There was a minimum of comment even in the newspapers. In fact, every effort was made to prevent the king from such a precipitous move. Why? One of the most important reasons was that the "power-hungry missionaries" weren't really power hungry at that time. Dr. Judd, who could have spear-headed a group toward the overthrow of the monarchy, was remarkably silent.

But more important, the country was suffering no economic problems: therefore, those in "royal power" could remain undisturbed.

Now, great sympathy arose for the grief-stricken monarch, who for two-and-a-half years, saw to Neilson's every need and waited on him personally. Neilson did not blame the king either, which is perhaps just as well, as Neilson was a member of the Harriman family, the American railroad magnate, and was related by marriage to Hamilton Fish, Secretary of State under President Grant.

Kamehameha IV decided, probably with some advice from R. C. Wyllie, that instead of abdicating, he would bend all his efforts toward securing an Anglican Bishop for Hawaii. As a kind of self-inflicted "penance," the king began translating the Anglican Prayer Book into Hawaiian.

✴ 4 ✴

In 1861 after Lady Franklin and her companion, Sophia Cracroft, arrived in Honolulu, R. C. Wyllie began again pressuring Kamehameha

—with the ladies' help—to request that an Anglican Bishop come to Hawaii to baptize the young prince.

Kamehameha was further urged to ask Queen Victoria to be the godmother to the young prince. Many hesitant letters were written by the king and as many, or more, dictated by Lady Franklin, for this daring request. The political ramifications were obvious.

Kamehameha remembered his cordial reception at the Court of St. James in 1848, but to ask the Queen to be godmother to his son—well, that was a bit overwhelming for Kamehameha, but with continuous promptings, he finally did so.

What Queen Victoria thought of the situation is obscured by her dwelling on her own grief—something she continued to do for too many years after her husband's death. Nevertheless, whatever transpired in the British royal court, Victoria agreed to send an Anglican Bishop to Hawaii and to be godmother to the prince.

While negotiations were underway, tragedy struck.

⚓ 5 ⚓

On August 17, 1862, Liliu was called to the palace by Queen Emma, who hysterically told her Liholiho (Kamehameha IV) had "killed the young prince." Liliu, shocked as well as puzzled, inasmuch as the young prince was still very much alive, though ill, tried to get a more coherent story from Emma. Gradually the tale emerged. The young prince in a burst of "Kamehameha temper" had refused to wear some boots his father had brought him. The king's patience tried beyond endurance, a rather minimal endurance, he had decided to "cool off" the young "tyrant" and had placed his head under a cold-water faucet. The result had been first a shock to the four-year-old child, and then, "brain fever" had developed—he was now dying.[5]

Royal secrets are never well kept, and on August 19, 1862, it was publicly announced that the Prince of Hawaii had become seriously ill. Bulletins were issued three times daily, but what was kept out of the press was that the king had been "responsible" for the illness. At all costs the king's reputation must be protected.

With painful irony, the British Commissioner and Consul-General, W. W. F. Synge, and his wife, arrived August 25, 1862, bearing a beautiful christening cup from Queen Victoria and were informed of the state of the young Prince's health by David Kalakaua, the King's chamberlain. The next day Kalakaua came to him, telling him that the Prince's situation had grown worse.

Mr. Synge's official report stated that he did not send a return message, but accompanied Kalakaua immediately to the palace.

> We were at once introduced to the King and Queen . . . The King asked me whom the Queen had appointed to be her Co-sponsor for the child. I told him at that time my Sovereign had not, I believed understood that it was His Majesty's wish that the Godfathers be chosen by her. He then said, "Do you think the Prince of Wales would consent to be Godfather, and will you act as his proxy?" At such a moment I thought I could not answer otherwise than I did, namely that I had little doubt that His Royal Highness would be glad to be associated with His Mother in the Sponsorship of a Prince in whom Her Majesty took so lively an interest, and that I would venture to act as His Proxy, subject to His future approval. The King then asked His brother Prince (Lot) Kamehameha to be the other Godfather; and the Baptismal Service was at once proceeded with in the antechamber—the King and Queen, the officiating Clergymen, the Sponsors and the Proxies only entering the Prince's apartment for a few seconds while the water was poured and the Sign of the Cross made, on his forehead, as he lay in bed. It was a most affecting Ceremony . . .[6]

There being no British Anglican Bishop yet in Hawaii—Dr. Staley was on his way—again an American pastor, Rev. Ephraim W. Clark of the First Congregational Church in Honolulu, performed the service, reading "portions of the Baptismal Service, omitting all the questions to the sponsors, and praying extempore." The little Prince was then officially christened Albert Edward Kauikeaouli Leiopapa a Kamehameha.

Two days later, on the 27th, he died. "Those present at his bedside besides his mother and father (the King and Queen) were Bernice Bishop, Mr. Wyllie and Lydia Paki." Liliu had replaced Madame Namakeha, somewhat unfairly, by Emma's placing the blame also on Madame Namakeha. Liliu, rightly or wrongly, never forgave the king for what she considered his blame in the death of the prince.

From nine o'clock on Thursday morning until noon, a continuous stream of people passed through the palace as the people grieved with the bereaved royal parents.

Kamehameha IV took the blame of his child's death upon himself, and others in the kingdom knew of his self-incriminations, for letters were written containing statements that "the king is nearly mad, blaming himself again . . ."—though no one else did, publicly. Kamehameha IV never recovered from his grief, becoming a recluse, and withdrawing from public life.

Queen Emma chose a different way. For four days she neither ate, nor drank, nor slept, but grieved in torrential tears at the tomb of her son. Then she arose, her grief cleansed, and began taking up her duties of every-day life as a queen.

✖ 6 ✖

Between 1854 and 1862 Liliu was also beginning to live the life of an *alii* in an "enlightened" Hawaiian society. Organizations were beginning to be formed, just as the *haole* had their organizations.

The most important one to Liliu was instituted by Victoria, while she was still in good standing with the Court: the Kaahumanu Society. Remembering that Hawaii had in the past basically recognized a matriarchal society, Victoria called together a group of high chiefesses whom she considered "leaders," to establish the Kaahumanu Society "for all time." It was to be an organization to preserve the old traditions and customs and especially to recognize the strength of womanhood. Hawaii was rapidly becoming, under the *haole,* a masculine-dominated country. Kamehameha IV had appointed no women to the privy council, as had always been done in the past. And although Victoria held the title of "kuhina nui," or premier, it was an honorary title after the death of Auhea, her aunt, who had "served" in her place, until she reached majority. Kaahumanu, the first *kuhina nui,* was the one to which the society turned for past leadership, a leadership they now hoped to extend into the present and future. It recognized "queenship" in the old way, with reverence and respect—and importance: *Moi wahine.*

The organization had a profound influence upon Liliu, who took naturally to becoming the "liberated woman;" she was both behind and ahead of her time. Her past ideas came from the liberated Kaahumanu, who was Kamehameha's confidante and adviser, but Liliu's future was to attempt to bring "equal rights" to women in both education and business long before she entered into government herself and long before such equality was generally acceptable anywhere in the world.

It was during this period of personal growth and court disruption that Liliuokalani became engaged to John Owen Dominis. A persistent belief had developed among her friends and family that she should marry.

In 1860, John Owen Dominis, as has already been seen, was a strange link between the Hawaiian royalty and the American *haole*. Growing up in the home that housed such strong annexationists as American Commissioner George Brown, who had been lost at sea with John's father, and Brown's successor, Anthony Ten-Eyck, John was also in the confidence of the strongly anti-annexationist, Prince Lot. John Owen Dominis emerges as an elusive character—he never seemed to be in the place where one might expect to find him; he never seemed to actually "take sides" in any given situation.

He was a good friend of the Bishops—that strangely royalist-*haole* couple. Charles Bishop's banking partner, W. A. Aldrich, had married John's cousin, Elizabeth Holt.[7] He had many other contacts on both sides of the annexation question. This unusual and contradictory man, now the secretary to Prince Lot, became the last suitor of Liliu Kamakaeha or Lydia Paki.

PART III
Changing Cultures Meet

❧ ❧

Mrs. John Owen Dominis
1862-1873

LYDIA PAKI

JOHN OWEN DOMINIS

CHAPTER 1

High Chiefess Lydia Paki Marries

❧ 1 ❧

Liliuokalani, in her *Story,* summarily dismisses her thirty years of married life in a scant ten pages. Her remarks relative to John Owen Dominis are terse: "I was engaged to Mr. Dominis for about two years; and it was our intention to be married the second day of September, 1862." There are few lines that are revealing about the marriage except those relating to his mother: "She clung with tenacity to the affection and constant attention of her son, and no man could be more devoted than General Dominis was to his mother."

Fragments exist of letters written to and from John between 1860 and 1862, the engagement period.[1] Early in 1861 he received a letter from a friend in California, who had been trying to persuade him to join him there: "What! you are considering marriage? Why?" It was certainly not an answer to a letter that told of impassioned love. A second letter asked a pertinent question: "Well, if you must. But what will Mama say?"

We do not know how John replied. One suspects he didn't, for one of his most irritating attributes was his silence and secrecy.

Between 1860 and 1862 John apparently lost favor with Prince Lot. In 1861 Prince Lot chose David Kalakaua as his adviser, friend, and companion to go to Canada to investigate the possibility of trade.

This period contains frequent requests from John to Lot for "a little more money in these hard times." In August 1861, a year and a month before his proposed marriage, John wrote Prince Lot that things were " . . . so jolly at home . . . only mother and myself . . . can't think of leaving home when having such a good time . . . such a good home . . . " Ominous words!

The time had come for Liliu to marry, and with it came her own unrealistic expectations and very real hidebound Victorian-missionary instilled attitudes of sexual morality. She entered marriage with the warring elements of being a woman capable of great passion—of love, hate, tenderness, resentment, joy, anger—all disciplined by both *aloha* and Victorianism.

Ever a victim of circumstances, Liliu found that her wedding date, originally set for September 2, 1862, her twenty-fourth birthday, had to be postponed until September 16th because of the tragic death of the Prince of Hawaii. The wedding was held in the home in which she lived for fourteen years and considered her own, Haleakala, but the newspapers told of it as a "small quiet wedding held at the home of the Bishop's."

All newspaper accounts were brief: "John Owen Dominis, his Majesty's Private Secretary, was married to Miss Lydia [Kamakaeha] Paki, adopted daughter of the late High Chief A. Paki," and mentioned the honored guests including the King. " . . . a bountiful repast was set out . . . and the center table was spread with a variety of elegant and costly bridal gifts."

Although some newspapers listed Mrs. Mary Dominis as a guest, one made the telling statement: "Mrs. Dominis, the groom's mother, waited at her home to greet her new daughter-in-law." Mary Dominis did not approve of the "kanaka" marriages. No doubt she would not have approved of anyone's marriage to her only son, but certainly not the marriage to a native, as later letters exchanged with Boston relatives reveal.[2] Although written about someone else, they include the fervent wish that "he" not marry a "kanaka."

❧ 2 ❧

Fortunately, Prince Lot almost immediately arranged a wedding trip. Although John was Prince Lot's friend and adviser, the true rapport lay between Lot and Liliu. Lot continued to be the royal "big brother" to her. While she had never had much enthusiasm for Kamehameha IV, she bore a great fondness for Prince Lot, and he, for her. They were much alike in their outlook on politics, foreigners, Hawaiians, music, and life in general.

From a picture taken at this time, she emerges as an attractive young woman dressed in a travelling suit right out of Lady Godey's Book, complete with feathered hat and long gloves. But the "glow of freedom," of which Julius Palmer spoke, was not yet upon her.

The wedding trip was joyous for Liliu. She was back into her "family"

—her atmosphere. Everywhere she and John travelled they were greeted as *alii*, and the retainers of Prince Lot provided marvelous hospitality to the newlyweds.

Unhappily, for Liliu, the joyous life of the wedding trip for the young *alii* and her husband in the company of the royal court could not last.

John and Liliu returned to Washington Place. It was described by Liliuokalani thirty-five years later " . . . a large square, white house, with pillars and portico on two sides, really a palatial dwelling, as comfortable in its appointments as it is inviting in its aspect; its front is distant from the street far enough to avoid the dust and noise. Trees shade its walls from the heat of the noonday and its ample gardens are filled with the choicest flowers and shrubs; it is, in fact, just as it appears, a choice tropical retreat in the midst of the chief city of the Hawaiian Islands."

Despite its attractive exterior, here Liliu, the new bride, found herself at a total loss. She had no training in the domestic areas of life, not even in those that had been offered to Bernice by Juliette Cooke. Liliu had been "studious," obviously preferring a book to a needle. Her cultural background gave her every reason to act in a way that must have appeared to Mrs. Dominis as that of a snobbish guest.

Mrs. Dominis, like her son, believed completely in the rightness of their own ways and ideas, and anyone who differed was definitely *wrong*. Liliu did not fall easily under the adamancy of the *haole* conduct and ways. Her *alii* upbringing led her to believe obstinately that she could not be *all* wrong. On the other hand her missionary training, and her natural childlike desire to please, plus her ingrained insecurity in herself that had been nourished from the Royal School days by the changing concept of *hanai*, gave her a determination to succeed on her own, a quality that later was to be called "stubborn wilfulness." The truth was that all her life she had a terrible feeling of not knowing where she belonged, also that if anything went wrong, it was somehow her fault, a belief Mrs. Dominis was only too happy to foster.

Liliu's first attempt at conformity in "helping" was disastrous. High on the Hawaiian list of loves is flowers. Liliu therefore looked out upon the beautiful rose garden of Washington Place. True to her own culture, she believed that flowers were to be picked to be fully enjoyed. So seizing a pair of shears, she went into the rose garden to snip off misty rose buds for a bouquet. Her heart lifted as she arranged these in a cut-glass vase (a wedding gift) to be placed on the table in the living room.

Mrs. Dominis was livid. How dared she go into her garden and cut the best buds? *How dared she!* Buds were not to be cut; only roses past their prime were cut off so others could bloom—the dying was to make room for the living. Didn't she know?

She never forgot this incident. When John saw the roses, he commented somewhat surprisedly, and Mrs. Dominis replied acidly that "Lydia" (for so she was known to Mrs. Dominis: that was her *Christian* name) had cut them. An intuitive man would have felt the electricity in the air, but John was not an intuitive man—nor perceptive, nor sensitive to another's reactions, surprisingly enough, not even to his mother's.

It was not the last time Liliu was to look to her husband in vain.

Liliuokalani wrote in her *Story,* with restraint typical of her: ". . . As she [Mrs. Dominis] felt that no one should step between her and her child, naturally I, as her son's wife, was considered an intruder; and I was forced to realize this from the beginning. My husband . . . would not swerve to one side or the other in any matter where there was any danger of hurting his mother's feelings. I respected the closeness of the tie between mother and son, and conformed my own ideas, so far as I could, to encourage and assist my husband in his devotion to his mother."

The situation did not improve during the early years of marriage and set the pattern for later years. From a small collection of letters of this period,[3] it is evident that Prince Lot afforded her opportunities to travel to other islands. It was undoubtedly a safety valve for her, but open rebellion sprouted from time to time, followed by quick repentance. She wrote John: "I didn't tell Mother goodby . . . forgive me . . ." and ". . . I didn't see mother . . . it was the hardest request and the saddest parting . . ." She wrote of giving her a locket ". . . but I'm afraid she won't like it . . . "

John, who spent time on the other islands or at Kailua on Oahu with Prince Lot, wrote letters that show he was constantly critical of her in one way or another. He criticized her handwriting and her use of English. "I will truely [sic] try to do better," she replied.

There can be little doubt that sexual incompatibility also existed between John and Liliu. Hawaiian by birth and nature and Victorian-missionary by up-bringing, Liliu was the woman-enigma of every age. Excitingly female, she was not sensual, erotic, nor flagrantly sexual. While naturally passionate, emotional, sensitive, and vibrantly alive to the world about her, she was also disciplined, controlled, scholarly, thoughtful, and wholly restrained by super-imposed conditions. In addition to her own nature, living in her mother-in-law's home was not conducive to the demonstrative affection, of which she was capable and which she desired so deeply.

Whether John had thought of her as the prototype of the sensuous Hawaiian woman when he married her, we cannot be sure. We can be sure, however, that he was not the sensuous man—of any nationality. Early letters—which could have been read aloud from the missionary pulpit and never added to the body of information of either good or evil—reveal nothing but everyday facts.

Years later, John in an unguarded and alcoholic moment accused her of being frigid.[4] It was a stark reflection of their incompatability.

Another tragedy of character existed for Liliu. She was not the kind of woman who could live without a man. She herself was not only not complete without masculine attention; she radiated a kind of need for a man's help. This led men of all walks of life to offer her assistance and aid and often to expect more than she was willing, or able, to give in return. It resulted throughout her life in disappointment, heartbreak, blackmail, and once in great joy.

Liliuokalani wanted children more than she wanted anything else in life. But none were forthcoming in her union with John. Had the old *hanai* system been acceptable, Liliu would have had as many children as she wanted, but John and his mother would hear of no such "pagan" thing.

Liliuokalani lived fifteen years in her barren and deprived state.

❦ 3 ❦

Between 1862 and 1864, the royal household was socially stagnant and politically indifferent. It was a poor time for the king to become a recluse with his own grief and penance; for Hawaii, lacking in strong leadership, was drifting further and further away from the control of the Hawaiian people.

The king's chief and only vital interest seemed to be in securing an Anglican clergyman. In 1863 Bishop Staley arrived from England, and Queen Emma and Kamehameha IV were baptized. It was the first royal break with the missionaries. A few days later David Kalakaua and other high chiefs were also baptized. Liliu was not. She retained a fierce loyalty to Kawaiahao Church.

The Americans considered the royal shift in church alliance a move on the part of the British to gain control. It was certainly hoped by Queen Emma and R.C. Wyllie that Great Britain would "now take more interest"; however, politically, nothing was done.

On November 30, 1863, Kamehameha IV died at the age of twenty-nine of "grief," and latent results of alcoholism, coupled with pulmonary problems. In the last two years Kamehameha IV had become abstemious, but depressed, morbid, and indifferent to his health. The Hawaiians had a different version. They felt the king, like many of them, could no longer cope with the *haole* world and had chosen to die. This attitude affected Prince Lot deeply. Annoyed with his brother for neglecting his governmental duties, he himself was becoming a strong element in the Hawaiian government, and dedicatedly growing more pro-Hawaiian.

While the observance of the king's death was subdued in Hawaiian fashion, it was markedly Episcopalian "on a scale unprecedented in (this) country," Manley Hopkins wrote hurriedly, trying to update his current history.

Kamehameha IV's remains were placed with those of his son's in the new Mausoleum in Nuuanu Valley. Here, for nine days, the grief-stricken Queen Emma slept in the vault along with the bodies of her husband and child. During the day she remained in a tent erected near the door of the vault. Entreated by the king, the Episcopal Bishop, and the father of the dead king to move to Rosebank, the home of R. C. Wyllie, nearby, she refused. She took no food nor drink except a "few sips of water and a taste of fruit" during this period of mourning.[5]

Then she rose from her asylum of grief, remarkably cleansed, and expressed her desire to Prince Lot, then Kamehameha V, to travel abroad. The royal purse, as well as the *alii* funds, was nearly exhausted. Kamehameha IV had spent great sums of not only royal (crown) and government funds, for improvements, but had also reached into his private funds and those of Prince Lot's in the Kamehameha *alii* land-revenues.

The new king reached now into his own private funds to send his sister-in-law abroad before he began his reign as the new monarch. His reign was to influence Liliuokalani's political views more than any other before had or any that would follow.

CHAPTER 2

Governor Dominis and Lady

❦ 1 ❦

Shortly after Lot became king, the Dominis' fortunes improved. John received the governorship of Oahu, a fairly lucrative and prestigious, if uninfluential, position, and newspapers carried accounts of social events that included "Governor Dominis and Lady."

Liliu thus began a new role in the drama of her history. These years were to be climactic for her and Hawaii—a period of intense reevaluation of what was happening to the country and the individual.

Unfortunately, these years are more scantily documented than any other period of her life. We can catch only brief, but revealing, glimpses of her in the letters and papers of Susan Tolman Mills and Abraham Fornander to support Lydia Aholo's later account and to place her in the milieu of her times. Even in her old age, Liliuokalani found it a painful period to remember.

The continued pressure from John regarding her inadequacies in education brought about her contact with Susan Mills. Perhaps a meeting of two such women of like interests is not coincidental. Susan Mills and her husband, Cyrus, had been missionaries in Ceylon; they were now teachers in Oahu College, formerly Punahou School.[1] They would later found Mills College in Oakland, California.

On a late February day in 1865, Liliu appeared at the door of Oahu College, correctly dressed as a Victorian matron, and requested admittance as a student. She proved to be something of a surprise, then and later, to Mrs. Mills, as she wrote that ". . . she had the marvelous bearing of a high chiefess, but she far surpassed her race in intelligence."[2]

Mrs. Mills' concepts of equal education for Caucasian women, instilled by her own remarkable teacher, Mary Lyons of Mount Holyoke College, had not yet extended to equal rights for women of all races. When Liliu made her prim request to be a student, Mrs. Mills felt it was unseemly, for Oahu College had been established for young *haole* men, primarily of missionary descent.

While no official record can be found of Lydia Dominis as enrolled in Oahu College, Susan Mills noted in her journal that "she became one of our pupils. We were impressed by her musical talent." Later years show that although Liliu continued her study of music, she became a student of much more. She caught the fire of a true educator and was to follow in the tradition of Mary Lyons and Susan Mills in ideals and purposes, although never allowed to carry them out as she wished despite her many attempts.

Liliu's latent spark of intellect was fanned far more than Mrs. Mills ever realized. Liliu perfected her handwriting; her English grammar and syntax improved as well. She began to read British and American poets, Susan's passion, and from Cyrus she once again plunged into Greek and Latin, and a smattering of French, for the French Consul Perrin was at the time working for a "parity of French with English." All these accomplishments were later to make her an invaluable aid to Abraham Fornander. But the greatest gift Susan Mills gave her was the wish to learn; to learn—always to learn more—became her intense desire. "Persevere through knowledge" was the motto she passed on to her *hanai* children, to have Lydia Aholo say, "When people foolishly ask if I were so close to the queen what did she *give* me, I tell them she gave me the greatest of all gifts—an education."

One day when Liliu was studying in the Mills' parlor, where she was a frequent visitor, Susan sensed something of the tension that existed for her at Washington Place. Neither of them, like good Victorian women, spoke of it, however. Suddenly Liliu looked up from her Greek grammar and said, "John once reminded me of Dr. Beckwith."[3]

This was Maurice Beckwith, with whom she had her first awakened love for knowledge and girlhood crush. There was a physical resemblance between the slight fair-haired Maurice and John, but there the likeness ceased. Was it that superficial resemblance that had capitulated Liliu into her painful marriage?

Abraham Fornander, Liliu's second mentor, fought his battle on the same grounds as hers—education. Fornander had for many years bitterly opposed the missionaries' method of education which he said was designed "to destroy the Hawaiian." While Lorenzo Lyons, a missionary himself, disagreed with Fornander that the missionaries were trying "to destroy the Hawaiians," he agreed that the changes in the old language resulted in a travesty of their culture.

Verbal battles were raging throughout the islands of whether Hawaii should be bilingual or only English speaking. There was no thought that the language, official or otherwise, should be Hawaiian. With the loss of a language, as Lyons pointed out, comes the destruction of cultural connotations and denotations. It was, however, becoming fairly obvious that a non-English speaking person could have no important government post. The country people began to cry to have English taught in their schools, "Or," they said, "we will be nothing."

Kamehameha V turned his attention to Abraham Fornander, Liliu, and David Kalakaua in his attempt for a cultural renaissance. But first he took care of the political situation.

❦ 2 ❦

Prince Lot became Kamehameha V without opposition or fanfare, although he had not been appointed successor by Kamehameha IV, who had done nothing in regard to an heir to the throne after the young Prince's death. The Hawaiians, ever conscious of the importance of women in government, looked briefly toward Princess Victoria, but Prince Lot proclaimed himself king without opposition. Then, to the consternation of the *haole* population, he refused to take the oath to uphold the Constitution of 1852. He said the people were not ready for such a liberal constitution; and he was quite right, if one thought of the "people" as being the Hawaiians. Lot did. The Constitution of 1852 was democratic in spirit and republic in form, a constitution designed for and by the Americans. The Hawaiians so close to the *alii* system were not ready "to step into a republic," as the past two reigns had shown. The monarchial form of government was a far better one for them.. They still looked to the king for *aloha,* for *mana,* for guidance and leadership, and they loved their chiefs with what Mark Twain termed "fanaticism."

The king requested in March, 1864, that consideration by the cabinet be given to a revision of the constitution. Both British R. C. Wyllie and American Attorney General C. C. Harris favored a revision. However, they were almost alone in doing so. Harris was called "a traitor," and

R. C. Wyllie dismissed as "an Englishman," by the Americans in government.

In May and June, Kamehameha V toured the outer islands. He asked *his* people—the Hawaiians of Hawaii, not the politicians nor the foreigners—what *their* wishes were. He found an enthusiastic response, a strong surge against the current restrictions on monarchial power, as well as the too liberal provisions in the 1852 Constitution. Mainly, he found the people intensely loyal to him and his purposes.[4]

Back in Honolulu, the King called for a Constitutional Convention. Nothing but acrimony resulted not only in the meetings, but also in newspapers. public meetings, and private conversations.

Kamehameha V took matters into his own hands and stated: "I will give you a Constitution." And so he did: the Constitution of 1864, a Constitution under which Hawaii was to be governed successfully for the next twenty-three years to the Bayonet Constitution (1887).

There was a serious and angry response from the foreigners, which Lot quietly overlooked. But he made one mistake: the foreigners suggested that a "military display of power" should be shown "lest the natives rebel." This was foolishness for Kamehameha V had given the natives exactly what they wanted: a strong autocratic, monarchial leadership.[5] He requested British and American ships to "stand by," and thereby set a precedent which would be recalled in 1893.

The new constitution gave greater power to the king and his appointed cabinet, curtailing the powers of the privy council and legislative assembly. It also abolished the honorary office of *kuhina nui* "as unnecessary and expensive."

The most controversial point, that of required educational and property qualifications for representatives and voters was settled. Kamehameha V did not believe that either the ignorant nor the thriftless should be allowed a voice in the government. Nor did he believe Hawaii was ready for universal suffrage.

On the surface it might appear that by this action the king was depriving the native Hawaiian of the right of holding offices and of voting. This, however, was not true. From earliest times the Hawaiians had been eager to learn to read and write,[6] they owned more small properties than many of the drifters of America or the European nations or the Asiatics, and, of the latter, the few who held land were often illiterate.

Kamehameha was becoming aware of ugly tales about Hawaii that were being spread abroad in the United States. Although Kamehameha V had no desire for a close association with the United States, he recognized the danger of losing the small prestige the country might have abroad.

During his late brother's reign the attacks had been "anti-British," "comic opera royalty," but now they were becoming viciously anti-Hawaiian, presenting the Hawaiians as still being pagans and savages.

The first jarring note of this type reached Kamehameha V when he read a dispatch sent by Mark Twain to the *Sacramento Union,* that quoted from the Jarves' history, telling of customs pre-dating the death of Kamehameha I, as if they were still being practiced.

Twain quoted from Jarves' *History of the Sandwich Islands:*

> The ceremonies observed on the death of any important personage were exceedingly barbarous. The hair was shaved or cut close, teeth knocked out and sometimes the ears were mangled. Some tattooed their tongues in a corresponding manner to the other parts of their bodies. Frequently the flesh was cut or burnt, eyes scooped out, and other even more painful personal outrages inflicted. But these usages, however shocking they may appear, were innocent compared with the horrid saturnalia which immediately followed the death of a chief of the highest rank. Then the most unbounded license prevailed; law and restraint were cast aside, and the whole people appeared more like demons than human beings. Every vice and crime was allowed. Property was destroyed, houses fired and old feuds revived and avenged. Gambling, theft and murder were as open as the day, clothing was cast aside as a useless incumbrance; drunkenness and promiscuous prostitution prevailed throughout the land, no women, excepting the widows of the deceased, being exempt from the grossest violation. There was no passion however lewd, no desire however wicked, but could be gratified with impunity during the continuance of this period which, happily, from its own violence soon spent itself. No other nation was ever witness to a custom which so entirely threw off all moral and legal restraints and incited the evil passions to unresisted riot and wanton debauchery.

These practices were accepted in the United States as being current even as late as 1895, and attributed erroneously to the time of Queen Liliuokalani's reign (1891-1893).

Twain described Kamehameha V as "short," (six-one isn't short, but Lot often slumped), "fat, dark, taciturn . . . not far removed from the savage."[7]

Kamehameha V was also aware of the recurrent theme that was heard that "we" (the American missionaries and their successors) "have given the good life to the Hawaiians—the language, the religion, the institutions, the commerce, and industry." But never a word was said that none of these "gifts" would have been possible without the *aloha* or the royal *alii* of giving first the land and later great sums of money to maintain the institutions; or the most important, but least recognized, permission—permission of freedom.

Kamehameha felt that the freedom granted by the largesse of his people was being misused, and he grew "more Hawaiian every day," as his opposition accused him. He also questioned what had happened to the *good* in the Hawaiian past. What about the "law of the splintered paddle," which gave safety "to young and old against marauders," not given by the missionaries, but by the "savage" Kamehameha The First?[8]

Something even more serious was coming to Kamehameha V's attention. There was a subtle influence at work among the Hawaiians, from the *alii* to the poorest worker, causing the concept of themselves and their self-worth to change. The confidence of being "Kane's [God's] best, His noblest works" and believing "The king and the land are our rock the storm cannot shatter" was becoming "The crab can never reach the top of the barrel. We are the crab," and "The big fish are coming up from the bottom of the ocean to eat up the little fish."[9]

Worst of all, Kamehameha I's dying prayer to future rulers of his people—"Increase their happiness, not their wants"—was being reversed.

The maturing Hawaiians recalled Kamakau's and Malo's warnings to Kamehameha III: "Do not shelter foreigners, for they are graspers of the land. We shall see that the strangers will complain of the natives as stupid, ignorant, and good-for-nothing, and this will embitter the race and degrade it."[10]

❧ 3 ❧

Just as it was becoming evident to Kamehameha V that the two differing cultures were clashing, not meshing, so Liliu was experiencing a cultural difference in her personal life. Her life at Washington Place was growing almost intolerable. It was the little things of everyday living that began to crowd in on her, to destroy *her* sense of self-worth and individuality, from the defeat of the warm *aloha* greeting to the irksome relegation of becoming merely (Governor Dominis) *and lady,* a *haole* phrasing. Her relations with her mother-in-law continued cool.

Had she been able to dissimulate more easily, she would have made a better politician; but, later as now, *aloha* was not a duty nor a ritual, but an ever-flowing expression of love. Such a glowing coal died in the cold ashes of Washington Place. Liliu could only express her dissatisfaction of being "Mrs. Dominis," by signing her songs and letters "Liliu Kamakaeha".[11]

Liliuokalani long remembered an exciting day when Kamehameha V had brought to Washington Place a large box of imports from Japan as gifts to the Dominises. Delightedly, she had plunged into the packing, scattering the wrappings about, as Mrs. Dominis stood by, picking up and folding the discarded papers properly.

They had been interrupted by the Rice family, a *haole* family, "coming to call." The young Rice daughters came into the parlor, and with them, the youngest and adored member of their family—Dora, four years old. Liliu had at that precise moment pulled a Japanese doll from the wrappings, and Dora's blue eyes grew round with amazement. She had never seen so beautiful a doll—only the rag doll that had come from "home" had been hers. Here was a doll that looked like a strange lady and was more beautifully clad than any Dora had ever seen.

Her eyes spoke with childlike yearning of the deprivation the missionary children experienced. She was much too well brought-up to ask to touch such a delicate, lovely thing, but her eyes hungered.

Liliu caught her expression and with a delightful laugh placed the doll in her hands, saying, "Here take it!" Dora backed away. Her aunt said, "Oh, no!" But Liliu came forward to fold the child-hands about the delicate silky figure, and say, "Dora, it's yours. I am giving it to you— to keep."[12]

And so it was ever in Liliuokalani's life. She never could—nor even thought of—withholding a present nor a desire from a child, or for that matter, from anyone, whether she was in riches or poverty. It was the tradition of giving in *mana,* a heritage of sharing the infinite riches which flowed through life.

Mary Dominis kept a starched smile on her face until the Rices had said their goodbyes, and then she flew into one of her controlled rages of trying "to civilize Lydia." One did not give gifts willy-nilly. Gifts were for proper times and proper places, birthdays, and yes, now that Christmas was being celebrated, then too. But for no reason at all—to anyone at all—No!

Most of all Liliu longed for the old Hawaiian custom of the chiefly family council. When a family problem arose among the Hawaiians, a member could bring his grievances to a family gathering and there lay them before his peers and elders. Each one had a right to express his opinion on the matter. Then whatever agreement was reached was abided by. The past was laid aside, and the feast was begun. The person lived by the decision reached—his own, his peers', his elders', or a compromise of all—whichever was agreed upon. Then it was over; once it was over, it was over.

With the Dominises there was no family council. Mrs. Dominis was *right,* so there was nothing to discuss. She merely set her pencil-slim lips in a straight line, and her nose grew thinner, longer, and sharper as silent disapproval oozed from her. Nothing was ever over; one carried forever the guilt of words said or unsaid, deeds done or undone.

Even her studies with the Mills and her music lessons did not remove Liliu from the repressive hand of the Dominises. But relief was in sight, although Liliu did not know it. A small respite came from the king.

❧ 4 ❧

One of Kamehameha V's first attempts to reinstate an entity for his country and establish Hawaii for Hawaiians was to have the old British National Anthem of "God Save the Queen" replaced with a Hawaiian National Anthem.

Thus it was one day, when Liliu saw little hope for herself, that relief came. It was raining that day, and she was especially depressed during rains; then the king came to Washington Place and made the most wonderful request: that *she* write a national anthem.

Although she was never free from the awareness of disapproval in Washington Place, her heart was caught in a quickening beat of delight at this prospect. With the rain beating down on the windows of her and John's sitting room, she began immediately to write.

The song she gave the king a few days later was *He Mele Lahui Hawaii*.

THE HAWAIIAN NATIONAL ANTHEM

1.   Almighty Father bend Thine ear,
       And 'list a nation's prayer,
       That lowly bows before Thy throne,
       And seeks Thy fostering care.

Chorus: Grant Thou Thy Peace, thr'out the land,
           O'er these sunny, sea-girt Isles,
       Keep the nation's life, oh Lord,
           And upon our Sovereign smile.

2.   Guard him with Thy tender care,
           Give him length of years to reign,
       On the throne his fathers won,
           Bless the nation once again.
       Give the King Thy loving grace,
           And with wisdom from on high,
       Prosperous lead his people on,
           As beneath Thy watchful eye.

Chorus: Grant Thou Thy Peace, etc.

3.   Bless oh Lord our country's chiefs,
           Grant them wisdom so to live,
       That our people may be saved,
           And to Thee the glory give,
       Watch Thou O'er us day by day,
           King and people with thy love,
       For our hope is all in Thee
           Bless Thou us who reign'st above.

It was a little too missionary-oriented for the king's taste, and certainly too much for Kalakaua's, who later rewrote it when he became king. But after hearing it sung in Kawaiahao Church, Kamehameha V praised it, giving praise that was dear to Liliu.

❦ 5 ❧

Kamehameha then turned his attention to Abraham Fornander as a close ally. He appointed Fornander to a position that on the surface one might have suspected would be the right one—Commissioner of Education. However, like Maurice Beckwith, Fornander was the scholar, not the administrator, and consequently achieved nothing. Where he could make a contribution was in studying the traditions, cultures, and language; and Kamehameha was wise enough to recognize this strength. After seeing Fornander comfortably settled economically, he sent him forth to "find the old Hawaii." He then chose and gave him the two best Hawaiian scholars: David Kalakaua and Liliu.

The "eccentric old gentleman," Abraham Fornander, had long been seen "riding his horse about the country side, shading himself with an umbrella while he read a book," and he was remembered as the gentleman who "wore a long black coat and top hat even on the hottest days."[13]

Born in Sweden in 1812, he had studied at the University of Uppsala— theology, classical languages, and history. Forced to leave the University by his father's untimely death, he took to the sea, arriving in Hawaii shortly after the missionaries. Almost at once he realized the missionaries were replacing the Hawaiian culture with their own.

By marrying an *alii* of Molokai,[14] he first became acquainted with the beauty of the rapidly dying culture. He assiduously collected legends, chants, *mele,* and by being extremely careful in using the original wording, he began to find comparisons of words in forty different languages. He added to his body of information, available to him in Hawaii, by a voluminous correspondence carried on with scholars in the United States and Europe.

He was now joined by the personable Kalakaua, who was to take him into the back country, away from the seaports, to talk with natives who intimately knew and remembered the past. Kalakaua's own family were "reciters of tradition and keepers of the past," and Kalakaua was respected and loved by the people, to which Sophia Cracroft bore an interesting record:

"Buckland [Lady Franklin's maid]," she wrote, "saw Col. Kalakaua (who is greatly loved by the natives for his amiable character and because he is one of the highest families of pure descent) seated by an old woman with his hands on her shoulders. She had drawn them forward and was kissing first one and then the other with every sign of affection."[15]

The old *mele,* the chants of tradition and legends, were brought to Liliu, who discovered a past she had only known vaguely from Konia and Paki. Her studious nature enabled her to lose herself in the translations and work with Fornander.

Fornander also bore record to her intelligence: "She has a remarkable grasp on the Hawaiian language although missionary taught," he wrote a correspondent in Sweden.

This was a beginning period of Hawaiian renaissance. If at any time in Hawaiian history the tide could have been turned, and Hawaii saved for the *Hawaiians* of their own culture, it was then.

But disaster struck. In the midst of Kamehameha's efforts to reestablish a respectability for Hawaii and a sense of self-worth for his people, there occurred an event that was to give the press the opportunity to set Hawaii back one hundred years.

Princess Victoria died on May 29, 1866. Her brother, the king, stood at the time with uncertain feet on the ground of two worlds and its peoples. There were the old ways to which Victoria had returned and in which he and his scholars had found much beauty and good. Then there were the *haole* ways, the ways of those who were uneducated in the mysteries of the old life, and who beheld all the old "heathenism," as "evil," full of "eroticism." It was they who held the pen that described Hawaii.

Kamehameha V decided his sister should have the old ways as she had wanted them, and a royal funeral was her due.

Victoria's body lay in state at the palace for nearly four weeks. The chamber was darkened, and the walls and ceilings draped and festooned with black. The *kahili* bearers, six on each side, stood as the honor guard in the command of David Kalakaua. Liliu shared the death-watch duties with Kapiolani (the former Madame Namakeha, now married to David Kalakaua), Bernice, Princess Ruth, and other high chiefesses, one of whom was in attendance at all times.

The tragedy of the situation was that Kamehameha V forgot the lack of respect that could come from the *haole*. The first evening the palace doors had been open for all to view the body and gather in the courtyard. It soon became evident that the foreigners did not respect the living or the dead and turned the scene into one of rowdy desecration, attempting to join the sacred hula dancers, and pushing wildly for "front row" views. Kamehameha promptly placed a ban on the *haole* spectators.

Disgruntled, they watched from the distance of a *haole* home to see inside the palace gates and write:

Hula girls attired in white bodices and full skirts, wreaths of white

flowers about their shoulders and garlands of green leaves on their
heads danced rhythmically, slowly, in the center of a large assembly.
The palace grounds were illuminated by candle-nut torches . . . a
dozen native women locked arms and swayed back and forth wailing the death songs.

On June 30, 1866, the funeral of the Princess took place from Kawaiahao Church, the services were read by Rev. H.H. Parker, later a
pulpit slanderer of Liliuokalani.

So the two cultures mingled, never merging, ever-divergent, to continue so for another uneasy eight years before clashing.

❦ 6 ❦

In 1868 Liliu inherited through her grandfather, Aikanaka, a piece
of land with two houses at Hamohamo (Waikiki). Hamohamo was the
popular "summer place" of many of the *haole,* but a few of the old *alii*
still held land along the beach. A langorous dirt street, lined with swaying coconut palms, ran along the beach front. Inland were duck ponds,
tropical foliage; and where the yards had not been landscaped, a kind
of old Hawaii restfulness remained. The ducks swam peacefully in their
lily ponds, and the hou trees grew, in some places, to the edge of the
water, reminding Liliu of her birthplace, now long replaced by frame
and brick houses.

The two houses, Paoakalani and Kealohilani, were one story, frame
buildings with large inviting living rooms where "all could gather in
joy and hospitality." Two sides, screened against flies and mosquitoes,
were open to invite in nature.

While the bedrooms were simple and the kitchen missionary style, the
living room bore the Victorian age-of-clutter look, filled also with all
things Hawaiian. Next to a satin pillow, embroidered in heavy thread
proclaiming "There Is No Place Like Home," stood a feathered *kahili.*
On a heavy oak table, side-by-side, were ornate silver services and koa
bowls, once high chiefesses' spittoons. A feather cape, a knitted afghan,
a dog's tooth necklace, a gold-plated bracelet—all intermingled in the
home Liliu came to love so dearly.

"I danced around the rooms. It was my own! Do you know what it
means to have a place that is your *own?* I felt I'd never be alone again,"
she later related to Lydia Aholo.

In those words Liliu revealed a deep-seated fear shared by everyone—

that of being alone. In her diary, years later, when she feared everyone would desert her, she wrote: "I wonder what it would be like to be left alone." "Alone" to Liliu was not having someone around who *understood* her. For, like Emerson, she could be alone in a crowd. At Washington Place there had been both John and his mother, but she was isolated from them by their own self-completeness.

At Hamohamo Liliu could begin to write without the silent disapproval of the Dominises peering over her shoulder. She gathered her songs together, commenced writing the "Tradition of Creation." She also began to accept that her marriage would never be all-fulfilling.

With the normal tendency to judge her marriage by comparison to a projected "ideal," she looked to what she felt was the Mills' perfect relationship. Her choice shows her idea of what a perfect marriage should be: it was one of like interests. Although the Mills had no children of their own, they had what Susan later said were "hundreds of beloved sons and daughters" in their schools. Liliu was to follow that example. The Mills shared a fervent love of educating, not merely teaching, but educating.

Vitally interested in this new idea, Liliu tried to interest John. She secretly cherished a belief that she could bring John into her sphere, if not in the Hawaiian way, then in the acceptable *haole*-teacher way. But John was not scholarly. He was perfectly content with what life gave him, as long as it was comfortable and satisfactory; and it had grown more comfortable and satisfactory, now that Liliu had Hamohamo.

Liliu had at first assumed that John would come to live with her at Paoakalani (Kealohilani was for the retainers). However, Mrs. Dominis and John had other ideas. Liliu's place was with her husband, and that was at Washington Place.

Liliu, after turbulent disagreements and humble pleadings[16] with her husband, had "high handedly" moved out of Washington Place. Actually, had John and Mrs. Dominis been honest with themselves, they would have realized this move was a happy one for them. Now John could again be "alone with mother . . . where things were so jolly . . . with just the two of them." They did not even have to worry about appearances, for in the Hawaiian society it was not unusual for the *alii* women to have their own homes; although, as with Queen Emma, the king shared her home and life in both the palace and the "summer palace" (Emma's home).

Shortly after Liliu was established at Hamohamo, her mother, Keohokalole, died. Keohokalole was the vessel that had carried and given birth to Liliu, but Konia was her "only mother," and Liliu's ingrained *hanai* love remained with Konia. In quite a different way, was it extended to Keohokalole.

As one of the highest chiefesses in the land, Keohokalole was privileged to the ceremony of Puna, and she was so honored by Liliu, in a *mele*,[17] written to commemorate the passing of a tradition, for Keohokalole was the last high chiefess to receive the ceremony.

At Puna were clear sparkling pools, which represented the miracle of water, a gift from the gods, to the Hawaiians. When a high chiefess planned to visit the pools, the message of her coming was sent to the people of Puna. Then the waters were decorated with lehua blossoms. Each blossom was stuck on a spear of pili grass, so that when the *alii* knelt to drink, the lehua blossom would brush her eyelashes. Thus nature, the gods, who were never separated from nature, blessed the *alii*. In return, the *alii* gave *mana* to the pools of water—so the circle was completed once again: nature, gods, man (or woman) gave, and received, in *aloha,* and thus gave, and received, the blessings of *mana*.

Liliu shed her easy flowing tears and wrote her *mele* of a passing tradition and a great chiefess, who only incidentally was her mother. She then planned to go on with life, not an onerous duty done, but an *aloha* one. However, Mrs. Dominis pointed out that no decent daughter refused to go into mourning for her *own* mother. Torn again between two divergent customs, and suddenly guilt-stricken by her lack of heart-felt grief, Liliu "went into mourning," as best she knew how by "retirement from society."[18]

❧ 7 ❧

In less than a year the exciting news came to Hawaii that the Duke of Edinburgh was to visit Honolulu. Despite Mark Twain's grumbling of the lack of sociability of the king, Kamehameha V made lavish preparations for the Duke, preparing and giving him his late father's home in typical Hawaiian hospitality.

He also desired to have a traditional feast prepared for the Duke. Kamehameha, the bachelor king, requested that Liliu have the feast at Hamohamo, for which duty she came "out of retirement."

On the appointed day, these magnificent chiefesses in their colorful dress "representing rank and clan by different colored leis, capes, tapa paus and royal feathers" marched in stately fashion along the sun-lit beach to Liliu's "sea-side home," where a large tent had been erected on the grounds.[19]

Representing her family, the Keawe line, was Liliu's younger sister, Likelike, who was at that time engaged to Prince Albert of Hawaii,[20] the illegitimate son of Kamehameha III and *hanai* to his widow, Dowager Queen Kalama.

Each high chiefess placed her calabash of fruits, pig in banana and ti leaves, fish, and flowers on the two long tables, covered with maile and anapuhi leaves. No other dishes or food was on the table, for each clan paid its *aloha* to the king with her dish or calabash, which was placed on the tables in order of rank of the presenter. The Duke watched with amazement, while the tables groaned with the abundance of food—*aloha* and *mana*.

The Duke of Edinburgh found himself blushing uncomfortably, when two of the most beautiful women in Hawaii, Mary Bush and Evelyn Townsend,[21] both "retainers" in Liliu's home, placed the flower leis about his neck and kissed him on the cheek. The "disconcerted" Duke, recovered his equilibrium, Liliu noted, and "graciously accepted the tributes of [our] islands."

After the feast the ladies "retired," and the king and the duke alone watched the king's hula dancer, Makua, dance in her loose blouse and full skirt[22] to the accompaniment of the chant of two men and the beat of native drums.

The contrast between two accounts of Hawaiian life, those the Duke brought to England and those Mark Twain sent to America, was as great as the views of the British denizens and the American, and no one could have foreseen the disastrous results.

The stay of the "sailor prince" of England was a happy round of activities. He later gave his own "entertainments," at which Liliu was always an honored guest. She and the Duke shared the happy experience, especially for her, of "exchanging musical compositions."

Lot
(Kamehameha V)

Lunalilo

CHAPTER 3

Last of the Kamehamehas

❧ 1 ❧

In 1872 Kamehameha V recognized several uncomfortable facts about Hawaii. The missionaries and their progeny had more than "taken the land away from the Hawaiians"; to him the problem was far more serious. They had taken away the ability of the Hawaiians to hold their land, their culture, their way of life by destroying their sense of self-worth. The seeds of helplessness, uselessness, and self-defeat had been sown despite the king's attempt through Fornander, Kalakaua, and Liliu to awaken a renewed hope, based on revival of the older traditions and customs. Appealing to the emotional and intellectual alone, in a new culture that was primarily materialistic, had proved to be the wrong approach.

Glimpsing the changing social and economic order, Kamehameha V had gone so far as to try to "force" his father's retainers, who had come to him in *alii* fashion at his father's death for care, to leave the palace to seek work elsewhere.

Many of the Hawaiians had by this time become adapted to plantation work, although they preferred working for the *alii* rather than the *haole*. For some, it was old loyalty, for the *haole* paid better. Other retainers found the native overseers less strict than the ones on the *haole* plantations, usually Portuguese. The women were becoming the "beloved domestic servants"[1] in missionary and other homes; and although these positions suited many of them, the *alii* felt that all the Hawaiians had fallen to an inferior position. When "liberal" *haoles* stated they were in favor of having "natives in position of authority," they nearly always added, "if they are fit."

Up to this time, no *alii* had been educated in the United States. They could in no way compete with the *haole* men from Yale, Harvard, Williams College, or other eastern colleges. These men returned with their Herbert Spencer-instilled belief that wealth was a criterion for leadership. They thought in broad terms of the populace, not the individual. Their efforts were bent to make a "better life" for the population in building roads and harbors, promoting commerce and industry, cultivating plantations and making use of natural resources. The Hawaiians still were individually oriented—their personal services were important as were their traditional background and culture.

On the *haole* side was also another attitude. Hawaii had become theirs, not just by having taken over land, administering political power, developing institutions and economy, but actually having "grown indigenous to the soil." As in no other country, a resident of Hawaii became Hawaiian, and fiercely loyal to his particular point of view as what was "best *for Hawaii*."[2]

This presumptuous attitude was becoming apparent in 1872. But the native high chiefs could not understand a "loyalty," that was so heavily overlaid by the new money-oriented culture that it removed itself completely from the concepts of *aloha* and *mana*.

Still another factor was appearing. The Hawaiians had welcomed peoples of all races, creeds, and color without thought to "differences." These ever-generous people were daily losing their grasp on their own status as a people, and as a result the word *haole,* in the early 1870's, took on an unpleasant connotation among the Hawaiians, for the first time. A *difference* was seen, and the difference, resented; consequently, racial problems arose. Only a few among the *alii* of the older Hawaiians retained their attitude of *aloha* toward all.

❦ 2 ❧

With Kamehameha V the native Hawaiian *alii* had begun to look to his beginnings, to his roots, for understanding and possibly to get answers to his country's problems. The natives were certainly expressing a wish for an entity of their own. The only tangible move that had taken place was that $100,000 had been appropriated for a new palace, but the building had not begun. There was great opposition by the *haole* to having a new *palace,* and the money was used for a new government building, instead.

On his deathbed Kamehameha V understood the old Hawaiian people better than any previous ruler, except Kamehameha I, and any to come, except Liliuokalani. He was faced, however, with a momentous decision: he was to choose his successor. Daily since the beginning of his illness, he had been entreated, coerced, and begged by the high chiefs to make his choice, as was his right, having no blood nor *hanai* heir of his own.

Kamehameha V, who had grown too fat, felt his country had grown too fat also—not strong, not vigorous, just fat. He felt overwhelming defeat, in spite of his efforts to bring Hawaii back to Hawaiians.

He had once loved Queen Emma, there can be little doubt; but he did not wish to appoint her as his successor. She was greatly loved by the Hawaiian people, but she was also too pro-British, as his brother had been. She could never hold the country against the Americans, who had no love for royalty, and even less for queens.

Although by lineal descent, his cousin, Lunalilo (Prince Bill), was next in eligibility, he distrusted this wastrel young man. There *was* another Kamehameha—Prince Albert, the illegitimate son of Kamehameha III, but the Constitution forbad illegitimate children from becoming heirs to the throne; besides, Prince Albert had too many personal problems of his own, having been brought up by the Dowager Queen, Kalama.

By staying true to his cultural custom, Kamehameha V should have appointed Bernice Pauahi Bishop, as the "last of the Kamehamehas," but even here he was reluctant. She was married to an American, and she had never shown any interest in governmental procedures. By this time, Lot realized fully that a novice to government should not be the head of it.

Princess Ruth, his half-sister, he considered completely incapable of ruling a country that was just developing a mind of its own. She had moved too far back into the old ways.

There was one whom he had himself said should be king—Leleiohoku, Liliu's brother; however, he was in his teens, attending a Catholic school in San Mateo, California. Most important, in the event of his appointment, until his majority, Ruth (his *hanai* mother) would be regent. Lot was well aware that the country expected one of two persons to succeed him—Lunalilo (Prince Bill) or David Kalakaua.

Lunalilo was an easy person to manipulate. His greatest talents, it seemed to Lot, were in music and alcoholic consumption. He was ambivalent. Lot remembered he sang at the Judd's; he poked fun at the British, and then when tension grew too much, he laughed and threw his arms about his host and they sang together with deep emotion the British "God Save the Queen." No one could doubt his sincerity; no one could believe in it.

Kamehameha V had never appointed him to any position of importance nor power. When Lunalilo asked about this "over-sight," Kamehameha V had replied, with his usual forthrightness, that he did not consider him capable of handling important matters.

He viewed David Kalakaua with uneasiness. Without doubt, among the eligible high chiefs, Kalakaua was the best educated, had through Lot's reign shown an insight into Old Hawaii, and had the most practical experience in the government. He was well liked, of high chiefly descent. One important thing he lacked: neither by birth nor *hanai* did he qualify as a Kamehameha, but neither did Lunalilo, although he was of lineal descent. The Kalakaua (Keawe) line was not. Two sisters and one brother of the Keawe (Kalakaua) line had been *hanai* to a Kamehameha. One sister, who had died in 1848, had been *hanai* to Kamehameha III, and a brother, *hanai,* to Princess Ruth, Leleiohoku. Another sister, much in the forefront both in Hawaiian life and in Kamehameha V's personal attention, was Liliu, *hanai* to Paki and Konia, the granddaughter of Kamehameha I. But Kalakaua had not been, by birth nor by *hanai,* a Kamehameha. It was a great obstacle to succession.

Lastly, Kamehameha V was forced to consider Liliu. But—there was always a "but" in Lot's thinking of a successor—she was contradictory, even more than the others. She was to all appearances loyal to a husband who divided his loyalties between two strong women with the remarkable ability of being almost oblivious of each as an individual. Kamehameha V felt that he favored his mother, but then that might have been because *he* favored Liliu. Liliu was *his* "family." She viewed, as he did, the American missionary descendants as a political threat to their country. At the same time, she was naive and trusting, and she was an exceedingly poor judge of character when it came to men of her own or the *haole* race.

She also had a certain amount of dedication to her husband's family. Of all the *haole,* John Owen Dominis was best known by Kamehameha V. He had chosen him as his private secretary and found him to be precise, careful, non-judgmental and non-committal to a point of exasperation. He was not a strong man, and had no political ambition.

Kamehameha V would have been surprised to have known that his death was the one thing that forced Dominis to apply his preciseness and exactness to the benefit of the Keawe line.

Kamehameha V knew there was another alternative: he could leave the selection of his successor to the high chiefs. Was this not the way "kings" had first been chosen, according to historian Malo? Thus no decision became a decision.

At his bedside, it was the accurate John Owen Dominis who recorded that Kamehameha V asked Bernice Bishop to succeed him.[3] She hesitated and then offered Ruth as an alternative, whom he declared "impossible." Queen Emma was then suggested, but Kamehameha V replied that she had been "Queen only by marriage." These were the damaging words of Kamehameha V that opened the door in 1873 to Kalakaua. It can be assumed that John did not foresee this; he was merely being "accurate."

On December 11, 1872, Kamehameha V died, without appointing a successor to the throne, saying only: "It is hard to die on one's birthday."

Kamehameha V also died without signing a will. As a result, the Kamehameha *alii* "crown" lands did not pass on to the next monarchial successor, only the income of the government lands, often confused with "crown" lands, went into the royal treasury to result in leading the country into serious financial problems.

❦ 3 ❦

Wildly enthusiastic, the "people"[4] chose their first king—the king of the populace—the king of the people—the popular king. The Hawaiian people were wild with freedom, but had no concept of its responsibilities. Kalakaua, Lunalilo's opponent, who at the time appealed to the intellect rather than the emotion, had little chance against Lunalilo.

Lunalilo! The man most likely not to succeed: Lunalilo, the popular "Prince Bill"—the chiefly Lunalilo.

Lunalilo had also made it plain in proclamations that *he* was the *rightful heir*, as Kamehameha V had suspected he would; but rather than make the claim himself, he was going to "allow" the people to proclaim him.

The *haole* population was well pleased with Lunalilo as king. He would be easily manipulated in their hands, while still being held popular in the minds of the Hawaiians. His charisma outshone his ability and blinded the Hawaiians, and encouraged the more perceptive *haole*.

Lunalilo rode to victory on his one promise: to restore the popular *haole* Constitution of 1852. David Kalakaua put forth his platform in Hawaiian rhetoric reminiscent of what he had learned was desirable among the Hawaiians, when he worked with Fornander. He pointed to the past, but also touched upon the current problems of the times:

> I shall obey the advice of our ancestor of Keaweahuelu, [sic] my grandfather, which he gave to Kamehameha I, to be the rule for his government: "The old men, the old women and the children shall

lie in safety on the highways."; preserve and increase the people; put native Hawaiians into Government offices; amend the Constitution of 1864.

Little attention was paid to Kalakaua, and Sanford Ballard Dole[5] wrote that as Lunalilo intended to proclaim himself king no matter what happened in the legislative election, "Therefore we supported him, paying little attention to Kalakaua."

The interesting fact that emerges from this election was that although Kamehameha V had worked assiduously for a revival of Hawaii for Hawaiians, in a rapidly disappearing Hawaii, he had been unable to awaken the people to the necessity of keeping social pace with governmental change. Kalakaua kept one hand on Old Hawaii, and the other on problems facing Hawaii in 1872. Despite the fact that Kamehameha V had been overwhelmingly supported in his new constitution, Lunalilo's one promise, based on only his own personal rancor against the Kamehameha's to destroy the Constitution going back to the 1852 one, won him the election.

The Hawaiian chiefs were still voting by tradition for the *High Chief* by lineage and not for a platform.

⚹ 4 ⚹

Once Lunalilo had been elected king, David Kalakaua moved gracefully to read in Hawaiian his own congratulations and the proclamations of the new king to the legislature.

The most surprising appointment of Lunalilo to his cabinet, was Charles Bishop, as minister of Foreign Affairs. He had resented Bishop as his guardian, but surpisingly, must have recognized him as a shrewd businessman. All his cabinet members were Americans, except one, Robert Stirling, who was a Scotsman. John Owen Dominis remained Governor of Oahu. It was the least Lunalilo could do for the husband of the woman he had once been engaged to marry.

Liliu had spent the last nine, disturbing years in a situation in which she had not even been able to hold her status as Princess Bernice Bishop had, nor acclimate herself to being a party to "Governor Dominis and lady," as the newspapers referred to her, not unlike every *haole* in Hawaii. She felt at this time she was "neither fish nor fowl nor even good red herring."

Nevertheless, she entered into Lunalilo's regime with the gaiety that predominated his life. Music, theater, singing clubs of the *alii* were all to her liking. Politically, she looked upon the situation as Kamehameha V would have—with dismay. Once again, annexation talk was begun, and a secret mission of Major General John M. Schofield, and Brevet Brigadier General B. S. Alexander[6] was sent by the United States Secretary of War to "ascertain the value of Pearl River Harbor." Talk was renewed for the cessation of Pearl Harbor, in return, possibly, for reciprocity on sugar sent to the United States. Charles Bishop, as minister of foreign affairs, said that such a move would not be a part of annexation; the natives, however, thought otherwise. Queen Emma spoke for them: "The reciprocity treaty, giving away land, is much discussed these days, . . . There is a feeling of bitterness against these rude people who dwell on our land and have high handed ideas of giving away somebody else's property as if it was theirs."[7]

Lunalilo remained in a peculiarly fatherly position of listening, and for a time committing himself to the proposition and then withdrawing his acquiescence ". . . no doubt influenced by the fear of revolution among [the] people; reports received from other Islands indicate excitement and turbulence of feeling among the Masses [against reciprocity]," C.R. Bishop wrote to Secretary Fish of the United States.[8] Other problems, such as the segregation of lepers, were a part of Lunalilo's reign, but no measurable steps were taken.

After a brief nine-month reign, Lunalilo became ill and was sent to Kailua. He was accompanied by his physician, Dr. Trousseau, who was later to be an important influence in Liliu's life; Charles Judd, his chamberlain; his father (Kanaina), Queen Emma, Liliu and others of the *alii*. "The Hawaiian band of native musicians and others did all they could to distract the king from his illness," Liliuokalani wrote. During this time he was frequently requested to appoint a successor—certainly a request not conducive to "distracting" from illness. His only comment had been that he "owed [his] sceptre to the people and [saw] no reason why the people should not elect [his] successor."

During his illness, a slight flurry of discontent arose that would hardly warrant the space to mention, if it were not that it involved, at least by rumor, David Kalakaua. The Household Troops (the entire standing army of about sixty men) mutinied. The cause was almost sophomoric in that they objected to some acts of their Hungarian drill-master and those of the adjutant general, Charles Judd. A small altercation ensued, and John Dominis was called in to quell the disturbance. He was either defied or simply disregarded. Dominis was not a strong arbitrator. The king, after several approaches by delegations, made peace with the mutineers, then disbanded the Household Troops, except the band, and thus left the kingdom without any regular organized military force. The native Hawaiians sympathized with the mutineers, and, as a consequence, the rather unlikely word went out of "race-war." This was a *haole* fear, not a Hawaiian one. In the end the "barracks mutiny" was labeled "humiliating" to the government and disgraceful, *but* supportive to David Kalakaua.[9]

Soon it became evident that Lunalilo was failing rapidly. He was brought to Honolulu with his royal court in attendance. When it became evident that the king was dying, Emma's advisors foresaw danger and encouraged Emma that she should influence Lunalilo, before his death, in her favor in succession. Emma, although not particularly politically oriented, agreed; however, nothing could have been more unfavorable to Lunalilo, who cared little for the Kamehameha-royal-Emma. Emma herself had no real desire to be a ruling queen. She became an innocent pawn in the hands of her advisors, who counted heavily on her popularity with the natives and their love for their queens.

Until this time, it should be noted, that Emma was quite fond of David Kalakaua, affectionally calling him "Taffy." Her letters to Liliu carried the same affection—addressing her as "Dear Liliu" and signing her name as "Kaleleonalani"—the name she had taken after the death of her son and her husband, meaning "flight of the chiefs." Later, she addressed Liliu as "Mrs. Dominis" and signed her name "Queen Emma." It was then, that in a letter, she wrote of Liliu: "She is a good person. She has done more than I have."

Lunalilo died slowly, but peacefully. He aroused several times before his "peaceful passing," to express his desire not to be "associated with his Kamehameha cousins." He requested that he not be buried in the Nuuanu Valley Mausoleum, but at Kawaiahao Churchyard, "among the common people who loved him." The night before his demise, he stated he wanted none of the royal trappings buried with him. He had all his kingly insignia destroyed. His final words in good Shakespearean tradition were: "Alien touch shall not finger my crown or traitor breath stir the feathers upon my raiment."

At eight o'clock on February 3, 1874, the guns from Punchbowl Hill announced the death of King Lunalilo. Notice was given that the remains of the king would lie in state between the hours of 10:00 a.m. and 2:00 p.m. in the palace. In front of the palace were drawn the Honolulu Rifles as a guard of honor. Within, were the ministers of state and the *alii*. It was a royal lying-in-state. Accompanied by a grieving multitude of natives, the body was taken during the night to the Nuuanu tombs, with *kahili* waving, and the cortege lighted by kukui-nut torches. At the time of his death, his family had no mausoleum and his remains had to be immured in the Kamehameha crypt to await a second burial, when his own tomb at Kawaiahao Church was completed two years later.

Lunalilo, after a year and twenty-five days of reign, left a Hawaiian nation strongly against annexation and cession of any territory; a newly elected legislative assembly of nearly all natives. He also left behind him men of diverse talents, but great strengths: David Kalakaua, Father Damien, Sanford Ballard Dole, Lorrin Thurston, Henry Berger, and one woman who was to know these men well and who was to experience the crises of the resulting problems of the next twenty years: Liliuokalani.

He left a will in which his property was to go to Kamehameha V, now deceased, to his father, Kanaina, and then to a home for the old, the poor, the indigent. Lunalilo, who claimed lineal descent from Kamehameha I, said in leaving his property thus, that he was continuing further along the line of the "law of the splintered paddle"; now the old should not only have the right to lie down on the wayside in safety, but in a home, in peace and contentment.

It was the typical liberal, the king of the people, the Lunalilo of the liberated *kahu:* the man who preferred to leave a country moving further toward bankruptcy than allow the people to think of him as less than "liberal humanitarian."

He left one other legacy, which he must have suspected, possibly even hoped, would fall to the recipient, even though *he* left no such provisions. He made it possible for Mrs. John Owen Dominis to become Princess Liliuokalani, to live and write peacefully at Hamohamo for a few short years.

PART IV
The Princess Period
❧ ❧
1874-1891

KING KALAKAUA

CHAPTER 1

A New Royal Line

❦ 1 ❦

Liliuokalani went into the period of her life as a princess with the greatest of ambivalence. All her life she had seen the difference of being a princess and a high chiefess. But this was not the way she preferred to become a princess—not through her brother, David Kalakaua. Theirs was from the beginning a conflicting relationship. She now owed him her allegiance as her brother and her king, but she did not like his personal habits, nor approve of his political ideas. She had a strong emotional attachment to the Kamehamehas as Konia's *hanai* child.

On February 12, 1874, it was something of a bitter victory for her, when she sat with David's wife, Kapiolani; her sister, Likelike; her brother-in-law, Archibald Cleghorn, and her own brother, Leleiohoku, at Kapiolani's home to await the news to be brought by her husband that David had been elected king.

Dominis reported that the election had not been a pleasant one, even at the moment, there was a "rebellion brewing." Queen Emma had put forth her claim to the throne. Many natives devoted to a queen, and particularly to Emma, had electioneered for her.

There was little doubt that of all the high chiefs of that time, David Kalakaua was qualified by birth, lineage, experience, and intelligence. Certainly, the majority of the natives recognized him as such, and he would receive the sufficient number of votes for election without appealing to the American vote. But David was always one to hedge his bets—and often over-reached himself.

After Kalakaua's legislative election (39 to 6) had been announced, the court house was attacked, and the legislators—particularly the native ones who had voted for him—were beaten. The offices were ransacked, papers were destroyed, and furniture, together with one delegate, thrown out of the windows. The action was a most unusual one for the quiescent and somewhat apathetic Hawaiian populace. Liliu was disturbed; her brother, annoyed, and a little frightened. Therefore at the suggestion of Dominis and Charles Bishop, who had come to join the waiting group, Kalakaua had asked for British and American ships to send seamen "to protect American and British property"—and his own. David Kalakaua was never known for his personal courage, while Liliuokalani was almost foolhardy. Another precedent was set for the eventual turmoil of 1893.

Peace was quickly restored. Hawaiian tempers never burned long, nor fiercely, unless fanned by *haole*. The French and English foreign ministers called upon Emma to notify her that their governments had acknowledged Kalakaua king. In the afternoon Emma sent a message to the king also "acknowledging him as sovereign and assuring him her people would do the same."

During the time of the electioneering Emma had written her cousin, Peter Kaeo, that one ". . . could not help but admire the way Taffy [Kalakaua] had worked for the election."[1] Liliuokalani, interestingly enough, was to echo those same words in regard to the men of the Provisional Government in 1895. It showed something of the regal simplicity that existed with these two women.

Liliu considered the "disturbance" totally un-Hawaiian, and, in a curious phrasing, she called Emma's later reactions examples of "feminine pettiness." Liliu had as small a grasp on politics, determined by elections, as Emma did.

On the day after his election, when quiet had been restored, at a small simple ceremony in the presence of the legislature, foreign representatives, influential citizens, both *haole* and Hawaiian, David Kalakaua took the oath of office required by the constitution and became King of Hawaii. He also took the oath of allegiance to the 1864 (Kamehameha V) constitution. The Kalakaua Dynasty was thus established.

On February 14, 1874, he appointed his younger brother, Prince William Pitt Leleiohoku, his successor, thus eliminating the possibility of the two previous interregnum periods and following elections. The decision was a wise one. According to *Thrum's Annual*,[2] two new princesses were designated: "Princess Likelike and Princess Kamakaeha Dominis." There is no evidence of an official act on the part of Kalakaua.

The papers began to view David Kalakaua favorably: they reviewed his past "of high rank as an *alii;* his parents, Kapaakea and Keohokalole of the Keawe line; his *hanai* parents as Kinimaka and Haaheo of Hawaii."

LIKELIKE CLEGHORN
Liliuokalani's younger sister

LELEIOHOKU II
(William Pitt)
Her younger brother

He had received, the papers continued, his "excellent education in the High Chiefs' School; had travelled on the Pacific Coast of America; had been employed in various government offices and thus had acquired valuable experience and familiarity with details of the government; he had been secretary to the privy council, chamberlain to Kamehameha V, and as a noble had been in close contact with the government from 1860 to the present." Generally, the personal comments regarding the new king followed those of Charles Nordhoff, a well-known traveler and writer: ". . . a man of education, of better physical stamina than the former kings, of good habits, vigorous will, and a strong determination to maintain the independence of the Islands."[3]

It is important that these views be mentioned, for in 1883 every item was to be severely attacked.

The new royal family members were completely different individuals. None of the family lacked charm. The young Prince Leleiohoku, as described by Liliuokalani "was a very popular young man, an amiable prince . . . had the same love (as all members of the family) for music . . . the like passion for poetry and song . . . a taste for social pleasures, and enjoyed the gay and festive element of life."

Likelike, described not by Liliuokalani but by other writers of the period, such as William Armstrong,[4] was high-tempered, easily hurt, and Hawaiian-oriented in a lackadaisical attitude toward life. Her personal life was anything but impeccable, and this later reflected on Liliu. Likelike had married Archibald Cleghorn in 1871, at Washington Place. Cleghorn was a Scotsman who had come to Hawaii in the 1850's. He had three older, illegitimate, daughters, who later moved into the household at Ainahou. At the time of their marriage, the Cleghorns lived on Emma Street, where their daughter, Kaiulani, was born in 1875. When Kaiulani was baptized in the Episcopal Church, Princess Ruth gave her the land and house of Ainahou, which was near Liliu's homes at Waikiki.

King David Kalakaua was shrewd, shrewd in a selfish way which is often self-defeating, easily influenced, especially if his own self-image could be enhanced, and an enigma to himself and Liliuokalani. His basic instincts were good, but his execution of them was marred by self-aggrandizement and bad advice.

Liliu still stood between the conflicting worlds of the missionary-Victorianism and the Hawaiian gaiety and dedication to her people.

The four had two divergent qualities in common: first, their talent and love of music; secondly, an incredible lack of ability to judge character judiciously, and a consequent fascinating capacity for choosing the wrong men—as friends and advisers—each for completely different reasons.

The new royal line also had new "royal" in-laws. David's wife, now Queen Kapiolani, was the granddaughter of the last king of Kauai and the widow of the High Chief Namakeha. She had two sisters, Poomaikelani and Kekaulike; Kekaulike had three sons: Edward, David, and Jonah—Edward Piikoi, David Kawananakoa (Piikoi), and Jonah Kuhio Kalanianaole (Piikoi). These all became members of the royal household, not altogether to the pleasure of Liliu, nor especially Likelike.[5] Kalakaua later appointed Poomaikelani governess of Hawaii and Kekaulike, governess of Kauai. The boys were considered "princes," although not officially so designated in 1874.

❧ 2 ❧

David Kalakaua began his reign with an action meant to satisfy his own personal desires and to achieve a diplomatic appeasement with the *haole* sugar plantation owners. A trip to the United States would serve both purposes. There Kalakaua was well aware of his own "personableness" and the effect his trip, as king, would have in the United States.

He was described as "having a striking appearance; he was a thick set man with black, kinky hair, long sideburns, and a drooping mustache." Both his intellect and social graces were highly praised, even by Americans.

November 16, 1874, had been declared a day of public thanksgiving and prayer in honor of the king's thirty-eighth birthday, Kalakaua's first congratulatory gesture to himself. At Kawaiahao Church he gave a farewell address, declaring that he was making this journey "in the endeavor to forward the best interest of you, my people . . ." He referred to the reciprocity treaty as a need "to ensure our material prosperity, and I believe that if such a treaty can be secured, the beneficial effects will soon be apparent to all classes, and our nation, under its reviving influences, will grow again."[6]

"All classes" did not, however, at the time, agree with him; most of the natives were *not* in favor of the treaty with the United States because of the possible existing loopholes that in return Pearl River Harbor would be ceded. Many Emmaites were against it and so was Liliu.

She conferred at one point with Sanford Ballard Dole, who assured her Pearl Harbor was not "the first step to Annexation"; Liliu thought differently. She commented about the camel being allowed to put its head in the tent. However, she had no authority, and if openly against Kalakaua's ideas, she would be considered "kipi"—traitor.

Quiet, however, was not something she could remain for long, and in a few years her opposition was to be taken by *haole* and natives alike to mean that she was willing to help dethrone her brother.

Of all the missionary-descendant *haole,* Liliuokalani trusted Sanford Ballard Dole most, and Lorrin A. Thurston, least. In these two instances her evaluation was accurate, though it was Sanford Dole who was to replace her as head of the Hawaiian government in 1893.

Sanford Ballard Dole, six years Liliu's junior, was born on April 23, 1844, as the second child of Daniel and Emily Dole. Daniel and his bride had arrived with the ninth company of missionaries in 1840, but by 1841 the need for a school for the missionaries' children was becoming so evident that the American Foreign Missions Board suggested a boarding school be built. This became Punahou School. The Doles were its first superintendent-teachers in 1842, when their first son, George, was an infant. Emily Dole died shortly after Sanford's birth, and he was taken by the Chamberlain (missionary) family to be cared for by a Hawaiian nurse. Here he first gained his interest in Hawaii's past for Hawaiian nurses *(kahu)* were a fount of folklore and stories for the impressionable young Sanford.

In 1846 Daniel married Charlotte Knapp, widow of Horton Knapp. Sanford was soon returned to the Dole household which moved to Kauai to establish another school.

When Sanford completed Punahou-Oahu College, in Honolulu, he was sent to Williams College in Massachusetts. Immediately afterward he "read law"[7] in the office of Massachusetts' Senator Brigham; he returned to Hawaii to practice and become involved in the government.

Liliuokalani's and Sanford Dole's paths were to cross frequently the whole of her remaining lifetime.

✕ 3 ✕

King Kalakaua, light of heart and eager to be on his way, left for the United States on November 17, 1874, in the company of John Owen Dominis and others of the royal entourage.

During Kalakaua's absence, Leleiohoku was regent. Leleiohoku had no political aspirations and his entire "regency" was marked only by the "musical clubs." Of the three members of the immediate royal household, each had formed separate clubs that "engaged in friendly rivalry to outdo each the other in poetry and song." These were Leleiohoku's, Princess Likelike's, and Liliu's.

Liliuokalani later stated that the Prince's Club far excelled those of his sisters, for "it consisted in a large degree of the very purest and sweetest male voices to be found amongst the native Hawaiians." Only Liliu, however, saw the importance of and made the attempt to write down the words and music of these original songs.

In the United States Kalakaua was received royally, and succeeded in gaining President Grant's ear. But the United States Congress was unconscionably slow in taking necessary action, and Kalakaua's first return in the blush of success began to fade quickly. The royal welcome home was followed in 1876 with reports from Marshall Parke that there were plans to assassinate the king, other members of the royal family, and even officials of the government. Only David Kalakaua seems to have taken the rumors seriously—directing Parke to place several persons under arrest for attempting to kill him with poisoned *poi* while he was attending a party.[8] Nothing, however, was done.

In September, 1876, Congress passed a motion to give effect to the reciprocity treaty. There was a great celebration in Hawaii with speakers praising the treaty and the new king. How the political pendulum swings!

David Kalakaua then came forth and called with heraldry typical of him for all to turn themselves to two major problems: 1) Increase the people (his motto was "Increase the Nation") and 2) Advance agriculture and commerce.

Kalakaua was a paradox; on one hand, he gave the Hawaiians exactly what they wanted: a flamboyant king, a leader reaching out to other nations, establishing an entity for his people; on the other, he gave the commercial classes exactly what they wanted: Hawaii's first economic boost—and an opening for annexation.

One would have thought that he'd prosper mightily, for he was giving everyone—for a while—what each wanted. Of course, when these came into conflict, it was Kalakaua who was to blame.

❧ 4 ❧

While Kamehameha V had begun to awaken the Hawaiians to an

entity of their own, the only ones in the current royal household or the government who had any grasp of this idea or what it meant were Liliu and Kalakaua. And these two differed considerably in what the interpretation should be. Liliu still believed that Hawaii belonged to the native Hawaiian to whom the royal *alii* were responsible. Kalakaua had this knowledge also but a tendency to agree that all denizens could claim Hawaii. Yet his idea of government was not so much a constitutional monarchy (1852 Constitution) as a king-centered one (1864 Constitution). And he was King.

The early missionaries who came never intended to *be* Hawaiians. They came simply to "Christianize the heathen." By economic need and by the request of the *alii* they entered into commerce and government but with their New England concepts of economy and prosperity. It is true many of them sincerely believed their own economic prosperity would be Hawaii's also: there was, only one way to prosper the country; that was to Americanize it. If the onus of the problem of the loss of Hawaii to the Hawaiians seem to fall upon the American commercial and missionary families, it is that they were the most influential in every area of life in 1874.

The new Hawaiian was defined by the white populace as "Anyone born here, naturalized under the Hawaiian laws, whether native Hawaiian, half-Hawaiian or *haole* [meaning white only, for Asiatics were excluded in the generosity of this movement] is Hawaiian—Hawaii is *his* country; his prosperity is Hawaiian prosperity . . ."

In that light, young W. R. Castle made a suggestion: that in the agricultural system of the islands the larger estates be broken up for the small farmer. It was to prevent "landed aristocracy and a restless, discontented population of ignorant and idle laborers."

Castle had two problems: the *haole* owners, now also "landed aristocracy," were not so easily influenced in giving up their holdings as the former Hawaiians had been; and secondly, the relaxed Hawaiian retainer system (*alii* and worker) was no match for the American pioneer spirit. Even Kalakaua, in a half-hearted attempt, tried to enter into the new system, but with failure.

❧ 5 ❧

In his own household Kalakaua continued to hold a constant threat over his princess-sisters that he could and would at any moment adopt and proclaim the young sons of Kekaulike, his sister-in-law, as heirs to the throne—provided he had no children of his own. It seemed unlikely that Kapiolani, who was older than thirty-eight-year-old Kalakaua, would bear children. The Constitution was strict that only legitimate children could be heirs to the throne.

Liliu was barren and so was Likelike in 1874; Leleiohoku was unmarried. Queen Emma wrote Flora Jones that "Mrs. Dominis and Mrs. Cleghorn constantly worry about the elevation of the boys above them."[9]

On October 16, 1875, when Likelike gave birth to Kaiulani,[10] she immediately demanded that Kalakaua proclaim Kaiulani next in line for succession. Kalakaua did not do so; but the Hawaiian people did. Guns were fired from Punch Bowl Hill and the people proclaimed a "new royal princess—the Hope of Hawaii." Kalakaua was wise enough to remain quiet.

Kalakaua, however, had made another unwise blunder in his relations with his subjects. When Lunalilo's remains were placed in their new resting place on the Kawaiahao Church grounds in 1873, as he had requested, Kalakaua denied a request for a twenty-one gun salute. In the stormy weather during the royal burial, twenty-one thunder claps were distinctly heard. "What man withholds the gods give" was often heard thereafter, and the new king's slight to his predecessor was remembered.

Kalakaua was uneasy. He was more uneasy six months later when Leleiohoku died of inflamatory rheumatism. Ruth was deeply upset by the death of her *hanai* son and demanded that royal honors be given him; which they were. But she demanded more, she said that as she was his *hanai* mother, she was to be declared his successor and the next heir to the throne.

Leleiohoku died on April 10, 1877, and on April 11, 1877, David Kalakaua officially declared Liliu Kamakaeha Dominis, "Princess Liliuokalani," heir apparent to the throne of Hawaii.

Princess Liliuokalani

CHAPTER 2

The "Birth" of Princess Liliuokalani

❧ 1 ❧

Kalakaua called Liliu to the palace to inform her she would be named heir apparent under the title of Princess Liliuokalani. Her first reaction was one of dismay and shock. "Liliuokalani," she wrote in her diary at the time she became Queen, is *"no name at all . . .* David chose it because it sounded more royal."[1]

With her usual stark, but naive and undiplomatic honesty, she refused the name that was "not her own." She could be named heir presumptive, of that there was no doubt, but as Liliu Kamakaeha, the name given her at birth. Kalakaua reminded her that the name meant "sore or smarting eyes"; she reminded him that Kalakaua meant "battle day."

The king then gave her the choice of being named heir presumptive as Princess Liliuokalani or not at all—he "would choose another to replace her."[2] So, at another moment of triumph Liliuokalani tasted again the bitter herbs of personal defeat. Thus, on April 11, 1877, she was officially "born" Princess Liliuokalani.

As heir apparent she immediately made use of her position, and began her visits to the outer islands as well as to travel around Oahu with John Owen Dominis, the governor. John, somewhat reluctant, suggested that Charles Wilson, the husband of Kitty Townsend, be appointed her "chamberlain," and accompany her on the trips. Wilson was part-Tahitian and a man of masculine charm, but not of great intelligence.

While the party was at Lahaina, John was recalled to Honolulu to be told he was being replaced by Charles Judd as chamberlain to the king and as manager of the "royal lands." In her *Story* Liliuokalani writes that David came to discuss the situation with her at Maui; actual evidence exists that he had grown nervous of his sister's popularity among the natives and feared her erupting anger when she heard about John's removal. Ever uneasy, David Kalakaua did go to Maui, and there Liliuo-

kalani tried to influence him to give John not only the governorship of
Oahu but also of Maui. The king acquiesced, but somewhat later.

It was on a second trip that Liliuokalani first met with the opposition
of her brother-in-law, Cleghorn, and began to see the fickleness of her
younger sister, Likelike. Liliuokalani was graciously received throughout
the island of Oahu.

The Edwin Boyds had prepared "an elongated visit for them with
receptions, entertainment, and a royal welcome indeed." It was here that
Liliuokalani realized that Likelike had a taste for forbidden fruit: James
Boyd, later to become the husband of Cleghorn's second daughter, became
quite entranced with the delightful Likelike, and she with him.

One afternoon during a horseback riding trip, Likelike and James
Boyd rode off together, leaving Liliuokalani alone as the rest of the party
had gone on ahead. Riding slowly along the path, and in looking out
across the valley to Honolulu and the sparkling waters, she espied Boyd
and her sister in the distance; it was obvious they were saying a fond
farewell. Liliuokalani reacted with both extreme annoyance, and with
the sensitive, compassionate understanding of how difficult it must be to
say goodbye to one someone loved. The latter emotion won out. She
began in her mind, and later wrote from memory, her best known song:
"Aloha Oe."

Shortly thereafter, a letter came from Cleghorn ordering Likelike to
return home, because it was his opinion that if the purpose was to meet
the people and cultivate their love it was a waste of time—the natives, in
his opinion, were all zealous partisans of Queen Emma.[3] Mr. Cleghorn,
undoubtedly, had other reasons for having his wife return; Liliuokalani
gave her sister her own choice, but finally prevailed upon her to continue
the journey.

Liliuokalani wrote in her *Story* that upon her return to Honolulu
throngs of people awaited her. "From Leleo to Alakea Street it was a
mass of moving heads, through which only slowly could our carriages,
horses, and outriders pass. It was understood and accepted as a victorious
procession; and out of sympathy for the disappointed dowager Queen
Emma our people refrained from noisy demonstrations and loud cheering . . ."

※ 2 ※

Liliuokalani was having her own problems with David Kalakaua. Her diaries and letters negate the subservient attitude which she implies in her *Story* she had toward her brother—or his generous attitude of confidence in her.

Her concern was largely with her husband's position. Her one word for John Owen Dominis during this period was "boring." He also "visited" her from time to time at Waikiki and her diary bears witness to such statements as: "He went home early. I'm glad. I couldn't stand any more of his dreary stories."

But politically she sought positions for him—these were also for economic reasons, for David Kalakaua had "taken most of our mother's lands and my sister and I said nothing."[4] Even what was left of these lands, he later willed to his wife, Kapiolani, who in turn willed them to her two nephews—David Kawananakoa and Jonah Kalanianaole. Edward had died in his teens.

❧ 3 ❧

By 1878 Liliuokalani had reached another crisis in her personal life. She was forty years old, and no child had been born to her.

John had appointed Luther Aholo as his private secretary for his new Maui post. Luther Aholo, a native Hawaiian, was declared at the time of his appointment and at his death a man of "outstanding abilities."

At Lahaina, Maui, Liliuokalani and John visited the Aholos, and in their royal party was Abraham Fornander. Here he played his role as protector, friend, and adviser to Old Hawaii. Fornander at this time was serving as Acting Governor of Maui as Dominis, the governor, was seldom there.

While walking on the same beach on which she had accepted Prince Bill's proposal, Liliuokalani confided to her old friend and mentor, her distress. Fornander, brought to her attention that Mrs. Aholo was pregnant, and in the old *hanai* system, it would be only natural for Liliuokalani to ask for the child, and for Keahi Aholo, to give her the child.

Liliuokalani assessed the situation practically. Keahi was Luther Aholo's second wife; there were three other children by his first wife, and two others had been born to Keahi, one who had died in 1868, now ten years later another child was expected. Would Keahi be willing to part with this child? Liliuokalani thought she might.

However, Liliuokalani, the ever-torn woman between Hawaiian and *haole* ways, spoke to John, against her better judgement, and as expected he was extremely annoyed and strictly forbade such a "ridiculous idea." Had he not continued his argument with "What would Mother say?" he might have won.

Then brother and sister closed ranks, as they on occasion did, and David Kalakaua gave not only his consent, but his blessing to the "old Hawaiian *hanai*." Liliuokalani was *so* completely overjoyed at the thought of having a child, she failed completely to realize what this action could later mean to her and the child.

The arrangements were made, but then David became "nervous again" and decided to send Liliuokalani to the United States "for her health."[5]

She was accompanied by a "royal party" that included Willian Allen, an annexationist and not a strong supporter of Kalakaua. It is possible Kalakaua wanted Allen out of the country also. The controversial Charles B. Wilson and his wife, Kitty Townsend Wilson, accompanied the party of Liliuokalani and her husband, John Owen Dominis. There was a hint of conspiracy between Kalakaua and Dominis in getting Liliuokalani's mind off *hanai,* for Kalakaua, ever fickle, had changed his mind. He undoubtedly feared a problem of succession.

While in San Francisco, her days were filled with sight-seeing. Visits were made to former Hawaiian residents and persons of prestige, such as former Governor Pacheco, relatives of James Lick of the Lick Observatory, and the Crocker family in Sacramento. Liliuokalani was impressed by the "elegant mansion" of the Crockers as well as with Mrs. Crocker's art gallery. She expressed her own feeling for art: ". . . works of genius indeed, so true to nature and so lifelike." Her childlike curiosity and attitude is heard in her words: "There were apartments devoted to the several branches of natural history; the cabinets of stuffed and mounted birds, as well as of quadrupeds and animals in great variety, these interested and amused me as if I had been a child of ten at a museum of curiosities."

The trip, however, had a far more important impact on Liliuokalani. An idea for a new venture came to her.

On March 16, 1878, Liliuokalani accompanied by Kitty Wilson, had gone to visit her old friend and teacher, Susan Tolman Mills at Mills Seminary. Mills Seminary-College, as it was then known, had moved the year before from Benecia to Oakland, California, and Susan Mills was as enthusiastic, as she ever became, over her new college. She was delighted to show her former pupil and now a princess about the grounds.

The visit had a profound effect on Liliuokalani. There, before the eucalyptus trees that enshrouded the campus, the view of the valleys and the Pacific Ocean lay before her, reminding her of Hawaii, and she visualized immediately a college for young women in Honolulu.

Mrs. Mills entertained her at a tea given at Kapiolani Cottage, a guest house built primarily for visiting former-missionary friends. Kapiolani Cottage had been named after the well-known early Christian convert High Chiefess Kapiolani, who had defied the Goddess Pele in the "Christian spirit" by picking forbidden berries from her hillside and then defiantly hurling them into the volcanic crater in which Pele lived. It was a mark of great Christian heroism noted by all the missionaries, as well as the poet, Tennyson.[6] Susan Mills was delighted to learn from Liliuokalani that Kapiolani was her great-grand-aunt.

At the tea was another old acquaintance of the princess,[7] E. G. Beckwith, who was on the board of trustees of Mills College. Beckwith remembered fondly Liliuokalani's "studiousness," and his brothers amorous problems with the young Liliu, but now an animated conversation ensued relative to Liliuokalani's plans for a girls' college in Hawaii. Liliuokalani knew only too well that many Hawaiian women had become domestic servants in the homes of the *haole,* and she felt a deep need that these young women should be trained as *ladies,* as they were at Mills College. The dream was to stay with her for many years, and gallant but abortive attempts were made to make it come true.

When Liliuokalani returned to Honolulu she learned that Mrs. Aholo had died eight days after the birth of her child—a girl. In Hawaiian fashion the child had been taken by her maternal grandparents, Loe and Kawahena. Liliuokalani departed immediately for Lahaina, and there, despite the protests of John and without the knowledge of Mrs. Dominis, she went to the grass structure of Loe and Kawahena and laid claim to her *hanai* child.

The grandparents had, by unspoken tradition, become *hanai* to the baby, so Liliuokalani without further thought instituted another Hawaiian custom: she immediately included Loe and Kawahena in her retinue, and together with the infant they returned to Honolulu to become her retainers—her family. Liliuokalani named her *hanai* child after herself; "Lydia," and gave her the Hawaiian name of Kaonohiponiponiokalani. But she remained true to the 1860 law that the child's last name should be that of the father—Aholo. Lydia Aholo was to live until 1979 (age 101), and would be the instigator of this book.

Liliuokalani saw, fondled and loved the infant Lydia every day, just as Konia had loved her forty years before. Old Hawaii was a vital part of Liliuokalani's life in 1878. One year later she held the "baby luau" to proclaim to all that Lydia was her child.

❧ 4 ❧

The political chaos to which Liliuokalani was to fall heir as queen began early in Kalakaua's reign. Through him three men were introduced into the governmental scene who were to bring nothing but problems to Hawaii: Walter Murray Gibson, Celso Moreno, and Robert Wilcox.

Walter Murray Gibson was an opportunist of the first order. He originally arrived in Hawaii as a missionary of high standing in the Mormon Church with commissions from Brigham Young and introductions to the rulers of Japan and Malaysia. He planned only to rest briefly in Hawaii before continuing on to direct the missions in Malaysia. He found, however, a comfortable nest and a ready reception, and decided to stay. His early years in the islands were marked by a masterful reorganization of the numerous native converts to the Mormon Church into a congregation and theology of his own making. He was able to convince the new saints, only recently abandoned by their *haole* missionaries when Young had recalled them to Utah, into turning over all their wealth and property to Gibson himself. With this considerable income he proceeded to purchase the major part of the island of Lanai and set up a small kingdom in the name of the Mormon Church.

This was too good to last, and upon investigation by three emissaries sent by Brigham Young, he was excommunicated and his followers drifted away to their original church home. He had, however, managed to gain an island home in the process.

Gibson was a "tall, thin old gentleman of sixty with white hair and beard, a mild, cold blue eye, a fine patrician nose and a tolerably port wine complexion . . . [his] voice was soft and low, and confidential to a rare extent. He was an unquestionably eminent-looking veteran, of smooth address, silky manners, and a somewhat fascinating mode of speech, in the estimation of the susceptible and sympathetic—a fine old fellow, I should say; wise as a serpent, but hardly as harmless as a dove," a journalist wrote of Gibson, after he became Kalakaua's Premier.

Gibson had met Celso Moreno in Washington during one of his trips to the United States following his Mormon debacle, and had praised the opportunities in the islands so highly that Moreno, who purported to being attached to the Italian diplomatic legation, decided he should personally look into the matter. A man equally as ingratiating and convincing as Gibson, he quickly gained the king's ear on arrival in Honolulu, and soon had displaced Gibson as a favorite in the court. Kalakaua considered him "a man of large and novel views in political and state affairs;" the king was frequently surprised to find "how exactly Mr. Moreno's views coincided with his own . . ." However, he was able to maintain his position, unlike Gibson, for only a few months.

Between these two men, Kalakaua's impulsive urge to lavish the wealth of the royal treasury was exploited and flattered. One of the schemes they instigated was the plan to educate the young *alii* abroad. Robert Kalani-Haipo Wilcox was one of these students. Along with two friends of Cleghorn, Robert Boyd and James Booth, this half-Hawaiian man was to be sent to study in Italy. The choice of this country was influenced by several factors. The king desired a "royal" country, rather than a republic. He was hesitant to appear pro-British, and Moreno was of course a great booster of his native country.

An apparently insignificant reason, but one that helped tilt the scale was a chance remark by John Dominis. During an evening gathering at Kalakaua's boat house near the palace, where John, Celso Moreno, Walter Murray Gibson and the king were enjoying cards and drink, John became uncharacteristically nostalgic. Apparently spurred by Gibson's tales of adventures, vied in turn by the exciting stories of Moreno's early life, John told of his father's running away to sea to escape the "royalty" of his "noble household in Italy." This slip of the tongue caused some little stir in Liliu's thoughts when she heard of it, but John would never discuss the matter when sober.

Whatever the reasons for the decision, Celso Moreno left with young Wilcox and his two cohorts on August 30, 1880. Moreno was actually leaving in some disgrace, having been removed as Premier, but was compensated by being named "ambassador to Italy and envoy extraordinary and minister plenipotentiary" for the purpose of negotiating with the powers of Europe and the United States. He safely deposited the young men in Italy and placed them in a military school.

⚓ 5 ⚓

By the end of 1882, after Moreno was forced to resign his portfolio, Gibson remained in office, despite great opposition to him on the part of the *haole*. Gibson gave to Kalakaua everything he needed to feed his ego—the idea of "uniting the entire Pacific Islands under the Primacy of Kalakaua"; the glory of a king; the majesty of a royal court. Kalakaua was in the haze of grandiose ideas.

Encouraged by Moreno and Gibson, Kalakaua, through a basic instinct of knowing that the Hawaiian people wanted their country an independent entity, a monarchy, worked for that end in three ways: First by planning a trip around the world ostensibly to "increase the nation" and find plantation workers, in a word, immigration. Second, by the completion of a new palace, which had had its beginnings with Kamehameha V. Third, by establishing a new dynasty and having himself and his queen "properly" crowned.

Liliuokalani was called by telephone to the palace on a rainy Saturday early in January of 1881. She had heard rumors that Kalakaua was planning a trip around the world. He would be the world's first reigning monarch to do so, and this fact had been received with mixed emotions among the people. The *haole* were not enthusiastic; they considered the whole idea a whim to satisfy the king's love for travel, and far too expensive.

Eighteen-eighty was the first year that it had become necessary for the legislature to provide funds for the royal family.[8] To that time the royal family had provided for their own incomes from the lands they personally owned.

But the land issue was exceedingly confused.[9] When Kamehameha III had instituted the land reform, he had retained one-third of all the land for the rulers in this manner: one-half of his third was to be used for maintaining the "crown," whoever wore it—these were the "government lands"; the other half of the third was known as the "crown lands," and they were for the personal use of the royal family that existed at that time. When the Kamehameha family line no longer held the crown, they retained all their "crown lands," last mentioned. The so-called government lands, for maintenance of the holder of the royal office, had slowly disappeared through use for various government projects, confusing land disbursements as the rulers succeeded one another, and a general reliance by most of the rulers on their own personal holdings.

Thus, by 1880, David Kalakaua actually had very few holdings in comparison with his predecessors on the throne, and the income was not enough to support the royal family. In addition to this, his tastes were very royal, and the flow of wealth from his office was great. His reliance on his inherited lands from his mother's father, Aikanaka, prompted Liliuokalani's comment that "He took our mother's lands and my sister and I said nothing."

Through this great confusion a once rich monarchy was being rapidly reduced to poverty. The Americans, who were trying so hard to make a "working republic" out of the monarchy balked at paying Kalakaua a salary even though the United States paid its president, and the British supported their royal family to some extent.

Liliuokalani, aware of the monetary situation as well as the unpopularity among the *haole,* of the trip, approached the palace meeting with trepidation. While the *haole* objected to Kalakaua's trip on their grounds, Liliuokalani was not too well satisfied with the persons whom he had chosen to accompany him: Charles Judd, former aid to Lunalilo and, the man who replaced John Owen Dominis as King Kalakaua's chamberlain; and a man who from the beginning of his government-attachment had negated and opposed everything Kalakaua stood for or believed in—Atty. Gen. William Armstrong. Kalakaua's choices were again examples of his inability to judge character. He may have thought that by conferring this honor he could win their loyalty. It did not work.

When Liliuokalani arrived at the palace, Kalakaua kept her waiting while he finished a card game in the boat house. She was met by Queen Kapiolani. Liliuokalani found her in tears. Yes. It was true. David was going around the world. And Kapiolani greatly feared the trip, remembering the deaths of Kamehameha II and his wife while in England.

Neither of Kapiolani's sisters could quiet her fears, and here Liliuokalani showed her strange practicality: she took control. She pointed out that Kalakaua had gone to the United States twice, Canada once; he was a strong, vigorous man and had been among the *haole* long enough not to be subject to their diseases. Those were the facts. And Liliuokalani could be quite adamant.

Kapiolani's fears lessened, and Kalakaua appeared. He greeted his sister with an *aloha* kiss; he was in high good humor—had probably won at cards, Liliuokalani suspected.

He told her at length about his trip—to visit Japan, China, Siam, India, France, Spain, Italy, England and of course, the United States. When he told her whom he was taking with him—something she already knew—she requested that he take John instead.

There can be little doubt that Liliuokalani would have been delighted to have John out of the country for a while, as well as feeling, politically, it would be a good move. However, Kalakaua refused. Instead he told her she would be regent while he was gone—"with a council of regency." She refused.

In her *Story* she indicates that the ensuing conversation was logical, pleasant, and unheated. Liliuokalani, according to her *hanai* daughter, never raised her voice in anger, but nevertheless that quiet, well-modulated voice could carry such determination, it brooked no rebuttal. It accomplished far more than shouting could have done.

With less restraint than usual, she wrote in her *Story*:

> As the king had sent for me with the express purpose of asking my opinion, I gave it in terms too plain to admit of the least misunderstanding between us. I told him that I did not admit either the necessity or the wisdom of any such organization as that of a council of regency; that to my view, if intrusted with the government during his absence I ought to be the sole regent.

And she *was* appointed sole regent.

In January, 1881, Kalakaua went off with a happy heart. Princess Liliuokalani, Regent, spent little of her precious moments, as her brother Leleiohoku had, in music, dance, and the "pleasantness of life." She immediately made plans to visit her people on all the islands.

Almost at once she was impeded by the outbreak of smallpox in Honolulu, and communication between the different islands was stopped at her command through the ministry. Immediately an attack was made on the ministry for such stringent measures; "dismissal and want of confidence" became the familiar cry. Liliuokalani not only stood firmly by the ministry, but in her speeches she was so effectively logical that the opposition stopped, and the epidemic, confined to Honolulu, was brought under control.

As soon as the privileges of travel were restored Liliuokalani set forth with her royal party which included Bernice Pauahi Bishop, Princess Ruth, and the Royal Hawaiian Band. She speaks lightly of her own reason for taking the Band in her *Story*: ". . . not for my pleasure especially, although music forms to me a great part of the enjoyment of life, but because I wished to bring with me, to my friends and my people on that island [Hawaii], a delight which I knew to them was quite rare, and in which I was quite sure all would find much satisfaction."

It was the first time the Band had made extensive trips, and it was also the first time Liliuokalani was to become acquainted with Henry

Berger, the band leader. The passing of time would prove this acquaintance special in a unique way.

As the excursion got under way, it quickly was confronted by a situation far more serious than was expected on such a royal visit to the people. On the big island of Hawaii, Mauna Loa had begun a volcanic eruption in 1880, and the lava flows were beginning to pose a serious threat to Hilo. The native people were in awe of the natural disaster, fascinated by the beauty and power of the lava flows, and terrified that their homes and fields would soon be destroyed.

Upon arrival of the royal party, a situation arose which reflected all too clearly the cultural and philosophical changes which had come to Hawaii in less than a century. Princess Ruth claimed to be a *kahuna,* and encouraged the fears of many of the people that Pele, fiery goddess who lived in the crater, desired appeasement. A sacrifice in the old tradition would be needed to satisfy her and rescue the lands.

The Princess Regent was disturbed as much by Ruth's claims as she was by the Hawaiian's return to Pele-worship. Though she held fast that the old traditions should be preserved and even revered for what they were, she held to the Christian doctrine in the areas of faith, and ordered all the churches to be opened for prayer meetings. She visited a church in Hilo, and in the red-edged smoke-filtered air, she led prayers. It was a dramatic moment—but one totally unplanned by Liliuokalani for mere drama.

Within a week the flow stopped a few miles from Hilo; cultivated lands and homes had been spared. The papers carried accounts of Liliuokalani's call for prayer meetings, and her attendance. They also told of her plans for earth barricades to divert the lava. They made no mention of Ruth and her supposed excursion to the edge of the lava flow or sacrifice to Pele. Later these stories would find their way into print, drawn from "oral" tales. It would be said that Ruth's actions were "suppressed" by the missionaries. More likely, the popularity and acceptance of Liliuokalani allowed her to dominate the news—if indeed Ruth ever had appeared at the fiery furnace.[10]

Initially the regent's trip through the islands was wonderfully successful, but her travels ended with a distressing accident on Oahu. She wrote:

> We were descending the steep side of a hill, and the result was that the driver had no longer control of the animals. Consequently the carriage came down the hill with such velocity that I was thrown

out, and landed between two rocks; but fortunately there was a bit
of marshy ground where I struck. It was a matter of immediate wonder that my life had been spared. Certainly no one could have been
nearer to instant death.

As a result, the tour was cut short, and she suffered for several months
from a severe back injury. While she lay in pain on her high Hawaiian
bed at Waikiki, she remembered her childhood accident, and the story
of Hina, the sea goddess, and her lameness resulting from the loss of her
calabash which had been stolen by the men of earth.

With the same determination she had used to overcome her own
childhood lameness, Liliuokalani once again overcame her injury, deciding that the new men of earth, the *haole,* would not take her calabash
nor leave her crippled. Contrary to the later reports of her adamancy,
"stubbornness," and "willfulness," her own words give a picture of a
woman whose religious and mystical orientation provided inner strength
to overcome great obstacles. Her recovery from this injury is closely related to *aloha*-love, recognizing that her painful "trial" was overshadowed
by her feeling of "the blessed consciousness that all this manifestation
[of care] was because my people loved me."[11] Her return from serious
injury and near-death to the arms of her people "left the impression
upon [her] that was too sacred for any description." It was typically
Hawaiian to retreat from "exposing" a deeply moving experience of joy,
sadness, love—a "sacred" moment.

The reign of the regent was not without its concerns for her brother,
for various rumors filtered back to Honolulu from his world trip. Kalakaua wrote her from time to time, but she also received other reports. One
in particular worried her: there was talk that Kalakaua would "sell" the
country and Liliuokalani was not at all sure he wouldn't try. He, of
course, did not have the power to do so—but try yes, for "How millions
would burn his fingers!" she wrote later.

Kalakaua returned; he had not tried to sell the country.

And Liliuokalani's regency received acclaim, not too joyfully received
by her brother. She was praised for "her prudence and tact" (refusing
to make a ministerial appointment while her brother was absent) and
her ability to make friends by the "simple dignity of her style and by her
accessibility to the people in public receptions and otherwise." The American minister contrasted her actions with the contrary course followed
by her brother. A slight flurry arose over her "preference" for the British,
but the snowflakes melted before they reached the ground.

In 1881 Liliuokalani completed her regency, well liked by Hawaiians and *haole* alike. She retired to a less comfortable personal life.

⚬ 6 ⚬

John Owen Dominis was what Dr. Trouseau later termed in the Blount Report, "an irregular husband . . . he had 'affairs' but never a regular mistress." Dr. Trouseau was probably correct. He was the family physician of the Kalakauas and the Dominises; he played cards, drank, and had his "evenings out" with the king and John. He certainly knew John well enough to know he was not the type of man to become committed to one woman; indeed if he wished extra-marital relationships, there was safety in numbers—or so he may have mistakenly believed.

Trouseau, despite his companionship with John, had a strong liking for Liliuokalani. He preferred to protect her. In the later Blount Report he stated: "She loved him [Dominis] and suffered great unhappiness by his inconsistencies. I tried to spare her much." He therefore attempted to keep John's "irregularities" from her until the latter part of 1882.

In November of 1882, Dr. Trouseau had the unpleasant duty of telling Liliuokalani that John Owen Dominis was about to have an illegitimate child born to a young half-Hawaiian woman, once intimately connected with the American historian Hale. She was even known in some quarters as "Mrs. Haley"—(the pronounciation of *hale* in Hawaiian was *hāley*.) Dowager Queen Emma wrote a friend that she was ". . . one of Mrs. Dominis' girls . . . or you may even know her as Mrs. D . . .—for so she is in truth."[12]

This young woman was a retainer of Liliuokalani's, a part of her "family"; she was also, however, officially married to a young Hawaiian by the name of John Lamiki Aimoku. Her *hanai* mother was a close friend of Liliuokalani—Mary Purdy, a relative of Sam Parker. Her name appears varyingly in later newspapers as Mary Purdy Pahau, Mary Hale Purdy Pahau.[13]

Liliu's first reaction was to claim the child as hers and John's—establishing a lineal descent to the throne, although this would have been illegal. Only John, the mother of the child, Dr. Trouseau, and Mary Purdy were to know of the birth. She was again also thinking of John, even putting him and his feelings ahead of what she knew was illegal in heritage. It was not an easy decision for her.

Out of bits and pieces of correspondence of Queen Emma, Dr. Trouseau to his brother, and Dr. Tisdale of Oakland, California, a strange conspiracy emerges; it is further strengthened by Liliuokalani's later diaries and by the corresponding dating by her *hanai* daughter, Lydia Aholo.[14]

On January 9, 1883, a child was born in the household of Liliuokalani at Waikiki. The mother gave her child in Hawaiian fashion in *hanai* to its maternal grandmother, Mary Purdy (Pahau), who was at the time fifty-three years old. She claimed him as her own—a remarkable woman, Mary Purdy (Pahau). Another remarkable woman, Princess Liliuokalani, took over his support, but she followed the letter of the law of 1860, as she had with Lydia, only this time the law read that a child born out of wedlock took the legal surname of his mother, Aimoku. Thus John Dominis Aimoku came into being. Not until after the death of John Owen Dominis did Liliuokalani officially adopt Aimoku (1910) and have his name changed to John Aimoku Dominis.

The preceding June (1882) another child had been born to another retainer of the Princess—Kaheo Aea, the wife of Joseph Aea. Both Joseph and Kaheo were pure Hawaiian and Liliuokalani had had a close friendship with Joseph, what some persons have hinted at as a lover relationship, but in nothing she wrote herself is there any indication that she even liked Joe Aea as a man—let alone loved him. He drank heavily, something Liliuokalani abhorred.

However, there was also to her advantage an old Hawaiian custom that if two women had sexual relations with the same man and one bore a child and did not wish to keep it and the other woman did, she could have the child as her own—the "child of two heads."[15]

Whether Joseph Kaipo Aea was such a child or not, Liliuokalani decided to take him in *hanai* after the birth of John Aimoku. There followed several years of varying dates in her diaries as to the year of the birth of these two children, as if she sometimes became confused which story was in vogue. It was also as if she had difficulty in keeping Aimoku as the elder—and well she might—for in 1887 the Aeas decided to blackmail her.

Love, which cannot be directed, but is won or lost by an individual, fell from Liliuokalani in full force upon Kaipo. He became her favorite of the three *hanai* children.

Lydia Aholo lived and travelled with her grandparents, in the retinue of Princess Liliuokalani, "just in case I ever became ill or anything," Lydia explained, but it was also custom. When she was four years old, she was placed at Kawaiahao Seminary, a school for young girls. Later Lydia came under the loving ministrations of Ida Pope. Ida Pope was to be to Lydia what Kaikai had been to Liliu—the one person who loved her without reservation. She also molded her character in a strict Puritanical form, one that was to separate her from Liliuokalani for a time.

Aimoku remained with Mary Purdy, who had two older sons, until he was nearly four, when he was placed with his "brother" Kaipo with a Mrs. Bush for proper care. Here is found an example of Liliuokalani's poor judgement. Mrs. Bush (the wife of J. E. Bush, a constant threat to Kalakaua), was a poor choice for the two boys.

℀ 7 ℁

Kalakaua returned from his trip around the world exceedingly well pleased with himself, but not so pleased with his sister's popularity. He suggested in good masculine fashion that she find "activities of her own" to engage herself in rather than in politics.

Liliuokalani was only too ready to do so, but they were not the activities that Kalakaua would have chosen for her. While he basked in the sunshine of his own grandiose and impractical dream of being the Napoleon of the Pacific, Liliuokalani turned to help Kapiolani with a project dear to both: that of establishing a maternity home to help keep babies alive, protect the mothers and—"Increase the Nation," Kalakaua's motto. In theory Kalakaua thought this was an excellent idea—Increase the Nation—in practicality his enthusiasm waned from time to time because it took monies away from his own projects. There was a time an ice cream social was planned with great care. Liliuokalani's diary tells of several days of planning. The ice cream ordered, invitations issued and all plans made for a money-raising ice cream social. Suddenly the entry reads, "The King says: Ice cream social pau [finished or ended]." Kalakaua evidently stopped the proceedings for reasons only he could give.

Kapiolani, however, was quite adamant: a maternity home *was* to be built. However, it was not until 1890 that she saw its completion.

In return for Liliu's support and aid for the maternity home, Liliuokalani enlisted Kapiolani's support in two projects of her own: a school for young girls—Liliuokalani College—where Hawaiian girls would learn not how to be domestics alone, as at Kawaiahoa Seminary; but to be ladies and scholars. It would be based on Mills Seminary-College. The students would also be taught the Hawaiian language, music, traditions, customs and history. She began having meetings with Princess Poomaikelani, sister of Kapiolani, her own sister, Likelike, and other *alii*.

Her second project was even more revolutionary for her time—it had no predecessor and no follower until in 1970, when Eileen Price had the same idea: a bank for women. Liliuokalani was an early feminist of the best type. She recognized that much of Hawaiian land-money was in the hands of the Hawaiian women. If they were allowed a bank in which to "conduct their own affairs," *haole* husbands would be less likely to dispose of their monies. Her strongest supporter was Bella Lyman, a part-Hawaiian woman married into a missionary descendant family.[16] Her strongest opponent was Charles Reed Bishop, her *hanai* brother-in-law.

With the beginning of putting these three projects into reality and her three *hanai* children close to her, Liliuokalani began the years of 1882 and 1883 with a peak of joy and satisfaction, all too soon to be crushed.

Kalakaua was busy with his own grand projects. On Queen Kapiolani's birthday, December 31, 1879, the cornerstone had been laid for the new Iolani Palace. It was done with complete Masonic rites. Kalakaua was a thirty-third degree Mason in the Scottish Rite and a Knight Templar in the York, as was John Owen Dominis. He had been told by the Order of Free Masons to "follow the ancient Masonic rites prescribed for proper cornerstone ceremonies," and he did so.

Present at the ceremony were Liliuokalani and John Owen Dominis, along with members of the royal household, representatives of the Hawaiian Chiefs, legislative and other political—foreign and domestic—representatives, as well as throngs of natives and *haole*.

The work had continued while Kalakaua was on his trip around the world. In celebration of Queen Kapiolani's birthday on December 27, 1882, he entertained for the first time: a dinner for his Masonic brothers.

The new palace was to have living quarters as well as official quarters for the royal family.

The palace was "palatial" in Hawaii, but compared to the palaces of Europe, and even Asia, it was modest. Liliuokalani had read and learned from foreign visitors of these palaces and Kalakaua had seen them, been entertained in them, but the Americans felt the new palace was much too grand for the "comic opera monarchy."

Kalakaua designated his coronation for February 12, 1883, exactly nine years to the day after he had signed the Constitution, proclaiming himself King. He also decreed the year of 1883 the Jubilee Year of Hawaii, "forever to be commemorated." There were snide remarks passed around about a king crowned nine years late. There were more caustic remarks about the cost.

Liliuokalani later defended in her *Story* the necessity of having the coronation in order to establish the *"stirps* of our family." At the time she was torn between this apparently right idea and money. Her later diaries form a dialogue of the need for establishing and maintaining a new dynasty and the cost.

Never before had the royal court—the *alii*—had to feel they were spending the "people's money." Now there was a constant haranguing in the legislature that the king was spending too much money. The native Hawaiians did not feel this way. To them, their king spent as he needed, the expenditures were an expression of *mana* and *aloha*.

Those were the native sentiments, but intrigue to overthrow all that was Hawaiian was at work in the land, influencing even some of the natives and many half-*haole* Hawaiians.

So stood the social-cultural-political conflict on February 12, 1883, the Coronation Day.

CHAPTER 3

The Coronation and the Genealogical Trial

❧ 1 ❧

The Coronation of 1883 was everything the Hawaiians could want—and the grumbling of "fluff and feathers" of the *haole* was blown away on the winds of Nature. It was also to the entire satisfaction of the royal household. Kalakaua had shown remarkable diplomacy in regard to his own—or possibly Walter Murray Gibson had; it was he who had planned the ceremony.

The weather, by which the Hawaiians judged the auspiciousness of any occasion, was for the three previous days unnerving, for it had been "anything but favorable, it having rained incessantly during that time—more especially on Saturday night."

Kalakaua had had a pavilion (now the bandstand) built on the palace grounds in which the ceremony was to take place. It was a work of art:

> Each of the eight sides bore the name of the respective Kings of Hawaii with the years during which they reigned, from the time of Kamehameha I to the present day. Each name and duration of the reign was encircled in laurel wreaths supported by two crossed palm leaves and surmounted by a crown. Over the front entrance to the pavilion were the following words: February 12, 1883, the day on which His Majesty King Kalakaua was crowned. The ceiling was decorated with paintings in oil and fresco work. The Hawaiian coat-of-arms was painted in the center of a white net work. This was considered without exception the finest specimen of this kind of work that has ever been produced in Honolulu.

The pavilion was surrounded by a spacious amphitheater for the accommodation of invited guests of the clergy, schools, institutions, societies, clubs, and the general public; it seated approximately 4,000 people.

The remaining palace grounds to the gates were open to spectators who had received no special invitation—to the people—mostly Hawaiians; it had a standing room of 7,000.

Upon the palace veranda on the right of the entrance were seated foreign representatives and on the left the government representatives and commanders of ships in port.

No stage lighting could have been planned more effectively; for Monday, February 12, 1883, dawned not in clouds, but the sun shown forth with "unwonted brilliancy . . . The brilliant weather continued, and strange to say, the morning star was seen in the heavens at 9 a.m., shining contemporaneously with the sun."

A guard of honor was formed in front of Iolani Palace. At ten o'clock, at points assigned, the Band formed on the right, in front of the line, facing the Pavilion.

"At the hour of 10:15 the King Street Gate of the Palace ground was thrown open to admit all persons who had received invitations." At eleven o'clock the sun was obstructed by a cloud and a hush fell over the waiting crowd. The sun remained hidden when their Majesties began their march to the pavilion, preceded by nine-year old Princess Kaiulani, "dressed in a light blue corded silk trimmed with lace, pale blue ribbons in her hair."

The cloudy sky remained, as if also hushed by the solemnity of the occasion, as the Procession, "headed by the Marshall of the Kingdom (W. C. Parke) and the honorable Marshall of Household, (J. M. Kapena) moved to the pavilion.

"At the appearance of His Majesty's Chamberlain the heralds of old and new Hawaii—conch shells and trumpets—proclaimed the approach of their Majesties."

Following the Chancellor, who was to administer the oath, came Her Royal Highness Princess Liliuokalani, with her ladies in waiting, and Governor John Owen Dominis. She "wore a Parisian toilette of gold brocade, the front part of white satin embroidered with gold, and a heavy crimson velvet train; the head-dress was a wreath of gold leaves and white feathers tipped with pearls; gold necklace with a diamond cross, and diamond earrings."

Following her was her sister, Her Royal Highness, Princess Likelike, with her attendants, and her husband, Archibald Cleghorn. There followed the sisters of Kapiolani, and other ladies of governmental importance.

Still in the cloudiness of the day, their Majesties approached the pavilion. The robe of the Queen was "of rich cardinal velvet, heavily embroidered in an elaborate design of fern leaves in gold, with ermine border, gloves and slippers, embroidered in green, a coronet of diamonds, bracelets of diamonds, emeralds, rubies, and amethysts, and she carried a superb, hand-painted fan trimmed with lace."

The Ceremony began with the singing of the Episcopalian Choir. The Marshal of the Household declared the king's accession and right to the throne by his lineages, "wohi" *(mana)* and numerous foreign and domestic royal orders.

"Princess Poomaikelani then advanced and presented his majesty with *Puloulou* (tabu stick) and the torch of Iwikauikaua and the *kahili* of King Pili, as symbols of ancient supreme chieftancy."

Chancellor Judd then undertook to have the king reaffirm his previous oath to the Constitution; Judd placed the sword of state in the king's hands as the "Ensign of Justice and Mercy"—it was an exact counterpart of that of England, fine Damascus steel inlaid with gold with the Hawaiian coat of arms and the motto of the realm. The hilt, guard and cord tassels were of gold, beautifully engraved.

After taking the sword, the king returned it to the chancellor, who unsheathed it and carried it "naked during the rest of the solemnity."

> Princess Kekaulike then advanced with the royal mantle and placed it in the hands of the Chancellor, who placed it on the king's shoulders saying: "Receive this ancient mantle of your predecessors as the Ensign of Knowledge and Wisdom." The mantle was one which was worn by the First Kamehameha, and was one of the most superb emblems of Royalty ever worn by King or Kaiser. It was a semi-circular cloak about four feet in length, covering an area of 25 square feet when spread out, and was made of the small golden-hued feathers of O'o. These feathers, each about the size of one's little finger nail were fastened to a fine net-work of fibre made from the bark of the Olana, in such a manner that they overlay each other.
>
> There were at least 5000 of these feathers used in the cloak, and, as there were but two taken from each bird, which have to be snared in the dense woods, where they are by no means abundant, it will be seen that the first cost of the cloak was very great, and that the keeping of it in order an endless task. This mantle was only worn by the reigning Sovereign . . .

The chancellor then put the ring on the fourth finger of his Majesty's right hand saying: "Receive this ring, the Ensign of Kingly Dignity." The chancellor delivered the Sceptre to the King saying: "Receive the royal Sceptre, the Ensign of Kingly Power of Justice."

All of the proceedings took place in the dimmed light of a hiding sun. Then Prince David Kawananakoa advanced with the crowns.

The choir sang the anthem:

> Almighty Father! we do bring
> Gold and gems for the King;
> Pure gold for the true Chief,
> The symbol of true Love.
> Gems of the hidden mine,
> Gleaming forth a glory;
> The glory of the unfolding Isles,
> That grow in wealth and peace—
> That come to crown their King,
> The heir of the farthest ages
> Chosen by the Almighty Father!
> To Whom the honor and the glory. Amen.

The Honorable President of the Legislative Assembly then took the king's crown and raised it up before the people and placed it in the hands of the chancellor, saying:

"I present this Crown to the rightful King of these Islands, approved by Acts of the Legislative Assembly in the Legislature of the Kingdom assembled of the years 1880 and 1882."

The chancellor then placed it in the king's hands, saying: "Receive this Crown of pure gold to adorn the high station wherein thou hast been placed."

The king then raised up the Crown and placed it upon his own head.

At that moment the sun broke through the clouds like a spotlight and illumined the whole scene—some said that a "single star appeared in the heavens" just previous to the brilliancy of the sun. In any event, the lighting effects were superb.

A sigh escaped the crowd and some fell on their knees.

The chancellor after a momentary pause took the second crown and placed it in the king's hands, who rose and placed it upon the queen's head, who after a slight moment of confusion as it caught in her diadem, reverently bowed to receive it, the king saying: "I place this Crown upon your head, to share the honors of my throne."

Criticism soon followed that Kalakaua in a Napoleonic fashion had crowned himself and his queen; however, in order for the chancellor to have done so, he would have had to cast his shadow upon the king, and

Kalakaua remaining true to the lingering native belief that no shadow should be cast upon the king, circumvented the situation by crowning himself and Kapiolani.

On that Monday, however, the crowd remained in stillness and awe as a prayer was offered, after which their Majesties then arose and resumed their places upon the throne. At the conclusion of the prayer, signals from the Palace towers announced the event, and a royal salvo of guns was fired from the battery and men-of-war in port. The Choir then sang an anthem dedicated to the King.

The Coronation Ceremony being completed, the king and queen, attended as before, retired to the Grand Hall, where the disrobing took place.

The procession left the pavilion; homage was paid in private to the King by the foreign and domestic members of the government.

> On the conclusion of the ceremonies, the band played Meyerbeer's celebrated "Coronation March," and as the people dispersed there was a general feeling of approbation expressed with successful manner in which the whole proceedings had been conducted. Flags were displayed in every direction, and the harbor presented an unusually gay appearance with four full-dressed men of war, and twenty-two merchantmen. The inter-island steamers and schooners also put forth all the bunting they possessed.

Coronation festivities continued all that week and the following week, and celebrations included the *Hookupu,* the presentation of gifts to the king, each giver contributing of his best, whether of the fruits of his land or the finest examples of his talents and skills. "On the 24th, at noon, the Grand *Luau* at the Palace began. Five thousand guests were fed and the feasting, hulas, and singing continued until 11:30 p.m."

On Wednesday, February 14, 1883, the statue of Kamehameha I, erected in front of Aliiolani Hale, opposite the palace on King Street, was unveiled by King Kalakaua. The statue had been ordered by the Legislature in 1878 from an American sculptor in Italy in order to commemorate the Centennial of the discovery of the Islands by Captain James Cook on January 18, 1778. Kamehameha the Great was supposed to have dated his career from that period. The first statue was lost off the Falkland Islands, and a replica had been ordered to be ready for unveiling during the coronation week.

The replica still stands on King Street before the State Judiciary across from the Iolani Palace. The original, eventually recovered, was erected at Kohala, Hawaii, the birthplace of Kamehameha.

❦ 2 ❦

Immediately after the Coronation, all the festering problems came to a head in a peculiar way. Kalakaua was attacked by what the newspapers called "a skillful genealogist," as not being of "sufficient *alii* lineage to be eligible for the throne. The contention was that Queen Emma alone was eligible.

It will probably never be known who the "skillful genealogist" was, but it is highly improbable that he was in the service of Queen Emma. Early in 1883 Emma had suffered a slight stroke, and neither her health nor her desires would have thrown her into the verbal newspaper fray that followed and became vicious and libelous. Emma was not a favorite of Liliuokalani, but she called Emma "petty," not malicious.

Kalakaua, against Liliuokalani's advice, picked up the gauntlet, not in his own defence, but to cast aspersions on Emma's reputation and genealogy. He thereby began losing his standing among the native Hawaiians, who still revered Queen Emma.

Only in the newspapers and "on the streets" was the case "tried"; varying papers carried both sides labelling the information "the genealogical trial."[1]

Kalakaua was first attacked as having no *wohi - mana* of ancient kings and gods on the basis that neither Keohokalole nor Kapaakea, his blood parents, had *wohi*. Neither did his *hanai* parents as they carried him, it was said, "on chest, backs, arms, and laps."

If the brother, as head of the family, had no *wohi*, it was declared, neither did the sister. Konia and Paki, who had recognized *wohi*, were totally discounted. Liliuokalani was not to be judged by the *hanai*. Keohokalole was fearfully slandered in every possible way. It was said that she had not been allowed to sit at the table of Kamehameha III—an absurd statement, for Keohokalole was one of the Councillors of Kamehameha III; she was also the last of the high chiefesses to be honored at *puna*. The stories went on even more absurdly that the Kalakauas never ate with Kamehameha V. The "trial" grew more and more vicious: it "was told" that before his death Kapaakea had denied being the father of all Keohokalole's children *except* Liliu Kamakaeha.

An old Hawaiian woman was supposed to have testified that she had seen Keohokalole in sexual relations with Blossom, a Negro blacksmith, and from the union had come Kalakaua. Later studies revealed that the Blossom family came to Hawaii in the 1850's when David Kalakaua was in his teens.

John Ii began to break the libelous statements, and probably could have ended the "trial" had not Kalakaua interferred. Ii stated that Kamehameha I had been placed as *hanai* in the keeping of the Keawe line and that as a result, a close relationship of the royal lines existed to the time of Kalakaua.[2] But Kalakaua turned his attack on Emma. Emma was accused of changing her genealogy, a Hawaiian "sin," to become "more royal."

The whole affair was belabored and would not be worth mentioning if it had not affected Liliuokalani in two ways: first, the fact she had not been "adopted," but *hanai* to Paki and Konia, denied her their *wohi*. Secondly, during the "trial" it was brought out that her grandfather Kamanawa had been hanged. This statement was true. In 1843 when she was only four years old and Kalakaua, six, Juliette Cooke told of "a man being hanged"—"someone who had something to do with one of the royal children," for he had asked to see David.

Kalakaua had never made a secret of his grandfather's (on his father's side) having been hanged for poisoning his wife. It was said he wanted to leave her for another and that missionary rule had declared divorce impossible. This story also varied in that Kamanawa had killed his wife in a fit of jealousy, when finding her with another man, an act some declared justifiable.

The story had been used against Liliuokalani while she served as regent. Told she had to sign a death warrant, she pleaded for postponement until Kalakaua returned from his world tour. It was said that although she favored stricter punishment for criminals, especially those who committed unprovoked crimes against the young or the elderly, she refused to sign the death warrant because it reminded her of her grandfather.

The truth was that she couldn't bear to be responsible for the loss of another human being's life. She never could—even when it came to the choice of losing her crown or sacrificing lives. She was, however, forced by the *haole* ministry, then in power, to sign the warrant. It haunted her all her life.

The "trial" rumbled on laying seeds of dissension for the Kalakaua family among the Kamehameha descendants. If it was *haole* instigated, as was suspected by some, it was succeeding in dividing the Hawaiians. If division could be achieved among the *alii* of various royal lines from the "conquered" islands, the Hawaiians would be a nation divided against itself. The "geneological trial" laid the groundwork for the first division among the Hawaiians that was to come into unhappy fruition during the overthrow ten years later.

Although Liliuokalani was somewhat tarnished by the brush, she came out least harmed of the Kalakaua family, as she alone was acknowledged the "legitimate child of Keohokalole and Kapaakea." The king came out worse, and an unpleasant light was cast upon Likelike and her daughter, Kaiulani.

Some of the *alii* grew tired of the haranguing that was going on in the papers, and after a consultation between Princess Ruth, an acknowledged Princess of the Kamehameha line, and an acknowledged Princess of the Keawe line, the two decided to put a stop to it.

While leaving a church service at St. Andrews Cathedral, the Keawe Princess stepped aside to allow Likelike and Kaiulani, to precede her, showing she gave them royal deference. They were then invited with Liliuokalani to her home.

> This visit took place just at noon and, just before the arrival of the Princesses. The High Chiefess ordered the flaming torch of Keawe to be lit in front of her home.
>
> After the princesses arrived Kekauluohi II [the high Chiefess] walked to the torch and extinguished it. Thereby she proclaimed, without a single word, that she recognized the exalted birth of the Princess Kaiulani.[3]

It was the stamp of approval for the Keawe-line-torch symbol as belonging to them.

The genealogical trial came to a simpering end and the newspapers had to look elsewhere for "their scandals," which, Liliuokalani said, "they termed 'news'."

❧ 3 ❧

Meanwhile in the government, Walter Murray Gibson was making strong in-roads. He was called by some people "King Gibson." Whatever else he was, he was a colorful person devoted to the king.

Liliuokalani knew another side of him, a warm human side, that history books omit. Liliuokalani with her inveterate interest in children came to know him through their mutual interest, the leper's orphanage. There she discovered him to be a man consumed by love for a woman he could not have: the Mother Superior of the orphanage. Whatever else may be believed or doubted about Gibson, his relationship with the Mother Superior cannot be doubted nor misunderstood by an honest observer.[4]

Gibson loved her with all the love he possessed. He regularly sent her and "her children" gifts of fruits and baked goods. He grieved every day he did not hear from her; he remained in constant torment of saying or doing anything that would prevent him from seeing her, or even spending a few moments talking with her over a cup of tea. His love remained platonic—whether by strict adherence of the nun to her vows or by simply not being emotionally touched, we don't know. But the Mother Superior had enormous compassion for the love-ridden man and gave him what she could of her companionship. In the midst of this affair of unrequited love, Gibson met a woman of dubious character. She sued him for breach of promise, something the papers made much of in order to discredit him as premier, without success. His denial of the relationship was not supported by the court's decision. He suspected his personal enemies of having "planted" the woman in the suit to humiliate him. Liliuokalani believed him completely; it was something, she was beginning to suspect, "they" *would* do.

Of his political faults she had little doubt. He supported the weakest side of Kalakaua—the vainglorious desire to be the Napoleon of the Pacific, encouraging the licensing of the lottery and opium. But it should be noted that many *haole* supported the latter two schemes also. She stated in her diary, "It is a shame all the fault should fall on Gibson . . . he did it all for the king."

Walter Murray Gibson expressed *his* feelings about Liliuokalani at her forty-eighth birthday party (1886), an elaborate luau at Muolaulani. Kalakaua first gave an eloquent toast to "all the ladies." Gibson responded that the guest should "cast reflection upon [his] singleness." He then turned to Liliuokalani: ". . . in honoring her, I desire to set forth how much I honor the good amongst the sex which she so worthily represents."[5]

While the government was moving disastrously on, Liliuokalani's projects were receiving little support. The maternity home, which was supported by Kalakaua, made the most progress, as the king arranged for tours to the outer islands and the royal princesses musical programs as benefits. But with her own projects he was most reluctant.

She struggled valiantly with the aid of both the *alii* such as Poomai-kelani (Kapiolani's sister) and missionary descendants, foremost Bella Lyman, for her educational society and the promotion of a bank for women.[6] She met great opposition from Charles Bishop in regard to the bank, but she persisted, even talking to Claus Spreckels about it, although he didn't show much enthusiasm either.

⚓ 4 ⚓

Claus Spreckels, born in Lambstedt, Germany, July 9, 1828, came to Hawaii in 1878. He persuaded Princess Ruth to sell him her disputed lands which he put under sugar cultivation. By bringing in specialized machinery and conniving with Kalakaua to receive special water rights, he was able to out-produce the other *haole* plantation owners.

He gave lavish parties and attended equally lavish luaus at the king's boat house and week-long sailing parties. He then entered into the government as another promoter of Kalakaua, causing Lorrin Thurston to ask: "Who is King—Spreckels or Kalakaua?" Speaking against Spreckels' support for Kalakaua's desire for a ship he said ". . . [the king] needs it no more than a cow needs a necklace."

It was a time when allegations against Thurston should have been seriously heeded. He was labelled as a "bitter, unscrupulous man [who] uses words for the street not in the legislature or in print." On June 1, 1886, because of Thurston's "alleged" election frauds and berating of Luther Aholo and other Hawaiians, both the *Daily Bulletin* and the *Advertiser* gave this warning that: "Thurston must be suspended." He was considered "dangerous" with his wild, unsubstantiated statements.[7] He proved how dangerous and unscrupulous he could be during the overthrow of the Hawaiian government in 1893.

Meanwhile Spreckels moved to introduce Hawaiian coinage through Kalakaua whereby he made a small fortune in minting fees for himself through the "king's vanity."

During this period Liliuokalani was infrequently brought into governmental discussions. When someone asked her to speak to the king in his favor, she wrote in her diary, "I have no more influence than the man in the moon."[8]

⚓ 5 ⚓

The ever-increasing problems of monies led Kalakaua into a political and personal dispute of Ruth's lands, after her death in 1883. This served only to further the breach between the Kamehameha family and the Kalakauas.

The king accused her of having used Kamehameha "crown land" monies which were not rightfully hers, but which should have come to the now royal purse. Yet there was no way he felt he could prove himself right while she was alive. Ruth lived only a few months in the magnificent home she had recently built. When she became ill, Liliuokalani joined the other *alii* in going to her bedside to remain there until her death, as was the old custom. Of course, Ruth had always been fond of Likelike and little Kaiulani, so they as well stayed with her during her last illness. Queen Emma came only intermittently for she herself was often ill. It was, to Liliuokalani's sadness and annoyance, Queen Kapiolani who could not reach into the recesses of the old Kamehameha family, yet she was of the highest chiefly line of Kauai. Strange and ugly things were happening among the *alii* to separate, cause dissention, and spread, without knowledge of facts, into the emotion of the commoners.

It was a difficult death watch with the estrangement that existed. Yet "it was Ruth's own indefatigable good humor that kept them safe from themselves, each other, and her impending death," Liliuokalani later wrote fondly of the chiefess.[9]

❧ 6 ❧

Ruth died on May 24, 1883, at the age of fifty-six. She was given a royal funeral, although attendance was less than expected.

Ruth willed most of her lands to Bernice with some *haole* exceptions. Then Kalakaua tried to secure a portion as he felt that all the lands would have gone to his younger brother Leleiohoku, as Ruth's *hanai* son, had he lived.

Liliuokalani protested against having Kalakaua contest the will as the lands had gone to her *hanai* sister, Bernice, but Kalakaua persisted. He lost, and left only further acrimony among the Hawaii *alii*.

"It was not the Hawaiian way to contest property, but I learned only too late that we were no longer under Hawaiian *aloha,* and David, as I use it now, was doing it the *haole* way," she later remarked, at a time her own will was being contested.

With the loss of the concept of *aloha* and *mana* had come the inevitable loss of its tangibles in monies and land. Even Queen Emma, for all the Hawaiian monarchial and Kamehameha wealth of Kamehameha III and IV, would die, leaving only small bequests and a Summer Home, later a museum. By 1884 Queen's Hospital was supported out of government funds.

For several months Bernice had not been well. She had gone to San Francisco with Likelike, and while there, was examined and told she had cancer. Following an operation, she returned to Hawaii and showed improvement, but the watch at Ruth's bedside had tired her.

Shortly after Ruth's death, Bernice began to decline rapidly. It was strange, Liliuokalani marvelled, for many years she "had seen them [Bernice and Charles Bishop] only infrequently, but now the Universal Equalizer, death, was bringing them together." She began to dine frequently at *Keoua Hale,* Ruth's home that had also been willed to Bernice.

John seldom joined them. He and Charles apparently were in disagreement of the government policy, although Liliuokalani doubted that John really favored her brother's actions either, but as he *said* nothing, it was difficult to know whose side he was on.

When Ruth had died, leaving Hawaii without a Governess, Liliuokalani had gone to John again to suggest he ask Kalakaua that he be "Generalissimo of all the Islands" as "we needed the money." He was stonily silent. All he would say was that if she would stop "giving away money" they wouldn't need so much. But she didn't know how to turn away an old friend without something in his hand. Many of the high *alii* were nearly starving. What else could she do? Her diary began carrying accounts of persons of high lineage coming to her to ask for money or goods. Liliuokalani never turned anyone away, whether she gave a few dollars or an all-purpose coconut.[10]

Her retainers were "living off her, impoverishing them," both John and Charles said. The social dislocation was creating paupers out of the retainers, and they had no skills to fall back on.

The retainers who had once been satisfied to live as retainers, serving as best they could, now were told they could live as *alii,* but they had no understanding of working for a higher position. They found it difficult in the new system to be productive—and allowed the Chinese and the *haole* to earn the money. Even the Japanese and Portuguese were surpassing them.

The new "democratic process" that was being taught them by the *haoles* told them they were as "good as the *alii,*" and as Liliuokalani was beginning to see it, they were in the sight of God, for she had given up her idea of the *alii* being the only God-descendants. She also felt one had to speak to the people in the language they could understand, and *they* still preferred the "god-descended" royalty to the "democratic royalty" the *haoles* were trying to project.

Many of the natives and especially half-natives rejected the *"good as the alii"* and substituted instead that they had the right to the same amount of money. Many of the older chiefs foresaw disaster in that their *wants,* not their needs, had been increased. It was the opposite of Kamehameha I's edict that would save his country.[11]

What the liberal new system did *not* teach was that many of the *haoles* had far more money than the royal family did, and if the average native wished to have *that* much he had to compete in the *haole* world, one totally foreign to him.

They were, indeed, as Malo had said, "cast adrift."

It was not therefore surprising that with the old retainer system gone and the desire for money increasing daily that the Hawaiians fell victim to the lottery system that in the end helped destroy them as a nation. Lottery was getting something for nothing and the people were beginning to forget that *service* was the finest labor and an end in itself.

Kalakaua was completely mesmerized by the lottery idea. It represented easy money to him. King Kalakaua loved and always needed money.

❦ 7 ❧

Liliuokalani was often accused by Kalakaua of "giving advice," but a great deal of advice was given her also. Charles told her she should stop paying for Kaipo, Aimoku, and even Lydia. He agreed reluctantly that if she insisted, she could continue with her "educational support" of Lydia and Aimoku, as Lydia was truly *hanai* and Aimoku was John's son. But Kaipo, no.

Kaipo, no? If she stopped supporting Kaipo she would lose him, something she could not bear. He was four years old and she adored him —a curly haired, bright-eyed toddler—her heart contracted every time she saw him. Kaheo, his mother, had threatened many times to take Kaipo from her, and each time Kaheo had gained a little more—for her other children. Liliuokalani was totally and completely at her mercy when it came to Kaipo. It was inconceivable that Charles should say she should not pay for him. She could not imagine his anger had he known she also put aside monies and bought stocks, not only for Kaipo but also for his brothers to appease Kaheo.

As Bernice grew weaker she expressed the desire to come to her home at Waikiki. Waikiki had always been considered "health giving," but Liliuokalani thought there was more than that: Bernice wanted to return to her own. So she came to where her *hanai* sister could be close to her.

In the long evening hours when her pain seemed less after the morphine shots Dr. Trouseau had given her, they talked of days of long past. The animosities of years past were gone now, for the young women who had a close *aloha* relationship were together in the tragic moments of when the life of one was coming to an end. Now as any two individuals of any time or place, they talked of the past.

Bernice's life hadn't been so perfect as Liliuokalani had thought, but she was satisfied, in a way. She and Charles, Bernice told her, had talked of establishing a school with monies from her land for young Hawaiian boys to learn a trade, and girls to learn "domestics."

Liliuokalani agreed a school was good, but the young Hawaiians needed to learn more than "trades" and how to be good wives and mothers and "domestics." They needed an *education* to cope with the *haole* world. Bernice said it was "too late," now if only the Hawaiian youth could learn a trade it would be sufficient. It took many years before Liliuokalani learned that there is no way to educate anyone who has been indoctrinated into not needing to be educated—and she had to learn it through her most precious possession—Kaipo.

As Liliuokalani dozed in the large Morris chair by Bernice's bed, she thought of death. Birth and death—the only two sure things that everyone experiences. "Of birth we ourselves know little—yet it is obviously very important," she said later. She must have thought of her own strange birth from the bodies of Keohokalole and Kapaakea so incidental in 1838 compared to her *hanai* to Paki and Konia; yet in 1886, with all the changes, *hanai* meant nothing in the eyes of New Hawaii, but everything in the hearts of Old Hawaiians. Even now her *hanai* sister had come "home."

She remembered the lines from Sarah Williams: "I've loved the stars too fondly to be fearful of the night." Yes, that was the Hawaiian way— they loved the stars, the moon, the moonlit sea, the lightly shaded forest of the dawn and dusk—

Bernice, do not fear the night: her heart must have cried out. As if the thoughts could penetrate Bernice's pain-dulled mind, she roused and smiled at her.

"I must return to Charles," Bernice said simply and Liliuokalani knew they had come full circle round.

Together they had lived again in their world as they stood on the edge of death and peered into its dark recesses, but now Bernice must return to a man and a life she had chosen for thirty-four years. She returned to Ruth's house on Emma Street, the house she had so recently inherited.

She seemed too young to die; in three months she would be fifty-three.

October 16, 1884, dawned reluctantly through misty rain. At noon Liliuokalani sat at her window and watched the downpour. When the phone rang, she knew before she lifted the receiver to hear Charles' voice that Bernice was gone.

Although it could be no surprise, she was shocked at the void she felt. Bernice was her last link with the Kamehamehas. Liliuokalani was the only one of that ruling house who now had even a tenuous hold, although had *hanai* lived on she would have held the strongest, and in her heart she did.

"The last of the Kamehamehas has left us . . ." the newspapers said. But before any newspapers had put ink on their presses all Honolulu knew of Bernice's death. Within an hour of her passing, business houses began to close, flags were lowered to half-mast at consulates and on ships, government buildings and schools had ceased to function. A beloved princess had died.

Charles did not wish a lying in state or a royal funeral. "But we must," he said, "for the sake of the people."[12]

"What crimes are committed in the name of the people," Liliuokalani had said to him, and although his glance had been sharp, she felt he knew what she meant, although he also detected an underlying current.

Some years later she said she didn't know *what* she meant. It was something she felt—but without clarity. As the years went on she had a better understanding and came to say at the time of the overthrow, "These crimes are committed not by the people but in the name of the people. We blamed the people for our crimes and we do strange things we call 'humanitarian' for the people. We never *ask* what the individual *wants*."[13]

If there ever were a time that she and Charles Bishop were close, it was then. They both desired "private grief."

What was happening? Was she becoming less Hawaiian? No, but *Hawaii* was becoming less Hawaiian. She looked out of the window of the Bishop home and saw the people gathering. The puzzle was that these people were not *their* people—yet among them *were their* people—"the Hawaiian people" who came to pay their last respects in mourning for their beautiful princess, of whatever race, were *their* people. Liliu could understand, because it was tradition, custom, not *color* that was involved.

Liliuokalani was no longer jealous of "the beautiful princess." Whatever had separated Bernice and her, whatever had caused her anguish in comparison to her had never been *aloha*. It had been missionary-imposed customs—*haole* ways. *Aloha* was unimpaired, and she ached with grief for the passing of her *hanai* sister and passing of their time.

Bernice's bier was placed in the center of the double drawing room. It was covered with folds of snowy white silk that seemed to symbolize Bernice. The candelabra, the white candles, the *kahili* bearers, were all there. King Kalakaua, Princess Liliuokalani, Queen Kapiolani, Princess Likelike and the other members of the royal family sat at the rear of the room. The walls were lined with Bernice's close friends and the lower floors were crowded with her retainers wailing and chanting their *mele*. Bernice's name song was sung again and again:

> Answer to thy name, Sun-Chasing Lady of Kaiona
> Chasing the mirage of ohia flowery desert
> My companion of the cold double night-rain of Koolau
> And of ki and Kukui shaded groves of Kahoiwai . . .

Yes, "Sun-Chasing Lady of Kaiona."[14]
Kaiona was a place name—but it had a meaning too.

Liliuokalani wondered how many even then knew what these place names meant and if anyone a generation from then would know the importance of place names in the *mele*.

"Sun-Chasing lady of troubled seas . . ." of "alluring seas" was a better translation. Liliuokalani again felt the pain of the lost language that had meant so much once—so many things—one word, one inflection—something different, so many different meanings . . .

For fifteen days the rain poured down, the chants continued, the wailing went on, and *kahili* were woven.

Then Bernice was to be laid at rest in the Royal Mausoleum beside Ruth. The rains persisted until the cortege moved up the Nuuanu Valley and then the sun burst forth brilliantly for the Sun-beam Chasing Lady for the place where "there was no more sea."

The newspapers printed, "The *meles* spoke of the pagan past; the

Christian watchers symbolized the progressive present, as Rev. Henry Parker spoke the funeral service words."

Four Sundays before, Rev. Henry Parker had stood in Kawaiahao Church pulpit and spoken words of slander (or are they slander from the pulpit?) against Walter Murray Gibson and Liliuokalani's brother calling them opportunists, thieves, pagans and even sorcerers.

After Bernice's funeral, the royal family and friends gathered at Charles Bishop's home. It was evident to everyone Bernice had been his whole life. What could make two people of such completely different backgrounds merge their lives totally, Liliuokalani wondered. Was it love? If so, what was love? Liliuokalani felt she had never known "love," with John, and she had never even known passion as Likelike had. Suddenly her life seemed lusterless and there was no way to polish it to a shiny, glossy glow. That was October, 1884.

Bernice left Liliuokalani lands in Hawaii and Kauai, but she did not leave what she wanted most—her childhood home—Haleakala.

In the days following, Charles came to bring her pieces of Bernice's jewelry—a broach, a ring—all of them carrying memories. Liliuokalani felt that Charles passed on some items with a sense of relief but ones she was to cherish: pairs of earrings woven from the hair of Paki or Konia. Charles undoubtedly considered them "pagan." Liliuokalani was deeply moved by them. She and Bishop were back on their old footing and found they had little to talk about. The visits were lonely ones. Something they had touched briefly at Bernice's death was gone. Yet she continued "to dine" with Charles at Keoua.

Bishop told her he would immediately begin building the Kamehameha Schools as Bernice desired, but that a small tuition would be charged.

Liliuokalani agreed that a tuition should be charged—there was already too much moral decay resulting from "free"—free everything. There was no doubt in her mind that things were more appreciated when paid for; yet she herself was the freest of givers.

✍ 8 ✍

Six months later Dowager Queen Emma died. She'd had several strokes and the rumor was she had "gone queer." Poomaikelani's husband, the keeper of her papers, was ordered to destroy all of them. This was the old Hawaiian custom. Someone apparently persuaded him to keep a few, for they were later to be brought to light.[15]

The king and Liliuokalani rode together in the carriage to the mausoleum to see Emma's coffin placed beside her husband's and son's. Suddenly Liliuokalani was overwhelmed with shame for grief she had not felt before. Who would grieve for Emma as she had grieved for her husband and son? There was no one left, not even her devoted R. C. Wyllie.

Yes, Liliuokalani decided she must always remember to put flowers on Emma's[16] grave when she went to Bernice's.

It was a period in which it seemed only right that life should give Liliuokalani a respite from death and sorrow, and it did.

CHAPTER 4

Grief and Joy

❦ 1 ❦

If a person is fortunate, she will have a small period of life—a year or a few years—which will shine as a solitary diamond in the ring of life. Liliuokalani was approaching such a period.

For a woman this time of fulfillment may come with society's acceptance of her place, with children coming into her life, with the fruition of a talent, or with a satisfying relationship. Liliuokalani was fortunate enough to have all of these. The setting for this gem is often a crown of thorns, and it was for Liliuokalani. Later she spoke of the years 1885-1886 as being "of great sorrow and greater joy."[1]

It has been generally thought by the students of Liliuokalani's life, no matter how briefly they have written or spoken of her, that she had a lover during this latter period. Sprinkled throughout her diary of 1886 are ambiguous entries that indicate a love-fulfillment, and guesses both contemporary and those of the past have missed the mark in naming the man involved.

Lydia Aholo's surmise is substantiated by recognizing three facets of Liliuokalani's character: her never ceasing love of music coupled with her genuine talent in this field; her Victorian upbringing begun in the High Chiefs' School, and most important, the situations through which she moved in her personal life.

By 1886 Liliuokalani had suffered innumerable personal and cultural shocks. She found herself confused, disturbed, and lonely. Her marriage relationship had not improved after John's illegitimate child had been born. Although she had taken Aimoku in old *hanai*, had tried to protect the conditions of his birth from becoming known, she realized she had failed in extending her affections to the new child as totally as she had to Lydia or Kaipo. None of these *hanai* situations had been smooth for Liliuokalani.

She often felt "lonely" and at times quite deserted, even by her retainers[2] who were beginning to lose their Hawaiian *aloha* to the more demanding and less serving attitude of the *haole*. The genealogical trial had helped create this new attitude.

Then the death of her only *hanai* sister, Bernice, had sent her into a period of depression.

In her personal life in 1886 she was extremely vulnerable.

In her public life she was frustrated by Kalakaua. He blocked her every effort toward her educational society and a women's bank; only reluctantly did he contribute to the project of the maternity home, yet she was becoming accepted among both *haole* and Hawaiian women for her efforts.[3] Her lands were rapidly being sold by the king. The only sale of Kapaakea's lands she approved of was the property at Molokai that was sold for $2000 for the establishment of Kalaupapa, the leper settlement.

The *haole* in the government were more and more strongly opposing Kalakaua's regime. Talk of annexation was again rampant and there were even more rumors of assassination of "all members of the Royal Family." She found her brother, her sister Likelike, and often herself vilified in the press and more painfully from the pulpit by Henry Parker of Kawaiahao Church. She recorded more than once in her diaries that she had missed church: "Although brought up differently—too much politics and sarcasm from pulpit." Again there followed her quick repentance. "May I be forgiven." The Hawaiian *aloha* crept in against the missionary adamancy. "I spent the day in the woods in the silence with One we have been taught to fear. I feel [His] presence."

Struggling with personal and public relationships she turned to that which never failed to bring her solace—her music. She longed for a companion who could appreciate and share with her her only untouched love. There was a companion, a man, in Hawaii—Henry Berger.

❧ 2 ❧

Heinrich Berger, seven years her junior, had come to Hawaii in 1872.[4]

Kamehameha V in his search to establish an entity for his country had, after Liliuokalani composed the national anthem, decided a Royal Band was needed to play the anthem at all state occasions. There existed already a dilettante band of loosely organized and undisciplined musicians, who played with greater enthusiasm than skill. Abraham Fornander mentioned to Kamehameha V that the Germans had given to the world great music and were known for discipline. Now in 1872, just before his own death, he was caught by the idea of "discipline" in music that a German bandmaster could supply.

Henry Berger (as he was to be known), at twenty-seven, came to Hawaii "on loan" from the German government. John Owen Dominis as Governor of Oahu was his immediate superior. Dominis, having failed to prove himself in many areas of leadership,[5] and without any concept of what he was asking, gave Berger the Herculean task of demanding that the band be ready to play for the King Kamehameha Day—one week after Berger arrived.

Berger accustomed to Prussian royalty considered the request, whether reasonable or not, a royal command. A group of recalcitrant young Hawaiians were "licked into shape" (Berger's favorite expression) by the remarkable bandmaster, and on Kamehameha Day, June 11, 1872, he was ready to give his first band concert in Hawaii.

The members of the royal party were seated on a small raised dais in an area just below Queen's Hospital. Flanking them on either side in a semi-circle almost reaching to the band were crowds of Hawaiians and *haole,* all waiting for the new band in their impressive white military-looking uniforms to begin. In the warm, still day, with only the soft rustling of the wind in the coconut trees, a tense Henry Berger bowed stiffly to the king, to the governor and to the latter's wife, Liliuokalani.

A breathless stillness swept over the crowd as the band began playing such music as the Hawaiians had never heard before. The Hawaiians' concept of music placed *words* above tunes; they often wrote lyrics and then "found" tunes to fit them. Now for the first time they heard tunes—music—without words! Berger bravely presented three numbers of his own composition—the "Governor of Oahu March," Hymn of Kamehameha I," and the "Hawaiian March."

No sound came from the crowd until the last number was played. A heavily perspiring Berger bowed again to the royal party, bowed to his band, turned to face the king, bowed and stepped back to wait. In a moment of silence in which Berger lived a lifetime, the new and the old met in the consciousness of the Hawaiians. The beat of gourd drums, the two-note *mele,* the atavistic rhythm had merged with something new.

Suddenly a thunderous applause broke from the crowd. A new and wonderful era of music had come to Hawaii. The old had met with skill and beauty to which the Hawaiians could respond spontaneously and unrestrainedly. The "new" music was not a clash in culture as the new missionary doctrine had been, but indeed a skillful blending of the old into a "disciplined" new.

Once the Hawaiians had given their total approval, the *haole* joined in the applause that grew and grew to echo in valleys. Henry Berger, although he only knew relief in a deep sigh at the moment, had come "home."

Liliuokalani was strangely moved by what she heard. She recognized a difference between a professional's work and her own and was seized by ambivalence of ceasing to write her quick compositions (she had written the national anthem in less than a week) and learning the new discipline of perfecting.

However, Berger stayed only four years—the four turbulent years of Liliuokalani's life (1872-1876) during which she moved from being the governor's wife to becoming a princess. He then returned to Germany as his "loan to Hawaii" from the German government was recalled. He left a grief-stricken band; even his most grumbling Hawaiian band members wept copious tears as he boarded the ship. The wharf was filled with Hawaiians placing leis about his shoulders and imploring him to return.

No one regretted his leaving more than Berger himself, and in six months he negotiated his release from the military, where he had served as a musician in the army medical corps from the age of seventeen, when he had left the Conservatory of Military Music in Berlin.

⚓ 3 ⚓

In 1876 Henry Berger was back in Hawaii. There was no question of where Berger's place was. Berger immediately rejoined his own band, many of whom had been scattered, and he recruited new members and again formed a Royal Hawaiian Band.

In the latter part of the 1870's Henry Berger and Liliuokalani's contacts became closer. They played the organ on alternate Sundays at the Kawaiahao Church. They conferred on the hymns to be sung, but Berger maintained a royalist attitude toward the princess. This deference was pleasing to her because it was lacking among most of the *haole*. She felt the warmth one feels by being treated "special."

Throughout their relationship he always included the "Governor's

March" in his programs and gave a quick bow to her as well as to Dominis before playing it. In later years a twinkle of ironic amusement passed between them as their eyes met briefly. After Dominis' death, if Berger omitted from his program the "March," the then-Queen Liliuokalani sent him a note requesting the "March" be played. They both understood.

By 1883 disappointments and frustration had seemed to surround Princess Liliuokalani to the point she thought she could take no more; her once highest ambition (to be a princess, equal to Bernice) had been achieved, and she had found it bitter fruit. With a sense of release from the "worldly vanities" of which Juliette Cooke had spoken, she turned to her first love—music. And she found herself thinking more and more about this man, especially in relation to her music. She craved someone with whom she could communicate on this level. The obsequiousness of Joe Aea coupled with Kaheo's threatening attitude toward Kaipo was beginning both to annoy and worry her. She was definitely disturbed by the romantic rumors linking C. B. Wilson, her chamberlain, and herself. In sharp retort she pointed out that Wilson's wife, Evelyn Townsend, had been as *hanai* in her home. The linking of Wilson's name and hers was absurd.[6] As her chamberlain he did, indeed, travel in her retinue, as did Joe Aea, her that-time agent. She had no sexual attachment to either, but the *haole* writers eager to smear the royalty in any way possible named these men as her lovers.[7] Strangely enough they never thought of Berger.

Liliuokalani at this time is best described by Julius Palmer, a Boston newspaperman who never forgot her from the first time he saw her until twenty years later when he wrote of her.

Palmer wrote in 1897 referring to the earlier period:

> The present Princess Lydia Dominis [sic], is one of the most graceful women I've ever seen move through a dance . . . To look at the face of (The Princess) Liliuokalani in repose, anyone of us of the stronger, yet more susceptible sex, would have said it presented nothing to excite or wish a second glance; but of all the fair women who moved through the dance on the great main deck of the frigate, she is the one that, from that moment to the present retains the strongest hold on my memory. Why? It is impossible to explain that mysterious magnetism which draws our affection towards one person and causes us to draw backward and inward in the presence of another . . . This element is not beauty, but it is grace . . . seen as

(the Princess) moved through the misty magic of the waltz ... it was
as if she were in love with every man she danced.[8]

Such a charismatic woman could and did attract men throughout her
life. Now she attracted Berger.

As early as 1883 she invited him to her home at Waikiki, knowing
he had been given the new national anthem of Kalakaua's composing,
borrowing from "The Hymn of Kamehameha I," to bring forth "Hawaii
Ponoi" as the new national anthem. No doubt this knowledge gave her
courage to talk with him about her own compositions. After much
thought—for a creative artist does not easily present his work to another
—she played and sang "Aloha Oe" for him. Although he had undoubtedly heard it before he was struck by its haunting beauty and her clear
soprano voice.

She timidly added that it had been told her the tune was similar to
"The Rock Beside the Sea." Berger, the master, paid her the highest
compliment she had had since Kamehameha V had asked her to write
a national anthem. He assured her that "Aloha Oe" was "quite original."
Three measures (1st, 2nd, 5th) were similar to "The Rock Beside the
Sea" but the remainder, especially the chorus, was uniquely Liliuokalani's.
He himself, he admitted, took many of his compositions from the tunes
hummed by the native Hawaiians as they went joyously off for a day of
fishing or surfing or even working happily in taro patches.

Later in 1883 Kalakaua sent Berger and the Royal Band to San Francisco, through the gratuity of Spreckels who provided a special rate on his
steamer for the band members. There the Royal Hawaiian Band won
first place in a competition sponsored by the Knights Templar.

But for Liliuokalani the greatest triumph of all was that "Aloha Oe"
had been sung for the first time in the United States, sung by the beautiful Hawaiian singer Nani Alapai. The song soon swept the nation, and
later the world. For a time it was forgotten she was its author, but she
and Henry Berger never forgot.

When the band returned, their friendship resumed. Liliuokalani's
missionary moral training had been very deep. Her situation with Berger
was both a delight and a torment. One needs little imagination to visualize
and feel the emotional flow between two people in perfect unity sitting
on the wide veranda of her Waikiki home, watching the moonlight sifting
through the trees and shimmering on the water, and talking, talking of
music, their language of love.

Liliuokalani marvelled that Berger was able to take so many of the Hawaiian songs and turn them into marches, even as he wrote the "Aloha Oe March." His reply was that the old two note *mele* was a great deal like the Gregorian Chant and was the basis of a march. He told her this was not the kind of music a Protestant would understand, and Liliuokalani was again reminded of Amos Starr Cooke's forbidding the singing of the "Battle Hymn of the Republic" at the Royal School because the children "created" "feather-cloaked pagan warriors marching in warlike tread" . . . not "saints." She and Berger could laugh together as she and John had never been able to do.

Berger's greatest joy as a young man had been when he had been allowed to study the Viennese Waltz with Johann Straus. Music was also for graceful dancing, was his contention, and Liliuokalani, recalling the old hulas full of grace and beauty, agreed.

As time moved on and Berger's and her friendship developed, Liliuokalani began the old Hawaiian custom of never mentioning a person emotionally close to her by name. He began to appear in her diaries as "my old friend"—as indeed he was.

Then Liliuokalani's love for codes, symbols, enigmatic words came into play, and we find curiously intertwined symbols representing a name, or names joined. These symbols occur similarly in Berger's journals, diaries, and even on his music. *Nua Lehua* appears as well as *Nua Aupuni*.[9] Never did she write his name, although, unfortunately, some misguided overly protective person later erased some telling passages.

Whatever the relationship between Liliuokalani and Henry Berger was, it was not surprising there should be a mutual attraction between them.

They each had charm. He seemed to be able to break through his German rigidity of discipline to emerge a gentle, somewhat naive and even child-like man. He was also generous to a fault with his "band boys." Although of moderate physical build, he was enormously sexually attractive to many women in Hawaii. He was apparently unhappily married, for the marriage ended in a divorce, but not before four children —one daughter and three sons—were born to the union.

Berger protected Liliuokalani by always referring to her as Mrs. Dominis or Princess Liliuokalani, though many of the references to "Mrs. Dominis" in his journals refer to John's mother, whom he was requested to "serenade" periodically. His "hidden" word for the one whom he loved was "mama," and anguish cries out from time to time in "How I miss mama."

Liliuokalani was not entirely free from guilt. Often her entry of "slept" . . . (erased) *Nua Lehua or Nua Aupuni* would be followed by *Kala-Kala,* "Forgive-forgive." *Kala-Kala* was a part of the *Hooponopono* "ritual."[10] It was the point at which all parties—injurer and injured —sought release and forgiveness. Both old Hawaiian *aloha* and missionary Victorianism came into play for Liliuokalani. Missionary Victorianism found her guilty, but without the release of "talking (it) over," without family counsel. She was left to her own *aloha* of facing the problem of guilt on her part, on Berger's, and on their relationship.

She worried a great deal about others knowing, and about what was being said about her. Other times her diary bore statements such as "came home in broad day light—I don't care."

During this time (1886) typical days of the Hawaiian princess emerge. She arose at 5:00 a.m., spent time alone in "meditation," breakfasted with one or more of her retainers to discuss business problems or chat in a friendly fashion or simply gossip. At 7:30 she had "devotionals" for her entire "family" of retainers. She read a passage from the Bible and asked each to "meditate" upon its meaning. Occasionally she asked for an idea to be expressed; other times she correlated a passage to an old Hawaiian precept. One of her favorites was from the Lord's prayer, "Forgive us our debts as we forgive our debtors," or "No one is free from his own sin until he has forgiven him who has sinned against him."

She retreated then to "Hinano bower," her thatched structure deep in the wood-foliage of Hamohamo, where she would spend the morning writing or gardening. She found inspiration in "puttering in [her] grotto."

Often she had luncheon guests or went out to lunch, followed by afternoon meetings of her "societies." Or in the afternoon she had her *hanai* children brought to her, Lydia from Kawaiahao Seminary and Aimoku and Kaipo from Mrs. Bush's. These were precious hours for her—and for them.

An abundant table was set, for Liliuokalani never forgot the days she "went to bed hungry" at the Royal School. The children could gorge themselves and then take the remaining fruits, sweets or whatever they wished back with them.

On rainy days her *hanai* as well as her retainer's children played their games around her. Lydia recalled playing hide-and-go-seek, during which the princess often said to her, "Come hide here." And Lydia slipped under the voluminous black skirt as the princess sat quietly watching the other children search. A giggle from Lydia was silenced by a gentle hand on her head. Everyone knew, after a time, where Lydia was, but no one dared look under the princess' skirt. Finally when utter frustration set in and the youngest, Liliuokalani's beloved Kaipo (four years old), began to cry and point a stubby finger at the princess' many-fold skirt, Lydia would emerge and Kaipo shared the victory.[11]

On sunny days that invited children to the beach, Liliuokalani joined them in "taking a salt water bath." When special *"haole"* amusements came to Hawaii, Liliuokalani gathered her young friends together and with the aid of her retainers, she took the "flock" to ride a roller coaster, see a balloonist, enjoy a magician or ventriloquist, or even visit a travelling circus.

Liliuokalani never forgot her young niece, Kaiulani, but she took her separately. Kaiulani was approaching her teens and preferred the company of her older cousins—David Kawananakoa and Jonah Kuhio Kalanianaole. Kaiulani also had her mother's quick temper and what Liliuokalani called her *"haole-*royalist *alii* temper," that resulted in angry scenes in which Kaiulani drew herself up in an imperious manner *of her* being a "royal princess." The results ranged from everyone bursting into angry and hurt tears to Kaiulani's physical violence of striking a retainer's child. Then her governess, Miss Gardner, whom Liliuokalani said had "the patience of a saint," would be called to return Kaiulani to Ainahou.

Her aunt took her to concerts in the evening, the theater, or the same "amusement" to which she had taken the children—but alone. In the evenings Liliuokalani also gave dancing parties for Kaiulani and the "young people."

Other evenings were spent in having "people" in to dinner, going out to dine, but often her diaries attested to a "lone cup of tea."

Two friends became more and more frequent evening visitors—Henry Berger and Fraulein Wolff. Although Berger has been consistently overlooked by Liliuokalani's attackers, or champions, she was regularly attacked for her association with Fraulein Wolff by those who were proponents of the Provisional Government and bitter enemies of the Royalists.

Fraulein Wolff first came into Liliuokalani's life as her German language teacher.[12] Liliuokalani, always aware of the semantic importance of language, had apparently decided she wanted to learn Henry Berger's native tongue. But Fraulein Wolff also dabbled in fortune-telling, cards, astrology, and dream-interpretations—all of which was condemned by the missionary-circle as resorting again to "heathenism and sorcery." Later, wild and unsubstantiated statements would be made that "the queen" ruled her government by a fortune teller's wiles.[13]

A careful study of Liliuokalani's diaries and letters reveal a fascination of the occult, for dream interpretation and "fortune telling" were deeply ingrained in the old Hawaiian beliefs. On the other hand, a note of scepticism runs parallel with the prophecies such as "If in ten days any wish is not realized, I'll consult no more."[14]

Another sparkling moment comes into her life in this period when she moved into a second home—Moulaulani, and writes: "How nice to be surrounded by everything luxurious in one's own home." Her tenuous hold on her husband's and his mother's home, Washington Place, was at the same time lost when she was asked by John to move her things out of the cottage, for Mrs. Dominis wished to have it for her Chinese servants.

Eighteen-eighty-six was to end with confusing beliefs of the old and the new violently at work in the royal household—during the last illness of Liliuokalani's sister, Likelike. The crown of thorns met in the setting of her jewel.

CHAPTER 5

A Queen's Invitation

❧ 1 ❧

Queen Victoria of England, preparing grumpily for her fiftieth year of reign and refusing to wear any hat but a bonnet,[1] could have had no idea of what a stir the invitation to attend her Jubilee made in far-away Hawaii.

King Kalakaua, uneasy about the accusations against his government, had suggested to Premier Gibson that Queen Kapiolani go to the Jubilee to "establish a closer relationship with England." Gibson did not like the idea because Kapiolani spoke no English. He liked it even less that Kalakaua toyed with the trip for himself; Gibson suggested Liliuokalani, whom Kalakaua dismissed with a movement of his hand, and the statement that she had her "hands full with her sister's illness." "Her" sister was also Kalakaua's—Likelike Cleghorn. And no one should have been more concerned than he, for whatever he may or may not have felt for his younger sister, the persistent rumor that he was having a *kahuna-ana-ana* praying her to death should have disturbed him even in his self-centered attitude.

It was true Liliuokalani was deeply concerned with her sister's illness. As a matter of fact, 1887 dawned with a multiplicity of emotions for Liliuokalani. Her closeness with Berger had come to an end; possibly the haunting guilt-system of the missionaries had convinced her that it "was her fault" that Likelike was so ill.

Liliuokalani was also, once again, trying to reach John, but she only succeeded in annoying him. Her diary bears a telling record of their relationship. First, that she was "harsh with John," and he "went to bed *huhu* [angry]," this entry is typically followed by "the next day went upstairs to ask John's forgiveness for my harsh words. He actually kissed me! Although he provoked me to say what I did in praise of Mr. Gibson whom everybody hates sometimes without cause for he bore it for the king."[2]

She began spending her nights as well as her days with Likelike. Her watches were spelled-off by other members of the royal household, including Kalakaua. It was obvious that Likelike was perturbed by natural events, whether or not she believed in the rumors that Kalakaua *was* having her "prayed to death." The eruption of the volcano, a sign that Pele wanted a sacrifice solidified her belief that her death was coming, and she in hopelessness began to refuse food.

Liliuokalani questioned her doctors—McKibben and Trouseau—and was told that the illness had initially been brought on by a miscarriage, as the result of a fall from a horse.[3]

In the midst of the struggle of trying to convince Likelike that no one was "praying her to death," the volcano's eruption was coincidental, and that she should cooperate with her doctors, Liliuokalani recorded that she dreamt "my husband came home last night"—only to follow it with: "all nonsense."

Likelike Cleghorn died on February 2, 1887, at 5:00 p.m. while Liliuokalani was alone with her, smoothing her sweat-drenched hair, and hearing her dying words: "Kaiulani must not marry one she does not love."

Liliuokalani's mind swept across the past to wonder why her sister would say this of her ten-year-old child. Was it that Kalakaua had attempted, unsuccessfully, to arrange an alliance marriage between Kaiulani and the Japanese prince? Was it that Likelike had loved someone else other than Cleghorn? Certainly not Prince Albert;[4] then Liliuokalani remembered James Boyd and "Aloha Oe." It made her infinitely sad.

The newspapers issued the statement first that Likelike had died of a heart attack and then ambiguously had changed it to "exhaustion."

Likelike was to be taken to the palace to lie-in-state in the throne room ". . . and all to satisfy Archie," Liliuokalani wrote, ". . . seems like making a publicity of our grief."[5]

Liliuokalani again wished the privacy of grief that she and Bishop had wanted at Bernice's death; however, Cleghorn prevailed.

"For Kaiulani's sake," he said; "Likelike is royal and so is Kaiulani." Cleghorn was a Scotsman and he had a western European feel for royalty, and Liliuokalani had to admit that from what she had read of other countries' state funerals, perhaps he was justified. But it puzzled her why the "republic minded" individuals hated the Hawaiian customs, even when theirs were similar.

Following the royal funeral, Cleghorn asked Liliuokalani to go through Likelike's things and "take what she wanted." It was a sad memory trip, and Liliuokalani found she wanted very little, a keepsake or two. The remainder should go to Kaiulani; Likelike had left Cleghorn and Kaiulani her sole heirs, whatever little there was left to go to them.

Liliuokalani was again keenly aware of how quickly the land was slipping away, for during this period she had had to sell between 77 and 100 acres of kalo and kula land on Oahu that had come to her from her mother, Keohokalole.[6] She was reluctant and sad because John and she had sold the land to Hawaiians but carried the mortgage which now, according to J. M. Monsarrat, the attorney-son of Victoria's lover, had said it had to be repossessed because no interest had been paid for several years and the land should also be open to sale or lease again. Somehow in the old system of land tenure this would not have been necessary. Of course they needed the money. They always needed money.

She wondered what these dispossessed Hawaiians would do.

❧ 2 ❧

After Likelike's death, Kalakaua invited Liliuokalani to go to Queen Victoria's Jubilee.

She implied in her *Story* that David had proposed that she accompany Queen Kapiolani to England to ease her grief. That no doubt was partially true, for Kalakaua had his moments of great kindness. There were, however, other factors involved. Early rumors had begun that Liliuokalani was preferred above Kalakaua and that she was *kipi* (traitor); unfortunately Kalakaua had a tendency to listen to the last word spoken to him.

When Kalakaua told her that he wanted her to go to London with Kapiolani as "a representative had been invited" she was extremely excited, for she loved travel as much as the king did. The later ugly rumor that the Hawaiian government had received "no invitation," but that the king took it upon himself to send "a representative," was not true. Until her papers were destroyed by members of the Provisional Government the invitation was shown frequently to her *hanai* children.[7] Those who said Hawaii—so small and insignificant in the world—had no invitation did not know about Queen Emma's visits with Queen Victoria and that Queen Victoria had called them "sisters in grief."[8] Nor did they know the history of Hawaii well enough to know of the Duke of Edinburgh's visit to Honolulu, nor of Kalakaua's cordial reception in England in 1881.

Liliuokalani asked if John could go also and received permission from Kalakaua.

Kapiolani was uncomfortable about going. She was a shy person and felt greatly inhibited because she spoke no English, only Hawaiian. Liliuokalani, somewhat annoyed with her, pointed out that it was her own fault for not having learned English and there was still time. Kapiolani, however, became terrified of such pressure, and her extraordinarily child-like gentleness and quiet reproach made Liliuokalani ashamed of her statements. Instead she reassured her that she herself would always be at her side and that Col. Curtis Iaukea would also be there. He was to "attend" her. Kapiolani was somewhat pacified.

The next jolt came when John insisted Liliuokalani take "a man along" as an attendant—he even chose him—Joseph Aea. She protested first and validly on the basis that it would cost too much money to add another person and she would rather have the money for other purposes.[9] Secondly, she did not want Joseph Aea; their lives had been too entwined, gossip too rampant, and problems too many—especially his drinking. Liliuokalani abhored people who drank; yet she had them on all sides— Joe Aea, Kaheo, Kalakaua, and John. She remembered all too vividly the disgrace and sorrows that had come from alcohol to Victoria, Lunalilo, Kamehameha IV, and even Kamehameha V.

John remained adamant in his choice of Joe Aea, as he so successfully could be when he set his mind to it; so Joseph Aea was included, much to Liliuokalani's later dismay and worry.

When the time of departure came, Liliuokalani set about saying her goodbyes. First she went to Kawaiahao Seminary to see Lydia Aholo, the Beckley girls, and others whom she supported there.

Miss Ida Pope, who was headmistress, had dressed the girls in their best white dresses. They were all presented to her in a group. Liliuokalani felt uneasy as she looked into the large dark eyes of Lydia and read in them the same ache that must have been in her own when she was "no one special" in the Royal School.[10]

Lydia, she was told, had been frequently absent and had been spending too much time with her grandparents. Perhaps, Liliuokalani thought, she should give more of her time and affection. She spoke to Miss Pope about her and asked that she be given "special treatment" while the princess was gone; it was to prove to be one of the worst personal mistakes she was ever to make.

Princess Liliuokalani addressed the girls in her moralistic fashion, cautioning them to be "good, studious, obedient to their teachers and loyal to their country." Her uneasiness increased as she rode in her carriage, with Joseph guiding the horses through the rough streets of Honolulu, to Washington Place. As she rang the bell at the front door, she was greeted by a distraught Miss Davis, Mrs. Dominis' nurse.

Mrs. Dominis was in bed; she had had a "serious fall" the night before. When Liliuokalani saw her, Mrs. Dominis was querulous and said that surely they wouldn't go now and leave her in that condition. Liliuokalani made no reply except to say she was sorry, but glad she had Miss Davis. She suspected she had fallen on purpose. Mary Dominis commanded John be sent to her. Liliuokalani never told John.[11] He would not learn of it until they reached Boston. Liliuokalani's party proceeded to the steamer where the king and the queen and others of their party were already on board. They passed through the immense crowd of loyal supporters and curious sightseers who were customarily on the wharves bidding goodbye and pleasant voyage.

❦ 3 ❦

An ocean voyage was always pleasant and relaxing for Liliuokalani. She spent time writing, reading, knitting, and talking with Kapiolani.

Nevertheless her concern for monies spent was noted even in her diary: ". . . written to Paris to have made dresses, corset, headdresses, black shoes—$500; mantella, bonnets, gloves—$50; 2 outdoor dresses—$75; $700 altogether . . . di . . . di"

The last four days before arriving in San Francisco John was attacked by rheumatism. At first Liliuokalani was annoyed, never being sure that John's attacks were real; then as she realized that he was completely immobilized with pain, she became greatly concerned.

The thrill of passing through the Golden Gate into the Golden City of San Francisco was one that never left her. From her first trip to her last she said she felt a "leap of gladness in my heart when approaching that city—I knew what Wordsworth meant when he saw his 'row of daffodils'. "[12]

Concern about John was abated when friends with a litter and a comfortable carriage took him to the Palace Hotel, where he stayed in bed for a week.

Liliuokalani was delighted to find that Kapiolani had put aside her fears and decided to use every possible moment for sightseeing. Having met the Mills the year before in Honolulu, she and her lady-in-waiting were graciously received by them at Mills College. To Liliuokalani's joy Kapiolani's interest in Liliu's college for women was increased as she saw first hand such a school.

When John was again able to travel they stopped in Sacramento to visit with the Crockers before crossing the Sierras.

One of the most exciting experiences in Liliuokalani's life came next. Crossing the summit they found the world was white, pure crystaline white. The trees carried their heavy burden of snow lightly and the ground was covered with cumulus clouds of snow.

The tops of the highest mountains of Hawaii carried snow, but not in its fur-white depth all around as it was in these mountains. Liliuokalani's poetic mind was stirred to John Greenleaf Whittier's words:

"I know not how in other lands, the changing seasons come and go; what splendors fall on Syrian sands, what purple lights on Alpine snow." The Hawaiians, who had no changing seasons, only "eternal summer," could only guess at the "changing seasons [which] come and go."

"As chaste as unsunn'd snow" Shakespeare had written, and Liliuokalani long remembered the ache that passed over her for Lunalilo who never knew what Shakespeare's words "As chaste as unsunn'd snow" meant. This, she decided was the worst part of the death of a dear one— seeing things they had missed—and being unable to share them.[13]

The train stopped after passing through the long snow sheds and the royal party tumbled out of the train, much to the amusement of the crew and other passengers, to make snowballs and pelt each other with them. Laughing and rubbing cold hands together for warmth they boarded the train to arrive at the Great Salt Lake.

Liliuokalani's curiosity of the world about her is apparent in her *Story* in which she relates in detail the trips across the United States. She questioned how a body of water like that could be in the center of the desert. Was it like the Red Sea? She spent time in contemplating the miracle of the parting of the Red Sea, and the differences in meaning of the word "faith."

At Walter Murray Gibson's request they stopped at the Mormon Tabernacle, "where we were met by several of their own people who had been converted to Mormonism." They were cordially received by the elders of the Church, as after Kamehameha V's cold rejection of the Mormons, Kalakaua had welcomed them to the islands, and Gibson, whatever his personal problems had been with the Church, admired the people enormously.

Liliuokalani sat in solemn awe as the huge organ pealed out tones she never believed an instrument could give. She was deeply moved and marvelled at modern technology.

As they crossed the vast unoccupied land she could not possibly believe that such a country could ever want to add a few small islands in the Pacific to its enormous possessions. No matter what the Americans in Hawaii said, surely the American government would never seize those little islands. It was too incongruous. She had no idea there could come a time when the desire of the majority of the people even in the United States would be ignored and only a handful would determine Hawaii's destiny.

She saw more of "changing seasons" as they came into the eastern part of the United States where spring was beginning—

> not a leaf appeared on the trees, no blossoms, no buds, no promise of what was hidden within those sentinels of life. It seemed a poverty-stricken country until Nature began to welcome us as we approached Washington, D.C. Then buds and blossoms peered forth to make us feel at home. It's been said that nature speaks in symbols and recently I have come to wonder if the cold, the harshness, the slow-coming into bloom and blossom and fullness of fruit of the American climate did not make their people hardier than our perpetual verdure and abundance of fruits and beauty, which lulled our people into a deceptiveness of security.
>
> Perhaps it is not good for a people to have things come too easily to them. Perhaps waiting patiently through a cold winter gives one a strength to resist a crop that fails. Our *alii*-system was failing and I feared our people would not be able to withstand a "crop failure."[14]

At Washington, D.C., she was to meet President Cleveland, who was to remain her friend throughout her life, and later she regretted the unkindness and ridicule that came upon him for her sake. Queen Kapiolani almost at once expressed her wish to meet the President, just as her husband had met President Arthur.

It can be clearly seen in Liliuokalani's writings that she thought of the President and his Lady as if they were the king and queen of the United States and not subject to the constraints of Congress. Liliuokalani wrote in 1897 that she should have been aware that "the Americans in Hawaii could no more understand our type of government than I could theirs, except they had a right to exercise *theirs* in *their* country, and we should have had the right to exercise *ours* in *our* country."[15]

The royal party experienced a happy social whirl with dinner at the White House, an artillery drill, social affairs and receptions given in their honor. Queen Kapiolani and she were most impressed by the visit of thirteen members of the Thirty-Third Degree Scottish Rite of the Masonic Order, headed by General Albert Pike. He was "a venerable old gentleman with a long flowing beard and silky white hair resting on his square shoulders."

When they arrived at Mount Vernon, coming down the Potomac, the steamer stopped as if in reverence; the men stood with their hats over their hearts as the band played the "Star Spangled Banner." Liliuokalani was as deeply touched as if she were hearing "Hawaii Ponoi." How the Americans loved their land in 1887, she implied in her *Story.* The Civil War was over and the great land was united just as Hawaii had become united in 1795 under Kamehameha I. She wrote a bit naively and over optimistically: "If we could see our likenesses, could we not learn to be tolerant of our differences?"[16]

From her *Story* we also see her profoundly moved as she heard the story of Martha Washington's sitting at her window in full view of her husband's grave from the day of his interment to the day of her death.

Her thoughts moved to John: would there come a day when she too would grieve by her window for a departed husband? A surge of compassion swept over her and she vowed to be more understanding of John and of Aimoku too.

In Boston receptions given by Mayor O'Brien and Governor Ames were grand affairs. Kapiolani's dress caught the attention of the press. "The toilet of her majesty Queen Kapiolani was of white silk brocade of the choicest Japanese manufacture, artistically embroidered with heavy raised and richly worked designs; it was cut in Hawaiian fashion, a loosely flowing robe of a pattern or mode very becoming to our women, whether made of inexpensive calico or print, or of the finest of silks or most lustrous of satins." They were entertained at a general reception held at the Mechanics Pavilion into which masses of people thronged to shake their hands in a democratic fashion. Hawaiian royalty were not unused to such a custom, although deeply deplored by Queen Emma's friend, Lady Franklin, for after the old customs had passed, kings and queens of Hawaii had always made themselves readily available to their people; however, they still touched them, often in reverence. Kalakaua had stated after he returned from his trip around the world that he was pleased that *unlike* the world over where royalty (or heads of state) had to be guarded "against their people," his people loved him so greatly he could walk alone and freely among them whenever he wished.

At this time Liliuokalani was inspired to write one of her most charming songs: "Mauna Wili Wili." It was about the curious machinations of the twirling of a water sprinkler. At the Waltham factory she was enchanted by the delicate mechanisms that came together to create a watch. Her simple yet deep philosophy also came forth: "what intricate work of thousands of pieces working together to tell the time—and the extraordinary simplicity of the sun dial that did the same thing!"[17]

Queen Kapiolani entered as avidly as Kalakaua would have into sightseeing, but for Liliuokalani the highlight was a Dominis' family gathering in Boston. There she met the Joneses, the Lees, the Snellings, the Jacobses, and the Emersons, many of whom were prominent educators and shared her enthusiasm for a college for women.

In New York, her usual stamina gave way to a severe cold, the first of many that were to follow. She remained in bed until Kapiolani's curious preoccupation with the mummies she had seen at the Metropolitan Museum aroused interest, and in spite of her illness, she accompanied Kapiolani and her suite to the museum. "The mummy hand, enfolded in yards and yards of linen was unwrapt and we beheld a small lifelike hand, dark colored but appearing as if the person had died recently." Everything—even the wrappings were in perfect preservation. It seemed almost wrong—as if someone who should go on was held back.

She was completely overcome by the sight for "it spoke too plainly of death and burial." No doubt she was reminded of Likelike and Bernice. How different the Egyptian ways were from the Hawaiian where flesh was burned and the bones hidden in caves; the soul had gone to join others; there was no constant reminder of death.

In June the royal party sailed on the *City of Rome*, the largest ship of the time, for England. Liliuokalani was quite impressed with the "strange mixture of humanity aboard and found I could indulge in my favorite pastime, that of studying those who surrounded me. How difficult it is to understand another person, especially those of different customs, but even our party in its setting became almost strangers in their indulgences of self and entertainment."[18]

The ship had an excellent library so Liliuokalani found her amusement there, in writing of her experiences and composing music. She began writing the song of the "Queen's Jubilee."

QUEEN KAPIOLANI AND LILIUOKALANI
Courtesy, Bishop Museum.

CHAPTER 6

A Queen's Jubilee

❧ 1 ❧

When Liliuokalani stepped off the *City of Rome* at Liverpool, England, for the first time in her life she knew what it meant to be "royal." Nothing could have prepared her for that moment; ". . . as far as eye could reach, on the right and on the left, could be seen thousands of heads,"[1] all turned to see the royal party disembark. This was not Hawaii where such crowds, though smaller in number, welcomed the royalty. It was England—a great foreign power waiting for a queen and her party.

Liliuokalani's childlike nature thrilled to the royal acclaim and her spirit soared to a different height of recognition of what a monarchial form of government could do for its people. And Liliuokalani began to understand Kalakaua's ambitions and at the same time tempered her own with *aloha* for her people.

A military escort of a hundred[2] soldiers presented arms and saluted the party as the royal carriage passed before the "tall, square shouldered, muscular looking fellows" while the band played "God Save the Queen," a tune that had once been Hawaii's. It was an anthem for the Queen of Hawaii as well as of England, and it was addressed to a Universal God, not the one of the missionaries, not the one of the Church of England, not the one of old Hawaii—but the One God. Liliuokalani could respond to this concept perfectly.

Festivity was everywhere and the atmosphere of royal respect permeated the air about Liliuokalani as it never had in Hawaii. The royal escort held her attention and especially the horses, so loved by the Hawaiians, "Rich brown, splendidly caparisoned, and with all their accoutrements of the neatest and most carefully furnished materials." Days of festivities followed. Always waiting with the quiet unassuming dignity that those who know their own intrinsic value have, Princess Liliuokalani awaited quietly to have the honors of the British court extended to her. All arrangements for the royal Hawaiian party had been provided by the British government through Lord Salisbury, then Prime Minister of England, and carried out by R.F. Synge of the Foreign Office, Queen Emma's long-time friend.

Neither Queen Kapiolani nor Liliuokalani considered a request for an audience with the Queen of England the least unusual. Liliuokalani expressed surprise that when Queen Victoria came from Scotland to Buckingham Palace, the streets were thronged with people, not only to welcome the queen but *to see her for the first time.* "Strange it seemed to me at the time to learn that many who had grown from youth to age in London during a whole lifetime had never seen their queen."[3]

Liliuokalani was impressed by the dark skinned "subjects" that had come from India, Persia, Siam, and other far-flung outposts of the British Empire, to pay tribute to the white-skinned queen. She thought of the role-reversal in Hawaii and found the *color* didn't matter as much as the attitudes, beliefs, and even more important that each had a right to his own, although often quite divergent custom. She never spoke of her enemies as "the whites" or even "the *haole*" but as the "missionary *party*" —*not* the *missionaries,* to whom she attributed much good, but the political party that developed through the sons of the missionaries into the members of the Provisional Government (1893-1895).

She expressed her political preference for the conservatism of Lord Salisbury over that of the "Grand Old Man" Gladstone. "If his rule has been less popular and more conservative, it has required no less devoted patriotism and lofty abilities." With these words she must have remembered Kamehameha V. She attributed the current prosperity of England to Lord Salisbury. With her eye for detail she saw the sixty-eight-year old Salisbury with "fire and brilliancy in his eyes which spoke of an active mind." She was no less kind, however, in her description of Gladstone, and her words are reminiscent of those spoken by Julius Palmer of her: ". . . certainly a countenance and a presence, once seen, not easily forgotten."[4]

But it was Mrs. Gladstone who caught and held her attention, most of all, and her relationship to her husband. Liliuokalani assumed "she must have been a valuable counsellor and a sympathetic confidant." Liliuokalani's own desire for sharing such a companionship is implicit in her words.

And certainly during the Jubilee each and every prince and princess was attentive to his consort, even the "irregular" Prince of Wales. Liliuokalani also saw only perfect forgiveness in unity after reading one of

Kapiolani's ever-loyal and loving letters to Kalakaua, addressing him as "my heavenly chief—you are mine and I am yours."[5]

Particularly poignant are her words describing the Grand Duchess of Mecklenberg-Strelitz a cousin of Queen Victoria. "There was a little lady who made her appearance accompanied by her husband who was blind; she seated him on a bench back of that we occupied; then she adjusted his necktie, she pulled down his coat and smoothed it out, and arranged other parts of his uniform to suit her own taste."[6]

Liliuokalani decided on a renewed effort to bring John closer to her. She began to watch him attentively and hopefully, remarking that the Marquis of Lorne took John's arm to walk about during a palace ball and become "engaged in a prolonged and pleasant conversation." She again noted him when he was at his best in the Masonic celebration where John Dominis sat in the third seat at the right of the Prince of Wales, The Grand Master.[7] These are gentle words from a gentle and hopeful woman, for in her diary she wrote on November 14, 1887, "For the first time in a whole year John was attentive."

John was not a totally ineffectual man; in his own milieu he could be quite personable and his accurate concern for facts and figures led him to be considered of executive timber. Facts and figures *per se* were his life—not a perceptive analysis nor a sensitive application of them. He had the type of diplomacy that infuriated the scholarly Fornander but sheltered him from confrontation shocks. He agreed with everyone while in their presence, and then quickly vanished when contradictory forces came together. He totally disliked making decisions that would cause dissension and managed somehow "not to be there" when such decisions were demanded, as he had with the election problems at Lahaina.[8]

However his never-failing recollections of persons' private lives—their positions, names and ages of their children, marital status, and other relationships, but avoidance of controversial issues, made him far more likeable than Liliuokalani, who had definite opinions about everything and little hesitancy in expressing them. Unfortunately for a biographer, he was "not a gossip."[9]

There is no evidence that John reached out to steady the rocky marriage between himself and Liliuokalani. Apparently it was sufficient in his mind that they were legally *married*.

🎵 2 🎵

The countryside of "Old England" was a series of pictures: the mustard fields stretching as an endless cloth of yellow-gold; quiet villages having "sturdy mortar" built houses under identifiable thatched roofs surrounding the parish church with its tall steeple. The charming country inns surprised her with their smallness and low-beamed ceilings unlike the inns in English novels she had read, but she found Clifton House of the Duke of Westminster more to her "ideal of a country house."

Her imagination took her as always to the people. "With the aid of a lifelike portrait of a noble lady," she visualized her "doing honors . . . making guests welcome . . . after the chase." Liliuokalani then made a Hawaiian transition in thought to write of provisions being made for the "sustenance and happiness . . . of retainers or tenantry . . . For these, their people, lived under their lords and mistresses with loving submission and loyal devotion, understanding their station in life, and therewith content; they looked to them for their maintenance and kind consideration, and asked for no more. The relation between master and retainer was one of love on both sides, of pure affection for trusted and faithful vassal, of devotion and desire to please from man to master."[10] This was the pure Hawaiian *alii* speaking.

No doubt with her thoughts on Hawaii she wrote of the changes that commerce and industrialization had brought, destroying gracious living for the sake of economics, and asks: "Is England better and happier for the extinction of a style of life read of in history but not today existing?" And she is sad, but at least there are "souvenirs" such as the manor she had just visited.

❧ 3 ❧

The day of the Jubilee dawned more auspiciously than Kalakaua's coronation, and we find Liliuokalani deeply impressed by the ceremony at Westminster Abbey. Carefully she related the form and ceremony of the entering kings and queens, princes and princesses, the world over, the high position given the Hawaiian party, but even in her heavily edited life story a sense of stillness and solemnity falls over the religious service. With her own blessing she wrote:

> " . . . a Gleam of God's sunshine penetrated through the windows, and finding its way from the casement across the grand temple, illumined with its radiance the bowed head of the royal worshipper. It was a beautiful emblem of divine favor, and reminded me of the coincidence . . . that occurred at the moment of coronation of my brother in Hawaii."[11]

While Liliuokalani beheld that the Universal God blessed all monarchies, large and small, at that very moment in Hawaii King Kalakaua was being humiliated and his life and power threatened. It was well she did not know, for she would have asked: "How can such things be?"

Although Liliuokalani was both a royalist and matriarchially oriented, she was not unaware of changes. Her own brand of feminism seen in her attempts for a women's college and a bank for women included a strong dislike for lack of gallantry and etiquette. The boatmen on the Thames who smoked idly while their women poled their boats through the locks caused her to exclaim "What lack of gallantry!" In the United States she puzzled over Martha Washington's apparent fall in esteem: "Why is it, by the way, that she is now 'Martha Washington,' when in that day she was always mentioned as 'Lady Washington'? Is it part of the etiquette of the new woman's era, or of the advancing democratic idea?"[12]

In the maze of complimentary and uncomplimentary descriptions of the "bonneted queen," Liliuokalani reveals much of herself in her description. She looked upon Queen Victoria "as a woman" outside of her appearances as a queen in pageants.

"She was sixty-eight years of age at this time, and seemed to be in the best of health. In walking she carried a little ebony cane on which she scarcely leaned. She had been represented to me as short, stout, and fat, and not at all graceful in appearance; but I did not at all agree with the truth of this representation. She was a well-proportioned, gracious, queenly woman. I would not call her handsome; yet she had a kind, winning expression on her face which gave evidence of the gentle spirit within."[13]

With this picture in mind, Liliuokalani returned with Queen Kapiolani and the royal party to the hotel to be greeted with the stunning news that "a revolutionary movement, inaugurated by those of foreign blood, or American blood . . ." had occurred in Hawaii.

A masterpiece of understatement followed: "It was a case of marked ingratitude."

Greatly disturbed, Liliuokalani attempted to talk over the Hawaiian situation with John. It seems to have been an empty attempt. Factual John merely implied that they had to wait to see what had really happened.

In the meantime, problems had arisen with Joseph Aea. While Liliuokalani abhored the attitude of money in the *haole,* she had become only too aware of its value and debts owed. To Joe Aea she mentioned a $780 debt, borrowed in 1882, "and a threat [was] made by Joe Aea." She continues, "Will wait until Monday to let me know—what does he mean?"[14]

The last question could imply extreme naievete on her part or it could mean—how far will he go? Intermittently from the birth of Kaipo, Joe and his wife had threatened to take Kaipo from Liliuokalani. The $780, no doubt "lent" for the child, was not a debt in Joe Aea's mind. However, the fact that Liliuokalani thought of it as a "debt" seems to substantiate the fact that Kaipo was not the "child of two heads" despite the rumors regarding her and Joe.

Aea knew enough of the Hawaiian politics to realize that Kalakaua had come close to being dethroned, and were he, Liliuokalani could conceivably become queen; such rumors had been going on even before the party left for England. If Liliuokalani became queen, her elder *hanai* son was Kaipo, not Aimoku, and Joe had an ace to play against a poor hand of only a $780 debt.

The newspapers in San Francisco had brought no solace to the royal party: The *San Francisco Chronicle* spoke of the Sandwich Islands being under a "military oligarchy, more domineering than Kalakaua ever was." Complaints were made of the new regime suppressing news with "military thoroughness . . . The freedom of the press of Honolulu is a myth." Even what the *Chronicle* considered a less biased version of the events published in American newspapers was prevented from reprint in Hawaiian newspapers, comments that would have been "very interesting reading to all Hawaiians."[15]

On July 24, 1887, Liliuokalani wrote in her diary "affairs at home seem sad—my poor brother—nearing home what lovely weather." The Hawaiian heart, like every heart, lifts when it nears home and hers was glad to leave a chilly-weathered England.

❧ 4 ❧

At the wharf the royal party was met with mixed emotions. Kalakaua and his party boarded the steamer to greet with leis and kisses his wife and his sister, but there were tears of sadness as well as joy in his wide dark eyes. Kapiolani clung to him in relief and fear, and Liliuokalani's heart went out to him in *aloha* and sadness. Crowds of people thronged the wharf as they had in England, but the atmosphere was different: it wasn't one of festivity and curiosity. There was *aloha*, welcome, but it was with a sense of tragedy. The Hawaiian and *haole*-oriented royalists were subdued and the new-*haole* American regime had a mixture of smugness of victory and hesitancy of showing their conquest too much among the Hawaiians. They had not yet recognized the true reason for the Hawaiian reluctance to open hostility.

Liliuokalani followed the king and queen down the gangplank and suddenly "her whole countenance glowed"[16] as her eyes fell on three immaculately turned out children: Lydia in her white dress with a blue sash, her large quiet questioning eyes, and by her side two small boys. Aimoku at four was a miniature John Owen Dominis, stiff, still, fair skinned, blondish hair, solemn and steady. Kaipo wriggled like a happy puppy on the end of a leash, all five years of him a bundle of energy. Curly black hair, huge brown eyes and a grin that split his dark-skinned face as a beam of sun breaks through a dark cloud.

Liliuokalani brushed aside her attendants and rushed toward her children; then she stopped short. In a carriage, watching the proceedings from a mental and physical distance was her niece, Princess Kaiulani.

With her in her carriage was her father, Archibald Cleghorn, who was now descending to bring his daughter to welcome her royal aunt. Liliuokalani was caught by a moment of infinite sadness as this was the first time since Likelike's funeral Liliuokalani had seen Kaiulani not surrounded by friends.

She approached the young girl moving toward her, kissed her smooth cheek and held her hands warmly in her own. Self-sufficient Kaiulani set her free to join the three *hanai* children and take them to Hamohamo. Liliuokalani was home.

CHAPTER 7

The Bayonet Constitution

❧ 1 ❧

Immediately upon Kalakaua's election (1874), in which the Americans had supported him against Queen Emma, the American and other sugar planters went to Kalakaua with dire foreboding that if a reciprocity treaty was not effected with the United States (it had been refused to all other reigning sovereigns of Hawaii to that time), the country would be bankrupt. It will be remembered that Kalakaua then visited the U.S. and although he took no part in the negotiations himself, his personableness and "royal appearance" no doubt influenced the American government. Another important factor was that although American capital had almost a monopoly on sugar, British influence was still strong. One-third of Hawaii's sugar was finding markets in New Zealand, Australia and in other British colonies. Wodehouse, the British Consul, remarked that soon all sugar would find its way into British markets. To prevent such action and consequent British influence in Hawaii, the American government decided to try reciprocity. The treaty, not lengthy, established two important provisions: while sugar, rice, and virtually all other Hawaiian products were to be admitted to the U.S. free of duties, (1) Hawaii was not to enter into the same type of agreement with any other country, and (2) the king was not to "lease or otherwise dispose of . . . any port, harbor, or other territory . . . or grant special privileges or rights of use therein . . . to any other power . . ."[1]

An unprecedented period of prosperity came to Hawaii through development of sugar plantations. Two of the three necessities for the sugar industry were met: a market and available capital. There was yet needed a supply of cheap labor.

The first and most important necessity — the market — had been achieved through the efforts of Kalakaua. American money brought in most of the capital.

The cheap labor problem was still acute. A look at the Hawaiian labor situation presents an interesting study: the native Hawaiian laborers were not lazy nor indifferent to work as has so often and erroneously been stated. But many of them could not make the rapid transition into the new *haole* world. Work as well as everything else in life is a state of mind, and the strong, rugged Hawaiian often preferred ranch work. There were many, of course, who were still retainer-*alii* oriented.

Another problem was that the population of Hawaii in 1875 was at its lowest; after that time it increased rapidly but not of native stock. The Hawaiians continued to decline in numbers. At the beginning of Kalakaua's reign they comprised 82 per cent of the population and at his end less than 50 per cent.

Kalakaua's government fought the decline through increased sanitation, medical knowledge, hospitals, efforts for leprosy segregation, but nothing could halt the effects of the cultural changes. Discouragement, confusion, Hawaiian self-negation as well as that of *haole* took its toll. Then in 1881 the already vulnerable Hawaiian fell victim to the smallpox epidemic.

It was during this period that Kalakaua was taking his trip around the world ostensibly to encourage immigration of "comparable Polynesian blood and attitudes." Walter Murray Gibson encouraged Malayasian immigration as being those persons closest to the Polynesians. The *haole* planters who merely wanted cheap labor continued to encourage Chinese immigration at slave wage and conditions; the initiative of the Chinese to move out of the fields into merchandizing and commerce was opposed by the *haole* planters. Soon fear arose that too many Chinese were coming into Hawaii from both China and California and "would change the character of Honolulu," so restrictions were placed on Chinese immigration. Most of the planters were also reluctant to admit the Japanese and were not displeased when the Japanese government resisted emigration despite Kalakaua's attempts to gain it. The resistance broke down in 1885. The Portuguese who were imported from the Portuguese islands in the Atlantic, became the most welcome, but the cost of bringing them to Hawaii was extremely high. Kalakaua did succeed in interesting immigrants from northern Europe—Germany and Scandinavia—as well as the South Seas.

There were also other problems not solved by 1887. Transportation and communication facilities had to be expanded in the newly industrialized and commercialized country. Shipping lines, roads, bridges, railroads—all became urgent.

In the opinion of the foreigner, against the monies for these needs, Kalakaua was "spending too much" on travel, a new palace, a coronation, and finally sending his queen and his sister to England to Victoria's Jubilee.

Kalakaua was thus rapidly losing his prestige among the *haole*. Most of the Hawaiians were still supporting him, however, through two political advisers, Celso Moreno and Walter Murray Gibson, he found himself engulfed in grandiose ideas and schemes. His first mistake was to abuse the right of the monarch to change his ministry without consent of the legislature. A cabinet change was his right under the 1864 (Kamehameha V) Constitution, but Kalakaua's choice was poor inasmuch as he turned the cabinet over to Celso Moreno, an incompetent, as Prime Minister. After a storm of protest Moreno was "dismissed" in five days and sent to Italy with the three boys, including Robert Wilcox, who were to be educated there. Kalakaua then went on his trip around the world and Liliuokalani became regent (1881). The fact that the King could be forced to change his ministry by cries of "lack of confidence" was almost immediately tried again with Liliuokalani during the smallpox epidemic. Liliuokalani stood firm against such action and caused some of the anti-royalists a few moments of worry of her potential strength as possible queen.

Upon Kalakaua's return he continued playing his game of being supreme ruler. In this action he was wholly supported by Gibson. It is difficult to judge without greater study of both men who was the more to blame for the political and financial fiascos that finally brought on the Bayonet Constitution in 1887.

Gibson encouraged Kalakaua in his far reaching dreams of being Primate of the Pacific and in establishing the entity of Hawaii through the coronation. Gibson was brilliant but unscrupulous—perhaps not more so than others—but in a position that spotlighted him and gave him the blame.

One of the most alarming weapons of Gibson was his cry of "Hawaii for Hawaiians," which served to stir up racial antagonism. Paradoxically, the *haole* population paraphrased the cry to "Hawaii for Gibson." Gibson was a *haole*—and logically, racism would then not be valid. However, the moment the word "racism" enters a nation's vocabulary it is frozen into hatred of color and nationality, not ideas, culture and traditions, and becomes a weapon for the illogical, unthinking, and violent.

"Racism" had been used much earlier in Hawaii by the *haole* and by American newspapers but had never been so conceived by the Hawaiian *alii*. Now the native Hawaiians and especially the *hapa-haole* (half Hawaiian) began falling into the vicious trap of racism. The *haole* found it an effective defense for themselves "as a minority."

Whatever race, color, or creed Kalakaua might have favored, he made some serious errors as head of state, be it a monarchy or a republic.

He favored Spreckels who gave him prestige in coinage—to Spreckels' own financial advantage; he entered into political intrigue in sale of offices, abuse of royal privilege in illegal leasing of land and defrauding of customs revenue, neglect of public facilities of roads, waterways, etc., and "exemption of lepers." Whether Kalakaua was guilty or not[2] of selling the opium license twice may not be known, but he accepted the responsibility of a $71,000 debt and added to his disgrace the anger of a money-conscious *haole* population.

The Hawaiian League, a secret political organization, was formed out of which was to grow the overthrow in 1893. There were two factions: the radicals who wished to overthrow the monarchy and annex the country to the United States, to which Lorrin Thurston belonged, and the conservatives (the majority) who wished Hawaii to remain a monarchy but with curtailed monarchial powers. Sanford Ballard Dole belonged to the latter group.

Immediately after the opium scandal broke, Thurston advocated a march on the palace by the League's riflemen. He was overruled, and instead a public mass meeting was held on June 30, 1887, at the Armory, where it was demanded that the king dismiss his Cabinet and sign a new Constitution—the so-called Bayonet Constitution.

The new Constitution prevented the king from dismissing his Cabinet except by vote of the legislature; nobles were to be elected by the voters of large land-holdings (most voters of foreign birth) and the king's veto could be overridden by the legislature. The right to vote was extended to all of American or European birth who took the oath to support the new Constitution (but not to the Orientals).

The new ministry contained two antagonistic and aggressive members —Clarence Ashford and Lorrin Thurston.

The native Hawaiians in general disliked the inferior position that had been forced upon their highest *alii*—the king, and their being largely disenfranchised by the voter-property restrictions. They were joined by the Asiatics, completely deprived of the right to vote. A rift was also beginning in the Reform party itself which included some half-Hawaiians and pro-royalists.

It was into this atmosphere that Liliuokalani stepped on her return from Queen Victoria's Jubilee.

⚥ 2 ⚥

Returning from England with strong royalist attachments coupled with understanding of the *native* Hawaiian and his needs, Liliuokalani was stunned by the actions of the foreign population. Without the benefit of the suffrage of her people, motivated solely by personal greed of the opposition, the king had been stripped of his powers. Although Kalakaua had misused his position, he was still held in high esteem among the Hawaiians. It was not so much that "the king could do no wrong," as "The king can make mistakes, but, right or wrong, we stand by our monarch" that was Hawaiian political *aloha* of 1887. It was their intrinsic feeling of forgiveness of *kala-kala,* and inherent respect for the *alii.* There was nevertheless a beginning of unrest among some of the natives.

Many of the natives came to Liliuokalani and requested that she influence the king toward reestablishing the 1864 Constitution.[3] Kalakaua, somewhat wiser and certainly more frightened because his life as well as throne had been threatened, would not hear of such a thing from her; however, later he listened to another more glib and less intelligent speaker.

Liliuokalani's distress against the situations surrounding the Bayonet Constitution were two-fold. She felt it extremely unjust that those under the guise of democracy had not given the people a choice in the decision. No vote had been taken—only a handful of men had demanded at the "point of a bayonet" the stripping of monarchial power.

Secondly, Liliuokalani visited Walter Murray Gibson's daughter and heard first hand a story that was being hastily squashed by the *haole.*[4] While Kalakaua was vulnerable, several men had forcibly entered the Gibson home where Gibson's daughter and son-in-law, the Fred Hay-seldens, lived. "Without regard for the gray hairs of the old gentleman," Liliuokalani wrote, they roughly shoved the two men to the wharf, where already were prepared two hanging ropes, the loops ominously threatening their lives, to the terror and horror of Gibson's daughter. The crowd around them was out of control and called "Hang them! Hang them!" It was the sobering hand of British Consul Wodehouse that stopped the insanity, and the two men were placed in prison. Later they were tried on every conceivable charge of misappropriation of government funds— and found innocent.

An exhausted old man and his son-in-law were sent out of the country. The word "banished" was quickly censored, a word that later, not censored but transcribed incorrectly against Liliuokalani, was to help to complete the overthrow of the monarchy in 1893. A terrified and sorrow-stricken Mrs. Hayselden gained Liliuokalani's sympathy and increased her enmity against the "reformists" far more than anything that had happened to Kalakaua. Now she condemned the *haole* for the lack of humane actions. Liliuokalani could not bear personal cruelty in any form. She gave Mrs. Hayselden money, comfort, and promise of her support in having her husband and father returned to Hawaii.

Fred Hayselden did return—but with his father-in-law's body. Walter Murray Gibson, interviewed, when he first reached San Francisco,[5] made remarkably quiet, calming, forgiving remarks for a man, who, from any point of view, had been despicably treated.

When Gibson's casket was opened in Honolulu it was discovered that through some defective embalming, Gibson's skin had turned black. Lorrin Thurston wrote in his *Memoirs* that now even God had seen him as the "black devil" he was.

There was, however, another feeling among the Hawaiians, now having become color conscious; they whispered, for whispers were all they dared, that "Now he is one of us."[6] Color and racism was incorrectly becoming the issue.

❧ 3 ❧

Liliuokalani's total sympathy with her brother was rudely halted on September 26, 1887, when she wrote with vehemence in her diary: "Today a day of importance in Hawaiian History—King signed a lease of Pearl River to United States for eight years to get reciprocity treaty—It should not have been done."

From the point of view of the Hawaiians retaining the monarchy and its independence, she was absolutely right. Her earlier worry that a Pearl Harbor concession would be merely the head of the camel in the tent of annexation was also correct.

A new relationship seemed to be developing between the king and his heir-apparent. For the first time Kalakaua began to recognize that his sister had an insight into government and was held in high regard

among the native Hawaiians. In November she wrote that Kalakaua
telephoned her to ask her to the palace to consult about ministers.[7] She
apparently favored Brown, Ashford, and Green but was dubious about
Wilder.

They talked for the first time in concrete and intelligent terms about
money and crown lands.[8] She wrote: "How sorry I am for him, he seems
anxious to make up for the past." No doubt, Kalakaua was hopeful to
"make up for the past," but he had already passed the point of no return.

In the meanwhile Liliuokalani, with her usual lack of correct character
evaluation, coupled with her *aloha,* took to her bosom and home Robert
Wilcox, now Italian educated, and his wife, a black-haired, brown-eyed
Italian beauty of a noble family, Signorina Gina Sobrero of the house
of Colonna di Stigliano, a countess.

Wilcox had been recalled from Italy, as were the others, by the Reform
Party who considered his "education" would be of little value to the
nation. An accurate evaluation.

However, he brought with him his bride. Having posed as a Hawaiian
prince, he had married the countess. Wilcox was destitute; so Liliuokalani
took them into her home at Moulaulani. When Kalakaua refused to give
money to the Wilcoxes, Liliuokalani made several attempts to find a
position for the half-Hawaiian Wilcox, but found none suitable to his
deficient abilities and high expectations. It was pregnant Gina that Liliuokalani befriended, giving the Wilcoxes the best rooms in her home and
taking one that was "cold"[9] for herself.

Here the countess cried herself to sleep night after night. Liliuokalani
finally asked Kalakaua for $1,000 so that Gina could go back to Italy,
as she begged to be allowed to do. "She is nearly heart broken and wishes
she had not married him."[10] Although Kalakaua refused again, somehow
Liliuokalani managed to reassure her that she would get the money. It
was then the beautiful young girl fell on her knees before the woman who
was her generous benefactor, promising that she would do anything to
repay her.

Liliuokalani pulled her to her feet, and sitting on the bed beside her
stroked her hair and asked only one small favor: that the child, if it were
a girl, be named Moulaulani.[11] Later she learned the child was a girl and
was named Moulaulani. Sufficient monies were garnered to send Wilcox
and his wife to San Francisco and through the Italian consul, Gina obtained a divorce and returned to Italy. Wilcox, unfortunately, returned
to Hawaii.

❦ 4 ❦

During the years of 1888-1890 Liliuokalani was drawn into the maelstorm of politics, not only by her brother but by those who opposed the king and attempted to use her as a pawn in overthrowing the government.

Ample evidence[12] exists that Lorrin Thurston and a few others of the radical wing of the Reform Party had already decided to overthrow the government and annex the country to the United States. Thurston had finally found an ally in the American government. Although an unsuspecting ally in anything so violent as a monarchial overthrow, James Blaine, Secretary of State of the United States, leaned as many men had from the time of Daniel Webster toward the idea that the Hawaiian Islands were already a part of the United States and used the real or convenient fear that Great Britain would take the Islands unless the United States did so first.

Blaine was thus instrumental in having John L. Stevens replace Merrill as American Minister in Hawaii. Stevens was Blaine's closest friend and business associate in publishing the *Daily Kennebec Journal,* a newspaper founded by an early annexationist, Luther Severance.[13]

Stevens had been "envoy extraordinary and minister plenipoteniary" to Paraguay and Uruguay in 1870-1874. There he had considered himself a master diplomat in calling in American troops to settle an uprising in Paraguay. He was, however, recalled by the United States government at the request of Paraguay. Later (1877-83) he served in the same capacity as ambassador in Norway and Sweden and was again recalled. From 1883 to 1888 he worked with Blaine and the *Journal.*

From the moment Stevens arrived in Honolulu he showed himself openly as an advocate of annexation—Lorrin Thurston had found his ally.

The split in the Reform Party (one for overthrow and the other for a modified monarchy) found two of the most influential American men in Hawaii, both of missionary descent, on opposite sides: Lorrin Thurston, the radical, and Sanford Ballard Dole, the moderate.

Dole appeared an impartial and fair judge on the Supreme Court bench in ruling for the king's right of veto, a right which if removed would have left Kalakaua completely without any power as head of state.

Whether Dole had anything to do with the approach to Liliuokalani to depose Kalakaua is questionable. He was certainly an acquaintance of those who came to her, but he was also a man who would have made his own overtures had he thought the action best. Furthermore he did not favor the destruction of the monarchy. Therefore it seems more likely that Liliuokalani was considered a convenient pawn by the opposition, rather than a choice for continuing the monarchy.

Whatever the underlying reasons may have been, James Dowsett came to Liliuokalani on December 20, 1887; Liliuokalani wrote in her diary that Dowsett, a royalist *haole,* "came today and told me that they wanted me to be queen—he said they could not do anything since the king vetoed military police bills—told particularly necessary if king abdicated if king was doing wrong—I would but not until then. In evening went and told king."

There is no evidence that Kalakaua took her particularly seriously; there is implicit evidence in her diary entry that she did not enter into intrigue with the opposition to overthrow her brother, as she was later accused of doing, "In the evening went and told king"—even the most naive conspirator does not tell his victim of his plans!

On January 14, 1888, she was again asked to take the throne. Her answer was the same as she "gave the League"[14]—would take it when *he* abdicates and not otherwise." The question arises again on January 16th when "W.W." (identified by Kuykendall as Robert Wilcox and Charles B. Wilson) came to consult her "on matter of importance." "I advise them to use only respectful words and no threats but to explain the situation to him [Kalakaua] how everything, the state of the country might be changed should he abdicate if only for a year, then he should take the reigns [sic] and reign peaceably the rest of his life. W. and W. went to the King . . ."

Liliuokalani then retreated to Hinano Bower, and there in quiet and meditation as was her custom during periods of stress, she waited for an answer from Kalakaua. The answer was that "he would think it over." The next day the subject was slightly enlarged upon with the king saying, "wait a while—I said yes, then wait."[15]

Certainly these entries speak of a most ineffectual type of conspiracy, yet before the month was out, Kalakaua had been convinced that Liliuokalani was *kipi* (a traitor). Liliuokalani attributed it to her reaction to the king's statement at a luau in which Kalakaua remarked with an alcoholic breath that if the dissension continued he would "sell the country." He had no power to do so, but it was certainly a dangerous statement to make in the presence of his enemies, and was seized upon. Liliuokalani wrote, "I looked displeased." Liliuokalani's looking "displeased" could carry a severe rebuke, and Kalakaua could interpret it, if he wished, as *kipi*. She continued angrily: "I don't care what he does but looks like millions will burn his fingers."

She was then visited by a native Hawaiian, Rev. J. Waiamu, who told her the "people [were] very much against the king's weakness and would take the throne if he abdicates. I said I would. Then said they could call a meeting to see the king—This is yet another party without knowing one another."

The latter statement seems a bit unlikely, but Liliuokalani no doubt believed it, especially if she received the information from a native. She was not yet ready to accept collusion or betrayal by native Hawaiians, considering all of them as loyal to the monarchy as she was.

❦ 5 ❦

In her private life Liliuokalani was struggling also with personal problems. Although she did not know it, her life was moving on toward a series of crises and changes.

She began her 1888 diary with these words: "Kawaiahao [church] to begin anew to wipe away all feeling of animosity of past year—maybe he [Henry Parker] will leave politics alone here after." Unfortunately, "he" did not, and shortly thereafter she wrote "was naughty all day—counted money instead of going to church—May I be forgiven—" and in July, "Stayed home—washing maile brushes—good way of spending Sunday." She also sought solace in making wreaths and floral arrangements for Bernice's and Likelike's graves and as usual one wreath for Emma's.

It was out of regard for her sister Likelike's memory that she and Archie Cleghorn clashed and began to part company. As was her monthly custom she planned the usual open reception for February 2, 1888, then she received a short note from Cleghorn saying that as the reception would fall on the anniversary of Likelike's death it "was in bad taste" to have it. Liliuokalani wrote annoyedly in her diary, "If he were only true to her memory! Heard he had proposed to Lou—."

However, Liliuokalani cancelled her reception and instead took Kaiulani with her to Likelike's grave. She at that time began to recognize Kaiulani's need for a mother. She "prevailed upon Archie to let Kaiulani stay with her a week."

It was a good week for Liliuokalani for it brought her into a children's world again. She called her *hanai* children to her and had her first glimpse of what could happen if children were parted from their *hanai* and only parents for too long. She was distressed to discover that Lydia had been absent a great deal from Kawaiahao Seminary, and then determined again to bring Lydia closer into her life—and the two boys, too.

It was time, she decided, that Mrs. Dominis should become acquainted with her grandchild. To this point, whether John had told his mother or not, rumors were well established about Aimoku, yet Mrs. Dominis had refused to acknowledge the child as her son's.

Mrs. Dominis had been ill for several months and Liliuokalani had intermittently visited her, stayed with her, nursed her, and become annoyed with her: "I think she tries to slide down on purpose."

Not infrequently did Liliuokalani take John, Mary (Pahau-Purdy), Kaipo and Aimoku for rides in her carriage and to visit friends. On January 15, 1887 she took it upon herself to "introduce" Aimoku to Mrs. Dominis as her grandchild. With Mrs. Dominis' gradual decline, she had told John that his mother should know about Aimoku—from him. John was reluctant.

Despite his reluctance, on a warm day with a slight tradewind moving gently across Honolulu, Liliuokalani, John, and Aimoku drove in a silent carriage to pay a call on Mrs. Dominis at Washington Place. Mrs. Dominis was in bed, querulous, and distracted.

Pulling the covers up to her chin so that only the aging face—she was to be 85-years-old that coming August—appeared under a white lace bed cap, she regarded Aimoku balefully. Liliuokalani who was beginning to overcome her dislike of being in a sickroom, having spent so many hours with her dying sisters and other *alii,* was once again assailed with repugnance, followed by guilt that she should feel that way. As a result she pulled Aimoku gently toward the bed and said to Mrs. Dominis, "Does he not look like John?"

Mrs. Dominis categorically denied such a likeness,[16] and implicit in her denial was the rejection that the child was John's. Before Mary Dominis died in the following year she acknowledged to Liliuokalani that she knew Aimoku was John's child and that no doubt there had been "some sacrifice" on Liliuokalani's part in the marriage.

On February 4, 1888, Liliuokalani had her birthday party for Lydia (Kaonoponi), then ten years, and included in the celebration Lydia's father Luther Aholo. (In 1885 Liliuokalani had used the abbreviation "Kaono(hi)poni"[17] for Lydia—a shortening of her Hawaiian name of Kaohohiponiponiokalani.) In the evening Luther Aholo and Liliuokalani discussed politics.[18] Luther Aholo also opposed Kalakaua's "weakness" in giving into the *haole* minority and signing the Bayonet Constitution.

Luther Aholo was to die shortly. Liliuokalani who had a type of pre-science in such matters may again have desired that father and daughter meet. The effect on Lydia was poor. For many years she believed that Kaipo as well as Aimoku were John Owen Dominis' sons and that as the children of the husband of "the queen" were "more royal" than she could ever be.[19] Not unlike her *hanai* mother, Liliuokalani, in her early years at the Royal School and "under the supervision of the Bishops," Lydia also took on a sense of inferiority—one that was to bring sorrow to both her and Liliuokalani in later years.

For all Liliuokalani's good intentions toward both Lydia and Aimoku, her heart never responded with the quickening beat of fright of their illnesses as it did with Kaipo. A call from Carrie Bush that Kaipo was ill caused an immediate visit to the Bush's, or a demand that Kaipo be sent home to her and her personally spending sleepless nights in worry and nursing a child who often had nothing more than an upset stomach.

❦ 6 ❦

Liliuokalani continued living through these years with Kalakaua's political problems, her changing relationships with her *hanai* children and her mother-in-law, her social and religious conflicts. She continued her efforts toward rapprochement with her husband. Often through Kaipo and Aimoku she attempted to bring John into her life, but she wrote, "John did not come on account of heavy rain but he did go to Captain Nichols ball." She did not.

On her fiftieth birthday she wrote "yet feel young," and as her jubilee birthday fell on a Sunday she had her celebration the following day, the 3rd of September. Her distrust of John's love was deep by then; she wrote "Heard John was sick, sent Lilia to see. They told me he *was* sick . . ."

The day began early: at 5:00 a.m. with the recitation of her geneology and the Royal Hawaiian Band playing. Close friends and relatives greeted her and were with her in these early morning hours.

John did, however, come at 10:00 a.m. to "breakfast" accompanied by the king, Prince David Kawananakoa and Kaiulani. In the afternoon the societies came, the band returned, and a reception was held. In the evening "friends" came to "supper" which could have been a light supper or a luau.

On April 26, 1889 Mary Dominis died at Washington Place. Liliuokalani's diaries[20] bear out that she had spent much time with her mother-in-law before her death and a healing of the breach had begun to take place between them. Mrs. Dominis in her last illness had become senile and dwelt on her past. She told Liliuokalani that her family dated back to William the Conqueror,[21] whose motto had been *Persevere.* Liliuokalani translating this into Hawaiian came up with *Onipaa,* which as all Hawaiian words, had a flow rather than a rigidity and conveyed the idea of going forward while standing steadfast on principles. She adopted it immediately for her Hawaii girls' college society adding the important words "in searching for knowledge."

After Mrs. Dominis' death, Liliuokalani moved to Washington Place to be close to her husband. John, however, moved to the cottage as the steps were too difficult for him to negotiate in his rheumatic condition.

In the meanwhile Robert Wilcox returned to Hawaii, again without money but now also lacking a wife. Liliuokalani allowed him to live again at Muolaulani. After a trip to Kauai, Liliuokalani returned to visit her home at Muolaulani and found a distraught young man who informed her that he, Robert Wilcox, had planned a revolution to "release the king from the thralldom."

Liliuokalani demanded to know what part her brother was playing in this revolution, and Wilcox informed her the king knew nothing about it. She insisted he should talk with the king and receive his "consent."

Wilcox, in a true revolutionist's flair waved his arms histrionically saying he would "gladly lay down his life for the king." She told him grimly he might have to. She apparently had no idea that the revolutionists would involve her, although she learned that her home had been used as the center of intrigue and that guns were buried in her garden.

Liliuokalani took no action. It may be that she didn't believe Wilcox, but the revolution took place the next day, and there was little time for warnings.

She wrote in her *Story* that she awoke early as was her habit and after dressing walked in the Washington Place rose garden—which was finally hers—before breakfasting. It was then she first noticed the rifle companies were hastily moving toward Punch Bowl Street Armory. She was informed by a young man hurrying by her gate that Wilcox "had taken possession of the palace."

Wilcox and his men had scaled the coral wall of the palace and entered the grounds. There he was held in abeyance by the palace guards. As he had possession of the government building across from the palace his *coup d'etat* seemed to depend on getting the king to the palace to sign a new constitution which Wilcox said the king had seen and was waiting to sign.

Kalakaua was not, however, to be enticed to the palace. He was at the time at Queen Kapiolani's home, corner of Queen and Punch Bowl streets; from there he retreated to the boathouse. Many conflicting stories circulated of why the king did not appear. The most likely but least true story was that he had heard that Wilcox planned to put Liliuokalani on the throne.

Liliuokalani's attitude at the time was a sense of annoyance with Kalakaua's "weakness," as she termed it, for having given in to the small *haole* group. She intermittently lost her patience with him and his drinking. Once she even went so far as to express impatience with Kapiolani, whom she found in tears because Kalakaua had not returned for a coronation anniversary, saying why should she care "she would be queen."[22]

But actually taking part in dethroning Kalakaua was not in keeping with her character. To take the "reigns" if he relinquished them, yes—but to take part in overthrowing him, no.

Her open disapproval of her brother's actions caused British Consul Wodehouse and others to assume she would enter a conspiracy against him. Many felt that she was also concerned about her rights to succession since Kaiulani had been given the title of "princess."

Nevertheless, Kalakaua apparently believed it, or else he had little faith in Wilcox's revolution.

After the abortive Wilcox revolution in which a few of the insurgents were killed and wounded and a great deal of property damage done, Kalakaua denied any knowledge of Wilcox's plans. Yet when Wilcox was tried by a native jury somewhat later, he was exonerated on the basis that as he had tried to "help the king"—he was a native hero to the Hawaiians. Also the testimony in the trials furnished no evidence of collusion between Liliuokalani and Wilcox.[23]

Thus stood the temper of the native Hawaiians in 1889. Serano Bishop, editor of *The Friend*, December, 1889, wrote ". . . a majority of the natives adhere to their hereditary and instinctive loyalty to the King . . ." Bishop then stated with implication of the defeat of the pro-royalist that "An appeal is soon to be made in the ballot."[24]

Before the "ballot" could prove Serano Bishop correct a serious split developed in the Reform Party. Although a truce was achieved between the king and the cabinet after Wilcox's abortive revolution, harmony was not established.

The most important cause of the split resulted from the difference of opinion regarding a new proposed treaty with the United States. In the United States there was a strong tide toward the repeal or reduction of the tariff on sugar and for adoption of the bounty system, both extremely damaging to Hawaiian trade.

H.A.P. Carter was dispatched to the United States in the hope of preventing a change in the favorable trade. Several proposed treaties, additions and changes—all more favorable to the United States than Hawaii were bandied about. British Consul Wodehouse protested that the United States was trying to make a protectorate of Hawaii.

The telling blow that parted the Reform Party, and led to its downfall, was a portion of the treaty proposal that provided "for a guarantee of Hawaii's independence by the United States and for the United States to be given full knowledge of treaties made between Hawaii and other countries."

Carter was disappointed with the opposition to the proposal, and expressed fear to Kalakaua[25] that "landing of foreign troops could not be prevented . . . if a revolution was started against the throne."

Cooperation with the United States and "absolute independence of the kingdom" broke the Reform Party, and a second party called the National Reformists, led by J.E. Bush and Robert Wilcox, was formed.

The death blow to the sugar planters came with the McKinley Tariff Bill which wiped out the differential advantage that Hawaiian sugar had enjoyed in the American market.[26]

It also strengthened the determination of the annexationists that the "only way to save the country," was to make Hawaii a part of the United States.

❧ 7 ❧

King Kalakaua's health had gradually been failing throughout the years 1888-1890. In November of 1890 it was reported that he planned to take a trip to the United States—a vacation in a cooler climate—for his health. There were intimations that Kalakaua planned to go also to Washington, D.C., and rumors were spread that he planned to "annex the Kingdom to the United States at a neat profit to himself."

R.S. Kuykendall wrote, "There was, in fact, not a scintilla of truth in the report . . ." Liliuokalani bore out the fact that Kalakaua did in fact plan to go to Washington, D.C., but to try to negotiate better arrangements for the planters.

Kalakaua was received in the United States with great ovations. He wrote James Robertson, January 1, 1891, "A spontaneous ovation (in Southern California). I have never seen the like before . . . not a moments rest. Travelling day and night . . . Wonder that I am not half dead yet . . ."

Robertson, the son-in-law of Archibald Cleghorn, was a close friend of Liliuokalani, and he immediately brought the letter to her. "She was deeply disturbed saying she hoped the king had not given his life for his enemies"—those who sought his help in changing the tariff, whom she called the "Missionary Party."

❦ 8 ❧

Liliuokalani again became regent during Kalakaua's absence. Her regency was less than three months and during the time she showed herself more British than Hawaiian, as her interests were directed toward social causes.

Liliuokalani had seen her brother off on his trip with great foreboding. While on his other trips she had been a tower of strength against Kapiolani's fears, she now pleaded that he not go, even offering as an excuse her own "feeble health"—a three week "fever" that had kept her in bed, but these excuses came from a woman who had declared her health excellent and two years before at fifty "felt young."

During the last week in January, 1891, Liliuokalani visited Kawaiahao Seminary where Lydia Aholo was enrolled. Lydia, then thirteen, vividly remembered that visit.[27]

The children in the Seminary had been busy all week preparing for the king's return. It was expected to be on January 29, and would, of course, be a holiday. Hawaiians love holidays—especially those commemorating the departure or arrival of royalty—and this one was to be a great celebration.

The teachers had discontinued classes to allow the children to make leis which would adorn everyone on the king's return.

On the twenty-seventh Lydia had a "most wonderful surprise;" Regent Liliuokalani came to the Seminary to take her to see the decorations on the streets of Honolulu.

Lydia could hardly control herself as the carriage came to a stop outside. All seven of the girls had been pressing their noses against the window, waiting, waiting, trying to keep their starched white dresses from wrinkling.

As the princess-regent's carriage arrived in the driveway, the teachers hushed the girls and then hurried them out to curtsy before the princess regent. Once set loose, they ran to the carriage in curiosity. Suddenly Lydia was overcome by the woman who was a princess and was now her regent. The girls all curtsied again and presented the regent with a lei, and returned to the school. Lydia alone remained.

As the coachman held open the door for her; she hesitated, trembling for a moment. This woman was so beautiful to her. Lydia had not seen her while the king had been away, she had only been sent messages which the other children—and even the teachers—had regarded with awe. Liliuokalani's position had grown closer to queenship.

Regal in black velvet, with diamonds and pearls adorning her Victorian dress and lovely black, wavy hair, she was suddenly Lydia's "Queen."

Stumblingly, she half-curtsied and whispered awkwardly, "Princess—Queen—"

Liliuokalani's dark eyes lit up from inside laughter as they often had before. "What has happened to 'Hanai'?" Lydia threw herself into the carriage. "Hanai!" Royalty fell away for the moment.

Against a tightly encased bosom, on the velvet of queens, she held the girl to her as Lydia had so often seen her grasp to her breast any and all children who came to her, in deepest tenderness and love. Lydia was overcome with joy.

"Lydia, Lydia," she said. "Have I so much neglected you with silly affairs of state?"

"No—no, Hanai," Lydia cried.

In her childish enthusiasm she accepted wholly "silly affairs of state" oblivious of the tensions in Hawaiian Government. Instead she settled down to see the city that was soon to welcome the king home.

"Is it true," she asked, "that the King might be ill?" Rumors had been rife about the king's health, but rumors were always rife in the Seminary —and in Hawaii. A fleeting look of sadness swept over Liliuokalani's expressive face.

"A little, maybe. Not much." And then as if she were talking to herself: "I wish the cable had been laid—so we would know." Lydia had no idea just what the trans-Pacific cable was, nor how hard Liliuokalani had worked to have it laid between the United States and Hawaii.

"But," Lydia cried, "The red fish came up from the sea." The red fish were a certain sign of death of royalty.

Liliuokalani took her hand tightly in hers. "Surely *you* do not believe in such old superstitions."

Lydia replied untruthfully that of course she didn't, but she later said she was also aware of the tightening of Liliuokalani's hand on hers. Old beliefs die hard. *And the red fish had come up, hadn't they?*

Liliuokalani spoke swiftly and precisely as she often did, especially under stress: "We shall drive from the Inter-Island Wharf, where the ministers of state will meet the King, to the palace, and you shall see it all."

The Inter-Island Wharf had been festooned with the first arch ever made in the Islands of evergreens. There was a transparency designed by Stratmeyer, of clasped hands indicating the cordial relationship that existed between the United States, which would be represented by Admiral Brown of the *Charleston* on which the king would arrive, and Hawaii, represented by the king himself.

A huge banner bearing the words "Hawaii Greets her King and Guests" spanned the arch. On the day of the king's arrival there were to be eight living persons on the arch, representing the Islands of the Kingdom. Banners and pictures of the king were throughout the City, with the royal arms extending the whole distance of Fort Street. Lydia's excitement increased with the step of the horses. She thought she should "surely burst."

At Merchant and Fort Street was a white banner bearing the words *Aloha Oe*—the regent's words, saying this time Love Forever.

Lydia recalled she was as excited by the crowds of people who wandered about the streets awaiting their king as she was about the decorations. To call her attention back to the coming festivities, Liliuokalani told her, "At the sighting of the *Charleston* the fire bells will ring. Other ships in port will fire, and the royal salute will be given from the battery at Punch Bowl."

"The King and Admiral Brown will be escorted in an open carriage by the Fire Brigade to the Palace, which has been 'somewhat'," she said with a smile, "renovated, completely decorated, and the royal apartments have been put in readiness for our guests."[28]

The festivities would begin then, culminating in the evening ball, invitations issued by Liliuokalani. She gave Lydia an invitation, although laughingly said she was too young to accept. But Lydia could proudly show it to her school friends.

> Acting Chairman of the Household is commanded by Her Royal Highness Princess Liliuokalani, Regent, to invite   LYDIA K. AHOLO to a ball to be given at the Iolani Palace at 8:30 in the evening at the Arrival of His Majesty the King. Full dress. R.S.V.P.

But there was to be no ball for anyone. No decorations. Instead the city would be draped in black mourning.

CHAPTER 8

The King is Dead -
A Queen is Born

❦ 1 ❦

On the morning of January 29, 1891, a chill of horror spread through Honolulu, for as the *Charleston* was sighted rounding Diamond Head with yards of cockbill, flags at half-mast, only the royal standard was not at half-mast—but that meant little—for the King never dies.

Was the king dying? Or dead?

No word had reached Honolulu from San Francisco or Washington, D.C., but it was obvious all was not well.

At the Iolani Palace the Ministers of State were already assembled in the Blue Room when Liliuokalani entered. On their faces was written the fear in her mind: *Is the King dead?* On some, the idea was engraved with grief; on others, suspicion; some, fear; on all, a touch of wariness. The voices were subdued, the undercurrents electric; *If the King is dead, what then?*

When the *Charleston* put into port, the dreaded rumor was verified and the city was hastily dismantled and the bright colors replaced with black. Newspapers were hurriedly printed and put out: *The King is Dead*. Heralds began moving about the streets proclaiming Liliuokalani Queen.

Few persons, if any, have faced a more difficult day than Liliuokalani did on January 29, 1891.

The last member, except for herself, of the nine throne-aligned children of the Royal School had died. The last adult member of the Kalakaua line, except herself, was now gone. Her brother, King Kalakaua, was dead. Liliuokalani was swept with the loneliness she often feared. The intricate web of grief, remorse, self-recriminations and shock of the reality of Kalakaua's death gripped her; her intellect was paralyzed. She was a woman so surprisingly unknowledgeable of the dangers of deceit, although she had been continually surrounded by them, that she had no idea a woman's grief could be used as a political weapon. But it was. She wrote in her *Story*: "I was so overcome by the death of my dear brother, so dazed with the suddenness of the news which had come upon us in a moment, that I hardly realized what was going on about me, nor did I at all appreciate for the moment my situation. Before my brother's remains were buried, a trap was sprung upon me by those who stood waiting as a wild beast watches for his prey."[1]

During her regency Liliuokalani should have had ample opportunity to awaken to the impending dangers surrounding her—deception, betrayal, and open threats.

Scarcely a day had gone by that a telephone call had not come, threatening either her life or an attack on the palace. She had been persuaded by her advisers, more alert to the plots, not to sleep in the guest rooms of the palace, where she had often stayed while Kalakaua was king, comforting Kapiolani. Now Kapiolani had wisely moved to her own home, and Liliuokalani had heeded strong warnings to spend her nights at Washington Place. Of the twenty-five palace guards, she took a few to stand by Washington Place, while the remainder stayed at the palace.

Despite this atmosphere of danger and the many warnings she received, Liliuokalani felt invulnerable. In a somewhat blind faith Liliuokalani had attended to official affairs of state every day, often walking from Washington Place to the palace without guards.

Then on January 29, 1891, before Kalakaua's body had been brought to the palace, before she had time to collect her thoughts, the ministers who waited for her at the palace forced her into making her first irrevocable mistake: taking the oath of office as queen by swearing allegiance to the Bayonet Constitution.

The moment she had heard the final news that Kalakaua was dead, she had sent for her husband who was "suffering with rheumatism" at Washington Place. He had come at once, much to her gratitude.

She questioned John the purpose of the unprecedented "meeting," which the ministers, not she, had called, and John merely told her she had to take the oath of office. Against her protest that she wished to wait until after her brother's funeral, his reply was typically factual: she must take it then. *They* had decided.

The oath was administered by the Chief Justice, Albert Francis Judd, and Princess Liliuokalani was proclaimed Queen by the Minister of Finance, Godfrey Brown:

> It having pleased the Almighty God to close the earthly career of King Kalakaua on 20th instant in San Francisco, California, United States of America, we the members of his late majesty's cabinet here-

by proclaim by virtue of the 22nd article of the Constitution, Her
Royal Highness The Princess Liliuokalani, Queen of the Hawaiian
Islands under the title of Liliuokalani.

God preserve the Queen Given at the Iolani
Palace This 29th day of January, A.D. 1891

Signed,   J. A. Cummins, Min. of Foreign Affairs
              Godfrey Brown, Min. of Finance
              C. N. Spencer, Min. of Interior
              A. P. Peterson, Atty. General

Godfrey Brown also read a statement that "The reign of our departed
King was memorable as an era of remarkable and increasing prosperity."
All would seem to be well, or was it: *Speak no ill of the dead.*

On the same day the group adjourned to the Blue Room where the
council moved to pay respect, give congratulations, and offer sympathy
to the new queen. However, A.F. Judd, Chief Justice, did more; he said:
"Should any of the members of your cabinet propose anything to you, say
'yes!' " Although the queen was first puzzled by the words, J.A. Cummins was soon to clarify them. In a half-stammering apologetic-lecture
tone he told her the cabinet wished to be allowed to remain; this was
further clarified by Godfrey Brown that "no changes could be made in
the cabinet except by the legislature." As Liliuokalani dismissed the discussions for later consideration, she was warned by the Attorney General
Peterson that she best "understand the situation and accept it."

Whether Liliuokalani did understand the underlying threat or not,
whether she at the time knew she had the right to dismiss the cabinet is
nowhere documented. However, there can be little doubt she did, but
had no intention of dealing with the problems at the moment.

She stated she would "defer all further notice of the matters until
after the king's burial." In the finality of the dismissal there was a touch
of Kaahumanu, who becoming angry with Rev. Bingham following her
long-delayed admittance to the church, in a gesture of contempt offered
him her little finger, not her hand, in departing.

Liliuokalani now did not wish the cabinet *aloha;* she merely nodded
her head in dismissal. And thus began the indictment of her being a
stubborn headstrong, willful, proud woman.

❧ 2 ❧

Between these morning hours and five in the afternoon when the
king's body was brought to the palace, Liliuokalani went through a

great deal of turmoil. She first visited Kapiolani who was inconsolable
and left her with her lady-in-waiting, Mrs. James Robertson.

She was upset, having signed an oath to the Bayonet Constitution, but
it was done, and now could not be changed. She knew that her people,
the Hawaiians, wanted a new constitution which would release them
from the control of the Missionary Party, but she would have to wait.
There was nothing else to do—only wait.

From a letter written by Ida Pope we learn that: "At three o'clock
in the afternoon the Queen sent for our girls to come to sing for her. The
girls sang 'Nearer My God to Thee' in native language. They sang in
English, 'Abide with Me,' 'Lead Kindly Light,' 'Rock of Ages,' and
'Safe in the Arms of Jesus.' They sang like seraphs.

"The natives stopped their working and listened with the most rapt
attention. I think it must have been quite a relief to the queen—the
wailing is kept up almost incessantly."[2]

Whether Miss Pope's evaluation of the queen's feelings regarding
the wailing is correct or not, her desire for the missionary songs to be
sung is an interesting comment about a woman whom Ida Pope knew
well, for it was she to whom the queen had now entrusted Lydia
"Ka(hi)poni" Aholo.

Among the girls was Lydia, and Queen Liliuokalani, as she embraced
each one as they passed before her, gave Lydia[3] a piece of paper on which
she had written the words from Sarah Williams:

> Is it so, O Christ, in heaven, that the
>   highest suffer most?
> That the strongest wander farthest and
>   most hopelessly are lost?
> That the mark of rank in nature is
>   capacity for pain,
> And the anguish of the singer
>   makes the sweetness of the strain?

Liliuokalani was particularly fond of the writings of the British woman who had been born just three years before herself but had died in
1868. She had once before, at Bernice's death bed, recalled the words:

> Though my soul be set in darkness, it
>   will rise in perfect light,
> I have loved the stars too fondly to be
>   fearful of the night.

Liliuokalani was not so much "comforted" by the Calvinistic doctrine of doubtful hope for her brother, as she was by Sarah Williams' words. She wrote her own *mele*,[4] part-old Hawaiian, part-Christian and part-mystical, but she did not present it to the chanters. It told of the hot red torch, the kindly gods who awaited Kalakaua with pomp and ceremony, the Calvinistic God who might have some corrective measures to take up with the "Merrie Monarch," and last a mystical, transcendental type of longing for him to rise above all ancient and Christian doctrine, as one who had "loved the stars too fondly to be fearful of the night."

At four o'clock she joined Kapiolani and the others to await her brother's body to be brought to the palace. Earlier Admiral Brown had told her Kalakaua had been given a funeral service at Trinity Church in San Francisco. Thirty-thousand people had crowded the church and the streets, for Kalakaua was the first monarch to die on American soil. How many firsts they'd had, Liliuokalani thought: Kalakaua the first reigning monarch to go around the world, Kapiolani the first queen to be a guest of a president of the United States; and Liliuokalani, the first ruling queen of Hawaii. But even now plans were in progress to make Liliuokalani the *last* reigning monarch of Hawaii.

The day continued gloomy and cloudy. Then as the procession passed through the gates of the palace a triple rainbow spanned the entire structure, embracing the palace. It was a royal sign. A good sign. All the native people knew it for that. Throngs of people crowded together, all silent, too full of grief to speak even to each other. When the cortege arrived at the palace steps, the casket was placed on the shoulders of the stoutest and best-picked men of the ship, and borne to a bier in the center of the Red Chamber. It was the royal reception room, and now it was the room in which the king would lie in state for three weeks.

❧ 3 ❧

People came from all the Islands to pay their final respects to their dead king. The cabinet and privy council carried out the details of the royal funeral for, as Liliuokalani wrote, the death and burial of a sovereign is "not a trivial matter" in Hawaii.

"The casket was placed on a cloth of royal feathers—these were the red and yellow feathers of the *oo* and *mamo* and the *iiwi* birds. The cloth was spread over a table in the center of the Red Chamber in the Iolani Palace, and guards were detailed for duty day and night. Twenty men were so honored by selection. They bore aloft the royal *ḳahilis,* the large feathered standards, which were never lowered during the entire course of the twenty-four hours. The attendants were, however, divided into four watches of three hours each. Those relieving formed a line and took their positions as the stations were vacated by their predecessors, who on resigning the plumes of state, returned to their homes. These watchers were selected from men who could claim ancestry from the chiefs."[5] His brother Masons also stood watch with the high chiefs.

While in attendance at the side of the royal casket, some sang the death-wail or old-time *mele* or chants belonging solely to the family of the deceased.

There were also younger attendants who composed dirges which were more in accord with the lyrics of the time. As Kalakaua was a member of the Masonic fraternity, two Masons as guard of honor always remained with the other watchers and were relieved in a similar manner.

The last morning of Kalakaua's lying in state began with the ceremonies of the *Hale Naua,* the much maligned Kalakaua's "secret organization." In an interview with Kalakaua a reporter of the *San Francisco Chronicle* of December 13, 1890, wrote that the king was in the process of writing a book to be called "The Temple of Wisdom of Diametrical Physiography."

> The book is based on the ancient wisdoms of Hawaii, long hidden and kept intact by the kahunas (priests) coupled with newly discovered scientific material relative to astronomy and astrology . . . An organization called the Hale Nuau [sic] works to bring the old and the new together. The inspiration for the mystical-modern scientific society is based, as is the structure of it, on the Masonic order of which the king is a Thirty-Third Degree of the Mystical Shrine . . .
>
> The king has also written a book of the legends of Hawaii with the help of former American Consul Daggett . . . The King gave little information of the contents of the book beyond saying it was preserving the beliefs and customs of the Hawaiians . . . He had many kind words for his wife, Queen Kapiolani, who spoke only Hawaiian, and for his sister, Princess Liliuokalani, who was a translator of no small consequence . . .

Liliuokalani wrote that the *Hale Naua* ceremony was one of the "most interesting and impressive . . . [she] had ever witnessed." The society honored its head and founder by prayer customs of the organization "similar [to] the Masonic and other fraternal organizations." The high priest who officiated was William Auld, assisted by two other lay priests.

> Then entered twelve women with lighted candles in their hands; each one of these bearing aloft her taper, offered a short prayer, the first words at the head, next at the shoulders, then the elbows, then the hands, and so on to the thighs, the knees, the ankles, and the feet. There were six of the torch bearers on each side; and after these formed they surrounded the remains and all repeated in unison prayers appropriate to the burial of the dead. They then withdrew in the most solemn manner. This service, so far from being, as has been alleged, idolatrous, had no more suggestion of paganism than can be found in the Masonic or other worship.

Later the state funeral services took place. An Anglican ritual service was conducted by the Bishop of Honolulu, presiding. The bier was carried in slow marching step through the Nuuanu Valley to the Royal Mausoleum. *Kahili* bearers bore the plumes of various colors above the heads of moving throngs that followed the procession.

At the mausoleum the casket was placed in the center of the tomb and the final prayers were offered by the Bishop and Rev. Beckwith of Kawaiahao Church.

The Masonic brethren then filed in slow procession about the bier; surrounding it, they stood in silence of regard and prayer. Then each member placed a sprig of green pine upon the casket as a final token of grief and farewell.

The members of the royal family were left alone for fifteen minutes behind closed doors in the recesses of the tomb. Kapiolani's sobbing verged on hysteria and she had to be raised by her lady-in-waiting and Liliuokalani from the casket upon which she had thrown herself to leave "my chief . . . my king . . . my love . . . I am yours and you are mine."

No doubt Liliuokalani remembered the nine days and nights during which Emma had loosed her grief upon the caskets of her son and husband. Now even grief was tempered and governed by the new ways of Christianity—yet had not Jesus wept at the tomb of Lazarus?

The royal family emerged and the guns of the military escort fired the final salute of three volleys fired above the grave. The funeral procession began its return.

And only now did Liliuokalani feel she was Queen of Hawaii—

Hawaii's first ruling queen. Hawaii's last monarch. The future withholds its vision until we can bear its icy fingers.

Long live the Queen!

A few days later Admiral Brown, after quietly paying his respects to the royal family, returned to his ship. There he was greeted by hundreds of Hawaiians who wished to show their gratitude for his kindness to their former king. Queen Liliuokalani had declared the day of the *Charleston's* departure one of appreciation. The Hawaiian people were allowed to go aboard the ship with their gifts.

Men, women and children came with an *aloha* memento dear to them: an old-fashioned spear, a calabash filled with poi, fruit, or fish, shells, necklaces, tapa—all telling of their love and gratitude—from the *mana* of each flowed his *aloha*.

This was on February 17, 1891; on March 6, 1891, Admiral Brown aboard the *Charleston* from San Francisco wrote to John L. Stevens, the American Minister, thanking him for his letter of the 23rd of February, and saying: "It looks to me as if Her Majesty should be taught a lesson which will do her good."[6] He went on to assure Stevens that a properly informed commander would have his ship in the Honolulu Harbor.

San Francisco Chronicle reported an interview with a "Mrs. Dr. Buli-King" of Hawaii, on January 31, 1891, that the new queen was not popular, did not get along well with her brother, had joined a band who were having the *kahunas* pray him to death.

Mrs. Dr. Buli-King ended her interview of arsenic with the sugar sweet words that she had been asked to stay for the festivities had the king lived and been assured "by the Princess [she] would be invited to the ball."

Such was the *aloha* of the foreigners toward the new queen.

PART V
Queen Liliuokalani

1891-1896

QUEEN LILIUOKALANI

CHAPTER 1

The New Queen

❦ 1 ❦

As she succeeded to the throne as the Queen of Hawaii in 1891, Lili-uokalani was described by Hawaiian and American papers as "well-educated," "tactful," a woman of "state craft," and even "handsome." She was without doubt the best educated woman in Hawaii, who had grown up in two cultures. As a missionary Christian, she was thoroughly approved of by her opponents who constantly sought her services in presenting church pageants and giving monies for church activities. She was the only member of the royal family since Kamehameha IV who had consistently and actively remained a member of the Kawaiahao Church. Yet her interests were broad and she contributed her time, services, and monies to the Catholic, Mormon, Episcopalian and other Protestant denominational activities. She commented that while the Kamehamehas tended to be "Protestants," she and Kalakaua believed all religions had their "rights" and were entitled to equal treatment and opportunities.

On the other hand she was a Hawaiian by blood and roots. If she loved anyone or anything unreservedly, it was the Hawaiian people. Yet strangely, she was not nationalistic to the exclusion of other peoples. It was *customs* she hoped to preserve. In that misunderstood desire lay the seeds of her destruction.

She was to her people *hanai*—the mother of her people—as no other Hawaiian ruler had been, for *hanai* was a term which usually referred to motherhood, not fatherhood, so a king was *alii moi* (highest chief-king), not "father." To her they were indeed her children; she was *moi wahine* in a basically matriarchal society. Ralph S. Kuykendall wrote: "The kindly humanitarian side of Liliuokalani's character is shown in her interest in the welfare of the humbler Hawaiians, especially in the proper training of native girls."[1]

In 1891 all the Hawaiians did not speak English—not even the Queen

Dowager Kapiolani; few of the *haole* spoke Hawaiian, and practically none understood the old *alii* language. The semantic breach was enormous. Liliuokalani from her early twenties had been aware that the use of the two languages caused a barrier to communication between her people and the foreigners.[2]

Although she was remarkably proficient in English, familiar with French and German, and had some knowledge of Greek and Latin, she said she frequently "thought in her own language."[3]

She recognized the danger of the words frozen into one concept and not allowed to remain fluid. In that way also she was a woman far ahead of her time.

Socially, she knew the native Hawaiian did not understand wealth as a criterion for position, as the *haole* held it to be. The current *haole* in government were graduates of Herbert Spencer's philosophy that wealth was might. The money "barons" (curious choice of word) were the leaders in America. The native Hawaiian had not the slightest understanding of such a society.

Politically, the Hawaiians preferred their *alii,* their king, as was proved when revolutionist Robert Wilcox, by merely saying he was acting on the king's behalf, was exonerated from all wrong by a native jury in 1889. From "creation" the Hawaiians had needed leaders.

The *Kumulipo*[4] told that out of the vast darkness rose the world and from the depths of the ocean came life in an orderly fashion, culminating in man. The greatest hero, the highest man, was the chief and because of his greatness he had to be a "god." From his "godly greatness" descended other chiefs of such lineage.[5]

Religiously, many Hawaiians held to the old *kahuna* beliefs of healing. In 1886 the *kahuna* had been legalized to practice medicine. But their medical practice was not restricted to herbs and foods; it involved "mental practice" and mental malpractice. It is worthy to note that with the *kahuna* (good) who opposed the *kahuna-ana-ana* (evil) there was a practical difference. The *kahuna-ana-ana* could be defeated by the *kahuna* because the former believed in the all-power of evil, and the latter believed that good could overcome evil. The *kahuna-ana-ana* had to possess a material belonging (hair, fingernail, piece of clothing) of his victim, but the *kahuna* needed no material possession; he went straight to his God to annul the evil belief and heal the patient. The Christian *kahuna,* of whom there were now many, made an easy transition to *one* God multiform in office but one in essence, from the many named gods performing various duties.[6] They made in many instances a leap over the prosaic doctrinal *haole* religions to a metaphysical and mystical oneness beyond doctrinal thoughts and words that fitted well into the fluid Hawaiian language.

This religious attitude fitted naturally with the ideologies of the past, the *mana* within flowing outward to the good of all who were receptive or in need in the *aloha*.

Liliuokalani was fully cognizant of what the Hawaiians believed to be true; she partook of its more mystical principles as her diary so often testified: "... in the stillness is the One whose presence I feel." "The better the day the better the deed"—Hawaiian oriented to the natural beauty surrounding one, a good day could bring forth a good deed. "I am sad . . . yet why—surrounded by beauty and flowers and sunshine." The goodness in nature was to be absorbed into the goodness of man to be a part of Oneness of God, man and nature. The Hawaiians had no division between the land, the sea, the sky—all were one and included man, rocks, trees, birds, animals—all fauna and flora.[7]

⚹ 2 ⚹

Liliuokalani was not a woman unaware of what was happening in her country. Kalakaua, no doubt anticipating the possibility of his own death, had taken her into his confidence.[8] A letter from Volney Ashford, whom the *haole* members of the government had driven out of the country just as they had Gibson, was precious to her; Volney had written that King Kalakaua had met in 1887 the members of the opposition who were demanding the Bayonet Constitution, with dignity, aplomb, and his usual graciousness, not with fear or cowardice. He had listened to them attentively but "with a thunder-cloud over his head."[9] Then as he saw no other way out he had signed *their* constitution—a constitution made up by a small group of foreigners headed by Lorrin A. Thurston—he had signed with, Ashford said, "dignity." Although it was a constitution that totally deprived him of his powers as a reigning king.

Kalakaua had also told her a disturbing story, that their grandfather Kamanawa, who had called young David to him before he had been hanged in 1842, had had a purpose. A high chief did not call his five-year-old grandson to him at a time like that for no reason: Kamanawa had told him that Liliha, a great prophetess, had seen in a vision that the Kamehameha line would die out; there would be no successors after Kinau's children ceased to rule. The prophecy had come true. But there was a more ominous one: The Kalakaua's (Keawe-a-Heule) line would succeed, but through them Hawaii would be lost to foreigners.

He had nearly lost the throne in 1887 and only saved it by giving in to the "*haole* greed." Inasmuch as the *haole* only wanted material prosperity, he would try once more to gain a more equitable tariff for them with the United States—then perhaps there would be peace.

It was these last words that caused Liliuokalani to write in her *Story:*

> If ever there was a man who was pure in spirit, if ever there was a mortal who had perfect charity, he was that man. In spite of all the revilings uttered against him, he never once opened his lips to speak against another, whomsoever it might be.
>
> So the King went cheerfully and patiently to work for the cause of those who had been and were his enemies. He sacrificed himself in the interests of the very people who had done him so much wrong, and given him such constant suffering. With an ever-forgiving heart he forgot his own sorrows, set aside all feelings of animosity, and to the last breath of his life he did all that lay in his power for those who had abused and injured him.[10]

He warned her against Robert Wilcox and J.E. Bush, although of some Hawaiian blood they had been indoctrinated into *haole* desire for acquisition of wealth and power. Wilcox was a revolutionist, an activist with little knowledge, and Bush was a follower of less knowledge of the damage the two were causing. They acted largely out of personal spite and greed for power, but they didn't have the discipline nor technique of the *haole*. Yet they plowed the ground for the overthrow.

Lorrin Thurston in one of his vituperative interviews with the *Washington Star* said in 1893 Liliuokalani was "pig-headed, stubborn, stupid . . . tricky . . . and totally without knowledge that there was trouble in the country."

Liliuokalani was not without such knowledge, but she approached her new position carefully and diplomatically. Before she could make one political appointment, she was, as has been seen, warned by her ministers and cabinet that such action would cause trouble. But beyond her ministers there was another dangerous man.

While all the foreign diplomats congratulated her and wished her well, and congratulations came from all over the world,[11] one man took it upon himself to, in her words, "scold her." Couched in the language of diplomacy Minister John L. Stevens laid down the rules:

The minister of the United States expresses his earnest opinion that your majesty has taken firm resolution to aid in making your reign a strictly constitutional reign, to maintain the constitutional right of your ministers to administer the laws, and always to acknowledge their responsibility to the Legislature in the performance of their sworn obligations. In the wish thus to respect the supreme authority of the Constitution and the Laws, Your Majesty places yourself in the exalted rank of the best Sovereigncy of the world and thus will avoid embarrassments and perplexities of countries not blessed with free and enlightened Constitutions.[12]

Stevens then wrote to United States Secretary of State Blaine:

The queen was surrounded by some of the worst elements in the country, persons of native and foreign birth . . . [the Queen] is trying to . . . get a Cabinet composed of her tools—she is well known to be much more stubborn in character than her brother . . . She will have to finally yield and place herself in the hands of the conservative and respectable men of the country as the only way to retain her throne.[13]

Liliuokalani not only objected to Stevens' harangue but also his manner: "He sat before me in a way no gentleman sits before a lady and certainly not a queen."

Judge Dole was finally appealed to and upheld the right of the queen to dismiss the cabinet: Under the 1887 constitution the king had no right to dismiss his ministers but at the decease of the king the new monarch did have the right to ask for their portfolios.

Liliuokalani's new cabinet did not change too radically: Charles N. Spencer was reappointed as Minister of Interior; Herman H. Widemann, a highly respected but elderly German whose wife was Hawaiian, Minister of Finance; William Austin Whiting, Attorney General, an American by birth and a lawyer of good-standing in the community. Even Samuel Parker, Minister of Foreign Affairs, later to come under general calumny, was a part-Hawaiian rancher from the big island, who had had legislative experience. John A. Stevens wrote of him: "Although a general favorite among the Hawaiians, very friendly to the United States."

The queen's next act was to proclaim her niece Kaiulani heir-apparent on March 9, 1891. Kaiulani was at the time in England studying. She was fifteen years old, the daughter of Liliuokalani's sister, Likelike, and Archibald Cleghorn.

Liliuokalani then conferred upon her husband John Owen Dominis the rank and privilege of "His Royal Highness the Prince Consort."

She also reappointed most of the old privy council members replacing only George MacFarlane with James Robertson as a new Chamberlain, and appointing Charles B. Wilson her new Marshal.

It was the last appointment that was to cause her the most trouble. Robert Wilcox, who had hoped to be the new Marshal, was livid. However, in view of Wilcox's past it was most unlikely that Liliuokalani would have chosen him to be close to her as her Marshal would naturally be. C.B. Wilson had been her trusted friend over many years and she certainly needed someone to trust at the time.

Her name had already, unfortunately been romantically linked with Wilson, but not a shred of evidence could ever be brought forth that he was anything but possibly an over-attentive admirer. He was married to Kitty Townsend, a girl who grew up in the Princess' home, and whose mother was a close friend to Liliuokalani. Later, C.B. Wilson's wife voluntarily went into prison with her as her attendant. Dr. Trouseau, who was as close as anyone could be to the Kalakaua-Liliuokalani household, categorically stated a romantic attachment between Wilson and the queen was absurd.[14]

Thus Queen Liliuokalani began her reign with accolades in the newspapers. She was hailed as "brilliant," "well-educated," "gracious," "moral," "wise," and even beautiful.

Charles Reed Bishop, who had known her from childhood, although he bore her no great affection, wrote in a letter, March 5, 1891:

> Although you have not asked for advice—I regard the moral influence which you can exert upon the community, and especially upon your race as much more important [than] anything you can do in politics or business of the country . . . In politics and routine of the Government the Ministers will have the responsibility, annoyances and blame—and usually very little praise. Let them have them, and do not worry yourself about them. You will live longer and happier and be more popular by not trying to do too much.[15]

❦ 3 ❦

The queen in the spring and summer of 1891 began her tour of the islands. Ida Pope wrote: "Her Majesty is just coming out of mourning [for her brother] (April 26, 1891) and like a wise sovereign, as she is, she intends making a tour of the islands. She desires the favor of her subjects and what better way to inspire them than to give them a glimpse of her most gracious self? Her first visit was to Molokai."

Liliuokalani was the first reigning monarch to visit the leper colony, and she was looked upon with awe, respect, and some fear, for leprosy was still a dreaded disease, and considered by some to be instantly contagious.

Many of her invited party did not wish to go. However, Ida Pope desired an invitation which she received from the queen, but was almost stopped by the President of the Board of Health. However, to Miss Pope's amusement and the president's chagrin, after his interview with "Her Majesty," he was sent personally to Miss Pope with the proper permits.

Ida Pope had a special relationship with the queen through her *hanai* daughter, Lydia Aholo. Just before leaving for the Jubilee in England, Liliuokalani had asked her to give Lydia "special attention," and Miss Pope had been more than willing to do so.

The trip to Molokai, which was later so severely criticized by the press—the press that also during the overthrow wrote of the "horrible, inhuman conditions of the lepers"—is best revealed in Miss Pope's own words. Ida Pope, it will be seen, was not blind to faults nor completely Hawaiian-oriented, but she was an honest reporter to her family:

> We went on the Likelike. It was to go at six Sunday evening April 26 . . . Everything was conducted in a quiet orderly manner.
>
> Miss Hoppin and I went to the wharf a few minutes before six boarded the boat and endeavored to secure a berth. I knew I should be sick and must have a place to lie down. Natives swarmed everywhere. Each one had his own bed—a piece of matting, blankets and pillows. Literally they took up their beds and walked. I began to feel dubious but Miss Hoppin said we would find a place and through the kindness of Prof. [Henry] Berger we secured comfortable places.
>
> The Queen did not come aboard until half past nine and we did not start until ten. I was sick most of the night, but it was not to be wondered at when there were natives talking and tobacco smoke thick enough to cut with a knife. There were three hundred and forty on the ship and it is a small inter-island steamer.
>
> The Queen slept on the deck on a rug. She was accompanied by her nephew, Prince — (his name is unpronounceable and unspellable) [Kalanianaole], Hon. Samuel Parker, Minister of Foreign Affairs, and her maids . . . We reached Molokai at six Monday

morning—anchored in the harbor. There is no wharf and we had
to be landed in row boats. In your mind's eye, Horatio, imagine me
clambering down the side of the Likelike, clutching the rope with one
hand and frantically holding on to my permit with the other. When
we reached the landing we were pulled up over the rocks by two
stalwart natives. The leper settlement that is one of theirs is clustered
about the landing. The lepers were at the landing. An arch was erected at the foot of the landing and twined with ropes of fern—and
branches of ti leaves. On the arch were these words—"Aloha ika
moi wahine" (Love to our Queen).

Prof. Berger escorted us to a place a little distance from the crowd
where we could see the Queen land. She came in the last boat. It was
a scene that baffles description. It seemed to me I was walking in a
charmed house.

When Her Majesty landed the leper band played "Hawaii Ponoi"
(national air) and greeted her with a wail. It sounded to me like the
soughing of the wind on a lonely night, but it is a cry of welcome
with the natives.

The meeting of the lepers with their friends was most pitiful. Husbands and wives—fathers, mothers, brothers and sisters that had not
met for years. They scattered about in little groups embracing each
other, sobbing and crying.

I felt like an intruder, as though I had no right to witness such a
scene.

The Queen has been criticized for taking the friends of the lepers
to Molokai. The natives have no fears of the disease and they kissed
diseased lips and cheeks without a shudder. But had we father,
mother, sister or brother there we would not do the same. If there
is ought to cure the hurt of this people I wish it would come to them
right speedily. They are such lovable gentle people but at the present
death rate they will be extinct in half a century.

The Hawaiian government should be held up as a model to all
nations—in at least one particular—and that is in her care of her
lepers. Molokai is wonderfully beautiful—but a prison shut in on
one side by the sea and on the other by a wall 1500 ft. high—not a
barren wall but a wall covered by the softest green verdure leading
into wooded vales where the pandau trees and guava bushes abound.

There is only one trail over this wall—steep and precipitous. None
but the strong ever attempt to scale it. They have fine horses and
must enjoy them. They are very fond of riding and are never so
happy as when in the saddle.

White poppies meet one's eye at every turn. There are not many trees in Kalapapa. In this village at the landing numbers have been planted, but at times the wind is too strong for them to thrive.

The Queen was taken to the Pres's house, where she addressed her people. The address was given in native tongue so Miss Hoppin and I did not go to hear it. We strolled about in search of the Bishop Home [for orphaned girls]. We had a letter for one of the little girls, Ella Bridges. She was in the Seminary three years ago. Her sister is with us now.

We went into the church yard and wandered about until we met a priest who directed us to the Sisters' Cottage. The Sisters have charge of the Girls' School at Kalapapa. The Mother Superior greeted us most cordially and we were refreshed with coffee and delicious bread and butter.

The cottage where the Sisters live is plain but neatly furnished, and everything about the premises is immaculate. The Mother Superior gathered some roses from her garden and asked us to arrange and tie them with a broad white ribbon which she gave us for that purpose. The bouquet was for the Queen so we "lay to" and arranged it "our prettiest."

There is no ice manufactured on Molokai and the water was so warm. Just before we started on our tour of investigation the Mother made us a delicious drink of acid phosphate. I wish I could write a eulogy of the Sisters. They are gentle, refined and elegant in appearance. We were welcomed as though we were of their own flesh and blood. I never experienced a more gracious hospitality . . .

They took us to the Bishop House. The school was not in session but we found Ella Bridges on the verandah and delivered the letter we had for her. She is a bright looking girl and has no sores. Her left hand is diseased—partially paralyzed. A number of the school children were on the verandah. They all—with the exception of Ella—showed marked evidence of the disease—faces swollen in bunches, many faces distorted and these looked like caricatures.

We went into the dormitories. They are small cottages with new beds in each, all neat and comfortable. In one dormitory, three patients were in bed. One—the Sisters told us—had been dying for several days. One of the Sisters went up and spoke to her. She seemed oblivious to all her surroundings. There was an unearthly pallor on her face. Her lips were parted and her great black eyes were looking into the Great Beyond.

At the foot of her bed was seated a little girl with one of her feet bandaged. The other one presented a horrible sight, swollen twice its natural size and of a bright purplish color. A sister said she had poulticed the foot and tried numerous remedies with no avail. Is it not wonderful that even in the most hopeless cases they do not give up trying to do something for them?

Have I ever written you about Margaret Powers? She is the brightest girl in the Seminary. Her mother and sister are lepers and live on Molokai. We were anxious to see them and found that they were living at Kalawao, three miles away. We could have had horses to ride, but I never rode cavalier fashion and no side saddles were to be had. So Miss H— and I walked. There is a good road between the villages. A gentle breeze was stirring, and I quite enjoyed the walk. The views were entrancing. Little hollows in the mountain looked so cool and inviting. I turned many times to look at the sapphire sea. It was dotted with white caps and the foaming spray dashed high on the rocks. It was a sight fit for the gods. I do not wonder that the natives love these purple spheres.

All along the way are cottages where families live. They were all out and greeted us with "Aloha nui." We met many horsemen who doffed their hats and smiled a greeting. I did not see an angry look or hear an unkind word, all the livelong day.

As we neared Kalawao we noted a neat cottage that had rose geraniums clambering over a window and a bed of flaming scarlet geraniums at the doorstep. We went in and found the house occupied by a white man. He was a leper . . . He did not know where Mrs. Powers lived but directed us to a house across the road. We crossed over and found it was the home of Mrs. Powers and her daughter, Emma. Such a family group! Emma was at one time one of the prettiest girls on the island. She is married to a leper and has a babe a week old. Both her husband and herself have the disease in a very bad form. Emma's face is swollen and covered with bunches as large as a hickory nut. She has the softest black eyes and pearly teeth and uses good English.

I felt so sorry for the mother. She was much affected when we told her we were from *Kawaiahoa* [Seminary]. Her grief was so silent and she looked so sad that my heart ached for her. A woman with her little boy was sitting on the verandah and holding the babe and fondling it, caressing it as though it were her own.

Emma with the brightest of smiles said the woman was her [Emma's] husband's first wife and the little boy her [Emma's] son. It was not a scene to inspire Tennyson to write a second *Enoch Arden*. There was no poetry in it, but an awful reality—an instance that God does surely punish those who transgress.

If this Hawaiian people would but mend their morals this terrible question of leprosy would be nearer its solution.

I tried not to look shocked but I was sick to my very soul. I think for about five minutes I was a good Presbyterian and believed in total depravity. It is not so that we are all born free and equal.

When I looked into the face of that little babe and thought of its possible future I felt like snatching it away. It looked so sweet and innocent—just like other babies—and what will it grow up to be in such a household where no moral right is recognized? I have not the same faith in the American Constitution that I once had. I think the clause about equality and freedom ought to be stricken out.

After leaving the Powers cottage we went on to the village of Kalawao and stopped at *Father Damien's grave*. We went into his church. Father Damien died a leper. He has been much criticised. He is said to have been unclean in his habits and morally impure, but this is but hearsay and he has gone to be judged by a more righteous judge than we are. He has been eulogized the world over and a statue is to be erected on Molokai to his memory. His grave is not marked by any stone but it is covered with flowers and rests in the shade of a pandanu tree . . .

We were all on board the steamer at five. We reached Honolulu at one in the morning of Tuesday, April 28, and have been talking Molokai ever since.[16]

The queen's tour was much more rigorous than Ida Pope's. Although she visited the same official places she did not pursue the journey with personal gratification but with the demands of state.

The "greeting" that Ida Pope avoided was simple and short: It was translated and read by Sam Parker:

My love to you all. Our visit is a mission full of sorrow. You are here away from your friends and birthplace. This is the most dreadful of all diseases which continually gnaws at the very vitality of our nation's life. But we have not given up the idea of finding a remedy for its cure. It is on account of this longing desire ever present in her heart to pay you her first visit among her people . . .

Other speeches were given by members of her party, encouraging the lepers that every effort was being made to find a cure: that "Dr. Matthew Makalua, a true Hawaiian is at present in England, studying medical sciences."

The Royal Hawaiian Band played between the speeches.

Only one political note was sounded, and that interestingly enough by a Hawaiian who was later to ally himself with Bush and Wilcox. The Honorable Joseph Nawahi, the last speaker said: "She ('our beloved queen') deeply grieves your afflictions. Your sorrows are hers, and your joys are hers, for a Queen is powerless without a people to rule over. Therefore let us unite in upholding her throne, for there are yet hopes for your tears."

Had Liliuokalani witnessed the scene at the Powers' home of a woman caressing the child of another woman, who was now married to her husband, she would not have shuddered as Ida Pope did, but would have considered the scene beautiful and full of *Aloha-hanai*.

Although John did not accompany her to Molokai, he did join her to visit Maui, where it was said "never a more lavish reception had been seen." The royal party was greeted by "all classes of people colorfully dressed to welcome the new Queen." Chinese and Japanese lanterns lighted the way, while hundreds of natives lined the walk-way. Luaus were given throughout the island and in the evening the queen attended the Catholic Church. The next day she was requested to address the children of the Austin's school. Here her words rang with her own philosophy:

"Dear Children . . . Remember the writing on your school wall 'Knowledge is power,' but remember also that without knowledge power is nothing. It follows that the next text is necessary to gain knowledge: 'Obey your teachers'."[17]

At the departure the small boat that was to take the party to the larger vessel slipped its moorings and Mr. Austin moved hastily to assist the queen. However several Hawaiian women moving more eagerly pushed Austin into the water. The queen safe in the boat "laughed the loudest." Often she had seen the *haole* miss the boat, but never before one pushed into the water by the women. She hoped it was prophetic.

On the return from Maui the party was greeted by a torchlight parade and John Dominis surprised her by having had built at Waialua a large wooden *lanai*, large enough to accommodate a hundred and fifty people.

Liliuokalani was deeply grateful. It seems that after Mrs. Dominis' death some restraint had dropped from between them. In justice to Dominis it might also be added that he now had monies he'd never had before, and John was ever-burdened with a New England concept of money.

At Kauai the queen was hailed with "universal enthusiasm." "Her generous and gracious demeanor—her fine sense that the kingdom is for her people—was evident." Three hundred natives lined the sides. Her *Story* interestingly enough relates mostly the hospitality of the missionary families and apparently one of her "most genial hosts" was W.H. Rice and family. Rice had been a bitter enemy of Gibson and later an active mover in the overthrow of the monarchy.[18]

Interesting shifts in policy can be seen in Liliuokalani's royal island visits from those of former monarchs. In the past the vessel was the monarch's and all those on board were the king's guests. Liliuokalani boarded a commercial vessel, and because of the strict health regulations for Molokai invitations and permits had to be granted. But it has been seen that Liliuokalani "invited" the natives who had relatives on the island, not those merely seeking royal privileges.

Her trip to Hawaii, the island she loved best, was aboard a commercial vessel and was almost insignificantly mentioned by Sanford Ballard Dole who was aboard going on a business trip to Hawaii.

> The Queen and Prince Consort with a small party and the band were aboard. At Mahukona they landed and were well received by something of a crowd, and the landing prettily decorated, and a royal salute of Chinese bombs. They went up to Kohala on the train where there was a big luau, and returned to Mahukona after dark . . .
>
> Hamokua and Hilo by daylight and close to the shore and a beautiful view of the coast with its multitudinous waterfalls, and its beautiful back country stretching away to the mountains. The sea was smooth and the day fine. Reached the landing between 1 and 2 P.M. A double canoe canopied with ferns came out to take the Queen ashore and a large crowd of people were at the beach. The next day, Friday there was a big luau in the court house yard at which 800 persons sat down at once. In the evening there was a ball in the court room—The queen and a large party drove up to the end of the new volcano road and had a picnic at Olaa. In the evening there was ice cream and the band at the "palace"—as John Baker's house[19] where the queen stays is called. The royal party leave this afternoon in the Kinau for Kau.[20]

❧ 4 ❧

Two angry men opened their "fire" upon the queen in their Hawaiian language newspaper[21] almost immediately upon her return.

J.E. Bush and Robert W. Wilcox, consumed with fury of having had no political appointments, railed that she favored "missionaries," "sugar barons" and of course the "queen's pets."

Bush wrote: "Her majesty means well but she unfortunately is a woman and in a position never ordained from the creation for other than a man, or one of masculine nature."

Liliuokalani was furious and in a moment of anger said she should send Wilson to "smash it [the presses] to pieces." Wilson unfortunately passed the information to Robertson[22] and thus the rumor of the queen's "ungovernable temper" began. Had Liliuokalani truly meant to "smash the presses," she would have done so, but there was nothing violent in her nature to carry out the anger and fury of her words. Actually, she felt no real apprehension against Wilcox and Bush. Wilcox she had known from his childhood; she had befriended him and his wife; she had watched his abortive 1889 revolution, she no doubt saw him as a child trying to play a grown-up's game.

J.E. Bush she recognized as having been double-dealing with Kalakaua. She had warned Kalakaua, who was totally blind to Bush's deceit. Bush's first wife had cared for her *hanai* sons, Kaipo and Aimoku, until they were six and seven.

One day during a surprise visit to Mrs. Bush, Liliuokalani had discovered the boys' rooms "totally unfit"[23]—dirty, unkempt, beds unmade, linens in need of washing. Then Princess Liliuokalani had made a sudden and final decision. The boys were to be moved out immediately; she brooked no argument from Mrs. Bush, because the boys had long been complaining. But now she saw for herself the conditions.

The boys stayed for a few months at Waikiki and then after Mrs. Dominis' death moved to Washington Place. They were later placed in the home of Carrie Bush, a relative by marriage to J.E. Bush.

Liliuokalani did not like Wilcox or Bush, but she was not afraid of them. She did not see that they could become the catalyst in a revolt against the monarchy.

Liliuokalani as a woman had an unknown champion who gave speeches to women throughout Honolulu exhorting them to "use their rights— women's rights—to stand by a great queen who stood in the highest position a woman could hold." The notes of the speeches are undated and unsigned[24] but there is little doubt their dates correspond to the attacks of Bush and Wilcox.

The writer went on to plead that "American suffrage had failed— although the women *had* the right to vote, they were not using it. Would the same happen in Hawaii—would the women fail to stand behind their queen?"

The same did happen. The matriarchal society of Kaahumanu, and even the reverence for Queen Emma, was gone. Princess Liliuokalani's struggle for women's rights in her attempting to have a college for Hawaiian girls and a bank for women had been only spasmodically supported.

What had happened? First, the pure Hawaiian population was rapidly dying out; the *hapa-haole* Hawaiian of the next generation was divided in its loyalties; and the *haole* population held the most influence.

Secondly, a rift which had begun shortly after Queen Emma's election-defeat to Kalakaua which the geneological trial had widened, resulted in the Hawaiians themselves being influenced by such men as Bush and Wilcox. "Kalakaua had not the 'lineage' to become king." In the same breath, without much thought, Wilcox called out he (Wilcox) was not an "annexationist but for a republic—a plebescite to elect him! Who is to be King?—Wilcox!"

In the midst of the sound and fury of the newspapers, Liliuokalani met again with death. John Owen Dominis died of pneumonia on August 27, 1891 at the age of sixty.

No one had anticipated the suddenness of his death although he had been ill for some time with rheumatism. The queen had had him moved from the cottage on Iolani Palace grounds into Washington Place and had prepared a downstairs bedroom for him so he could again avoid the stairs.

Liliuokalani had made arrangements shortly after she became queen to have a gate constructed in one corner of the palace grounds through which John could come and go at will. He also preferred living in the cottage as it saved his walking up the long koa stairway of the palace, so he said.

The day of his death had been a hot sultry one, and Queen Liliuokalani, who had watched at his bedside for several days, had taken a carriage ride to Waikiki with her Chamberlain, C.B. Wilson. Wilson later said that she had been exceeding nervous and "taut." Her calm that she usually found at Waikiki was absent. She spoke hurriedly to her retainers and paused alone in Hinano Bower where, Wilson later reported, she dropped on her knees and prayed. She returned to the two houses as if in search of someone. Finally she ordered Wilson to find

Kapoli and Mary Purdy (Pahau) and bring them to Washington Place. She had already dispatched Joseph Aea to go to the St. Albans school to have Aimoku and Kaipo also brought to Washington Place.[25]

Liliuokalani returned to Washington Place and was told by Dr. Trouseau that John was exceedingly ill. Major Seaward, a close friend of John, and Sam Parker were already there as were some of the Queen's "young lady friends."[26] She wrote in her *Story:*

> Dr. Trouseau, the physician in charge of the case, soon entered, and after a brief examination said he thought the patient needed rest, and motioned to those who were present that they be excused from the chamber. Accordingly they retired to the veranda, leaving me alone by my husband's bedside . . . I drew near the foot of the bed, and stood where I could easily watch him while he was apparently sleeping. I had been thus standing but a few minutes when, noticing a slight quivering motion pass over his frame, I immediately went to his side, and then hastily called the friends in attendance and summoned the doctor. He examined the patient and said it was all over. Just a few minutes before my husband passed away he made a peculiar motion of his hand which I have seen brethren of the Masonic fraternity use in prayer. It will be noticed that I was entirely alone by the side of my husband when he died; but there have been words of the cruelest import uttered by those who were not there, and could have known nothing of the facts. May they be forgiven for the wrong done to me and to my husband's memory.[27]

The words of "cruelest import" were that John's mistress, Mary Purdy, was at his bedside, holding his hand and sobbing bitterly while the Queen merely looked on. It was true Liliuokalani had sent for both Kapoli and Mary—it was a gesture of old-Hawaii as well as that of a magnanimous woman—but it must be remembered that Mary had often been present with John, Aimoku, and Liliuokalani in carriage rides and visits to Waikiki.[28] However, Kapoli Aimoku refused to come, but Mary was something of a remarkable woman herself for until her death she allowed it to be believed she was Aimoku's mother. She was old Hawaiian; her daughter was born new Hawaiian. It would be interesting to know what Kapoli thought, but there is no further record of her except her signature on a petition sent to the queen in 1892 requesting that she veto the lottery bill.[29] When Liliuokalani wrote her book in 1897, she never mentioned Kapoli, Mary Purdy nor John's son, John Dominis Aimoku.

The children also arrived after his death and it was then Aimoku was told that John was his father, but not Kaipo's. It later led to dissension between them and once, to the consternation of Liliuokalani, Kaipo in the heat of argument called Aimoku a bastard.[30]

Almost two years to the day before John's death Mary Dominis had died, and Liliuokalani must have felt a hope of release for John from his mother's domination. Although it was physically gone, the indoctrination of the beliefs apparently remained, except for the one gesture of the *lanai* at Waialua.

One almost has a feeling that Liliuokalani literally attempted to raise John above himself when she became queen to be *her* royal consort. But it was too late, both because of John's physical condition and his long interment in his mother's influence.

One gesture of Mrs. Dominis' defiance was removed on the day Liliuokalani became queen—the American flag was lowered from Washington Place from where it had flown continuously since 1843, when it had been raised by Com. TenEyck and the house named "Washington Place" so there "would always be a piece of American soil in Hawaii."

Now the Hawaiian flag fluttered on the flagpole of Washington Place as Liliuokalani's mind and heart fluttered, folded and waved in the winds of the past.

John Dominis lay-in-state until September 6, 1891. Queen Liliuokalani's first birthday as queen was marked with one word: "gloomy." She requested that no celebration be held.

The intervening days had been painfully hot. A preliminary viewing was held for the "notables of the Kingdom—Princes, Judges, members of the Privy Council, representatives of friendly states." The coffin had been placed in the throne room "on a raised foundation covered below by a cloth of blue satin and above by a rich yellow robe. Over the coffin was a mantle of broad alternate bands of red and yellow feathers. The coffin was of Kou and Koa wood, with the Hawaiian Coat of Arms surmounted by a crown at the top, and at the bottom, the Masonic emblem."

> At 12:40 Her Majesty entered the throne room . . . All rose while the Queen, clothed in deep mourning, proceeded to the head of the bier and took her place there, one of the princes on her left hand and the other on her right . . .
>
> The Rev. Dr. Beckwith read from the Bible followed by a prayer . . . The queen and her party withdrew, followed by the others. After the firing of guns the procession wended its slow way along King Street, up Nuuanu Avenue to the Mausoleum.

Crowds of people thronged the streets. There was only one difference —there was no wailing. At the mausoleum the services followed those of Kalakaua's and the coffin was placed next to Kalakaua's. A short service was held followed by the concluding Masonic Ceremony. Three volleys were fired by the household troops. Then Liliuokalani was left alone for fifteen minutes in the mausoleum.

Grief, remorse, the intricate ambiguities attending the death of a loved one raged in her. Things said, unsaid, things done, undone. Then, as all through her life, she drew her strength from the Bible ". . . If it is the Father's will in heaven, I must submit, for the Bible teaches us 'he doeth all things well' . . ."[31]

She emerged, her face hidden in a black veil and her hat lowered; the doors were closed and the funeral party led by the Royal Hawaiian Band returned to Honolulu.

¥ 5 ¥

Two days after John Dominis' death on August 31, 1891, Liliuokalani had appointed to the Privy Council: H.R.H. Prince David Kawananakoa, Hon. Sanford Ballard Dole, George C. Beckley, Abraham Fernandez, D.P.R. Isenberg, and John Richardson.[32]

By the fall of 1891 Liliuokalani was making every possible effort to secure a stable cooperative government. She had learned from Kalakaua that he had sold most of the *alii* lands that might have eventually become hers as well as much of the remaining crown lands that had come to the crown in 1874. These had been auctioned off in 1890 and the monies had been used to pay Kalakaua's personal debts as well as some he had incurred to the country.

Liliuokalani had entered her reign at a most inauspicious moment. Because of the United States' McKinley Tarriff Bill, the country was in a state of depression. The crown and government monies had had heavy drains placed on them.

The queen therefore began her reign with a policy of economy and retrenchment. She began by proposing to reduce the royal appropriations. The appropriations for 1890-1892 (appropriations were made for two-year periods) had already been considerably curtailed: The king was to receive $40,000; the queen $10,000; Princess Liliuokalani $10,000; Kaiulani $4,800; ministers, $10,000; John O. Dominis, a permanent settlement of $3,600; household expenses stood at $12,000. She planned to reduce her own appropriation as queen to $30,000; cancelled Queen Kapiolani's in that she inherited from Kalakaua's personal *alii* lands and had wealth in her own right. This action began a period of exceeding coolness between the once close friends and sisters-in-law. John O. Dominis' salary was halted by his death and while Archibald Cleghorn was appointed Governor of Oahu his monetary compensation was minimal, $2,000 yearly. Princess Kaiulani's appropriation as heir-apparent was increased to $8,000 ($2,000 less than Liliuokalani's as heir-apparent). The ministers were greatly disturbed by the rumor that the queen was suggesting a cut of $2,000 for them, Thrum wrote in his "notes."[33]

Business, Thrum reported publicly, was "generally good." The proposed government retrenchment program had apparently given an impetus to business, despite the sugar situation.

One of Liliuokalani's first acts was to direct the Crown Land Commissioner to "set aside choice sections of crown lands for homestead subdivision in 10 acre lots on a 30 years term for lease and cultivation; first 5 years to be rent free, balance at nominal yearly rent of $1.00 per acre."[34] These were set aside primarily for Hawaiians.

Thrum also wrote factually of two events which would become disasterous to the queen: "At this writing politics are in the ascendent, preparatory to the coming elections, February, next . . . Commission was to take steps for participation in World's Columbian Exposition in 1893 at Chicago invited by the United States."

First and foremost Liliuokalani believed in the old Hawaiian adage that the king must do the will of his people. Therefore, she sent representatives among the native population to ask what their wishes were—just as Kamehameha V had done—and the answer was the same. The "people" wanted a strong monarchial form of government, one they could understand as they did the *alii,* and trust as they always had their "leaders" who were high chiefs. They wanted a voice in government, yes, but not as the *haole* had determined it by the Bayonet Constitution, determined by "much money and property."

By the end of 1891 there could be little doubt what the Hawaiian people themselves wished: A strong monarchy, a stronger voice for themselves in government through leadership, and *no* annexation to a foreign power.

There were two warring political parties in Hawaii in 1891; the National Reform and the Reform. The National Reform supported the monarchy; the Reform leaned toward annexation. From both would come a troublesome third party called the Liberal.

By the end of 1891, Liliuokalani had been lulled into a false sense of security by her own naiveté, her faith in her people—and her trust in the United States Government.

Mott-Smith, the Hawaii Minister to the United States, wrote the Minister of Foreign Affairs Parker that Secretary of State Blaine

> assures me that the United States are ready to support the Queen in her authority and in the preservation of internal order with the view that our native Sovereigns and our native government should stand in the front as long as possible. You may rest assured that the United States will not interfere in our affairs except by the desire of the Queen, in times of pilikia (trouble), and then only to withdraw when order shall have been restored. I want you to understand this, for it is a guarantee, that if we cannot head off any emeute or violence of home demagogues, . . . Her Majesty can have the help of the United States for the asking and that without prejudice to her rights. . . .[35]

What was not within the purview of Liliuokalani's political sphere was that individual men defy governments, men double-deal, and hatred of a position can lead illogically to hatred of the person who holds the position.

CHAPTER 2

The Longest Legislature

❧ 1 ❧

In 1892 Liliuokalani faced the crucial moment of her political life. Kalakaua's last advice to her had been that she return the control of the government to the terms of the 1864 Constitution, or Hawaii would be forever lost to the Hawaiians as a people.

But like most good counsel, it was hedged about with admonitions that would make the goal almost impossible to obtain. He warned that such results could only be achieved through legislative sanctions. Although he had tried himself, for nearly two years, to hold a constitutional convention to bring about a change within the organic law and had failed, he insisted that his sister should take the same path.

Liliuokalani was not without political acumen. After a year of establishing herself in the hearts of her people, and carefully handling the *haole* population by a program of retrenchment, she too introduced the idea of a constitutional convention.

The convention was as effectively forestalled as it had been under her brother's rule. Even in 1891 it was becoming evident that no change would be tolerated in the Bayonet Constitution, by which a small portion of *haole* had, without legislative, ministerial, nor populace approval, deprived King Kalakaua of most of his power.

The destruction, by the *haole,* of the matriarchal society of Old Hawaii had also been conclusive. No woman had held any position of political importance for nearly fifty years, not from the time of Liliuokalani's mother, who had served on Kamehameha III's privy council along with Liliuokalani's *hanai* mother, Konia, in 1843. Although Victoria had succeeded as *kuhina nui* (premier) under Kamehameha V, she had done so in name only.

Liliuokalani was looked upon by the *haole* population and some of the *hapa-haole* (Wilcox-Bush faction), by the mere fact of being a woman, as unsuitable for any position of political importance—and certainly not that of a ruling queen. Under the thin veneer of "she may reign but not rule," was also the rock-ribbed American antagonism toward royalty.

The Hawaiians themselves were monarchial and matriarchial in their reverence for their queens. Liliuokalani was well aware that she stood at the focal point of old Hawaiian traditions, customs, desires, and above all, their *need* of a strong monarchy. The Hawaiian people as a race, she realized, could not survive under any leadership less than that. Their way of life had been too radically and too quickly changed for them to cope with further change. They were at a breaking point.

Liliuokalani had none of her brother's grandiose ideas of being "empress of the Pacific." She merely wanted for her people what Kamehameha The First had advised: "To supply their needs but not increase their wants." As the best educated person in both cultures, she was eminently qualified for Hawaiian leadership; but strange fingers were to play upon her personal and political life. As a result she was to make mistakes, that, had they been made by an elected man, might have been tolerated. Made by a woman, a queen, they were magnified and added substantially to her downfall.

Entries in her diary reveal her personal life as intermingled with the political. She continued her dedication to church work and benevolence. On January 1, 1892, she began the year by giving her famous Liliuokalani clock to Waialua Church.

She continued to socialize with both Hawaiian and *haole* women. Mrs. Kitty Wilson, the wife of Marshal C.B. Wilson, was one of her constant companions. Several times she attended lectures by women who spoke in *haole* homes. At such a lecture, on the French Revolution, given at Mrs. Sanford B. Dole's home, to her intense mortification, she fell asleep. She wrote: "I was so ashamed but I could not help myself . . . After a hard days [sic] work of thinking and excitement, naturally when in a room where everything is still a sense of drowsiness comes over one."[1]

State expenditures as well as personal ones were becoming an increasing problem for her. Reluctantly, she agreed to government monies being spent for the first anniversary celebration of her ascension to the throne. Yet newspaper reports complained that it lacked the "elegance" and "lavishness" of Kalakaua's entertainments, which before they had so vigorously criticized.

One entertainment which she did not stint on was a fancy dress ball for children, at which, interestingly enough, most of the parents were *haole*. "Only the parents of the children and a small number of grown up friends were kindly invited by the queen to enjoy the rare spectacle."[2]

She continued to support the Liliuokalani Educational Society with her own monies, and send Hawaiian children to Kawaiahao Seminary from monies from the modest Dominis Fund, a trust from her husband's estate. She made provisions for her two *hanai* sons to be educated at St. Albans, later Iolani College. Lydia was left, under Ida Pope's careful eye, at Kawaiahao Seminary and later at Kamehameha Schools.

It was not uncommon for her to lend money to private individuals, who were, in one way or another, about to lose their homes in mortgages, held by wealthy *haole,* including Charles R. Bishop.

A constant thorn in her side was her brother-in-law, Archie Cleghorn, who took it upon himself to interfere in personal and political matters, and become particularly cantankerous in questions of protocol.

He made an effort to secure some of the crown lands, which he felt had been illegally sold or confiscated, and even to have some transferred to his daughter, Princess Kaiulani. Liliuokalani wrote in her diary, "I do not think it is a wise thing to do as they [the legislature] tried to take the crown lands away from the king last session and it is risky to stir up the question again. . . . We are just as likely to lose it as Mr. Wideman is a prominent party to turning them over and becoming government land."[3]

Personal aggrandizement was sought by *haole* and *hapa-haole*. Liliuokalani wished to present the Grand Cross of the Order of Kamehameha the Great to Sam Parker. She felt he had been the prime person in keeping the government on "steady keel" during 1891. Archibald Cleghorn and Charles Bishop made themselves a committee of two to prevent the presentation. She wrote in her diary: ". . . The king *has the right* to confer an Order on anyone he likes." She decided not to do so, because of her "respect [for] his [Charles Bishop's] age and connection with his wife's family."[4]

❧ 2 ❧

January 28th, the day of preparation for the celebration of her ascension, Liliuokalani termed "a disagreeable day." There had been a constant harassment by both *haole* and Cleghorn for "place." Cleghorn wished to stand on the dais next to her, a position she said should remain empty until Kaiulani came of age. Cleghorn, she felt, certainly did not "represent his daughter," the heir-apparent, who was in England. She chose for the highest honors in banquet-seating preferential arrangements for the two princes: David Kawananakoa and Kuhio (Jonah) Kalanianaole, of whom she preferred David. He was also the elder. Her choice of the princes was two-fold. If Kaiulani should pre-decease them, they would be regents under a council of regency until they reached their maturity. Secondly, she gave a typical revealing statement of her attitude toward Hawaiians in high or low positions: "they should have pride in themselves."

The day was not unmixed with sadness, for she remembered well the past year—the death of her brother and her husband. She recorded: "It has been a sad year to me."

Outwardly, the day was regarded as a success. From early morning until late afternoon, the queen received callers. From eleven in the morning until midafternoon she received foreign diplomats, government officials and the residents of all the islands. At three o'clock the luau was opened in a "huge lanai in the palace grounds," and in Liliuokalani's hospitable words, "everyone on the ground had something to eat."

❧ 3 ❧

At this point it is necessary to step back a few months to the election day, February 3, 1892, in order to understand the underlying causes of the turmoil that was to continue to exist during the entire legislative year of 1892.

Liliuokalani had been warned by Sam Parker that the Liberals, if not elected, would cause trouble. She called them "the roughs," recognized them as the Wilcox-Bush faction, and dismissed them from her mind as being more verbal than active. Despite their angry threats against her, she felt their Hawaiian-ness would prevail, and no harm would come to her person nor her position from them.

Early in the year it looked as if the Liberals would win through *haole* indifference. Virtually, the whole business community thought night and day about the economic plight in which the United States' McKinley tariff [passed in October, 1890] had placed on Hawaii. The act, by admitting to the United States free of duty all foreign sugars and awarding a two-cents-a-pound bounty to domestic growers, had destroyed the value to Hawaii of the treaty of reciprocity. Hawaiian profits had vanished, and already Honolulu enterprises of all kinds reflected the depression. Planters sought cheaper labor;

bankers grew cautious about loans; iron works failed; mechanics went unemployed. Yet many *haole* believed that, given a stable, conservative, business-men's government, Hawaii could ride out the storm, particularly if her diplomatic representative in Washington [Mott-Smith] could persuade a protectionist-minded administration there, to revise and broaden the trade treaty, placing more items—especially preserved fruits—on the free list. Thus occupied, their eyes on Washington, the conservative citizens simply had refused to take the Liberals seriously. Then suddenly the prospects were appalling. All over Oahu Wilcox and his followers campaigned exuberantly. The other two parties had not even named candidates.

Lorrin A. Thurston called for a coalition. Let the Reformers swallow their pride and unite with all who would stand for a free-trade treaty and against a constitutional convention. In response there was a last-minute attempt at a so-called citizens' ticket. But the National Reformers were not ready to follow Thurston's lead. They believed in the free-trade treaty, yes. But they were emphatically against conceding anything at Pearl Harbor to get it. So belatedly they began their own campaign.[5]

For this election Hawaii first used the Australian secret ballot, and, when the returns were in, it was evident no party would control the legislature despite whatever bribery might have gone on previously, as accusations on all sides had been made since 1887.

The *Advertiser*, on February 10, complacently reported that ". . . National Reformers and Reformers have been placed under one head of Conservatives . . . against the Party of Anarchy (Liberals)."

The Liberals went into verbal and press action again, but this time blamed Marshal C.B. Wilson rather than the queen for all that was wrong.

Although they were largely inspired in their tirades by personal envy of not having been chosen by the queen for appointments, they placed a strong political weapon in the hands of the opposition, by their derogatory remarks against the queen and her Marshal and supposed lover.

Liliuokalani was not so complacent as the *Advertiser*. She recognized that if the National Reformers joined the Reformers, she would receive no support whatsoever, for the Liberals were openly against her. Liliuokalani had been reluctant to take a political side to this point. On January 21, John Ena had called on her to solicit campaign contributions, as well as support the merging of Hawaiian newspapers *Holomua* and *Elele Poakulu*. She wrote in her diary she had "promised $100 to each," but continued: "They say I must for the good of the Public. But I think I hadn't ought to give any for the campaign because I would just be in politics or assisting it, which I should not do."

Soon, however, Liliuokalani *was* "in politics," whether she "should" or not. Her first "political" move was based on what was preeminently important to her—to give the people a new constitution.

She quoted in her diary from a sermon by Kawaiahao's Church minister, Henry Parker, "The voice of the people is the voice of God." But in her *Story* she spoke of the voice of the people, the voice of God, as being "Hawaiian tradition."[6] The word "people," heard by the queen and the *haole,* was interpreted diametrically opposite. To Liliuokalani of "Hawaiian tradition," "the people" were the Hawaiians; to the *haole* (to whom Parker spoke), "the people" were the anti-royalists. Many were not even naturalized citizens of Hawaii, but were still able to vote and hold public office.

Liliuokalani's first open move was to gain the support of the Hui Kalaiaina—the Hawaiian political society that Robert Wilcox had failed to win over—and to enlarge its membership. The queen, through Charles B. Wilson, her Marshal; Samuel Nowlein, commander of her Household Guards; and Joseph Nawahi, a Representative-elect from Hilo, let it be known that her people need not revolt against her in order to get what they wanted. But by the first of May, Wilson warned her that some of the new members of the Hui were of dubious loyalty—that, in fact, they were Wilcox's counterspies.

On April 28, Liliuokalani wrote Princess Kaiulani a letter in which she gave no indication, nor advice, of political manuevering, but revealed, rather, her reliance on genealogy—an old Hawaii custom. The letter also showed where her first love lay—not in politics but in the development of a person,

> . . . preferably of literary or musical talent. The superior intelligence of Keawe-a-Heulu is I am confident handed down to us & we must use it wisely. You are studying literature. It will also be of great advantage to you. To be able to write a history, to compose a poem, to write anything which will prove a fertile & cultivated mind is an accomplishment which one in your station ought to be master of . . .[7]

The queen's diaries, pertaining to the complicated intrigues that were going on in Hawaiian political circles of Reformers versus Liberals-and-National-Reformers of dubious loyalties, reveal her growing suspicions.

The annexationists, with excellent legerdemain, directed the queen's marshal's attentions toward the Liberals and their "treason." The Liberals, not the best of conspirators, did not attempt to keep their meetings secret. In May, the queen's marshal, C.B. Wilson, learned that the Liberals were ordering guns and pistols and tried to convince the queen that she should have them arrested.

On the morning of May 19 the Marshal was advised by Liliuokalani to force a showdown. He sent two messengers to request Wilcox to come immediately to the palace to consult with Her Majesty about a constitution. Caught off guard, Wilcox tried to gain time. The Marshal's men stood firm; the interview grew quarrelsome; in the end, Wilcox sent a defiant refusal. At once, warrants were issued for arrests on the basis that Wilcox had "in his possession guns and pistols."

On the same day (May 19th) Liliuokalani wrote in her diary:

> Wilson informed W. R. Castle secretly of this matter [of proposed arrest of Wilcox and Ashford] what should he [Castle] do but go and inform Ashford of it and when arrests were made all the guns had disappeared—what does this mean? It looks as if the Missionary Party are really at bottom of all these disturbances & the Ashfords & R. W. Wilcox are their tools.

If they were not directly "their tools," they certainly served to attract attention away from the major danger.

By May 21, the Liberal leaders (Wilcox and V. Ashford) had been arrested for treason. It was then Liliuokalani wrote that a "Miss Julia Smith" from Kauai came to the queen, sent ostensibly by Alfred S. Hartwell, an attorney, and later an avowed enemy of the queen, to assure the queen that "her [Miss Smith's] school" would be "out of harms way" of the Liberals.

Liliuokalani replied she was not concerned regarding any rebellion of the Liberals. Promptly the next day Miss Smith reappeared again, as Hartwell's emissary, to say that Wilcox and Ashford would be sent out of the country. Liliuokalani recorded in her diary: "And yet, all Mr. Hartwell's pleadings were in favor of the prisoners saying their actions were not [t]rea[s]onable[sic]." On June 10 and 11 Liliuokalani wrote that rumors persisted that V.V. Ashford had been released from prison and had left the country, having been paid $25,000 to leave so as not to expose the "Annexation Party."

Later the accusation was strongly denied by the annexationists; however, so much intrigue was going on between the annexationists and the vacillating Liberals that it is impossible to separate fact from fiction. It is possible the rumor had some truth in it.

The Ashfords, Wilcox, and Bush had been formally arrested by C.B. Wilson, thus their hatred of him increased. They were, however, freed from all charges of "treason" by Chief Justice A.F. Judd and Judge Sanford Ballard Dole.

🎎 4 🎎

Between the time of the election (February 3) and the convening of the 1892 Legislature (May 28th), Liliuokalani had an important personal visitor, whom she impressed deeply and whose opinions were to influence the British in her favor. And his philosophical views were to become a part of her meditations in her latter years. This man was Sir Edwin Arnold, publisher and founder of the *London Daily Telegraph* and author of *The Light of Asia.* He gave a copy of his book to the queen at this time.

He wrote, on March 8th, a glowing account of "Paradise," seeing none of its serpents, but questioning, as Lady Franklin had, the "brusque treatment" of the queen. He reported both for London and Hawaiian papers:

> As for her Majesty, she is "every inch a queen" and bears with noble grace and lofty gentleness the lonely honours of her rank . . . The queen rose, with all the simplicity of a lady welcoming friends, to receive us and shook hands cordially, dressed in complete mourning [for her husband]. She wore a black robe of silk crape, cut loose below the bosom . . . carried a black edged lace handkerchief, no ornaments except a magnificent diamond ring. Her countenance— distinctly handsome—has a coffee color and is surmounted by thick black hair, growing luxuriantly, touched here and there with silver flecks.[8]

At the same time of Sir Edwin Arnold's dispatches to London, the *San Francisco Examiner* wrote flagrantly of "treason," "stratagems," "spoils," "riots," "sorcery," "a black pagan queen, who wanted nothing short of absolute monarchy in the obeisance of the uncivilized kings of Hawaii." Its writers stressed the extreme dangers to all the white populace from the "savage queen."

Even the *Paradise of the Pacific* began to take exception to the *Examiner,* saying, "The *Examiner* writers can only become original when they become unnatural." The *Paradise of the Pacific* went on to point out that, at the very moment riots of a most dangerous kind were supposedly taking place, the correspondent had attended a quiet day at a picnic, enjoying the hospitality of Hawaii.

In the meantime the annexations led by Lorrin Thurston were at work laying the foundation for the overthrow. The Annexation Club, as it was called, was begun in January of 1892, as revealed in an interview between Thurston and Secretary of State Gresham: "As early as July [sic] 1892 myself [Thurston] and several others had a consultation upon the subject of Hawaiian affairs, and after an interchange of views we agreed it was only a question of time when the Islands would have to be annexed to the United States, and we formed an annexation league for that purpose . . ."[9]

Thurston later managed to have himself sent to the United States, on government monies, under the guise of having Hawaii represented at the World's Columbian Exposition in Chicago to be held in 1893. Thurston's main project was to go to Washington, D.C., to test the American climate toward annexation. He intended to persuade the President that the "entire Hawaiian population was in favor of annexation." In truth, practically none of the natives wanted annexation and only a few of the radicals of the *hapa-haole* group. Most of the planters were opposed to annexation, as were many of the commercial and businessmen. Only two persons were adamantly in favor of it—Lorrin A. Thurston and John L. Stevens, American minister to Hawaii. Thurston had, however, won over a few followers in Hawaii, among whom was W.O. Smith, attorney-at-law. Smith had become associated in law practice with Thurston in 1887. Thurston was then a member of the Hawaiian League, which had opposed King Kalakaua. Smith did not at that time join the League, but became a member of the Annexation Club in 1892.

Smith played a most important role in the overthrow of the monarchy by his use of Willie Kaae, one of the queen's minor secretaries. As early as the 17th of February 1892, Smith began paying Willie's debts (which were many), but one also to the queen of $250 plus $17.50 interest.[10] It was a cheap price for what he was later to receive from Willie.

❡ 5 ❡

On May 28, 1892, Hawaii's legislature opened with fanfare as carriages rolled through the gates of Ali'iolani Hale, past the black and gold statue of the first Kamehameha, the Queen's Household

Guards in battle array presented arms, and opposite them across the drive the Royal Hawaiian Band played one lively tune after another. Indoors there were kahilis and great bouquets of lilies. There were special seats for the dignitaries, and the throne was draped with a golden feather cloak.

When the Queen's coach left Iolani Palace, a salute resounded from Punchbowl, and when, drawn by a span of black horses, it arrived at Ali'olani's entrance, the band swung majestically into "Hawaii Pono'i."[11]

This was Liliuokalani's first legislature, though she had been queen a year and four months; for the sessions were biennial. It was also her last, and it was destined to become the longest on record—171 turbulent days from opening to prorogation.

With grace and spirit, Liliuokalani delivered her address, in English, touching upon the problems the nation faced and pledging herself to reign as a constitutional monarch, and "firmly to endeavor to preserve the autonomy and . . . independence" of the kingdom. In closing she invoked the blessing of Divine Providence upon the deliberations about to commence. The holiday mood was barely skin-deep, and below the surface were grave concern, shrewd calculations, passionate loyalties, smoldering resentments, feverish longings, and political antagonisms somewhat beyond the usual portion of such a body on its opening day.

On June 4 Lorrin Thurston, returning from the United States, brought encouraging, if biased, news to the Annexationist League. Thurston reported "if conditions in Hawaii compel you people to act as you have indicated, and you come to Washington with an annexation proposition, you will find an exceedingly sympathetic administration here."[12] He had not seen President Benjamin Harrison, but he had talked with Senator Cushman K. Davis, a member of the Committee on Foreign Relations; with Representative James H. Blount, chairman of the Committee of Foreign Affairs; with Secretary of the Navy B.F. Tracy; and with Secretary of State James G. Blaine. It was Tracy who had brought him the encouraging message theoretically from the President. Tracy had no authority to set forth American policy—nor Hawaiian.

Secretary Blaine was ill and unable to keep a second appointment he had made with Thurston. To that fact history owes the seven-page letter, dated San Francisco, May 27, 1892, in which Thurston, on his way home, spelled out his thoughts to Blaine about annexation.

Thurston outlined the means by which he thought he could bring matters to a head. In the course of the next few months he hoped to secure the appointment at the Islands of a cabinet "committed to annexation," proceed with the "education" of the people, win "the adhesion of as many native leaders as possible," and have the legislature adjourn in August or September instead of being prorogued. This maneuver would allow the House to reconvene on its own volition without being called into extra session by the queen. Then, when the time was ripe—perhaps in December when the American Congress had expressed itself in favor of annexation—Thurston proposed either to submit the question to the people in a general election or to take action in the reassembled legislature.[13]

Although Thurston's dream plans of quick action were impeded by the February election results, from it began a series of removals of the queen's appointed cabinets by "want-of-confidence" by the House.

As the threat of a Wilcox-Ashford uprising diminished, Liliuokalani realized that it was necessary to keep the party dedicated to her in power —the National Reformers. Although later highly condemned for such "personal interest," it appears to have been a sound move.

One of her most important strengths, as she saw it at the time, was to keep Marshal C.B. Wilson in office. In command of the police and the military, Wilson was a sure and potent ally against any force that might endanger the throne—in Liliuokalani's view an essential ally. Yet the Marshal held his appointive position under the attorney-general, and by that cabinet officer he could be dismissed. Reduced to its simplest terms, then, the queen's problem for the duration of the session was to keep Attorney General Whiting in office or, if necessary, to replace him with a man who would promise to continue Wilson as marshal.

Unfortunately Wilson had enemies among the Liberals, who resented his influence on the queen and hated him for the arrests in May; and among the Reformers, who accused him of incompetence and corruption, of dealing illicitly with opium smugglers and gamblers.

Against the barrage of accusations of his being in league with the opium smugglers, Wilson presented to the queen a list of names of these so-called smugglers. This list included a surprising number of important *haole* men in the community,[14] who had made these accusations themselves. The subject was dropped.

There was another crucial problem for Liliuokalani, a misconception on her part that went back to what she considered the "illegality" of the 1887 Constitution. She believed that in order to promulgate a new constitution *legally* she must have the signatures of the majority of the ministers appointed under the old (Bayonet) constitution, to which she had, to her regret, sworn allegiance. This political naiveté or fanatical desire to stay "within the law" as much as possible was to be her greatest detriment.

Liliuokalani, once reluctant to enter politics, was deeply involved by June. Some writers have stated that "the Queen who might have kept her crown indefinitely if she had been content to reign as a constitutional monarch—a ceremonial and symbolic personage rather than a ruler— was by disposition and circumstance impelled toward a power struggle with the legislature."[15]

These writers are only partially correct. A careful look into the history of the times shows that no queen—no matter how subservient to the legislature—would have been tolerated. The machinery to destroy the monarchy and to commit, by design or accident, total Hawaiian genocide had begun before Liliuokalani's birth. She had no choice. The Hawaiians would have no respect for a puppet-queen, and Americans had no toler-ance for any queen, constitutional or otherwise. Her "disposition" was, indeed, to preserve the Hawaiian monarchy and what was left of the Hawaiian way of life. The "circumstances" were partly fortuitous, but used effectively by the *haole* to gain their end.

Strangely enough, she won her struggle with the recalcitrant legislature of 1892 through compromise; only to arouse such antagonism by her victory that the foe in ambush waited for her slightest movement in order to make its final attack.

During the entire year, the Legislature had been in constant turmoil. The Sam Parker cabinet, appointed at Liliuokalani's accession, operated smoothly in its early days. Then two "circumstances" occurred. First, Joseph Nawahi, a new leader of the Liberals, began introducing "race consciousness," as opposed to nationalism, as a weapon against the annexa-tionists. Secondly, upon Robert Wilcox's release from prison, he began making astonishing speeches on the Pearl Harbor question, which sound-ed more like Thurston than Wilcox. He also reversed himself to defend the 1887 Constitution.

Wilcox moved on July 13 for a "want-of-confidence" of the Parker cabinet. The cabinet survived, but the damage was done. It began losing popularity, especially its attorney general, W.S. Whiting, who had kept C.B. Wilson as marshal. He was suspected of being the queen's "tool."

For the more than 17,000 arrests and the more than 13,000 convictions since he took office, Charles B. Wilson was said to be "blaming the laws." Desertion of contract by laborers, drunkenness, opium smuggling, and gambling, he described as "offenses created by statute, upon the commission of which the moral sense of the community apparently casts but little stigma."[16]

A howl of indignation rose in the House and echoed through the town. "Does Mr. Wilson," the *Advertiser* asked, "wish the public, whom he serves, to understand that gambling has become open, public, notorious, and all but universal . . . because it is right enough in itself but is simply forbidden by law . . . ?"

Wilson's words were unfortunate, to say the least; but his explanation to the queen, who was rigidly moral, despite later accusations, was that he "was misquoted." What he meant, he said, was not that the arrests (he had ordered them himself) and the convictions were wrong, but that until the community itself would take a moral stand, the arrests and convictions would continue to create unnecessary expense for the government. If that is what Wilson meant, he was correct; but the public is seldom willing to exert its own moral influence. The opposition was more than ready to pounce on any statement made by Wilson that could be used against him or anyone else. In this case it toppled Whiting.

On July 27 Liliuokalani accepted Whiting's resignation. She, however, gives a different reason. Mollie Sheldon was pregnant by Whiting and "now that it is all known I cannot appoint [sic] him."[17]

The cabinet was rocking, and the legislature, by design of a few or by "circumstance," decided to keep it unstable to support their contention that "no stable government can be achieved under the Queen."

Paul Neumann was selected to take Whiting's place—he served thirty-six hours and was voted out by 31 to 10. The queen could appoint, but the Legislature could dismiss. Against such odds, Liliuokalani had to walk a sagging tight rope.

A second bombshell hit on August 30. Representative White of Lahaina introduced a bill to grant franchise to the newly organized Hawaiian Lottery Company.

Not until after the imprisonment of the queen, did Liliuokalani's diaries come to light; however, as they are still consistently quoted regarding her entanglement in the Lottery problem and the accusation that she was influenced by "supernatural forces," they are worthy of reexamination.

Accusations were made that the queen was completely under the "sorcery" power of a medium by the name of Fraulein Wolf, and that the queen *never* made an appointment without her advice.

❧ 6 ❧

Fraulein Wolf, the medium, who had come into Liliuokalani's life several years earlier as her German teacher, had now ingratiated herself to become a confidante. It should be noted that the queen had no one else in whom to confide. She had even come to suspect C.B. Wilson by this time.

Fraulein played upon a universal interest of the day—fortune-telling, astrology, mind-reading and second-sight. Although the queen has been unmercifully criticized for her interest in Fraulein's "gifts," nothing has been said about *haole* who consulted the Fraulein. Nor was anything said of the popularity of Mr. and Mrs. Edward Steen, "clairvoyants and mind-readers," having "second sight equal only to Helen and Herman" (a well-known team of mind-readers). The Steens were enormously popular among the *haole*.[18]

Fraulein Wolf custom-tailored her arts to old Hawaii. One day in the midst of a German lesson, while Liliuokalani patiently recited gutteral German verbs against the gentle musical breezes of Hawaii, Fraulein caught her attention with a "trance," in which she said she saw Kamehameha I, who had come to advise the new queen.

Liliuokalani, partly skeptical and partly intrigued, put aside German verbs to listen to the Fraulein's description of Kamehameha the Great. At that time, the Fraulein revealed little not already known among the Hawaiians about Kamehameha the Great. However, Liliuokalani was surprised and pleased to find a *haole* with the information.

Fraulein Wolf then caught the unsuspecting queen, much as Rasputin had caught Empress Alexandra, on a subject dear to her. In Liliuokalani's case it was her husband's lineage and background. Most of the information Fraulein gave Liliuokalani was "substantiated" by a "yellow piece of paper," that the queen had thought lost, and which was later remarkably found by Fraulein. This was a paper of which, Liliuokalani wrote in her diary, "John discovered twenty-eight yrs ago—latterly he wanted to show it to me and one day we had a quarrel and so he made up his mind never to disclose to me who he was, and before he died he hid the paper so I shouldn't find it."[19]

Keeping Liliuokalani's interest in the "high rank" and "ducal crown," and information readily available in newspapers, Fraulein set the queen off on a curious correspondence to Trieste[20] to learn more of her husband's relatives. The last that was heard of this fruitless effort was a letter from "Dominis' first wife and now the rightful queen of Hawaii."[21]

Meanwhile Fraulein began her political maneuvers. She told of a man who was to come from across the sea bringing great wealth. His initials were "C.S." Liliuokalani readily supplied "Claus Spreckels." It was not unknown that Spreckels was on his way to Hawaii. It was no secret that, as a royalist, he would offer monetary support to the queen.

There was always enough truth and "foresight" in Fraulein's prophecies to keep Liliuokalani on the edge. And well there might be, because Fraulein was an active member in the community, and a shrewd guesser, if not actually a pawn of those who were manipulating the government behind the scenes.

Liliuokalani wrote in her diary later of the Fraulein's prediction of another man who would come with an opportunity for great wealth—which would pull her country out of its depression. Her diary indicates that she completely succumbed, when the very next day a gentleman, who was to be known for many years only as Mr. T.E.E., came to her, and presented a lottery scheme. Much degradation has been placed upon the queen because Mr. T.E.E. was not only supposed to bring great wealth to her country but $10,000 for "pocket money." Considering the number of personal and public charities that Liliuokalani supported from her "pocket money," the amount was small and certainly not "selfish," as has been implied.

Perhaps it was no small coincidence that Mr. T.E.E. was actually T.E. Evans, the brother of James Evans,[22] who was later married to Fraulein Wolf in San Francisco.[23]

Although from the hue and cry that has since followed one would think that Mr. T.E.E. and the queen were solely responsible for initiating a "lottery scheme," this is not true. A bill had been considered during Kalakaua's reign in regard to a lottery, but now it took on vicious proportions, and Liliuokalani was petitioned by the "best ladies" in Honolulu not to sign the "gambling bill." These women included her former Royal School teacher, Juliette Cooke, and, interestingly enough, Mrs. Lamiki Aimoku, John Dominis Aimoku's mother.

Juliette Cooke, who went to see her personally, reported that the queen was gracious and they talked of many happy memories of the Royal School days, but she would not agree to withhold her signature from the bill if it passed in the legislature. It passed and Liliuokalani signed it. There never seemed to be any doubt in Liliuokalani's mind (as there was apparently none in the many pro-bill signers) that the lottery would bring in a million dollars or more for general building, road maintenance, and other government expenditures. The wrath of the opposition (many of whom had voted for the bill) fell on her.

"Giving natives who were 'natural gamblers' and 'who had continually sought to get something for nothing' [the bill] was pulling out the last brick in the wall of morality which the missionaries had tried so hard to build," Serano Bishop wrote in one of his "messages" to the American papers.

The rumors that "the queen never made a single governmental appointment without the approval of the medium" came from her diary records. However, these entries bear out no such indictment. During the first part of 1892 she wrote of conferences with Samuel Parker, Sam Damon, Curtis Iaukea, and James Wodehouse, British Minister to Hawaii.

It was true her diaries reveal that Fraulein warned the queen against three men and suggested others from whom she was to choose her cabinet. The three men, whom the medium warned Liliuokalani against, could have been no surprise to the queen for they were Lorrin Thurston, W.O. Smith and Alexander Young, all known enemies and all annexationists.

Using only initials, Fraulein recommended S.P. (Sam Parker), C.S. (Charles Spencer or Claus Spreckels), J.E. (either John Ena or possibly her own friend, James Evans), S.D. (Sam Damon or Sanford Dole) and A.P. (Arthur Peterson.)

She said nothing about Paul Neumann; yet it was he, whom we saw earlier, that the queen appointed and who was so peremptorily dismissed. John Ena or James Evans and Sam Damon or Sanford Dole were never chosen by the queen. It seems Fraulein's "second-sight" advice had less weight than what the queen's detractors would believe. Although there is no doubt that Liliuokalani believed in the medium's second sight to a degree, her acceptance was based largely on supported gossip regarding persons in the community. In the opinion of this writer, the queen was more intrigued by the idea of "second sight," common among the Hawaiians, than she was directly influenced by Fraulein's advice, except in the case of the Dominis' search.

The queen's diary also records that she held consultations regarding appointments with Parker, who was already in the ministry, and Charles Spencer, a carry-over from the Kalakaua ministry.

❧ 7 ❧

When the Parker cabinet was voted out by want of confidence in September the opposition sent the queen three names acceptable to them. She rejected these, and chose Arthur Peterson, a National Reformer—coincidentally found on Fraulein's list, it was later pointed out. Liliuokalani chose him, according to her, as "one of her friends." She was then immediately accused of putting her "personal interests first."

The die had been cast. The Reformers would not go into a cabinet with Nationals. Nationals would not accept Wilcox or Bush; lottery candidates would not join anti-lottery zealots. No one would compromise, cooperate, or attempt to help keep even the semblance of a stable government. One might question if it was the queen alone who was "obstinate."

Peterson gave up trying to form a cabinet. Then E.C. MacFarlane, also a National Reformer, on September 14 presented his handiwork to the House: himself as premier and minister of finance, Paul Neumann as attorney-general, Samuel Parker and Charles T. Gulick in the other positions. Few legislators were satisfied; many were violently displeased, for MacFarlane had not submitted his slate to the caucus for approval. For this omission one can hardly blame him, since the caucus had split into half a dozen hostile factions. But the Reformers did blame him, and their want-of-confidence motion came after only three days. The motion lost by one vote.

The MacFarlane cabinet hung by a thread. Nevertheless, the legislature made a token attempt at business which included the lottery and opium-licensing questions.

In October at a caucus of the Reform party to discuss the "constitutional principle,"[24] which essentially meant to them their right to appoint the cabinet, it was decided "to dethrone the queen with the help of the *USS Boston* through the machinations of J.L. Stevens."[25]

The queen ceased writing in her diary in August 1892. She may have begun to recognize the dangers to her privacy and decided to stop writing altogether, or she may have begun another journal, not yet found. The latter is possible because many of her own reactions were later recorded in *Moi Wahine*[26] and her own bits of "historical truths," some of which were reiterated by James Robertson in his *Some Historical Truths*.

After a month the MacFarlane cabinet was voted out. MacFarlane's last act was to attack Brown, who was said to be a prime mover in rounding up native legislators to vote against the ministry.[27]

The breach between the *haole* and the Hawaiians was growing more obvious daily. For of the "rounding up [of] natives" Serano Bishop, a later bitter vilifier of the queen, wrote

> . . . the native members, who have been the uncertain element, have undergone a very wholesome education since they meekly yielded and permitted the new Cabinet to remain in, last month . . . they are now very resolute, and will stand no more nonsense. They certainly kept their secret well, during last week, when they were organizing their movement . . .[28]

Once more Liliuokalani faced the task of selecting a cabinet that would serve her interests, yet satisfy a militant majority. This time the contest of wills lasted three weeks. The queen had no intention of bowing to the Reformers' "principle," which many of her closest friends assured her had not a shred of validity. But it was not easy to find anyone, either in or out of the legislature, willing to go before that body with a cabinet of her choosing.

At the end of October, Joseph Nawahi was willing to try. But when he led in William Cornwell, Charles T. Gulick, and Robert Creighton to take the long-vacant chairs, a buzz of protest ran through the chamber, and a want-of-confidence resolution followed immediately. By noon they were out. By a vote of 26 to 13 they went down in history as the Nancy Hanks cabinet, named for the horse that lately had broken the world's trotting record. They finished "the course" in just over two hours.

The struggle went on. Until the House had a cabinet they could approve, the majority would not permit other business to be done. Government employees went unpaid and a hopperful of bills waited, while each day the legislature met only to adjourn.

Liliuokalani's position had been untenable since January. There was no possible way she could run a government against the constant opposition that the 1887 constitution allowed the Legislature. She was constantly accused of "making deals" to keep Wilson in office or to promote the lottery. Nothing, however, was, or has been, said about the annexationists' "deals" to elect men only friendly to annexation. Even their "principle" demanded that she choose her cabinet leader, who then chose the cabinet, from her opposition party.

Liliuokalani turned to the one foreign ambassador she trusted—British Minister Wodehouse. Wodehouse firmly believed the queen had the right to choose her "personal favorites" for a cabinet. But Wodehouse was also concerned that American Minister Stevens would land troops from the *USS Boston*. In no communications with Great Britain is there any evidence that the British had the slightest interest in destroying Hawaii's independence. The later arguments of the Americans that either Britain or Japan planned to "take" Hawaii are proved completely false by official records of the Japanese and the British of this time.[29] The British even trusted the American government, despite Wodehouse's fears, to the degree that on the day of the overthrow of the monarchy, Lord Rosebery wrote the Japanese ministry that there was not the slightest danger of the Americans taking Hawaii.[30]

After an interview with Wodehouse on November 4, 1892, Liliuokalani had decided on a compromise. She showed him her new appointments: G.N. Wilcox, premier and minister of interior; Peter C. Jones, minister of finance; Mark Robinson, minister of foreign affairs; Cecil Brown, attorney general. The latter was no relation to Andrew Brown, who was on the Committee of Safety.

"They are men of weight and influence in the community," Wodehouse wrote his government, "and will be acceptable to the 'moderate' men of all parties."[31]

Wodehouse was correct. The House accepted the new cabinet. The Reformers declared the queen's conduct was in accord with all "constitutional monarchies." The Liberals remained somewhat obstinate. The Nationals recognized "a compromise," but agreed it was an excellent cabinet.

The demand for the dismissal of Wilson, led by Henry Castle, editor of the *Advertiser*, once again was heard. After a year of total chaos, the blame was placed entirely on the queen. Inasmuch as now she had appointed an "acceptable cabinet," and could not be defaulted on that account, the legislature continued to forestall on other basic constitutional change, debates on opium licensing, the question of the lottery, and Chinese immigration.

Nothing had been settled by the end of 1892, but two dangerous appropriations were made: one of $5,000 to send a commission to Washington, D.C., ostensibly in regard to the tariff question but in actuality, for annexation. Twelve thousand dollars was appropriated to send the Royal Band to Chicago for the Exposition. Liliuokalani had written earlier to the effect "that if the country was poor why send to Chicago or why should Hawaii be represented there [at the Exposition]."[32]

Rifts were beginning to occur between the queen and the cabinet. One was caused by their failure to report to the legislature the queen's reason for not signing the Chinese Immigration Bill. She did not veto the bill, but allowed it to become a law without her signature. The reason for her action was that the bill was "too restrictive."[33] The planters desired cheap Chinese labor, but did not wish to have Chinese competition in commerce. The bill restricted Chinese immigrants to field-work and, reluctantly, to domestic help. It forbade them from entering into commerce or business of any kind for themselves.

Doubts regarding the cabinet were being surreptitiously implanted in the queen's mind by her supporters. During the month of November, the queen was privately informed by note, "that it was the intention of the American Minister, with the aid of some of our residents, to perfect a scheme of annexation, and that the Cabinet had knowledge of the fact." On the 17th of December, the queen received the following letter from the same informant: (identified as A. Marques by Kuykendall).

> Referring to the confidential communication I took the liberty to address Your Majesty a few weeks ago, about the attitude and utterances of American representatives here, the perfect correctness of which has been confirmed by subsequent information I now beg to be allowed to state, that through the same trustworthy source I have been informed that in a very late moment of effusion, some American official gave to understand that he had instructions to press and hurry up an annexation scheme, which he confidently expected to carry through at no distant date, with the help and assistance of the present Cabinet. If Your Majesty will kindly weigh this information by the side of the bold open declarations and annexation campaign made at the present time in the Bulletin, by the Rev. Sereno Bishop, the well-known mouthpiece of the annexation party, I think that Your Majesty will be able to draw conclusions for yourself, and realize not only that there is yet danger ahead, but that the enemy is in the household, and that the strictest watch ought to be kept on the members of the present Cabinet.[34]

Hawaii was at a collision point. The queen could see but one way to preserve her country, and the *haole* could see but one way to preserve "their" country. Two trains were coming toward each other on the same track.

Three Days of Revolution

❦ 1 ❦

The end of the year of 1892 merged with the beginning of the new year of 1893. The queen had been duly warned against annexationists. Thurston, the prime mover, was apparently not sure of the stand Stevens would take toward annexation, and wrote Archibald Hopkins on board the *SS Australia* that (they) should ". . . induce the queen to give up the throne for $250,000. . . . annexation doesn't look so good now."

Early in January, Stevens and one of his daughters took a trip to Hilo. Later he said it was the first time he had felt it safe for the United States minister and naval commander to be away from Honolulu, and that he believed the G.N. Wilcox cabinet would carry the country through the next eighteen months safely.[1]

Mr. Stevens, usually so knowledgeable about affairs of state, seemed determined to appear ignorant of what he later accused the queen of knowing: that the opposition had enough votes lined up for a "lack of confidence" against the cabinet. He later stated that "Queen Liliuokalani knows of this, is in sympathy with the dissatisfied, has conferred with them and agreed to all plans . . ."[2] The lack of confidence lost by six votes on this first attempt.

It was, however, extremely important that everything on the surface would appear as if neither Stevens nor Thurston anticipated anything but harmony. It was even proposed by W.O. Smith that a committee of politically assorted persons be sent to Washington to discuss "commercial relations." These included the unlikely bedfellows: L.A. Thurston, R.W. Wilcox, and Joseph Nawahi.

It was no secret that the queen was going to propose a new constitution. As early as August of 1892 she had begun work with Joseph Nawahi, Sam Nowlein and William White.[3]

The only person who could be trusted not to go immediately to the opposition with this information was Sam Nowlein. Certainly neither

White nor Nawahi could be trusted. It can only be guessed that the queen worked to quiet their vociferous demands—and possibly, if she were as "clever" as the opposition said, to have the rumors spread among the natives that she *was* preparing a more equitable constitution for them.

The G.N. Wilcox cabinet had been presented with copies of the queen's proposed constitution. Thurston and W.O. Smith also had copies supplied them by Willie Kaae,[4] one of the queen's secretaries, whose debts W.O. Smith had so conveniently previously paid, and thus put Willie in his camp. He was now collecting his payment with interest.

❧ 2 ❧

The political skies were darkened by the January 4, 1893, legislature passing the lottery bill and again adopting a want of confidence to force the resignation of the G.N. Wilcox cabinet. The queen immediately appointed Sam Parker, John F. Colburn, William Cornwell, and Arthur Peterson, who were to become the last monarchial cabinet.

Although later the queen was blamed for the passage of the lottery bill, it might be noted that several opponents who knew of the upcoming vote were absent. Consequently, the bill passed, "due to absenteeism." Perhaps the attitude of Dr. McGrew, who proudly proclaimed himself as the "father of annexation," is of significance. Sanford Ballard Dole quoted McGrew as "happy over the lottery bill because he thinks it will demoralize things here and hasten annexation."[5]

Liliuokalani herself was somewhat in doubt about the passage of the lottery and opium bills, because there had been so much animosity among the people on account of them. She stated that White "railroaded them through."[6] Cleghorn wrote his daughter he hoped the queen would not sign the bills. However, she did sign, later telling Commissioner James Blount that as her cabinet had advised her to do so, "she had no other option." It has been said she did. "It was a well-recognized principle that the veto was a personal prerogative of the sovereign, not limited in any way by the advice of the cabinet." On the other hand, she was under the constant threat of Article 78 of the Bayonet Constitution, which required that all official acts of the sovereign be performed "with the advice and consent of the Cabinet." Also she had been thoroughly convinced by both the cabinet and the manuevering threesome—White, Nawahi and R.W. Wilcox—that it was the wish of the Hawaiian people. In the latter they were probably correct, because by this time the average native Hawaiian was completely confused by the disorder in the community.

There was also another reason. Liliuokalani had deeply imbedded in her a characteristic which some might consider a flaw. Implanted and nourished from the days of the Royal School, through her marriage years, she had been strongly indoctrinated in obedience and the terrible "sin" of disobedience. Her diaries which always included expressions of deep sorrow for the death of children, carried one discordant note of a child who had drowned because he was "disobedient."

Minister Stevens' opposition to the lottery, interestingly enough, had nothing to do with "morality," so loudly proclaimed, but that it would create a serious "postal problem in the United States as the American government had forbidden lottery literature."[7] It was evident where Stevens' eye was directed.

In testimony regarding the days between January 14 and 17, on both sides, inaccuracies and inconsistencies abound, depending on individual predilections. It has been said the Blount Report on the ensuing events was a lawyer's brief in defense of the queen and against Stevens, and the later Morgan report was a rebuttal for the provisional government and Stevens against the queen. If the accusation is true that Blount consulted primarily the Hawaiians, it is certainly true Morgan interviewed only the members of the Provisional Government; although he, unlike Blount, did not hesitate to accept the hospitality of the queen. Lydia Aholo's memories of a luau that Morgan attended remained distasteful to her. "He sat next to me and he was so drunk he couldn't keep his hands off me. I signalled the queen of what was happening and she nodded her permission that I might leave."[8]

By January 14, 1893, Liliuokalani had reached exactly the same conclusion the revolutionists had. There was no longer a neutral zone of cooperation or appeasement between the monarchy, dedicated to Hawaiian heritage, and the *haole* businessmen, dedicated to commercial progress.

Historians have generally agreed that any country is ripe for revolution if there is: 1) a "rotten door" to break down; 2) strong opposition leadership, and 3) as little as three percent of the population willing to follow. The revolutionists had a door badly weakened, if not completely rotten, one which Liliuokalani had inherited from her brother Kalakaua, one which the *haole* and *hapa-haole* and even a few Hawaiians had continued to splinter further during the past two years of her reign. The revolutionists had at least determined leaders in such men as L.A. Thurston, labelled by more than one unbiased historian as a "rabid radical." The three percent followers were found primarily among the Americans born in Hawaii, second generation missionary sons, American businessmen who were not even naturalized citizens, and a few naturalized foreigners.

Liliuokalani was not unaware of the weakened door. But she believed that by a return to a strong monarchy of pre-1887, she could give again Hawaii to the Hawiians as there was no doubt the majority of the whole population, and 90 per cent of the natives, wished for such government. She had, however, no strong leaders. Her advisers were vacillating and unreliable men, and in the end proved themselves traitors.

She took the stand that she, and she alone, could turn back the clock to live by Kamehameha the Great's words: "Do not give the land to the foreigners," and Kamehameha V's method of "promulgating" a new constitution. His had been a constitution under which Hawaii had been successfully governed for twenty-three years in prosperity for all—until the *haole* grew more power-and-money-hungry.

Liliuokalani also believed that no foreign *government* was her enemy, but Juliette Cooke expressed the truth in 1843 at the time of Paulet's "conquest." "The chiefs will give up all in the face of a cannon." It was true. They were not fighters in that sense. Negotiations between "high chiefs," or the *moi* (kings), and "high chiefs" of foreign countries (queens or presidents) was the answer to serious disputes. In the latter, Liliuokalani believed as firmly as Kamehameha III had in 1843. The two political times were, however, entirely different.

She believed the only way to save her small country from being given away by "guests" was to change the form of government to a strong monarchy, by promulgating a new constitution.

Her constitution was remarkably mild compared to what could have been expected of the "stubborn, vicious, 'determined to rule'" queen. The major changes were that it: (1) increased the franchise to her people by restricting voting to Hawaiian born or naturalized; (2) it restricted the terms of justices to the supreme court to six years rather than for life. Third, it increased the power of the queen by having (a) nobles appointed for life by the queen instead of elected for a number of years, and (b) cabinet ministers serve "during the queen's pleasure," *but also subject to impeachment and to removal by legislative want of confidence.* (author's italics). Article 78 of the 1887 constitution, the one that had caused her so much confusion, was to be removed: "all official acts of the sovereign to be performed with the advice and consent of the Cabinet." The last was essential, if she was to have any control whatsoever.

On the morning of January 14, 1893, Liliuokalani, before ten o'clock, called her cabinet members together to inform them that she planned to proclaim the new constitution and instructed them to be present at the palace to sign the document with her after the prorogation of the Legislature.

It was then Minister Colburn, according to the queen, "acted the part of a traitor." He immediately went downtown to the offices of Henry Waterhouse; then to A.S. Hartwell, who called in L.A. Thurston and W.O. Smith to consult about the constitution he later said he had never seen!

Attorney General Peterson, who later said he had had the constitution "in his pocket for sometime but hadn't read it," joined the group. Peterson and Colburn were advised not to sign the constitution and, under no circumstances resign from the cabinet, for then the queen could appoint others who would support her, who would sign the constitution, and thus make it legal. The queen believed firmly that the cabinet must approve of her actions—again the problem of Article 78. Both the cabinet and opposition did all they could to foster this belief.

Colburn and Peterson returned to the Government Building. The queen, dressed in a "gorgeous lavender silk robe with pages bearing her train" prorogued the Legislature. All was quiet.

In the meantime the *USS Boston* conveniently came in from Hilo, bringing J.L. Stevens. Judge Hartwell sent a message to Captain Wiltse to make preliminary arrangements for the landing of military forces to "protect American lives and property." It was evident that the queen would be opposed by revolutionists whatever happened, because, if the constitution were promulgated, there would have been no need for "protection of American lives or property"; the Hawaiians would have been totally satisfied.

Without a word of warning to the queen, the cabinet ministers walked to Iolani Palace to keep their appointment with the queen *to sign the constitution*. Foreign and native guests had gathered in the throne room to await the promulgation. "The constitution was carried by a messenger from the Territorial Building to the palace on a blue satin pillow."

The ministers met the queen in the Blue Room ostensibly to sign the constitution. Here they refused, saying they had "not read it." Such a statement was either an out-and-out lie or a blatant disregard of the queen's request. They went so far as to say they did not know of her intention until that morning. Nevertheless, the throne room filled with guests who knew of it, as well as the crowds of natives, who waited outside on the palace grounds. The cabinet "debated" with one objective in view: to refuse to sign the constitution. The queen said, and not without justifiable bitterness, they had encouraged her in this undertaking and had "led her to the edge of the precipice, and now left her to leap alone."[9]

The ministers left the queen with Sam Parker, and again joined the annexationists (Smith, Thurston, Hartwell and Waterhouse) to discuss the matter. After a five-hour wait, the queen again summoned the ministers to the Blue Room. She brought her fist down on the table and stated in her clear, quiet voice: "Gentlemen, I have no desire to listen to any advice from you. I have decided to promulgate this constitution and do it now!"[10]

It was then that the cabinet members began again to disclaim having ever seen the constitution before; so she had it read aloud. *Then* specific objections began and Peterson, according to her diary, "begged [she] should wait two weeks and then [she] was assured a new constitution would be presented to [her]." She stated, "with these assurances" she would yield, and she adjourned to the Throne Room to speak to the guests there. She was without doubt not assured, but there was nothing else she could do.

With remarkable equanimity she entered the throne room, and in the quiet, expectant silence spoke to her guests with sadness but sincerity:

> I have listened to thousands of voices of my people that have come to me and I am prepared to grant their request. The present constitution is full of defects as the Chief Justice here will testify as the questions have come so often before him for settlement. It is so faulty that I think a new one should be granted. I have prepared one in which the rights of all have been regarded, a constitution suited to the wishes of the dear people. I was ready and expected to proclaim a new constitution today as a suitable occasion for my dear people. But with regret I say I have met with obstacles that prevented it. Return to your homes peaceably and quietly and continue to look toward me and I will look toward you. Keep me ever in your love. I am obliged to postpone the granting of a constitution for a few days. I must confer with my cabinet and when after you return home you may see it received graciously you have my love and with sorrow I dismiss you.[11]

She then went to the second-floor veranda of the palace and spoke in Hawaiian to the crowd below, for most of them were her petitioners. She said essentially the same (as translated by Chief Justice Judd for the *Advertiser*) but promised more strongly that their wishes would be granted at "some future date." The Hawaiian newspaper, in translation, quoted her as telling her people "go with good hope, and do not be disturbed or troubled in your minds because within these next few days now coming I will proclaim the new constitution." Whatever the queen said regarding the new constitution, as reported by the newspapers, it is generally agreed she did say "Retire to your homes and maintain the peace."

The queen retired to her chambers, and the members of the Annexation Club went into action. Thurston later testified that this was the first formal attempt to seek "protection from the queen's forces."

The "committee of thirteen" (or the "Committee of Safety") were made up of W.O. Smith, L.A. Thurston, W.R. Castle and A.S. Wilcox, Hawaiian born of American parents; W.C. Wilder, American; C. Bolte, German; and Henry Waterhouse, Tasmanian, naturalized Hawaiian citizens; Andrew Brown, Scotsman, and H.F. Glade, who were not naturalized; and H.E. Cooper (chairman), F.W. McChesney, T.F. Lansing, and J.A. Candless, who were Americans.[12] *There were no Hawaiians on the committee.* These thirteen men took it upon themselves to declare that the action of the queen was revolutionary and that she was likely to persist in this manner. Therefore, "the intelligent part of the community had got to take matters into their own hands and establish law and order." Thurston's motion was approved that "preliminary steps be taken at once to form and declare a Provisional Government with view to annexation to the United States."[13]

It was then decided to consult Minister Stevens to learn what protection the U.S. forces would afford because of the "unanimous sentiment and feeling that [American] life and property were in imminent danger."[14]

Stevens replied that he considered the queen's actions "revolutionary," and although he had previously promised to support *her*, now he would recognize the *Cabinet as the government*, and would give them the same assistance "that had always been afforded the Hawaiian government by the U.S. Representatives."[15]

On Sunday, January 15, 1893, Thurston, Colburn and Peterson met with Stevens, and it was decided as the "queen was in Revolution against the government [apparently now the cabinet] the Throne should be declared vacant." Here more contradictions begin. Stevens supposedly agreed to the recognition of the *de facto* government if they held "any building." Later he denied this agreement, and stated they must hold "the government building, the executive departments, (Palace) Archives, and the police station."

Queen Liliuokalani wrote nothing in her diary of the days January 14 to 17th. What was she doing? Why were these men who were engaged in what was, from the standpoint of any government, a treasonable enterprise, not arrested?

We can see by hindsight that the queen had too much trust in her cabinet (who, supposedly, were now "the government"), in the United States, despite her suspicions of Stevens himself, and in the old Hawaiian tradition of negotiations. Liliuokalani remembered the stories told her of the long-ago battles among the *moi*. When the battles grew too bloody, a truce was called, a *kahuna* intervened with prayer, and negotiations were begun. Liliuokalani believed in negotiations.

But she did not remember these men, who now opposed her, were outside enemies, not within her household. They were not of the same "family" as of old, when *aloha, mana* and *hanai* existed.

Marshal C.B. Wilson stated later to Blount that he was ready to swear out warrants for the arrest of the ringleaders of the plot, but he was persuaded against doing so by the cabinet, particularly Peterson.[16]

In the cabinet Sam Parker and Cornwell were holding out against Peterson. Colburn, refusing to capitulate, desired that "conservative businessmen" be consulted. With the queen's consent, the following men met to consider the situation: F.A. Schaefer, J.O. Carter, S.M. Damon, W.M. Giffard, S.C. Allen, E.C. MacFarlane.

They reviewed the whole problem and came to the erroneous conclusion that the crucial issue was the constitution. They drafted a proclamation for the queen to sign in which she assured the community the "matter [of the new constitution] was at an end."[17]

Liliuokalani was reluctant, but had begun to realize that, like her brother, King Kalakaua, the only way to "keep peace" was by appeasement. Humiliated, she bowed to what she supposed were the wishes of the Committee of Safety as well as the cabinet's. The cabinet informed the diplomatic corps (Stevens was not present) of the queen's decision and then proceeded to have the proclamation printed. However, for some reason it did not appear until Monday morning January 16th. The twenty-four-hour delay gave the Committee the time needed to complete what they had planned to do since 1887—overthrow the monarchy.

Parker and Peterson called on Stevens on January 15 to discover where he stood. To them he replied he "would not take the side of the queen." Later he said he "promised nothing."[18] Upon receiving this information, Wilson proposed martial law and the arrest of the Committee of Safety. Peterson, who had now been joined by Paul Neumann, opposed the suggestion on the ground that "it might precipitate a conflict." Liliuo-kalani stood firm that there should be "no bloodshed." Instead it was decided that mass meetings of the people should be held to counter the Committee of Safety. Based on the sentiment expressed at the mass meetings, further decision would be made.

Meanwhile the Committee moved faster than the cabinet to announce and hold their mass meetings. Notices were posted Sunday night (before the queen's proclamation had been publicly printed); and although the Committee knew of it, they pretended ignorance.

At a meeting at W.R. Castle's before the "mass meeting," the Committee went ahead planning for a provisional government. It was suggested that Thurston be the head. Fortunately, he declined as "being too radical and having too many business arrangements." The latter included the Volcano House project, which he and others had requested and accepted the queen's support in financing.

Although the Committee had collected some rifles and ammunition, they realized that if there were open confrontation, they needed to secure all the arms that the "queen's forces" had—pitiably few. Nevertheless, it caused them some concern as Stevens, almost certainly on their side, had not yet fully committed himself to landing American forces.

On Monday morning Wilson called on Thurston to assure him the queen would do nothing further about a constitution. Thurston, however, refused to listen and replied "they intend[ed] to settle the matter once and for all." The Committee then sent a letter to Stevens requesting that troops be landed from the *USS Boston*. The text of the letter included the astonishing words: "The queen with the aid of armed force and accompanied by threats of violence and bloodshed from those with whom she was acting, attempted to proclaim a new constitution . . . This conduct and action . . . have created general alarm and terror . . . We are unable to protect ourselves without aid, and therefore, pray for the protection of the United States forces."[19]

On Monday afternoon the two mass meetings were held with notable differences.[20] The meeting of the Committee held in the Honolulu Rifles'

Armory chaired by W.C. Wilder was composed of nearly all "male white foreign element . . . The language was incendiary and led by Thurston, who referred to 1887 as the 'starting point'."

The Royalist meeting at the Palace Square was quiet and orderly. The queen and Marshal Wilson had ordered the speakers to be extremely cautious. Women as well as men were present and the group was composed of Hawaiians, and some of the "foreign element," who drifted in and out, finding the meeting less exciting than the one at the armory. This time Bush, Nawahi, White, and Wilcox addressed the group in favor of the queen. Robert Wilcox, with his chameleon character, declaimed that "any man that would speak against a woman, especially a queen, is an animal, and a fit companion for a hog."[21]

On Monday, January 16, shortly after the mass meetings had disbanded, before any negotiations could be considered, the American forces from the *USS Boston* landed. While much controversy exists by whose authority the American marines came ashore and for what reason, the facts remain.

At two o'clock, before the mass meetings were held, Stevens had made up his mind to land the troops. At three o'clock he handed the written request to Captain Wiltse, who had already composed his order to land the troops as close to five o'clock as possible.[22]

No one except Thurston had requested the landing of troops.

Ostensibly the troops were to protect American lives and property. The 162-man marine force landed at the foot of Nuuanu Avenue, marched past the palace on King Street to the J.B. Atherton estate. Only a few stayed at the American legation and at J.L. Stevens' home, next door to Waterhouse—thus "American life and property" was protected.

At ten in the evening, Stevens secured accommodations for the troops at Arion Hall, a small building along side the government building out of sight of the palace and separated from it by the Music Hall on King Street. According to Admiral Skerret[23] ". . . it was unadvisable to locate the troops there; if they were landed for the protection of United States citizens . . . if they were landed to support the Provisional Government troops, . . . it was a wise choice."

The landing of the troops could not have been a complete surprise to the queen's supporters. However, in the face of 162-fully equipped fighting men, a handful of poorly equipped "royal guards" and weaponless natives had little chance in opposing them. Furthermore, the queen still insisted on "peaceful means."

She sent Governor Cleghorn with her two still-trusted cabinet members—Parker and Colburn—to Stevens to ask his intentions; was it annexation? He replied "no." When they protested the troops and asked, "by the queen's request," that the troops be withdrawn, he told them to put their request in writing and if it were in a "friendly spirit," he would reply in kind. Stevens' reply, January 17, was even more ambiguous than his oral communications, and Cleghorn concluded, "our independence is gone."[24]

Not a shot had been fired; not a legal document signed; not a single consultation held outside its own small group. On these negative premises the Provisional Government set itself up as a *de facto* ("actually exercising power") rather than a *de jure* ("according to law; legal, by right") government. The Committee met at eight o'clock, Monday night, January 17, 1893, at Henry Waterhouse's residence to finalize the Provisional Government's "cabinet" and officers.

Thurston, Wilder, and Castle were ill, a fact which probably allowed Sanford Ballard Dole to take a last stand to save the monarchy. Knowing the personal animosity directed toward the queen, Dole agreed she should be dethroned, for her own safety, if nothing else. He also knew the Hawaiians' love for the monarchy was as great as the Americans' hatred for it; therefore, he suggested that Princess Kaiulani be named the queen's successor under a regency. He was immediately shouted down.

Dole was then asked to be president of the new government. He hesitated, but was later influenced by Soper, once chief of police under the queen, agreeing to command the military forces. He was further influenced by Sam Damon, who had been close to the queen and was a "very conservative man." Damon had spoken to the queen about his offer, and she had told him to go ahead as it probably would save bloodshed. She wrote in her diary: "I attribute the leniency of the Council to his interposition with them."

❧ 3 ❧

The queen has been accused of being (but only by the kindest people) naive. There is no doubt she was, but an interesting observation is that probably the most naive, certainly the least vicious or predatory of all the *haole* in opposition to her was her successor—Sanford Ballard Dole. Was it the hand of Providence that brought Dole to a position he didn't want, and which probably carried out the queen's deepest desire that there be no bloodshed? Liliuokalani in her latter years believed it to be so.[25] One hesitates to speculate what might have happened had Lorrin Thurston been placed in Sanford B. Dole's position.

Dole was finally chosen to head the government in meetings during which neither Thurston nor Stevens could be present—illness struck in each instance.

For an attorney, Dole was indeed naive to have written during that fateful day when he became head of the Provisional Government:

> At 10 o'clock I went downtown. I remember a letter I had in my pocket which Thurston had given me that morning, addressed to Mr. Stevens, setting forth our intended movement, and proposing to ask his recognition, or something like that. I went in and handed the letter to him. He did not say much, but I remember that he said: "I think you have a great opportunity."[26]

Certainly, it was "understood" by the Committee of Safety that Stevens would support the new government, or they would never have dared go as far as they did.

While the newly formed Provisional Government was being organized, the queen's marshal's police force patrolled the streets for vandalism or incendiarism. There was none. Wilson was also to watch all stores that sold ammunition, but guards were removed on Peterson's orders.

Wilson, suspicious of Peterson's actions, alerted Captain Nowlein, commander of the queen's troops and household guards. At a last second opportunity to move against the Committee, Wilson did not act because he was forbidden by the cabinet to do so. W.D. Alexander wrote:

> To judge from their conduct, the queen's cabinet were overawed by the unanimity of and determination of the foreign community [about fifty active men, but the three percent!], and probably had an exaggerated idea of the force of the command of safety. They shrank from the responsibility of causing fruitless bloodshed and sought a valid excuse for inaction, which they thought they found in the presence of the United States troops on shore, and in the well known sympathy of the American minister with the opposition.

The queen's cabinet (still the legal government) called together the members of the diplomatic and consular corps for a meeting, at which Stevens was conspicuously absent, pleading illness. The diplomats advised against resistance by force. The queen sent a note to Stevens giving again her assurance to uphold the present constitution. Stevens did not answer. The queen sent the entire cabinet to Stevens of whom he saw only

Peterson, who argued as they (the cabinet) were the legal government, would it not be possible for Stevens to sustain the queen. Stevens, still under the guise of protecting "American life and property only," said that if the "insurgents were attacked or arrested by the queen's forces, the United States troops would intervene."[27]

Too late, the queen's ministers took their eyes off Stevens, now that he had made his choice clear, to look upon the acts of treason of the Committee. Thurston dictated a proclamation to be used in deposing the queen, abrogating the monarchy, and establishing a provisional government to exist "until annexation with the United States had been arranged."[28]

A revolutionist, John Good, had been collecting arms and ammunitions from stores all morning. Whether by prearrangement or not, a native policeman grabbed the reins of Good's team at Fort and King streets, and was shot by Good.[29]

At the sound of the shot, all the queen's guards ran toward Fort and King streets, thus enabling the Committee members to proceed unobserved to the government building. Lt. Commander Swinburne of the *USS Boston* had been alerted by C.L. Carter to watch for the moment Dole took possession of the government building. This was the "moment."

The strategic "moment" took place coincidentally while the queen's ministers were at the police station drafting their note to Stevens. The queen's ministers later stated they were ready to repress the revolt, but Stevens kept them waiting. Stevens hedged considerably under questioning about the time of his recognition of the Provisional Government. His final report before the Morgan committee stated that "sometime between 4:20 and 5:00 p.m.", *before the queen had yielded* (author's italics). And long before the police station surrendered, a note from Mr. Stevens to Dole announced that,

> A Provisional Government having been duly constituted in the place of the recent Government of Queen Liliuokalani and said Provisional Government being in full possession of the Government Building, the Archives, and the Treasury and in control of the capital of the Hawaiian Islands, I hereby recognize said Provisional Government as the *de facto* Government of the Hawaiian Islands.

Dole reported to his brother, George, that taking over the government building was comparatively simple. "Our soldiers began to arrive before the reading of the proclamation was over . . . we proclaimed martial law . . . demanded the station house. The queen gave up her authority under protest."

Wilson refused to give up the police station without written orders from the queen. The cabinet again persuaded the queen to prevent bloodshed. Damon told her she could protest to the Provisional Government.

Liliuokalani, however, protested *not* to the Provisional Government but to the United States government in Washington for redress.

It was an astonishingly shrewd move and equally shrewdly drafted:

> I, Liliuokalani, by the Grace of God and under the Constitution of the Kingdom, Queen, do hereby solemnly protest against any and all acts done against myself and the constitutional Government of the Hawaiian Kingdom by certain persons claiming to have established a provisional government of and for this Kingdom.
>
> That I yield to the superior force of the United States of America, whose minister plenipotentiary, His Excellency John L. Stevens, has caused United States troops to be landed at Honolulu and declared that he would support the said provisional government.
>
> Now, to avoid any collision of armed forces and perhaps the loss of life, I do under this protest, and impelled by said force, yield my authority until such time as the Government of the United States shall, upon the facts being presented to it, undo the action of its representatives and reinstate me in the authority which I claim as the constitutional sovereign of the Hawaiian Islands.

At seven in the evening Dole accepted the queen's protest, *apparently without reading it,* possibly believing it was a protest of the Provisional Government, which would have proved entirely futile. Therefore, unfortunately for the Provisional Government, Dole without challenging the queen's assertion that she surrendered to the "superior forces of the United States," endorsed the written protest, "Received this day by the hands of the late cabinet 17 day of January AD 1893."[30]

The queen noted later in her diary: "Things turned out better than I expected."[31]

And the *coup* of the three-day revolution was not the *fait accompli* the Provisional Government hoped it to be when Stevens raised the American flag over Hawaii on February 1, 1893.

CHAPTER 4

The Provisional Government

❦ 1 ❦

The final act of the executive and advisory council of the self-appointed Provisional Government was to send commissioners to Washington to "negotiate a treaty of political union between the Hawaii and the United States." The steamer *Claudine* was chartered by monies from the royal treasury. L.A. Thurston, W.R. Castle, and W.C. Wilder were to be the commissioners.

By this time no doubt someone had read the queen's "protest," for before the *Claudine* left, she was carefully searched to make certain no royalist nor envoy was aboard. The queen's commissioners were openly denied passage. The queen was allowed to send a written appeal to President Harrison asking that no conclusions be reached until her envoys could arrive. However, as the next ship to leave Honolulu was February 2, (two weeks later), the P.G.'s had an excellent opportunity to place their case before President Harrison without any rebuttal.

The commissioners, now increased to five, adding Charles L. Carter and Joseph Marsden, were enthusiastically received in Washington, D.C., by Charles Reed Bishop who wrote of Liliuokalani that she was "deceitful and treacherous" and of poor moral character (yet it was he, two years before, who advised her to "continue to be a moral example to [her] people.") He now could not believe, for all her faults, "She could be so concerted."[1]

When his comments reached her she replied with characteristic generosity, "C.R. Bishop is not pleased—I forgot I've been accused falsely, perhaps he believed them to be true . . . forgotten also that they had not hesitated to vilify my character . . . would have corrected all but he had to leave . . . a chasm between [us] only time can heal."[2]

W.N. Armstrong (the former world-traveller with King Kalakaua and later defamer of the king's character in his book), Archibald Hopkins and John Mott-Smith, Hawaiian minister—all welcomed the commissioners. John Mott-Smith could bear closer scrutiny than this book allows. All during Thurston's previous "negotiations" and ground-work laying, he had without doubt been in touch with Mott-Smith. Yet Mott-Smith played a game of "no knowledge" of any of Thurston's machinations. On February 3, 1893, however, he was on hand to greet Thurston and the other commissioners.

A strange difference of opinion had begun to arise between the Provisional Government and its representatives. Although explicitly directed to ask for territorial status, but as a last resort accept a protectorate, W.R. Castle stated "we have nothing whatsoever to do with a protectorate." Yet C.R. Bishop (not a commissioner) felt "the Treaty gave too much to the United States" and that a protectorate, "keeping its hands off our labor laws, would be best for us." At no time was statehood mentioned, although fancifully hoped for by some.

On February 4, 1893, the commission proposed a plan, very much to their benefit, that: 1) the United States would assume the Hawaiian national debt; 2) all government land (in which they included not only Crown Lands but personal *alii* lands of Liliuokalani) would remain in possession of the local government; 3) the planters would expect to share in any bounty on sugar. The United States was 4) to improve and use Pearl Harbor and lay a submarine cable from the Pacific Coast to Hawaii; 5) provide for the ex-queen and Princess Kaiulani. On the other hand all Hawaiian immigration and labor contracts were to be kept inviolate, as well as all other laws "inconsistent with the proposed treaty or the Constitution of the United States."

These demands were a bit strong for even United States Secretary of State Foster. He called them "serious embarrassments" and difficult to reconcile with the Constitution and laws of the United States. The "headstrong willfulness" of Queen Liliuokalani seems to have taken root in the commission.

President Benjamin Harrison (who would be succeeded by Grover Cleveland in about sixty days, March 4, 1893) suggested a "plebiscite in the islands in order to give 'the transaction the semblance of having been the universal will of the people'." Secretary of State Foster apparently realized, as did the commissioners that such a move would "dethrone" the Provisional Government and reinstate Liliuokalani—and must be prevented. In negotiations between Harrison and the commissioners,

Foster persuaded the President that a plebiscite would be "unnecessary." He then convinced the commissioners that issues on tariff and the bounty of sugar be omitted; that all references to coaling stations and oceanic cables be removed. "Existing labor system was to continue until changed by positive legislation at Washington." In a hurry to rush the treaty of annexation through the Senate, the commissioners accepted the compromise. Later (1897) when annexation was again considered they were also to cede all government and crown lands to the United States.

In a message in which all responsibility of the United States or its representative in the Revolution was denied, prompt and favorable action was asked of the Senate. Harrison said later (May 20, 1898) in an interview with Indianapolis *News* that he believed that "to have recognized the monarchy there would have been to go back to barbarism."

The second generation of Hawaiian monarchial reign of nearly fifty years, from Kamehameha III's signing the first American-dictated constitution in 1838 through the constitutional monarchies of five succeeding rulers, acceptable to the Hawaiian people themselves and recognized by all major countries of the world—was forgotten. Every dispatch issued by the opposition newspapers in Hawaii, but especially in the United States, attempted to present Hawaii negatively as it had existed *pre*-Kamehameha I; *pre*-overthrow of the old gods by Kaahumanu and Kamehameha II, and even *pre*-missionary arrival.

✲ 2 ✲

When the queen's envoys reached Washington the treaty had already been sent to the Senate. The envoys included the queen's most trusted advisor, Paul Neumann, who had her "power of attorney," which unfortunately read as if he could "sell" the country if he wished. The queen had no such intentions. She was well versed in United States history and was now being daily reminded that the United States was filling out its own contiguous borders. This she could understand. It was not unlike Kamehameha the Great's uniting the islands.

However, no one could offer her enough money for her people's rights. Yet the Provisional Government thought that her country could be "bought" for a mere $250,000.

She was warned of another potential danger: Monarchies were disappearing, and she herself supposedly had no royal blood. The two statements were, of course, contradictory, but they caused her concern.

She found uneasy, but true comparisons in contemporary European history, where new constitutions were radically changing the old monarchial systems.

Other members of the queen's commission who knew no sale was possible, were the Dowager Queen Kapiolani's nephew, Prince David Kawananakoa, characterized by Castle as "a very pleasant fellow" but "purely ornamental." The real adversary to the opposition was E.C. MacFarlane against whom Stevens failed to warn the new Secretary of State, Walter Q. Gresham, until it was too late.[3]

It was as a result of MarFarlane, who was unable to reach President-elect Cleveland except through his secretary, that the royalist version of the revolution appeared in New York *World* (March 1, 1893). MacFarlane squarely placed the blame of the overthrow on Stevens. Neumann, speaking to Foster, asserted flatly that without Stevens and the troops from the *Boston* the queen would not have been dethroned. The general appeal of the royalist agents was that: 1) the request for annexation had not come from the natives; 2) the Provisional Government had tried to prevent the queen's side from being heard; 3) the queen's personal lands had been confused with the Crown Lands and had been confiscated by the Provisional Government.[4]

There was little said about the second-generation Hawaii, possibly because the royalist thought the American government and its people were historically aware of the changes between 1789 (Captain Cook's unfortunate visit) and 1893. They couldn't have been more wrong, and, consequently, lost the opportunity of presenting a true picture of Hawaii and her queen.[5]

They minimized the insistence of the Provisional Government that the British were about "to take Hawaii." Major Wodehouse, British consul in Hawaii, stated firmly that Great Britain would never have tried to "annex so civilized a nation."[6] However, Wodehouse on the other hand encouraged Princess Kaiulani to return to Hawaii from England, for the people would certainly welcome her. Her guardian, Theo. H. Davies, who held extensive commercial enterprises in Hawaii, was concerned his ward would not be properly provided for by the Provisional Government. He misread, by mistake or intent, Wodehouse's advice and brought Kaiulani to Washington, to the jubilation of Thurston and Carter, who could now point to her as "a potential English sovereign for Hawaii."[7]

Kaiulani was somewhat indifferently received, although she did attract some attention from the press and the President. Liliuokalani would have preferred she remained in England, but blamed Davies more than the princess for her coming.[8] Kaiulani returned to England March 18, 1893.

❦ 3 ❦

While Queen Liliuokalani's fate was being decided in Washington, she was having her own problems at home. She wrote in her diary of sending for her *hanai* sons, Kaipo and Aimoku, to be with her. Ida Pope wrote that she did not think it wise that "Kaiponi [sic] (Lydia) be with the queen at this time . . . too many threats."[9]

On February 5 it rained almost continuously—the rains Liliuokalani had always disliked. This one particularly so. She decided again "never going to church." Henry Parker was in full stride against her, as he had been against her brother: "never saw a more unchristianlike . . . missionaries abuse me from the pulpit. Is it godly?"

On the tenth anniversary of the day King Kalakaua had ordained as beginning of the "Jubilee Year" for all time [February 12, 1883] Liliuokalani drove to Waikiki and remained there "alone with (her) own values." She lunched with her retainers and then regretfully returned to Washington Place ". . . how lovely too lovely to come home but had to." Words like these and others in her writings, her songs, and her reminiscences to Lydia Aholo reveal a serenity of spirit that could only have come from the "mysticism" of *Aloha* of Old Hawaii. She had a peace within herself that no circumstance nor person could totally destroy—although every conceivable attempt was made to do so to the end of her life.

The next day a group of *kahuna* came to Washington Place. She wrote "3 women came—dressed all in white with yellow handkerchiefs on neck red bands on hats . . . but I wish they hadn't come here."

It was reported[10] that "a great gathering of kahunas," curiously enough presided over by Kahuila Wilcox (R.W. Wilcox's mother) and the former anti-queen Bipikane (Pipikane), met in Honolulu to propose a method by which the queen could be restored. They fully believed that the gods as well as the people had been offended. The god of the missionaries, which many of them had begun to worship, now seemed so partial to the missionary sons that they returned to their old ways. Three "particularly powerful kahuna women," who were present at the Council gathering, prophesied that the queen would be restored if she followed the instructions of Hiiaka (member of the Pele family).

The *kahuna* conference adjourned and the three women went to Washington Place. They offered themselves to the queen as human sacrifices.

> They proposed that the three with the queen form a procession and enter Iolani Palace from King Street gate. The three would chant their way in through the gate, up past the walk, past the guards and soldiers into the throne room . . . "we in front . . . the queen behind" and "we will stop the mouth of the gun."
>
> Once inside the throne room the three would lead the queen to the throne, seat her on it and then die. "Perhaps!" they said, "death will not come at once but it will come within a few days" and the queen will know that the gods have accepted their sacrifice.

Liliuokalani refused their offer. They concluded the queen's "faith in the old ways had been shaken and she did not have sufficient faith in the Christian religion to overcome obstacles."

Liliuokalani offered a different reason. First she was no longer naive enough to believe the soldiers would hesitate to shoot women—herself included. Secondly, she knew that "traps" of all kinds were being set for her. An agreement with the *kahuna* proposition would certainly label her as "heathen," even though such upright citizens as Cecil Brown had a *kahuna*. She wrote in her diary on April 27th "Aiku asked if he could send a kahuna . . . kahuna is Kaika . . . Cecil Brown's kahuna . . .There's a catch. I told him the Bible was my only guide . . . will get my instructions from there."

The queen, who Thurston said was "wealthy" and "needed no money for she had several homes—and as for the princess her good looks should be sufficient for her to secure a wealthy husband," showed not only his disregard for the royalty he thought he had so peremptorily disposed of, but also his ignorance.

Liliuokalani's diary of 1893 bears frantic statements of having signed mortgage notes on her homes and "all lands left by Bernice" to Damon "for money borrowed for commissioners." The sum came to $10,000. She paid Nawahi's insurance of $140 commenting ". . . mercy only knows how I'm trying to stint myself to pay off what I owe."[11]

She, despite warnings of danger, continued to ride in her carriage. One day, in the unpleasant rain, she "drove by the Palace but would not look at the American flag over the building." She wrote, "The feelings of injury may wear off by and by . . . my dear flag . . . that ever a foreign flag should wave over it. May heaven look down on the missionaries and punish them for their deeds."

Here she too made the mistake of blaming the parents for their sons' deeds. It was the missionaries' sons who were bringing about her torment; however, it cannot be overlooked that the later missionaries did leave their fields of "saving souls" to till the soils of commerce, and they also turned the Hawaiians away from the *alii* monarchial form of government to a republican form, which they did not understand. It is true many early missionaries left "without a cent in their pockets," but of those who stayed, their sons prospered mightily, with the exception of Sanford Ballard Dole (not to be confused with Dole pineapple—a distant cousin of Sanford Dole, who arrived in Hawaii in 1898). The missionaries and their sons were not without the help of United States representatives, all of whom with the exception of Consul Miller (1853) were from the beginning annexationists. Although the queen continued to call the opposition the "missionary party" and later in writing a comic opera the "mischicanery party," she was well aware that other American citizens were involved in her problems. She merely felt, as she often expressed, that one should expect something better—more Christlike—from the "Christian" indoctrinated men.

From January 17 to March 9, 1893, at which time Cleveland withdrew the annexation treaty from the Senate "for the purpose of reexamination," and ordered Secretary of State Gresham to send a fact-finding, impartial person to Hawaii, Liliuokalani was harrassed at home by persons suggesting abdication or resistance, and bringing her the most discouraging news. C.W. Ashford came to her insisting she'd never be restored—"thought to startle me . . . but gave him only a look of unconcern." He made note of the fact she still had her guard of honor under Captain Nowlein. However, two weeks later Sanford Dole decided to remove her guards because "they'd seen people come in after midnight."

The Provisional Government was uneasy, and persons backing it came to her telling her she should abdicate and accept the money from the Provisional Government. She replied she would rather be "poor with [her] people" than "sell the country." Hawaiian civil rights groups suggested resistance and she replied, "No." Her confidential diary stated she felt they were not moved by patriotism but for their own rights—"This will end in all being arrested."

The queen waited for news from Washington, writing songs, and after the Hawaiian band had resigned, refusing to work under the Provisional Government, she "spent time on back veranda listening to the Portuguese band."

⚜ 4 ⚜

James H. Blount was appointed by Cleveland to go to Hawaii. Assertions that Blount was already prejudiced toward restoring the queen may be reviewed by the fact that Blount did not want the position and only accepted the commission when he was told by his son that the climate of Hawaii would add five years to his ailing wife's life.

He was described as a man of "unswerving integrity and devotion to duty."[12] Physically he was a man "of medium stature, florid complexion, a penetrating steel-gray eye before which falsehood and deceit trembled. His fine head of hair became snowy white very early in life, giving him distinction in the House."[13] He was born in Georgia and had served in the Confederate Army. Both situations were to be held against him by the Provisional Government.

Upon their arrival in Honolulu, he and his wife were greeted in full force by the members of the Provisional Government; offers of housing and all conveniences were made. He politely declined.

The queen had also sent a carriage, which he also declined, but accepted graciously the flower leis placed about his and his wife's shoulders.

On April 1, 1893, Blount ordered the American flag taken down and naval forces returned to their ships. The Hawaiian flag was then raised. In contrast to the wild cheering of the opposition on February 1, 1893, when Stevens had the American flag raised, now two months later, there was complete silence. The Hawaiian men stood with their hats in their hands. Tears streamed down the cheeks of both men and women.

James Blount began his investigations by interviewing persons of all stations. He questioned Liliuokalani as well as members of the Provisional Government, but he chose to make his final decision from the testimony of the general populace.

Blount quickly acquired the uncomplimentary name of "Paramount Blount" by the Provisional Government supporters, because he had, to their dissatisfaction, "paramount authority to represent the United States." Privately, he expressed surprise of how well the natives spoke English and how knowledgeable and intelligent they were. Socially he kept his distance from both the royalists and the Provisional Government people.

American newspaper reporters now began to flock to the Islands.

Among them were Charles Nordhoff of the New York *Herald,* Dr. Willam S. Bowen of the New York *World,* Julius Palmer of the Boston *Transcript* and Harold M. Sewall of the *World.* None of these men had the right to interfere in Blount's investigation nor in advising anyone. However, such was not the case. Bowen and Sewall both took it upon themselves to try to persuade Paul Neumann to prevail upon the queen to give up her throne. Dole heartily approved their plan and gave his official sanction. In defense of Dole's actions but not his wisdom, it can be noted they had given him the impression they had equal official status with Blount.[14]

The queen was puzzled by Neumann, whom she said she was sure was loyal to her—yet—another time she called him "an old snake." She refused to give up the throne—"It is not for me; it is for my people," she stated.

On the other hand Nordhoff strongly favored the queen. He reported that she was well-read, intelligent, and answered questions "worthy of a lawyer."

Nordhoff had nothing but problems. His every word was carefully read in the *Herald,* and he was threatened to be "tarred and feathered." He was sued for libel because he "falsely stated" three men of the Provisional Government had signed the lottery bill. Blount pointed out that Nordhoff could not be held liable in Hawaii for libel published in the United States. Nevertheless Nordhoff retracted his statements, but Blount stated that the Provisional Government crushed out "all opposing opinions by forceful methods."

While Nordhoff was apologizing for his indiscretion, Serano Bishop and Dr. Hyde[15] were sending messages picked up by Smith of the San Francisco *Examiner* to the United States declaring the queen "savage", "immoral", "heathenish", "incapable of ruling a civilized—or any— nation," "foul-mouthed," "dangerous", "a dirty squaw", and "bloodthirsty." To which she commented in her diary on April 29th, "All my friends know what is true . . . am above such allegations." Some *Examiner* reporters in Hawaii were surprised she "spoke English . . . had thought they'd need an interpreter."[16]

Liliuokalani was then accused of "joining with Spreckels and Nordhoff and Blount." Her own comments regarding Spreckels were in essence that she wished he'd mind his own business. In reply to whether he were going to help restore her to the throne, Spreckels said he "hoped she wouldn't take part in anything like lottery or interfere with plantation workers." She wrote "cannot see why I shouldn't see that the working class can better themselves . . . to watch for Mr. S's interest only within the law is all he can expect and only what law provides . . . I said nothing . . . I do not like to make promises . . . will not say who I'll appoint as ministers . . . those for good of the country not a private individual or firm."[17]

Right or wrong, Liliuokalani believed the lottery would help the common people. Right or wrong, she thought the "slave labor" on the plantations was "inhuman." Right or wrong, she believed the Chinese should have a right to "improve themselves" in commerce and trade. And right or wrong, she was firmly dedicated to seeing that the Hawaiian commoner had an opportunity to gain some sense of self-worth and esteem rather than continually being negated and placed in a subordinate position. She believed with all her heart in education for values and not money.

She was, of course, out of step with her times that were influenced by acquisition. She was following the innate beliefs of the Hawaiians that had always held relationships of greater importance than ownership. It was one of their "flaws" of character.

James Blount made his assessment of the Hawaiian situation. If he had taken a personal dislike to the Provisional Government, they without doubt hated him enough to have the newly appointed band play "Marching Through Georgia" when he left.

The Blount Report of well over two-thousand pages was delivered to President Cleveland as a full account of the points which he had been sent to gather: 1) causes of the revolution; 2) a hard look at the part played by Minister Stevens; and 3) the attitude of the people of Hawaii toward the Provisional Government.

He stated unequivocally that the: 1) causes of the revolution stemmed from the dissatisfaction of the white businessmen; 2) without Stevens' interference there could not have been a revolution; 3) only a small minority of the people of Hawaii approved of the "oligarchy" of the Provisional Government. A majority of native and white favored a monarchy.[18]

Secretary Walter Q. Gresham made his report to Cleveland on October 18, 1893. In doing so he also laid the blame for the revolution directly on Stevens, advised against the resubmission of the treaty and, in the name of justice, asked whether "a great wrong done a feeble state by the authority of the United States should not be undone by restoring the "legitimate" government."[19]

Cleveland had met the queen and was aware of the second generation of Hawaiian rulers as cultured, well-educated and dedicated to what *they* considered best for the changing times in Hawaii for *their* people. He accepted Gresham's recommendation. Later, in 1898, Cleveland would say that from the time annexation had first been suggested he had "been utterly and constantly opposed to it . . . our interference in the Hawaiian Revolution in 1893 was disgraceful . . . on behalf of national honor and our fair name." After Hawaii was annexed, he wrote General Richard Olney, "I am ashamed of the whole affair."

The American press attacked Cleveland as viciously as it did the queen—freedom of press, under which the Provisional Government supposedly also functioned, operated to save the writers from the "libel" of Charles Nordhoff.

The restoration of the queen would be "a very delicate task" according to *Harper's* monthly writer Carl Schurz. General Olney warned Gresham that "it is *our* government; set up by *our* minister by the aid of *our* naval and military forces . . . (protected) by *our* flag," and finally that President Harrison had "practically sanctioned everything Minister Stevens took it upon himself to do."

In the final analysis it was decided that in order to restore the queen she must agree to all conditions of the United States including giving full amnesty to all those who had opposed her and her government. It was believed that these suggestions would be acceptable to both sides, and therefore force would be unnecessary, although a tacit promise was present that the United States forces this time stood behind the queen.

But it was not known that Dole signed the queen's protest without having read it; that none of the supporters of the Provisional Government *now* cared what the United States government decided, unless, of course, if it were in their favor. No one seemed to recall that although the queen had immediately acceded to Blount's request to await the decision of the United States, Dole had been non-committal.

At this point the United States government was as ignorant—or naive—of the determination of the Provisional Government as Liliuokalani had been when she first began to bow to their wishes with her "protest" to "keep peace and avoid bloodshed."

❦ 5 ❦

Albert S. Willis was the choice for the new minister to be sent to Hawaii. Willis was from the beginning uncomfortable in his position. He was warned that the men of the Provisional Government were angry men and that the natives were "blood-thirsty." Willis at best was not a brave man and his mission called for a man of great courage. Blount himself had told Willis that he feared for the queen's life if she were restored.

Serano Bishop wrote Gorham Gilman on September 25, 1893, that "They (the Provisional Government) are not going to cut their own throats nor submit the welfare of the country's civilization to the arbitrament of ignr't, superstitious haole hating natives." Both Bishop and Gilman had been treated with nothing but the kindest hospitality from the "ignr't, superstitious, haole-hating natives."

Willis arrived on November 4th with his orders to restore the queen. The intensity of the atmosphere into which he walked caused him to delay any action until "things were more quiet." As a result of his delay both sides were confused and rumors flew about Honolulu, not decreasing but increasing the anxiety and tension.

Finally on November 13, Willis decided to see the queen. He, however, had no intentions of going to her but asked her to call on him at the American legation. "All Honolulu seemed to think this improper and not according to protocol" and many protested to the queen. Liliuokalani wrote in her diary: "I said nothing."

Liliuokalani was ushered into a small office-sitting room and was told that Grover Cleveland, the President of the United States, sent kind greetings, expressed his regret for the "unauthorized intervention" that caused her to lose her sovereignty. He hoped now with her cooperation, the wrong done her would be righted. She bowed her acknowledgements.

Queen Liliuokalani, suddenly aware of a stirring in the room that separated her and Mr. Willis by a Japanese screen, questioned if this interview was, as he said, "alone and in confidence." Mr. Willis replied that indeed it was. His wife, he assured her, was in the next room and would not disturb them and his secretary Ellis Mills was "somewhere in the house." The queen wrote in her diary that she suspected Mrs. Willis was taking notes on their conversation.

She was asked if she would give full amnesty of life and property to all persons "who have been or who are now in the Provisional Government, or who have been instrumental in the overthrow of your government." Willis reported, "She hesitated a moment and then slowly and calmly answered: 'There are certain laws of my government by which I shall abide'." Liliuokalani wrote she would have to consult her cabinet. There had been too much trouble for her before when supposedly not consulting her cabinet.

Willis then pressed for an answer from her alone. How did she feel? This was a confidential conversation between just the two of them, he assured her. She replied according to her diary, that

> our laws read that "those who are guilty of treason shall suffer the penalty of death, and their property confiscated by the government." If any amnesty was to be made, it was that they should leave the country forever—for if they were permitted to remain, they would commit the same offense over again, seeing that they had once caused a revolution in 1887 and this was a second offense and the next I feared would be more serious for our country and our people.

The queen was correct in that the Hawaiian law made treason punishable by death and confiscation of property.

From this "alone and confidential" interview, "just between the two of them," Mr. Willis compiled extensive notes from which he quoted that the queen had said "such persons should be beheaded." He said he repeated the word "beheaded," and she agreed.

Later Liliuokalani said she had never used the word "beheaded" because it was not a method by which Hawaiians had ever used for execution. In her *Story* she said the "interview" was read to her and had she *seen* not *heard* the word she would have without doubt corrected it.

Many explanations have been given by numerous writers: one that the queen said "banished," and it was transcribed as "beheaded." The fact still remains first that this interview was *not* to have been "transcribed," and secondly, Liliuokalani was suspicious of "every word being taken down." Such suspicions would have made her alert in her responses. In the opinion of this writer, the queen possibly said "banished," but if "beheaded" were repeated to her, *caught unawares,* she might have unwittingly acquiesced.[20]

Willis sent his confidential report to Gresham and the secretary instructed Willis to question the queen again. This time she was allowed to bring a representative of her own with her. She chose J.O. Carter, a long-time friend and now her agent. This time Mr. Mills was visibly present. Mr. Willis read from the previous interview and then asked if the queen were willing to rescind the death penalty, inasmuch as the United States government would not recognize her sovereignty if she did not. She replied she would do so. He pressed for full pardon, and when the queen hesitated, he gave her one day in which to make her decision.

That night was one of terror for Queen Liliuokalani. The "confidential statement" had already reached the newspapers, and at home and abroad was the news that the "savage queen planned to behead all the whites." The civilized whites then took up arms to "shoot the queen on sight." J.O. Carter warned her of her danger, pointing out that there were men stationed on Kawaiahao Church's roof with guns aimed on Washington Place. It was at this time Liliuokalani began turning from the church she had attended and loved from childhood, to the Episcopal Church, bordering her property. With the aid of James Robertson, E.C. MarFarlane and the bishop of the Episcopal Church, Liliuokalani made her escape. Dressed in the habit of a nun she walked with two nuns through her gate into the Episcopal Church and entered a carriage driven by Robertson and accompanied by MacFarlane.[21]

She was taken in the dark of night to a downtown hotel, where she was guarded throughout the night by the two men. She wrote in her diary: ". . . left to own thoughts . . . great struggle . . . after reading the Bible idea crossed my mind—immediately adopted it . . . sent Capt. Nowlein to Carter. Decided to accede to President . . ."

The next day she made her only *official* communication

> To His Excellency Albert S. Willis, Envoy Extraordinary and Minister Plenipotentiary:
> Sir: Since I had the interview with you this morning I have given the most careful and conscientious thought as to my duty and I now of my own free will give you my conclusions. I must not feel vengeful to any of my people. If I am restored by the United States, I must forget myself and remember my dear people and my country. I must forgive and forget the past, permitting no proscription or punishment of anyone but trusting that all will hereafter work together in peace and friendship for the good and for the glory of our beautiful and once happy land. Asking you to bear to the President and to the Government he represents a message of gratitude from me and from my people, and promising with Gods [sic] grace, to prove worthy of the confidence and friendship of your people I am
>
> > With Assurance of Respect
> > Liliuokalani
>
> Washington Place, Dec. 18, 1893

Willis, reluctantly, took the reply to the leaders of Provisional Government. The queen had accepted all conditions imposed upon her by the United States government. Was the Provisional Government willing to do the same by restoring the queen?

Instead of Willis giving the Provisional Government a time limit, they gave him one: They would "take the matter under consideration."

Four days later at midnight, the reply to Cleveland was delivered by Dole to Willis. With toned-down language of Thurston and legalese of Dole and Smith, the answer made the American government look ridiculous. Refuted by arguments based on international law, justice, equity, and history of Hawaiian-American affairs, all of Blount's, Cleveland's, and Willis' points were demolished. The astounding statement was then made that the right of the President to interfere in "our domestic affairs" was repudiated and denounced as contrary to America's traditional policies, and to Blount's instructions.

Stevens was absolved from all blame. In conclusion, the letter upheld the Provisional Government's position as impregnable—legally, diplomatically, and ethically—and pointed out:

> We have done your Government no wrong; no charge of discourtesy is or can be brought against us. Our only issue with your people has been that, because we revered its institutions of civil liberty, we have desired to have them extended to our distracted country, and because we honor its flag and deeming that its beneficent and authoritative presence would be for the best interests of all of our people, we have stood ready to add our country, a new star, to its glory, and to consummate a union which we believed would be as much for the benefit of your country as ours. If this is an offense, we plead guilty to it.

And, as a final thrust, the Provisional Government "respectfully and unhesitatingly declines to entertain the proposition of the President of the United States that it should surrender its authority to the ex-Queen."[22]

Like a horse with the bit in its mouth the Provisional Government took off to denounce Willis for "secretiveness," "unfriendliness," and "ambiguousness," having thus caused "much distress and anxiety."

Cleveland called the letter "most extraordinary." Written no doubt by Thurston, but signed by Dole, it spared no one; but as nothing short of "unprovoked" war would now aid the monarchy, Cleveland "left the matter in the hands of Congress."

Liliuokalani ended her diary of 1893 with the words: "1893 over-look to 1894. Thankful to Creator and pray that land might be restored to people and our just rights—my prayer."

SANFORD BALLARD DOLE

CHAPTER 5

Mrs. Dominis vs. the Queen

❧ 1 ❧

While the "question of Hawaii" and the fate of its queen, Liliuokalani, was in the hands of the United States Congress, the woman herself, although stunned by the reaction of the Provisional Government, did not lose hope. As long as Hawaii was not annexed to the United States, the Provisional Government was insecure and the royalists hopeful.

Even before the Provisional Government had refused to accept President Cleveland's "edict," John Tyler Morgan, annexationist and chairman of the Senate Committee on foreign relations, had asked to have the question referred to his committee, as it later was.

C.B. Wilson, interviewed by Col. W.T. Cooper, stated that "ninety-percent of the Hawaiians were strongly opposed and irreconcilably opposed to the unauthorized 'bargain' by which their country lost its independence." He equated annexation with conquest. He stated here the queen's point of view.

"They [the P.G.'s] have no consideration for anything except money — they take away land, birthright, and wreck the peace of mind of the native Hawaiian all for wealth and power."[1]

To this Morgan answered: "If the United States want these islands she will annex them without consulting the native Hawaiian's wishes on the subject."[2]

That statement was in essence the basis of the Morgan report. Blount wrote, "[Morgan] can reach the witnesses on one side only, and even these are deeply implicated in the so-called revolution on holding offices under the new government." Senator George Gray of Delaware remarked that Morgan examined witnesses "in a very partial and unfair way . . . to aid the annexationists and injure the President."

Gresham, who had taken an intense dislike to Thurston because of his fifty-one page typically uncourteous letter of December 27, 1893, was also opposed to Morgan.

"In the hands of Congress" the Hawaii issue became more of a domestic American in-fighting than a question of annexation or the cause of the revolution. Morgan's guides-and-mentors were Thurston and W.D. Alexander, who had been paid by the Provisional Government to "lecture" on the Hawaiian question all in their favor.

Morgan was thus able to refute the charges of Blount against the revolutionists. Although he would eventually completely exonerate Stevens and blame only the queen, the final report had not a single recommendation for future action.

The oligarchy continued in Hawaii, holding everyone in the strictest control to their wishes. Between January 1, 1894 and July 4, 1894, both royalists and annexationists (the P.G.'s) were uneasy. On February 3, 1894, Sanford B. Dole wrote commisserating with his brother George in Riverside, California, that "It is one of the worst of misfortunes to lose one's [grip] on good spirits." Dole, in the same letter, gave glowing reports of "his" government, and the desperation of the royalists now that the "exposure of Mrs. Dominis [sic] fond desire to chop off our heads and confiscate our property" has deprived their cause of the "last vestige of sympathy."[3]

Rumors of danger to both the P.G.'s and the queen continued to fly about Honolulu. Dole had written in an earlier letter to his brother that he and his wife did not dare sleep in the same house two nights in succession. Liliuokalani requested "native guards" as she would never feel safe until she had Hawaiian police about her. Again and again she ignored the many warnings against going out because she would be "shot on sight."

Ulrich Thompson, a teacher at Kamehameha Schools, wrote of her visit there. He spoke of giving a "Public Objective Lesson" . . . on "a cup of coffee."

> I had brought in a beautiful set of child's cups and saucers, with cream and coffee pot to match, given one of our children by the Cookes, intending to give each boy a cup of coffee. There was a kerosene stove upon which to boil the water. The room was crowded; and I was just beginning to locate the great coffee countries on the map; and to tell why Mocha and Java coffee were considered better than any other blend;—when the Queen, Liliuokalani and her ladies in waiting, entered. Soon they were seated and listening attentively as the lesson progressed and the aroma of fresh coffee filled the class

room. I poured a cup of coffee and presented it to her Majesty, who
received it as only she knew how to accept homage. Then, I poured
a cup for each of her ladies. They seemed pleased and interested.
Finally after they had taken gracious leave—I returned to the thought
of serving each boy with a cup of coffee. The cups were washed and
coffee poured and offered to the boys. Not one of the boys would
touch the coffee or the cups.—At the moment I could not understand
why.—But later, I solved the matter, at least to my own satisfaction.
The Queen had drunk of that coffee. It was *not for them!*

That was the most delicate compliment to a Queen, that I ever
heard of. Sir Walter Raleigh, throwing down his cloak for Queen
Elizabeth, was not more gallant.[4]

Apparently, the native boys at Kamehameha School recognized one
Queen and *no* Mrs. Dominis.

The queen wrote in her diary (January 17) "Year ago signed away
right to throne under protest . . . PGs celebrate . . . horrible . . . parade,
reception, illumination." It was gratifying to the queen that most of the
Diplomatic Corps refused to attend the activities.

Despite their celebration of "First Anniversary" of the Provisional
Government, the men were not completely secure. Thurston contemplated
the suggestion of "restoring" the queen for forty-eight hours and then
overthrowing her—accepting *no protest.*

This ridiculous suggestion was followed by offering the queen $20,000
a year and Kaiulani $10,000 if she would just abdicate quietly. Her reply
was she would "not accept one cent and sacrifice the rights of [her]
people."[5]

In the meantime the oligarchy in Hawaii had officially proclaimed
themselves as the Provisional Government and declared martial law.
They realized, of course, that they needed the United States, and as a
better bait decided to "form" a Republic by advice of Frank P. Hastings,
Hawaiian chargé in Washington: "The very idea of a young Republic,
no matter how formed is in itself a tower of strength in America . . .
the American people look for the star and not the crown."

On March 15, 1894, the Provisional Government called a convention
to draft a constitution for the "Republic of Hawaii," guided by Thurston.

The revolutionary leaders made sure they would retain control. The
president and the executive and advisory council were automatically
named the majority. The voters were then allowed to elect the minority
members. The voters, however, were limited to those of wealth, who had

to take an oath of allegiance to the Provisional Government and to oppose any attempt to reestablish the monarchy.

The Provisional Government were to hold its constitutional convention in April. Sam Parker suggested to the queen that the royalists call a mass meeting to prevent the people from voting. Liliuokalani recommended: "Stick to principles . . . people should be cautious and stay away . . ." She advised the Hawaiian Patriotic Society not to go to any mass meetings and certainly not allow the "natives to be used as a cat's paw." She maintained that Cleveland was "doing all."

The Provisional Government even by its restrictions on franchise came to believe that even the few thousand voters who had approved the constitution could not be trusted to endorse it, so the constitution became law not by plebiscite (such as it was), but by proclamation. The queen had lost her throne for trying to alter the constitution by proclamation; now the Revolutionaries (P.G.'s) in the name of "liberty" did substantially the same thing.[6]

In the final constitution the qualifications for voting or holding office were so strict that comparatively few natives and no Orientals could vote. Fewer still could serve in either house of the legislature.

President Cleveland jokingly expressed contempt in a proclamation:

FOOLS' DAY A FAST DAY

To My People: Whereas, my good and great sister and fellow sovereign, her gracious majesty, Liliuokalani, queen of Hawaii, has been wickedly and unlawfully dethroned by the machinations of Americans and persons of American descent in those islands, being instigated thereto by the devil, one John L. Stevens; and whereas, my well-conceived plans for the restoration of her sacred majesty have not had the result they deserved but her majesty is still defrauded of her legal rights by her refractory and rebellious subjects, and her position is a just cause of sympathy and alarm; now, therefore, I, Grover Cleveland, President of the United States, do hereby ordain and appoint the last day of April next as a day of solemn fasting, humiliation and prayer. Let my people humble themselves and repent for their injustice to me and my great and good sister, and pray, without distinction of color, for her speedy return to the throne and the discomfiture of the miserable herd of missionaries and their sons, her enemies and traducers.

Long Live Liliuokalani, the de jure queen of Hawaii!

Done at our mansion in Washington this 25th day of February, 1894.

Grover Cleveland

A true copy. Attest,
Walter Q. Gresham,
Secretary of State.[7]

Liliuokalani even before learning of this, had spent "three hours fasting, meditation, and prayer."

She continued hopefully planning for restoration, appointing a cabinet, and then being met with the surprising resistance of some of the Provisional Government that she must prove she had royal blood. She wrote the following letter to Poomaikelani, whose husband had kept the genealogical records of Kalakaua and Kapiolani. The salutation of "mother" and closing of "your loving daughter," were complimentary.

Mother Poomaikelani,
My love to you.

The question regarding my royal birth has been raised again, and this is the reason why I am repeating my former request to you to lend me the books definitely telling about our genealogy. Will you kindly hand them to Kaimana and he will bring them to me. I should like to read them for a short while and when I am finished using them Kaimana will return them to you in perfect condition.

Leaders of the provisional government have made comments that I have no royal blood in my veins, whatsoever, consequently I have no claim to the throne and so are Kawananakoa and Kalanianaole, my nephews, whom I have designated in my constitution to ascend the throne, if Kaiulani passes away without any issue.

Hearing of these untrue comments, Mr. Willis, the American Consul, wishes me to produce my genealogy.

May I ask you again to lend me those books? Kaimana will return them to you.

Your loving daughter,
Liliuokalani[8]

Mar. 28, 1894.

By June 6, 1894, talk of "fighting" for restoration came to the queen. Her reply was "Don't feel [it's] particularly bright."

Her serenity is expressed on June 7th when she wrote ". . . am surrounded by everything that is beautiful, the lovely foliage, the flowers, birds sing so sweetly. All tend to make life contentment—and Maker of all watches over me and makes my life happy."

Still a child of nature, her mystical hopes remained that if nature was so beautiful, unfolding in its natural order, was it possible that man could reverse these laws?

❧ 2 ❧

Letters from C.L. Carter flowed to J.L. Stevens giving the shaky side of the Provisional Government. On February 3, 1894, he argued that Paul Neumann's bitterness was personal against Stevens. He then refuted his own case for Stevens by saying that it was Stevens' interference in opposing Neumann for election to the legislature (nearly causing him to lose) that brought about Neumann's bitterness. Stevens seems to have had his fingers in personal plots as well as Hawaiian.

In April Carter wrote:

> Your counsel with regard to holding together has had a very good effect upon me and has given me patience to continue an active enthusiasm which I would not otherwise have had. The feeble and vacillating course of the Provisional Government in many recent local affairs has been a sore disappointment. Mr. Dole has been too ill to exercise that calm judgment which is ordinarily his strongest characteristic, and the Attorney General [W. O. Smith] has been too busy and tactless to control affairs even could he have done so with Mr. Damon constantly making most costly blunders.
>
> The experience of the last two or three months has gone far to satisfy me that politics are a practical occupation and that they cannot be safely left to the guidance of men who consider them contemptible. We all hoped that when Mr. Hatch went in he would strengthen the situation, but he has carried out his declaration of making the public business secondary to his professional affairs with the result that he has been of little practical value. The government has done wisely in sending for Mr. Thurston. I think the gentlemen commenced to realize that affairs were slipping beyond their control and so sent for him to lead and he will be exceedingly valuable in the days to come, although the want of a practical leader has led to many unfortunate complications and vastly too much unnecessary friction.
>
> The power of the Hawaiian League is broken, although the element which it represents may combine at any time with as much effect as ever. You can see how all of these things have been very dis-

couraging and might have led me to the point of abandoning any active part in the situation, but I have gone on and have now secured a nomination for election as a delegate to the constitutional convention, and if elected shall do all that I can for the best interests of the country and the cause of annexation. There is a very considerable revulsion of feeling among the planters on the subject of annexation, and it is entirely within the range of possibilities that they may attempt to indefinitely postpone the matter, but if so they will find a most determined opposition to contend against. The other islands to which we have always looked for the strongest support are disorganized and largely disgruntled all for lack of having a practical man to go among them and keep them posted. Mr. Baldwin is of course a tower of strength, as he always is, and he has rallied the Islands of Maui and Kauai into practical and satisfactory action so far as the delegates are concerned but the registration is meagre. On Oahu the delegates are far from satisfactory whereas they might have been highly so, but the registration here has been exceedingly satisfactory. You will note that we have some 1700 on the Island. The largest registration under the old regime was about 2800. This gives us a decided majority and when it is considered that nearly a thousand otherwise qualified for registration had not and could not pay their taxes but very generally stated that if their taxes were paid for them they would register, you can understand how with the use of a little money the Provisional Government would have had an overwhelming support.

In spite of all these difficulties I see a bright future ahead of us and do not doubt that the friends of all that is best in the country will stand together in the struggle.

Charles L. Carter[9]

On July 4, 1894, the Provisional Government proclaimed itself a Republic—although even Thurston admitted it did not have "all the elements" of a republic, an understatement at best.

Sanford Ballard Dole took the oath of office of President. A.F. Judd, who had administered Kalakaua's oath and Liliuokalani's, now administered Dole's:

I, Sanford B. Dole, President of Provisional Government of Hawaiian Islands, by virtue of the charge to me given by the Executive and Advisory Councils of the Provisional Government and by the Act dated July 3, 1894, proclaim the Republic of Hawaii as the sovereign authority over and throughout the Hawaiian Islands from this time forth. And I declare the Constitution framed and adopted by the Constitutional Convention of 1894 to be the Constitution and the supreme law of the Republic of Hawaii, and by virtue of this Constitution I now assume office and authority of President thereof.

On August 27, Willis wrote to Dole: "The right of the people of the Hawaiian Islands to establish their own form of government has been formally acknowledged both by Executive and Legislature departments of the United States. I extend recognition of the Republic of Hawaii."

The Hawaiian flag was raised as the flag of the Republic. The Hawaiians refused to look at it as they passed by. It was not, they declared, "their flag."

Becoming a republic did not automatically change anything from the oligarchy regime of the Provisional Government. Financially there were problems: the United States had not been "willing to take over the debt." The debt of the monarchy in 1892 was $122,000 with the sale of bonds of $27,700, but from January 17, 1893, the debt had nearly doubled. The trip to Washington alone had cost the government another $14,000. Total income from crown lands amounted yearly to $48,769.75, which the Republic now took along with all government land revenues.[10]

Liliuokalani's *alii* lands remained in constant debate and were held largely by the Republic.

The lands were not the only factors under "debate." That which wounded the royalists and native Hawaiians most was the new government taking over the Iolani Palace as the Executive Building. Inasmuch as the Republic had few if any military reinforcements after the United States withdrew their troops, they "recruited" the "Portuguese Army" and any beach bums or other footloose wanderers as military guards. As a result these men destroyed priceless treasures in the palace. They had been instructed to "do away with all the royal trappings," but Dole soon became aware of the wanton destruction and stopped it. Feather *kahilis,* priceless feathered cloaks, invaluable pieces of art were destroyed. Queen Liliuokalani had attempted on January 17, 1893, to wrap and secure some of the royal treasures, but she had been ordered out of the palace and told to return to Washington Place.[11]

It was in the basement that a half-drunk recruit by the name of Riley had found King Kalakaua's crown. Riley had watched the other men "play" king with the swords and the capes and now he had found what he—typical of his station—believed to be a "play" crown. So he systematically began to pry loose the "pretty baubles" of rubies, emeralds, and diamonds. These he put to a more practical use of payment in lieu of money in a game of dice. A more knowledgeable "officer" discovered the game and "bought back" most of the jewels. However, Riley hid one big glittering glass stone, which he sent to his girl friend on the mainland. It was one of the biggest diamonds in Kalakaua's crown. Years later a representative of the government tracked down the diamond and "bought" it back from a naive mid-western girl who once had held a king's ransom.[12]

The royalists had not given up. On July 30 there were still rumors that the council of the Republic considered restoring the queen. Liliuo-kalani had hopes of restoration until the Republic was recognized by foreign powers. The "foreign powers" did recognize the Republic as "defacto government" on July 23rd. Paul Neumann insisted that *defacto* government versus the *de jure* government was not legal. Liliuokalani mistakenly believed that power lay with this legality and not "might" and so continued to believe, encouraged by Widemann, Parker, and Cummins, that she could be restored. However, against her better judgment, she signed "commissions" for the men to go to Washington, D.C. She wrote "felt it was working against me as had left all to Pres. Cleveland."[13]

She even wrote a new constitution which she gave to Robertson to go over on November 10, 1894. On December 26, Sam Parker suggested she confer with Wideman, Campbell, and Carter. On the 27th she wrote in her diary that she didn't wish to confer with those men: ". . . told him it was treason." On that day, however, she signed what was to be the crux of her trial for misprision, changed from treason: "signed eleven commissions."

Throughout the year the men of the Republic had been uneasy. Twice Dole had gone aboard ships—one American and one British—asking if armed force would be available in case of national uprising. In each instance he was refused. Dole was far from satisfied that the "people of Hawaii" were in favor of the Republic. He wrote his brother: "For most of the time for the past 18 months I have felt anxious about the possibility of a hostile attack and we have made the Executive Building well nigh impregnable against such an attack unless some of our own men should become traitors."[14] He went on to say with more assurety that the "next" step to be taken was "to pass a new land law providing for the management and disposition of government lands including Crown Lands. I intend to provide for different methods of furnishing land to settlers, and to make it well nigh impossible for speculators to get a chance at the public lands." There was to be no repetition of what the *haole* had done under the monarchy.

As late as December 8, 1894, Dole was not completely secure that the Republic was a "recognized" government. He wrote that Cleveland's recognition had helped and that "generally we have been acknowledged by the great powers, with the exception of T.H. Davies and he says he will follow in the wake of the British Empire, so we feel quite easy now."

It is significant in what was to follow in 1895 to note that the year of 1894 ended with the Republic's lack of complete surety of its own "legality," and its expressed fears of "Mrs. Dominis." On the other hand, the Royalists hoped that the monarchy could be restored and pressed Liliuokalani to send commissioners, write constitutions, and sign—in what was later to be interpreted as treason—"Commissions." Liliuokalani, not too sure that her advisors were correct, warned against anything that could be considered "treason."

The natives still held her as *Moi Wahine* and the royalists as queen, and detested with a passion the derogatory term of "Mrs. Dominis."

CHAPTER 6

The Queen is Arrested

❧ 1 ❧

The curt dismissal by the P.G.'s of President Cleveland's "command" that she be restored was inconceivable to Liliuokalani. Her great "crime" had been that she had attempted what seemed to her not only her right but her duty—to gain a more equitable constitution for *her* people, and at *their* request. She failed to do so through the legislative means under the Bayonet Constitution of 1887—*not* instituted by legislative means. Only then did she use the historical precedence of Kamehameha V of promulgating a new constitution by monarchial edict.

This proposed action brought the United States' armed forces against her in what she considered an unjustifiable action.

All during the year of 1893, the "Restoration Hymn" of 1843 was repeatedly published in newspapers.[1] It may have been printed as a "fifty-year anniversary," or to encourage the queen. But just as likely, it was a subtle "refined cruelty" on the part of her enemies. In 1843 the "Restoration Hymn" spoke of justice from "across the sea," and peace.

President Cleveland was maligned almost as severely as the queen, and he was to be proved powerless by a group of people—the Congress. Less than one percent of the members of Congress had any firsthand, or even intelligent second hand, knowledge of Hawaii. They were influenced by the press; the press had approximately the same amount of correct information.

Never allowing truth to stand in the way of a good story, the press condemned Hawaii and her queen as "primitive," "outmoded," "savage," but the physical islands, a delicious fruit to be picked for commercial purposes.

There was enough opposition to annexation in the United States however, plus general political apathy toward some "unimportant little islands in the Pacific," to delay any move by Congress toward annexation.

Such reluctance seemed to the queen a hopeful sign, but the oligarchy of the Provisional Government became the oligarchy of the Republic, and with or without annexation, the hope of an independent Hawaii *for the Hawaiians* was gone.

The attitude of the "missionary party," "reform party," "anti-royalists," or "pro-annexationists," by whatever name they were known among the natives or themselves, has been thoroughly set forth in many books written by missionary descendants and others of their persuasion.[2] In short, they believed, as they had before Liliuokalani's birth, that not only was their way the right way, but that there was no other way. They took up the idea of "what was best for Hawaii."

By the time Liliuokalani was in her teens the word was already out: "Hawaii is *ours; we* have given them the language, the civilization, the Christianization. Hawaii is *ours*."[3]

Liliuokalani could no more turn back the clock to pre-1887 than she single-handedly could have held back a tidal wave.

❧ 2 ❧

In 1895 Liliuokalani was still in a state of shock. Physically, she had suffered several "nervous exhaustions" from the strain imposed upon her. Her enemies continued to call her "foolish," "naive," even "stupid."[4] However, she was first and foremost Hawaiian *alii,* whose "first duty," according to early historian Malo, was to serve *her people.* That was the way she saw her duty—give to *her* people what they wanted, but do so by as peaceful means as possible, even if peace had to be assured by humiliation to herself in acceding to demands of the opposition. Her betrayal would continue.

Robert Wilcox, that perpetual chameleon revolutionist, came to Liliuokalani to tell her he planned "to have her restored." Liliuokalani, clinging to a tenuous vine of her health, unfortunately dismissed Robert Wilcox with the attitude she had long held toward him. She thought of him as a child, never taking him seriously.

One can easily assume she dismissed him with a pat on the head of "Go play your games, Robert." It can be said she should have known better, but Wilcox was rather like a perpetual teenage rebel. King Kalakaua had had him "educated" in Italy, and he had brought back an unhappy wife, whom Liliuokalani had befriended. When he could get no position "suitable to his station," he had sulkily gone off to San Francisco, where his Italian Countess wife left him. Upon his return he had begun the badly organized and fluke rebellion "for" King Kalakaua

against the Bayonet Constitution in 1889. Even Kalakaua in his most believing moments had shied away from Wilcox's actions. Wilcox had then
turned against Liliuokalani when she had become queen and he had
not received political appointments he desired. He demanded a new
constitution; he wanted to be *"king"* of a new republic. After the queen
was threatened by the incipient Provisional Government after the announcement of her new constitution, Wilcox led rallies in *support* of the
queen.

Now, with the Republic established, Robert Wilcox plotted a counter-
revolution. It was this information he brought to Liliuokalani. It was this
information that was to lead to her being arrested for treason.

At the time Wilcox gave her the information there can be little doubt
she put small faith in his "revolution." However, there were others of
her household who heard Wilcox, believed in him, and whose loyalty
to the queen was as weak as her cabinet's had been. These were her
supposed-lover, Charles B. Wilson, and her trusted household guard, Sam
Nowlein, who by some writers[5] had been given the dubious credit of
beginning the revolution, with Wilcox only joining later. Liliuokalani *did*
tell Sam Nowlein that if the people wished to throw off their yoke
they should, but she would not stand for "mere rioting." The counter-
revolution began.

A group of poorly equipped "revolutionists," having procured guns
that had been sent from San Francisco on the schooner *Walhberg* (Wal-
berg), met at Henry F. Bertleman's home, near Diamond Head, to plan
strategy. The moving toward the "secret meeting" was so carefully planned
and so stealthily carried out that *armed* natives walked through the
streets of Honolulu as fishermen! The new government, which had been
uneasy since its inception, was hardly oblivious to such manueverings.

The police immediately began to follow the men to Bertleman's home.
On the way they met a young man, Charles Carter (son of H.A.P. Carter), who "wanted to join the fun." Carter's fun was short-lived. Having
taken a pistol of his own, he approached the Bertleman home and saw
a movement in the bushes. Carter fired and a return shot killed him. The
shot, it was determined later, was fired by a "half-white named Poole . . .
it was probably rightly considered by the commission that he was not
more guilty than others who were shooting at our men and missed them,"
Dole wrote his brother on February 23, 1895.[6] As a result no "murderers"
were brought to the later trial. But now there was "full-scale war."

Shots were exchanged and the Hawaiians hastened to the craggy sides of Diamond Head and into the valleys. The armed forces of the Republic enjoyed the chase, but the royalists, among whom were many *haole* and *hapa-haole* as well as Hawaiians, found little joy in hiding in the gulches.

On January 16, 1895, Queen Liliuokalani sat uneasily and unhappily in her living room at Washington Place with her companions, Mrs. Charles Clark and Mrs. Evelyn Wilson. They talked in low tones about the abortive "revolution" that had ended so tragically in the imprisonment of over a hundred Hawaiian and *haole* sympathizers, taken from their homes and families on suspicion to be put in prison.

Liliuokalani's uneasiness stemmed from concern for her supporters; not for a moment did she believe any harm could come to her directly. Although often warned, she had been so infected by the age-old belief that the person of the queen was sacred that no amount of *haole* indoctrination, personal insult, or even open threats of bodily harm, had destroyed this ingrained certainty. It was this self-delusion that gave her that strange naiveté that made the P.G.'s call her "willful" and "opinionated." But it did not disguise the latent fear that caused her knuckles, gripping the arm of her chair, to turn white.

From January 7th until the 16th the *Bulletin* published a list of those arrested. Dan Logan, its editor, occasionally made a caustic comment against the P.G.'s while the *Star,* a "republic" newspaper, raved and ranted against the "bloodthirsty rebels."

That Liliuokalani knew of the planned uprising is no doubt correct, though there is no evidence that she actually *believed* in its success or took an active part in it. She indirectly admitted her knowledge at her trial, although advised against such an admission by her attorney, Paul Neumann. To suppose her "guilty" of hoping for restoration seems quite normal and a bit absurd to be a charge levied against her. Nevertheless it was.

Little was said that there was always in her desires the prayer of avoidance of bloodshed. Absurdly naive? Impossibly foolish? So the P.G.'s thought. Yet it must be remembered Liliuokalani lived by a different faith—the faith in the spirit of *Aloha*—God as Love, despite the missionaries' vengeful God. Lorrin Thurston speaks of *their* success as "fate"[7] and perhaps therein lies the key to the greatest difference in attitudes.

The "inevitability," of the twentieth century movement against monarchies, the manifest destiny of the United States, the supposed impossibility of the existence of a small country having its own culture, the rightness of genocide under the guise of "civilization"—these may all be summed up as "fate."

"Faith" however, as the Hawaiians knew it, was individual, and the results are only evident when the ruins of battle have been cleared away and the small phoenix of *aloha* can rise again.

Faith belongs to God's laws. Faith is mystical, and leaves the outcome with God.

Fate belongs to man's preconceived ideas and is often materialistically aided. S.B. Dole caught a glimpse of this when he wrote his brother: "I have my anxious times. We are queer combinations in our imperfect human character. I suppose that one trouble with me is that I get away from God through worldliness and so lose the strengthening influence of a consciousness of His presence."[8]

Liliuokalani's champions in the counter-revolution, many of them *hapa-haole,* had taken on the attitude of the revolutionists of 1893, that blood must and would be shed. It was unfortunately to be mostly theirs. Liliuokalani, as she sat in her living room with Mrs. Clark, whose husband had been taken prisoner, regretted the whole affair.

The women had heard the ominous clatter of horses' hooves coming to a halt at the gate of Washington Place. No one spoke aloud her fears.

The chime of the doorbell echoed ominously through Washington Place—the bell that had heralded so many exciting, famous, friendly people with a gay note of welcome. It now took on a tolling sound. Mrs. Wilson, who had glimpsed through the drawn drapes the visitors coming up the path, informed the queen that Deputy Marshal Brown and Captain Robert Parker of the police were at the door. "Bring them in," she declared, and all the royal command was there.

Deputy Marshal Brown, with Captain Parker, the cousin of Sam Parker, entered clumsily and stated he had a warrant for the queen's arrest.

When she asked to see the warrant, he refused. He knew it was for imprisonment, and he knew she thought it was for "questioning."[9] But it was just as well to leave the warrant in doubt.

Again that strange trust that all would be well—that nothing could really happen to *her* ascended over both her anger and intuitive suspicions she had of the two men. Calmly she instructed Mrs. Clark to make preparations for her to go to the police station "for the questioning." The two men exchanged glances, but said nothing. Mrs. Clark left to return promptly with the queen's handbag, a Victorian bonnet, and a shawl, because the day was cool with intermittent squalls.

Liliuokalani felt the first premonition of real fear brush her, but even then as lightly as the trade winds, when the men told her Mrs. Clark could accompany and *stay* with her if she wished. Yet this was not so unusual, she struggled to believe. She nearly always had a lady-in-waiting with her. It was the way in which Captain Parker had said *stay*—and the tears in Mrs. Clark's eyes that frightened her. Mrs. Clark's husband had been taken away not to return. Had it been in this manner? But, of course not; she was the Queen.

A silent crowd had gathered at the gates of Washington Place. They were mostly Hawaiians and their faces were solemn, forbidding; yet questioning: *What should we do?*

Liliuokalani remembered the Old Hawaii tales of Captain Cook's death and the adage: *No one must take away our Chief.* But Captain Cook had taken the Chief. It had been a successful ploy of Cook's to hold a chief hostage (he had done so in Tahiti), until the natives responded to his wishes. In Hawaii he found an unexpectedly fierce loyalty to the *Moi* when he had tried to take him captive. There had been resistance to death. But her people must not kill, not even one man. Times were different now. A new society existed. More than a hundred years had passed since that first Chief had been taken away—in what the P.G.'s called that "ignominious affair of Captain Cook." She, *Moi wahine,* had kept her people from bloodshed—and it was her duty to do so now.

She raised a black-gloved hand to the people and bowed her head in recognition of their loyalty. They moved back, but the heart-rendering wailing of Old Hawaii filled the air.

As the carriage turned the corner, Liliuokalani looked back to see the crowds dispersed by P.G. guards, but she saw something else that struck a spear of terror through her heart of grief: Chief Justice Albert F. Judd was entering her home.

Shaken, she was scarcely aware of the people who crowded the streets —silently weeping Hawaiians, curious *haole,* grinning, but weary, P.G. soldiers.

Her horror and apprehension increased as the carriage took the route to the Iolani Palace instead of the police station. The palace grounds looked like a badly kept military camp. Tents had been pitched and soldiers lay on the grass on their backs, exhausted; half-lying, leaning on their arms; chewing blades of grass—*on the palace grounds*—their guns scattered about. No one stood up as the carriage approached.

Directly aimed at her from the lower veranda of the palace were two brass fieldpieces. As the carriage neared the gates of the palace, she saw the lines of guards, not to protect her—but to protect the men *from* her. For a moment she felt ridiculous, hysterical, laughter bubble up inside her, but it was quickly quelled, for cutting through the distant wails of Hawaiians and the throb of fear that had begun in her ears, was the sound of the Government Band playing in derision "Marching Through Georgia," their insult to Blount, now to her.

She was met by Colonel J.H. Fisher on the palace steps. She looked neither to the left nor the right as she walked through the rooms in which she had once reigned as queen, nor did she speak. She was taken to a corner room, the guest room often used by Princess Poomaikelani, and other royal relatives, once beautifully furnished in Japanese decor. Now her first glance saw it as bare, uncarpeted, and meagerly furnished.

Colonel Fisher, who obviously did not like his job, tried to soften his words in telling her that this was to be her "place," her "living quarters" from now on. She was a prisoner of the state, being held for treason. She turned to look into his eyes, her face expressionless: "My prison," she corrected him.

Colonel Fisher fidgeted. "President Dole . . ." he hesitated, then went on when the queen refused to react to this title. "President Dole has said you may have anything you wish—only ask the guard—the officer on duty."

"I would like to have Mrs. Clark stay with me. And I prefer to have my meals prepared at my own home and brought here." The fear of being poisoned had finally penetrated her trust.

"I'm sure it can be arranged," Colonel Fisher hurried his way to the door.

"Thank *Mr.* Dole for me," she said coolly, as he had almost made his escape. She still had the power to make the P.G.'s feel uncomfortable, and one who has this ability is not easily forgiven. Nor was she to be.

Once the doors closed, Mrs. Nahinu Clark, who had not the queen's stamina, began to weep. Liliuokalani quieted her weeping and fears by the same practicality she had used with Queen Kapiolani regarding her fears of King Kalakaua. She suggested they use their time immediately to take stock of what they had.

They did not have much, besides the few items of furniture of a single bed, a chair, a sofa, a bureau and a small table, there was a cupboard, intended for food, made of wood with wire screening to allow the circulation of the air through the food. Adjoining the main room was a bathroom, a small corner room. There was also a large balcony extending off from the windows, a balcony which was to prove both a curse and a blessing to the queen.

By nightfall the enormity of her situation had fallen full upon her. The constant tramping of the guards not only outside her door, but also along the veranda, was a continuous reminder that she was a prisoner. The first night she often spoke of as "the longest night of her life." It was spent mostly in prayer. Nahinu and she read from the Episcopal Book of Common Prayer, which had been placed in her bag earlier in the day.

Toward dawn Nahinu Clark lay down on the sofa after having helped the queen onto her bed. Neither of them slept.

The queen's mind wandered and struggled with an unbelievable situation, with hope, prayer confusion. She thought of Lot Lane, the bravest of the counter-revolutionists. He was somewhere out on the Pali, cold and hungry, praying to his Catholic God; she, to her now Episcopalian God; and President Dole, to his Congregational-Presbyterian-Calvinistic God, the Mormons to theirs, and so over the Islands. Were there, indeed, no longer *many gods? Was* there just *one?*

She sighed and turned on her uncomfortable bed and thought again of her one human hope—Lot Lane. Lane, one of eight Irish-Hawaiian children, took to his fighting Irish blood his father's advice to "fight to the death for their mother's land." Lot was the last of the hidden counter-revolutionists sought by the new Republic. Even when the last few surrendered, he had climbed higher into the mountains to hide in crevices, to be soaked by torrential rains, to eat wild bananas. Without shoes, clothes in shreds, evading bloodhounds and bullets, he had given no thought to surrender.

Liliuokalani did not know that that very dawn she awaited, with trembling hope of a new day, would bring Lot down from his mountain cave. Deceived by the cease-fire in the city, he was to descend with a cry of gratitude that "the foreigners had come to rescue the Hawaiians as they had promised" only to meet a friend who told him: "Our queen was arrested."

On January 17th Lot Lane, unshaven, barefoot, and fierce of countenance went to the only place he could be of help—the police station. Not *for* help. *To* help. For there in one room were over a hundred Hawaiians and *haole* royalists who had had no news of their wives and children, a deprivation that was worse than their semi-starvation.

Lot gave himself up. He refused to give information demanded of him of the *haole* who had supported the Hawaiians. "You will be put to death as a traitor," the nervous guard threatened him, his finger not far from the gun on his desk.

"No, I am not the traitor. You are. I choose with my heart and head to fight for my country—and I will not tell of my friends," he was reported to have said.[10]

However, with Lane's surrender, the "rebellion" was over.

But Lot did what he came to do. He terrified the guards into bringing food—*poi* and meat—for men who had lived for days on hardtack and coffee. And he brought them as much news of their families as he knew, and railed furiously against fate that had not made him omniscient enough to know about everyone. He blamed himself for the sorrow of the men who wept in the crowded corners whose hope of news about a loved one had been dashed more severely than their bodies against the prison walls.

⚓ 3 ⚓

Meanwhile, during and after that first, long night, when Liliuokalani managed to bring her thoughts to a halt, to shut out her own heartache and problems, she became aware of the incessant sighs coming from Mrs. Clark. Her husband was in prison; her children might be alone, if the friends who had taken them had also been imprisoned. She decided immediately that Mrs. Clark should return to her children. She once again placed the needs of others before her own.

Marshal C.B. Wilson, having turned himself over to the authorities of the Republic, was made Liliuokalani's liaison officer. The following day he came to her to say his wife had volunteered to remain in prison with her. Even the most malicious of gossip mongers must have had to think twice to believe that the wife of the man with whom Liliuokalani was supposed to have had her flagrant love affairs would have voluntarily gone into prison with her. Dr. Trouseau had characterized Evelyn Townsend Wilson, "pretty kitty," as "extremely jealous and would never have tolerated an affair between her husband and even the queen." While Trouseau's testimony to Blount was dismissed with scorn, the action of Evelyn Wilson could not be.

It was from Mrs. Wilson that Liliuokalani learned that her home, Washington Place, had been thoroughly ransacked ostensibly for the purpose of finding treasonable evidence against her. All her personal papers, diaries, purported constitutions, all petitions from her people, her late brother's and her late husband's papers were confiscated. Only her will was returned to her. She was, however, later allowed to "buy back" certain pieces of jewelry of "sentimental value." The building itself was so violently assaulted by the Portuguese militia that the foundation and underpinnings had to be later repaired to make it livable again. The same type of senseless vandalism and destruction occurred as had been begun at the Palace in 1893.

Liliuokalani was sick at heart to hear that her last stronghold of hope had been senselessly ravaged. Even her songs had been confiscated under the pretext that they might contain "hidden messages" to her people.[11]

She was told that her agent Joseph Helehue had been taken prisoner and was under "severe examination," including placement in a dark cell and deprived of food and water.

Liliuokalani was assured she would be given a trial to determine her guilt. A brief hope was kindled in her, that if she were found "not guilty," she might even be restored. Liliuokalani had not abdicated and felt that until she did, she was still queen. Many of the natives felt the same.

Liliuokalani also had another false hope. She remembered that over a period of years the foreigners had insisted that any one of their members brought to trial should have a jury of his own countrymen. Many a person had gone free on that basis.

It was evident to Liliuokalani that, tried by a native jury, she would be immediately exonerated. It was also evident to the new government.

Liliuokalani was not to be tried by a jury of natives nor of her peers. She would be tried by a military commission composed almost entirely of "officers" of the army of the Republic:

1. Colonel William Austin Whiting, First Regiment, N.G.H.
2. Lt. Col. J.H. Fisher, First Regiment, N.G.H.
3. Captain C.W. Ziegler, Company F, N.G.H.
4. Captain J.M. Camara, Jr., Company C, N.G.H.
5. Captain J.W. Pratt, Adjutant, N.G.H.
6. Captain W.C. Wilder, Jr., Company D, N.G.H.
7. First Lt. J.W. Jones, Company D, N.G.H.
8. Captain William A. Kinney, Aide-de-Camp on General Staff, Judge Advocate.[12]

CHAPTER 7

On Trial

Martial law was declared on January 7, 1895, suspending the right of *Habeas Corpus,* and a military commission was appointed and ordered to meet on January 17, 1895 (the day after Liliuokalani was arrested) for the purpose of court martial.

Paul Neumann protested throughout the trials the "legality" of a Republic not at war trying prisoners by a military commission. He fought vigorously on this premise during the trial of Prince Jonah Kalanianaole, whose trial was hoped to be a "test" trial. He was defeated by A.S. Hartwell and L.A. Thurston.[1]

Liliuokalani was arraigned before the military commission on the morning of February 5, 1895, for treason. The charge was changed through what had become known as "plea bargaining" to misprision of treason, of having knowledge of treason, but not disclosing it. Liliuokalani, however, upon being asked in the court of her stand pleaded, "not guilty." It was her own decision, one that upset both the court and her attorney.

She had made the decision in private upon learning of several deceptions of which she had been the victim.

On January 19th she had been "told" to sign an abdication on the promise that "all her supporters would then be set free." It was later scoffed at that she could not possibly have believed it would be that simple. Yet had *she* not acted on the same "simplicity" in bowing to the withdrawal of her constitution and later in giving complete amnesty to her traitors? Liliuokalani was "simple" in that she *believed* the "promises" of the opposition.

Shortly before signing the abdication, she was told her action would *not* free her supporters but would save their lives. "For myself I would have chosen death rather than have signed it," she wrote in her *Story;* but "to stay the flow of blood," she signed.

Still later the much publicized abdication was said to be worthless as she was no longer "queen" as of January 16, 1893! Yet a great deal of effort had been spent for so worthless a piece of paper. The abdication exists:

> After full and free consultation with my personal friends and with my legal advisers . . . and acting in conformity with their advice, and also upon my own free volition, and in pursuance of my . . . understanding of my duty to the people of Hawaii, and to their highest and best interests, . . . and without any claim that I shall become entitled, by reason anything that I may now say or do, to any other or different treatment or consideration at the hands of the Government than I otherwise could and might legally receive, I . . . do hereby make known . . .

She then asserted that: (1) Hawaii was in the lawful hands of the Republic; (2) she relinquished all rights for herself and her heirs to the throne; (3) she pleaded for clemency for the "rebels"; (4) she preferred to live in retirement; (5) she gave her oath of allegiance to the Republic; (6) she had signed without undue influence from the President of Hawaii.

Whether or not she understood the document's legalese, she had *no choice* but to sign the already prepared abdication. Her "friends"—William G. Irwin, H.L. Widemann, Samuel Parker, Paul Neumann and C.B. Wilson—with whom she had "conferred" knew exactly what she was signing. They too knew she had no choice but to sign the carefully prepared document written by the Republic's man, A.S. Hartwell.

The trial of Liliuokalani was held in the Throne Room of the Iolani Palace. Except for the chandeliers, all the "royal trappings" were gone—the *kahili,* the portraits, the rugs, the gold and crimson chairs. These had given place to a stark room worthy of a military court, as barren of royal trappings as of courtesy.

Every prisoner who had preceded the queen had been found guilty of treason or misprision, had been sentenced to fines, hard labor, or death. Liliuokalani had no doubt that no matter what the court decided was her crime, she would be found guilty. Yet in the most hopeless times, there is in most of us a faint glimmer of faith. Many of the prisoners had turned states evidence, most notably Sam Nowlein and Charles Clark.

Liliuokalani was arraigned before the military commission on February 5th. She entered the throne room where the press took delight in pointing out she had once "worn the purple, been greeted by sovereigns from all parts of the globe, and had extended her hand to be kissed." She was now a prisoner.

They reluctantly admitted that she entered "with firm step, although 57 years of age . . . while her movements are slow and deliberate she still has the haughty carriage." The court was filled to capacity among whom was Joaquin Miller, California's "Poet of the Sierras," who sent to the United States some blistering comments concerning the court. He was captivated by the queen's dignity, quiet beauty, and complete self-possession. He was asked to leave Hawaii.

"Many ladies were present," the papers stated. The report could have continued that not all were in sympathy with the "ex-queen." There seems to be nothing so delightful as to see the great fallen.

"The defendant," "ex-queen," "Mrs. Dominis," "the lady," "that woman," or "Liliuokalani," as she was called, was attended by Mrs. Clark, whose husband had turned states evidence. There was indeed something truly remarkable about these two women.

It was said "Mrs. Dominis was composed, throughout, an attentive listener, a keen observer and a helpful aid to her counsel." Paul Neumann, her counsel, tried in both the preliminaries and throughout the trial to discredit the rights of the military commission to try the case; he also protested on the basis of circumstantial evidence. He was generally overruled.

The case for the prosecution was tailor-made by Captain Robert Parker of the police; Kaae, the queen's treacherous "private secretary"; Sam Nowlein, her trusted guard; Charles Clark, who long had "eaten bread from the queen's table"; Chief Justice Judd, and an insignificant guard by the name of Joseph Kaaewai.[2]

Parker testified that his search of Washington Place had uncovered bombs, rifles, revolvers and ammunition. Also in the queen's private desk was found a fragment of a shell case, a part of a bomb buried in the garden. Thereby she "knew" of the treason.

Kaae testified to "copying" constitutions (he did not mention the ones he had previously surreptitiously given to W.O. Smith, and others of the opposition *before* the 1893 revolution). He spoke only of the "planned constitutions" of the queen between 1893-1895 and the suggestive fact that she had burned some papers before being arrested. His most damaging statement was that she had signed in December of 1894 (*before* the counter-revolution began) "eleven commissions" for political offices. This one statement, supported by the diary,[3] taken from her ransacked home, became the basis of her guilt of misprision.

Sam Nowlein took it upon himself to say he was the organizer of the revolt. Having turned states evidence, he had nothing to fear. Yet never did Sam Nowlein say directly that he had informed Liliuokalani that there was to be an uprising. By innuendo he implied she "must have known."

Charles Clark's testimony was somewhat more damaging to Liliuokalani. He said he had seen Mrs. Dominis and told her Nowlein had told him "The time had come . . . She said Nowlein had told her the same thing, and she hoped it would be a success." Nowlein under cross examination denied Clark's statement of the queen and of his conversation with her.

Chief Justice Judd brought "Mrs. Dominis'" diary, which he had "found" and read the revealing lines of December 28, 1894, "Have signed eleven commissions."

Joseph Kaaewai's testimony consisted primarily of his statement that the queen had inquired of him the "news of last night." He had replied it had gone unfavorably and she had said, "yes."

Paul Neumann considered Clark's words the only evidence tending to implicate his client. Eleven witnesses, including Sam Nowlein, were called. All swore that Clark's word could not be believed even under oath. Neumann dismissed Kaaewai as a "gardener" and hardly a confidant of the queen.

Liliuokalani was on the stand a few minutes. "Her examination in chief was so skillfully made that the cross examination was resultless."

In essence she denied Clark's testimony and the talk with Kaaewai.

She then spoke in Hawaiian—as if in disgust to the non-Hawaiian speaking people, she talked directly to her own people. It was to them and no one else to whom she owed an explanation:

> In the year 1893, on the 15th day of January, at the request of a large majority of the Hawaiian people, and by and with the consent of my cabinet, I proposed to make certain changes in the Constitution of the Hawaiian Kingdom, for the advantage and benefit of the Kingdom, and subjects and residents thereof. These proposed changes did not deprive foreigners of any rights or privileges enjoyed by them under the Constitution of 1887, promulgated by King Kalakaua and his Cabinet without the consent of the people or ratified by their votes.
>
> My ministers at the last moment changed their views and requested me to defer all action in connection with the Constitution, and I yielded to the advice as bound to do by the existing constitution and laws.
>
> A foreign minority of the foreign population made my action the

pretext for overthrowing the Monarchy, and aided by the United States Naval forces and representative, established a new government.

I owed no allegiance to the Provisional Government so established nor to any power or to any one save the will of my people and the welfare of my country.

The wishes of my people were not consulted as to this change of government, and only those who were in practical rebellion against the Constitutional Government were allowed to vote upon the question whether the Monarchy should exist or not.

To prevent the shedding of the blood of my people, natives and foreigners alike, I opposed armed interference and quietly yielded to the armed forces brought against my throne, and submitted to the arbitratement of the Government of the United States the decision of my rights and those of the Hawaiian people. Since then, as is well known to all, I have pursued the path of peace and diplomatic discussion and not that of internal strife.

The United States having first interfered in the interest of those founding the Government of 1893 upon the basis of revolution, concluded to leave to the Hawaiian people the selection of their own form of Government. A plebiscite was suggested but denied by the Provisional Government.

The movement undertaken by the Hawaiians last month was absolutely commenced without my knowledge, sanction, consent, or assistance, directly or indirectly, and this fact is in truth well known to those who took part in it.

I received no information from anyone in regard to arms which were or which were to be procured, nor of any men who were induced, or to be induced, to join in any such uprising.

I do not know why this information should have been withheld from me, unless it was with a view to my personal safety or as a precautionary measure.

It would not have received my sanction and I can assure the gentlemen of this commission that, had I known of any such intention, I would have dissuaded the promoters from such a venture. But I will add that had I known, their secrets would have been mine and inviolately preserved.

That I intended to change my cabinet and to appoint certain officers of the Kingdom, in the event of my restoration, I will admit. Before the 24th of January, 1895, the day upon which I formally abdicated and called upon my people to recognize the Republic of Hawaii as the only lawful government of these Islands, I claim that I had the right to select a cabinet in anticipation of a possibility of my restoration to the throne. I was not intimidated into abdicating, but followed my own council. I deemed that such an act would restore peace and good will among my people.

I acted of my own free will, and wish the world to know that I have asked no immunity or favor for myself nor plead my abdication as a petition for mercy. My actions were dictated by the sole aim of doing good to my beloved country and of alleviating the positions and pains of those who unhappily and unwisely resorted to arms.

As you deal with them, so I pray that the Almighty God may deal with you in your hours of trial. The behavior of the rebels to those foreigners whom they captured and held shows that there was no malignancy in the hearts of the Hawaiians at all. It would have been sad indeed if the doctrine of the Christian Missionary Fathers, taught to my people by them and those who succeeded them, should have fallen like the seed in the parable, upon barren ground.

You are commencing a new era in our history. May the Divine Providence grant you the wisdom to lead the nation into the paths of forbearance, forgiveness and peace, and to create and consolidate a united people ever anxious to advance in the way of civilization outlined by the American fathers of liberty and religion.

In concluding my statement I thank you for the courtesy you have shown to me, not as your former Queen, but as an humble citizen of this land and as a woman. I assure you, who believe you are faithfully fulfilling a public duty, that I shall never harbor any resentment or cherish any ill feeling towards you whatever may be your decision.

After deliberation of the court translation of the statement, the following portions were ordered to be withdrawn:

One: that a minority of the foreign population overthrew the monarchy. Two: that they were aided by the United States Naval forces to establish a new government. Three: that the defendant owed no allegiance to the Provisional Government prior to the signing of the January 24th, 1895 abdication papers. Four: that she pursued the path of peace and diplomatic discussion, and not that of internal strife. Five: that the Provisional Government prevented a plebiscite. Six: that she received no information from any one in regard to arms which were procured for the purpose of insurrection. Seven: that she did not plan to take part in establishing a new government, and eight: that before her abdication on the 24th of January she did not have to recognize any government but her own.

Neumann argued that none of the passages should be stricken with the exception that "and only those who were in practical rebellion against the government (Neumann restated it as "rebellion against the Constitution of the state") were allowed to vote etc. "The court had reworded the material to be stricken as "government"; the queen's words were "the constitutional government"—which would have placed it against the 1887 Bayonet Constitution, not against that of the Republic.

Nevertheless, the court remained adamant. With the portions "stricken" Liliuokalani's defense was worthless. Paul Neumann made a last attempt toward what he considered justice. He reiterated his question of the constitutionality of the proceedings and the authority of the court to try the defendant on "such a crime of which she is accused." He pointed out that if she were guilty "the time at which the offense became completed antedated the proclamation of martial law" (her commissions were dated December 28, 1894; martial law was instituted January 7, 1895.) Consequently she should be tried by civil law and not martial law. He quoted extensively from precedence of Winthrop and Greenleaf[4] to prove his point. He denied that there was a "war"; it was a "riot" to prevent a home (Bertleman's) from being illegally searched—and therefore no reason for martial law: no justification for misprision.

Neumann disclaimed Clark's testimony; accepted Nowlein's which was not damaging; pointed out that Kaaewai was not listed as a witness, when such a list was requested by the defense on February 2, 1895. He also pointed out that Kaaewai had been placed in jail as a witness and suggested that all witnesses had been "intimidated." He denied that he alluded to the rumors that witnesses had been "put in dark cells," and quoted instead Robertson's statement[5] in brief that they were placed in jail on treason and would be subject to being put to death. (The *Star* had published the sentences), and therefore they must tell the "truth." It was obvious to "frightened, ignorant men" what the "truth" was. He contended that the witnesses had been suborned.

He then argued the queen's points in her statement.

Neumann's last appeal was that the queen be tried *on evidence*, not by "moral conviction," nor "predetermination" nor "hatred."

In his closing remarks Neumann said:

> By a conviction you heap upon her an indelible shame, a shame because she has been tried after having relinquished all rights which she possessed before, and relinquished them for what? The tranquilization of the country, for the benefit of the people here—for leniency —for those imprisoned on her behalf.

Judge Advocate Kinney's answer to the legality of the court was "answered" by the fact that there had been for "some long months mutterings, agitation, and incitement on the part of the press and the supporters of the late monarchy"; arms had been collected; an "army formed"; commissions had been signed in preparation of restoration. These factors, however, he admitted could be considered as "history."

Kinney then lunged into an attack full of venom and sarcasm against "Her Majesty," as presenting herself, "Spotless and immaculate." His evidence began with the fact that the "uprising was in behalf of the accused." He colored his words by saying it was no doubt to be "a surprise party" for her, ". . . the whole affair was hidden in a Christmas stocking . . . to be opened when fully ripened on Christmas morning." He spoke derogatorily of her "will-of-wisp innocence." He pointed out that Clark and Nowlein were members of her household and certainly knew what was going on while she was supposedly "pursuing the path of peace and diplomatic discussion and not that of internal strife."

Kinney continued, after a recess, in the same vein. The "lady" knew about the rebellion; she had "signed commissions preparatory to restoration"; if her actions were "for peace, what would they have been if she had turned her mind to war?" He denied what the newspapers had continually since 1893 purported: that he or the court or any of the members of the Republic had ever called the Hawaiians "bloodthirsty." Mr. Kinney no doubt had no recollection of the many references to a "beheading." It is possible that between the time of Liliuokalani's arrest and the trial, her diary entries of those days of interviews with Willis had been read, and could hardly be used as evidence for "beheading." It must have seemed best to Kinney to remain innocent of words such as "savage" and "bloodthirsty."[6]

Then he turned his attack upon the queen's quotation of the "seed on barren ground," to twist it to his own purpose: "Indeed, the Hawaiians had been barren ground." He moved fiercely against her household traitors referring to Elijah whose lament was that "there was not one in Israel who had not bowed to Baal." Like many indiscriminate quoters of the Scriptures he forgot the loyal 7,000 who were later shown to Elijah.

The attorney general's conclusion is interesting. He speaks of her "paper" as having a good deal of the heroic. "She waives all right to any immunity or any consideration for herself. There is a good deal of the heroic line that has been put here, but the lady knows, if she knows anything, that with the men she is dealing with she can file packets of papers

of that kind with perfect impunity, *and it will be considered for what
it is worth*" (author's italics).

His closing remarks were:

> The accused has reminded us and it is well to put it to the Com-
> mission that she is a woman, and much that is in her statement may
> well be passed by, leaving to your consideration whether this is any
> statement to make to the charge on which she is on trial. I submit
> to the Commission that by all the rules of evidence she is guilty of
> the charges preferred against her and that she should be so found.

After a three-day trial Liliuokalani was given the maximum sentence
for misprision of treason of a $5,000 fine and five years imprisonment at
hard labor.

CHAPTER 8

A Queen Imprisoned

Liliuokalani, after her conviction of misprision, returned to her prison, sometimes referred to by the Republic writers as the "spacious apartment in the left wing of the Iolani Palace." To Liliuokalani, who was forbidden visitors or news of any kind, and allowed merely to walk under guard on the balcony and never to leave the "spacious quarters"—this was her prison.

Sanford Ballard Dole, after a two-week review period, commuted her sentence from the $5,000 fine and five years "imprisonment at hard labor" to mere imprisonment. In fact all the death sentences were remitted and many of the fines. By March 19, 1895, martial law was ended, and the military commission adjourned *sine die*. Of the 190 prisoners (37 for "treason and open rebellion"; 141, "treason"; and 12, "misprision"), twenty-two had been exiled to the United States, three were deported to Canada, five received suspended sentences, five were acquited, among them Sam Nowlein, and the remainder served short sentences usually without either fines or hard labor.

By January 1, 1896,[1] all were "freed", except Liliuokalani. She remained nearly eight months in her Iolani Palace prison (January 16 to September 6, 1895); five months more under "house arrest" at Washington Place (September 6, 1895, to February 6, 1896—a little over a month after all the others had been released); then island-restricted from February 6, 1896, to October 6, 1896—nearly twenty-one months total.

Overthrowing the Hawaiian constitutional monarchy, putting down the counter-revolution, imprisoning the queen—none of these solved the problems for the Republic nor brought about their success. It was annexation that was wanted—and always had been.

Sanford Ballard Dole wrote his brother that things were not going too well and had his brother been there the *past* three years, he would have realized that the revolution of 1893 had been for the specific purpose of gaining annexation.[2]

Several factors preventing annexation were involved. First was the disinterest of the United States; the little "kingdom of Hawaii" could rise and fall in whatever way fate might decree. Its cast of characters were at worst savage chiefs and at best despicable royalists, against whom the freedom-hearted people of America rebelled. Now, however, that the question of annexation fell squarely on the United States government, a little more serious thought was being taken. It involved direct action on the part of the United States government—all such action had been officially denied to this point.

Secondly, a doubt was beginning to creep into the minds of the American public as to the fairness of the overthrow by the P.G.'s and the establishment of the Republic of Hawaii. Even some of the silent majority in Hawaii were becoming restless. The planters had not benefited as they supposed they would; the labor situation had remained unchanged; and discrimination against the Orientals was becoming acute. The Orientals were, of course, not permitted to vote; but this problem was allowed to drift as many Hawaiians were also kept from the polls. Japan, however, took exception to the exclusion of Japanese, as being in violation with their treaty agreement.

The Republic in 1897 paid the Japanese Government $75,000 in indemnity.[3] During the years of 1896-1898 the Republic soothed the planters as best they could. The labor-problem they tried to solve by giving "government-crown lands" for homesteading to "anyone who wanted them." The Republic was still an oligarchy, and Thurston was one of the first to admit that the populace of Hawaii was "not ready for self-rule." The natives particularly needed "protection," guidance. Pro-Republic writers said the government was "paternal" to the natives.[4] The Hawaiians remained resentful of a "patriarchal society" and were bitter about their *Moi wahine* being in prison.

The need for annexation became so great that *now*, that which was feared *before* the overthrow of the monarchy, was indeed upon them— that one of the foreign powers would take the "poor little Republic" out in the Pacific. Dole wrote, "moreover, if the U.S. lets go of us, we will immediately become a prize for England, Japan, or Russia. It will be most unlikely that without U.S. aid we would remain independent for any length of time."[5]

The United States government, in general, but especially Secretary of State Gresham, had become so tired of the "gadfly Thurston" that he had requested the man be sent home as *persona non grata*. Thurston devoted some forty pages in his *Memoirs*[6] denying this allegation. He contended that President Dole had refused to recall him; Gresham's reactions to him (Thurston) were "personal"; there was no official request for recall. Nevertheless, Thurston returned to Hawaii, not entirely by his own decision.

Serano Bishop took his unofficial place as a "journalist," revealing the "true" situation in Hawaii. It is interesting to note that Serano Bishop had written one of the most glowing accounts of Liliuokalani ever to appear in print in 1891, in the *Review of Reviews,* when she became queen. Then beginning in 1893 and continuing viciously through 1898, Serano Bishop accused Liliuokalani of every conceivable personal and political crime *except misprision!* In American newspapers he called her a sorceress: she had sacrificed a black pig. Her diaries, which were now in the hands of the opposition, told of a small black pig being killed for a luau for John Aimoku's fourth birthday.[7]

Despite the accounts to the contrary, as reported in 1881 when Princess Liliuokalani was regent and led prayers during the eruption of the volcano near Hilo, she was now accused of worshipping Madame Pele.[8] Every line in her diaries that could be turned to defamation of character was used against her as "pagan." Later, when Liliuokalani could reply, she said, "Perhaps I have 'indulged' in harmless 'superstitions' of our native customs in hoping to preserve some of our old traditions. Nevertheless, while the missionaries have ornamented their Christmas trees we have never called them Druids."[9]

Bishop continued to attack her morals, bringing up the old chestnut of C.B. Wilson and Joseph Aea. He defamed her character by the "lascivious hula," the "sensual meles" and even chose words of her own compositions. Lasciviousness, it seems, as well as beauty, can be found in the eye of the beholder.

Somehow Serano Bishop felt that he could, by spotlighting Liliuokalani's defects, bring into a paradoxically distorted focus the entire Hawaiian population. However, while she was "over-ambitious," they were without ambition, thriftless, lazy and shiftless. While she was "conniving," "clever," "sly," "scheming," they were stupid, ignorant, and scarcely capable of being educated beyond menial tasks. All were, of course, thieves, a most interesting word for Bishop to have used. The brush was indeed dipped in different pots of paint.

Serano Bishop easily reached his already receptive audience, but he infuriated others. Hundreds of letters came from individuals and organizations offering to help restore the queen. These ranged all the way from "citizens of the Cherokee Nation"—somewhat ironic because there was discussion of placing the Hawaiians on "reservations"—to the "Texas Women."[10]

Liliuokalani was not allowed to see any of these, and all newspaper articles in her favor or against the Republic were kept from her. Her retainers began to send her flowers wrapped in newspapers, having articles in her favor,[11] which she eagerly read. It was not long before her guards realized what was happening. Actually, the information came from her "companion in prison, Evelyn Wilson," who "let slip" some information to C.B. Wilson, still the queen's guard.

Through the ambiguity of different sources[12] the fact remains that Johnny Wilson, Evelyn and C.B. Wilson's young son, continued to bring the queen flowers from her own garden, wrapped in "harmless newsprint." But slipped in among the stems and hidden by the foliage surrounding the flowers were secreted clippings and messages—often just "We love you, Hanai."

Liliuokalani, who like every true Hawaiian, valued above all things the freedom to come and go in God's open universe, accepted her prison life with almost unbelievable equanimity.

She again "took stock of her surroundings and to what [she] had access." Although denied reading material, she was given paper and pencil. If it is true that at the point of deepest despair the ever-glowing faintest gleam of light can—if pursued—grow to sunlight that floods the prison cell, it was true for Liliuokalani. For the first time in her life she was free from burdens imposed by others: political, social, family, retainers, and even "friends."

Some people may rail against such a period; some may become depressed and let the time disintegrate and some can use it. Liliuokalani used it, taking her blank sheets of paper she drew the lines of the staff for musical notes. Without an instrument, she transcribed the notes by her voice—that voice of perfect pitch. She returned to her first love—composing, and her second love—writing of history and preservation of the Hawaiian tradition and culture.

Her major endeavor in prose was for the heritage of the Hawaiian people, the translation of Kalakaua's *Kumulipo*, the "Tradition of Creation." She also wrote "Bits of History" and began two possible autobiographies, one the "Variegated Leaves" and the other "Petals of the Flowers."[13]

The latter prose writings did not come into print until several years later as part of her autobiography It was her music, her songs, that slipped out beyond the prison walls. Every line she wrote was studied by the Republic for possible "messages of treason" to her people.

As late as 1957, Ethel Damon wrote in her biography of Sanford Ballard Dole that the "ex-queen was at that time plotting dissension and 'rebellion' against the Republic and showing it through her music."

If nothing treasonable could be found, the magnifying glass was focussed on "lasciviousness and lewdness".

Even the most suspicious minded person could not find fault with the first song that Evelyn Wilson sent out; except, of course, it dealt with love—and love was sensual, wasn't it?

It was "Aloha Oe." This song Liliuokalani had first written with a touch of envy for her sister Likelike, who found love so easily. It was the same song that later had brought love into her own life through Henry Berger. This beloved song she now rewrote.

Berger had warned her against trying to promulgate a new constitution. He had resigned from the band—along with all the other members —when the P.G.'s took over. During the interim period when the Portuguese Band played, he had gone to San Francisco. He later returned to Honolulu where he married his second wife, Rose.

Upon returning to his beloved Hawaii, he again took charge of the band for the Republic, with the strange words, "We still play for *her*."[14] It was more than that: music, flowers and natural beauty were the three things that could never be taken from the Hawaiians. Liliuokalani later said, that like her motto, *Onipaa,* they belonged to the soul, and were indestructible.[15]

On the ersatz music paper Liliuokalani worked with her song:

Aloha Oe

Proudly the rain on the cliffs
Creeps into the forest
Seeking the buds
And miniature *lehua* flowers of
the uplands

Chorus
Farewell to you, farewell to you,
O fragrance in the blue depths
One fond embrace and I leave
To meet again.

Sweet memories come
Sound softly in my heart.
You are my beloved sweetheart
Felt within.

I understand the beauty
Of rose blossoms at Mauna-wili.
There the birds delight,
Alert the beauty of this flower.[16]

The Republic's interpretation of "Aloha Oe" was primarily Liliuokalani's farewell to her country, a most satisfying interpretation. Others found it—and it now remains—a great love song.

There however were, as in all true Hawaiian songs, three interpretations. The obvious one: beautiful description of the rain, the cliffs, the flowers. The analogy the Hawaiians knew: union of man-woman-nature-gods. And the mystical, the *kahuna* knew: the union of all-in-all, the "Christ" revelation of man's individual unity with God. Therefore only a few of the older, knowledgeable Hawaiians recognized the meaning of the rain striking the *lehua* blossom signifying marital union and unity of the people and the land, and further the mystical marriage of Christ, revealed in the old *mele*, but also in Revelations. A few also remembered that Konia's name song for her *hanai* child spoke of the "blossoms of mauna-wili."[17]

A second piece of music came about through bitterness, overcome. Liliuokalani had ample reason to hate the men of the Republic who had brought about her dethronement and the overthrow of her government, subjected her to unnecessary personal humiliation, and left her people in a condition worse than they had ever been before.

Forgive, forgive—had that not always been her creed? She made every effort to find in her heart forgiveness. Each day she spent in devotions, prayers, meditations. She received inspiration from Rt. Rev. Alfred Willis of the Episcopal Church, the only man of the cloth who came to visit her in prison.

Yet it was difficult. Then as it often happens, the "circumstances deemed most afflictive becomes an angel entertained unawares." Later when Liliuokalani was to become acquainted with the writings of Mary Baker Eddy, founder of Christian Science, she found this passage her favorite.[18] One day she overheard Charles Wilson tell his wife of an incident.[19] It was about the queen's retainer Wakeki, who brought Liliuokalani her freshly washed clothes each week.

Wakeki was searched before entering and when leaving the palace prison. Each item of clothing, belonging to the queen, was carefully inspected to see that no messages were sewn into the garments. Wakeki hated with maniacal bitterness the guards who searched thoroughly the clothing she considered them unfit to look upon, let alone touch.

On a particularly difficult day, she spat in the face of one of the guards as *he* "lasciviously" felt in the breast of the queen's corset for she knew not what. He struck her a sharp blow across the face.

She fell, cursing him by the old gods of Hawaii—and so strengthened the rumor that the *queen* practiced sorcery, especially as the guard became ill shortly thereafter and was taken off duty. The "spell" was apparently not complete, for he recovered.

A second guard, either fearing the result of such action, because all guards had been firmly instructed against violence of any kind (the government's position was still precarious with the United States), or else taking pity on the woman, pulled the first guard back and told her she should not return but send someone else thereafter.

"Someone else" replaced Wakeki but the "intense furious temper of the queen" was indeed aroused. Men had gone to prison for her, men had possibly been tortured to be persuaded to give evidence against her, she herself had been sarcastically demeaned, viciously vilified—but to strike a retainer! That was too much. Liliuokalani struck out angrily at the furniture about her, called the guards by her strongest epithet: "snakes." She wept furiously and impotently.

Evelyn let her spend her fury and then watched with heartbreak, as Liliuokalani dropped—as she oftentimes did—on her childhood-crippled unbending knee to pray to God for forgiveness for herself, and to find in her heart forgiveness for others.

It was then she turned to look at Evelyn. "Is it possible," she asked, "that to pray on bended knee is only 'to be seen of men?' Is forgiveness truly only a state of mind as we have been taught of Old? Standing, walking, dancing, riding, surfing, if the mind is stayed on God,—one prays?"[20]

Evelyn remained silent.

Liliuokalani laughed—that joyous, silvery laugh—Evelyn hadn't heard for many months. True to her own nature, Liliuokalani had wrenched her thoughts from self-pity. She asked for pencil and paper to write a "name song" for Johnny Wilson and the beautiful flowers he brought.

My Flower at Paoakalani[21]

O gentle breeze waft hither
And remind me
Of my sweet never fading flower
That has bloomed in the depths of Paoakalani
See forever the beauty of the flowers
Inland at Uluhaimalama
None the equal
Of my gentle flower of
Paoakalani

Dainty face
With softest eyes as black as jet,
Pink cheeks so delicate of hue
Growing in the depths of
Paoakalani

My love delights.
O gentle breeze, waft hither,
Come to me my beloved
Growing in the depths of
Paoakalani

Flowers and lovers—was it truly Johnny—or C.B. Wilson, the interpreters of vice questioned. Was there a message to her people to "arise"? Finding nothing "revolutionary," only what they hoped might apply to Wilson, the powers of the Republic allowed the song outside the prison walls.

Shortly after this time Liliuokalani became seriously ill, and Evelyn Wilson requested that she might have "some air" in a carriage ride. Although granted permission, Liliuokalani refused to ride through the streets of Honolulu under guard. Instead she began her regular walks on the balcony outside her prison rooms. From there she could look down upon the guards below. She could see Honolulu lose its gaiety of song and music and take on the staid rigidity of the Republic government.

Forgive, forgive, forgive—

Liliuokalani, whose heart and body both bent to forgiveness, wrote "A Queen's Prayer."[22] This song she dedicated to her niece, her heir-apparent, Kaiulani, who was still abroad.

It was by her, it seemed, that forgiveness must also be made, for it was she who had been deprived of her birthright—to be queen.

The Queen's Prayer

Your love
Is in heaven,
And your truth
So perfect.

I live in sorrow
Imprisoned,
You are my light,
Your glory my support.

Behold not with malevolence
The sins of man
But forgive
And cleanse.

And so, O Lord,
Beneath your wings
Be our peace
Forever more.

Surely, no one could read double meanings of sensuality, heresy, lasciviousness or lewdness into this song. Yet in the years that followed it was so construed.

At the time it was allowed to go out into the streets of Honolulu. But Liliuokalani, still not satisfied, followed her words with deeds.

In August Asiatic Cholera had broken out and many died. Both Mrs. Wilson and Liliuokalani were stricken. Rumors declared that Orientals had brought it in, a statement resented by Chinatown residents, as many of the sailors who were ill were not Orientals.

Whatever the truth was, both Hawaiian and *haole* women organized relief stations. It was then that Liliuokalani called Captain Good and C.B. Wilson to her.[23]

She told them she wished to help the poor and homeless. Here she echoed the words of the man she once loved—Lunalilo. As she could not go out, she designated Mrs. James Campbell and Mrs. Douglass who had charge of the Waikiki district to accept a house and a lot on her place at Waikiki for carrying on their work.

It was rumored that from that time forward the queen never suffered from a stiff knee—a knee that would not bend. Pictures of her after this time no longer show her unable to sit comfortably on the ground, as "Hawaiians do."

Liliuokalani never wrote a word of bitterness of her imprisonment. She spoke instead of "courtesies shown her," of her time occupied with crocheting, music, writing, devotions—and the special pleasure she had in her canary. Always with gratitude for gifts daily sent her, whether she always received them or not.

Two men—one in England, Sir Edwin Arnold, and one in Boston, Julius Palmer—wrote almost identical words of her: "every inch a queen" and "the most gracious woman I have ever met."

Yet the *haole* continued to fear her to the extent they hired writers such as Kate Field and Mary Krout to defame her. Everything was done to destroy her personally if not bodily. What but fear could inspire such action?

Yet carried on the tradewinds, riffling through the palm fronds, riding on the waves, passing through the smoke-filled air of burning Honolulu Chinatown, went the soft strains of "Aloha Oe" and "A Queen's Prayer" to every island of the Republic of Hawaii—to Hawaii Nei.

The following month Liliuokalani was released to house-arrest at Washington Place. She was told she would later be pardoned, but for the time being she was "under parole" and could be arrested and recommitted at any time.

Liliuokalani was still in the custody of C.B. Wilson. She was granted "servants," but none of her former retainers were to approach her. She was prohibited from having any "gathering" in her home, go to church, or to any other public place.

At this time she made a final decision to leave her childhood church, Kawaiahao, and become a communicant of the Episcopal Church.[24]

On February 6, 1896, Liliuokalani received her release from parole as a prisoner but was forbidden to leave the Island of Oahu. She found a childlike thrill in being able to once again enjoy her country home at Waialua and even more happily to be at Waikiki, where she found Wakeki awaiting her and where "we caught fish, and placed them immediately on hot coals, supplementing our picnic with bread and butter, and our native *poi*."

Thus was the "imprisonment" of Queen Liliuokalani. On October 6, 1896, twenty-one months less ten days, after her arrest she was completely freed of all restrictions and her "civil rights restored."

PART VI

Ex-Queen or Moi Wahine

❧ ❧

1896-1917

CHAPTER 1

The "Ex-Queen" Becomes an Author

1

"No sooner had we released her than the terrible woman went to the United States to cause more trouble," wrote a member of the Republic press.

On December 6, 1896, Liliuokalani appealed to Sanford Ballard Dole for permission to visit the United States. She was carefully questioned as to her intentions. She said her visit would be first to San Francisco; further pressed, she admitted she hoped to see her relatives in Boston. Smiling, she added she would like to see her niece in England. The Doles, she wrote in her *Story,* were solicitous and gracious, warning her only of the cold New England winters.

Liliuokalani later wrote that once aboard the steamship, *China,* bound for San Francisco she drew "for the first time in years a long breath of freedom."[1] Unfortunately, Liliuokalani was not yet free.

It was true she was no longer a prisoner of the Republic, nor a queen under the threat of assassination; however, this threat was to follow her to Washington, D.C. And she was still under the Hawaiian social pressure of being *moi wahine,* distorted now by the Americanized term of "queen."

Once the life of the high chiefesses of Hawaii had been, like the life of most of the Hawaiians, easy, uncomplicated, and, above and beyond all things, free; but "free" with understood duties and privileges. By blood-rank a woman became at birth a high chiefess; by *hanai* her position was often elevated. But now the terminology had changed. The "highest high chiefs" and "chiefesses" the *moi* and *moi wahine* had become incorrectly anglicized terms to be "kings" and "queens," and bore all the irrational and ambivalent hatred that existed among the Americans against "royalty." Even worse, sometimes the word "chiefs" was equated with Indian chiefs, and "chiefesses" with "squaws." No "monarchy" at all was recognized, only tribal rule. There was no correct translation, nor place, for *moi* nor *moi wahine.*

As Liliuokalani drew her "first breath of freedom," she was about to face the most difficult period of her life. One would have felt that the years of physical and mental pressures of turbulent rule, dethronement, and imprisonment would have been the most difficult. But they were not. The twenty-one years to follow were to be far more devastating to her as a person. She was to live the role of "ex-queen" in a social, political, economic world that was against everything *moi wahine* stood for, because not a single cultural trait embodied in the term was understood by the *haole* world. Even if it could have been intellectually perceived, it could never have been emotionally discerned. Eighteen ninety-six was a year void of emotional understanding for Queen Liliuokalani. She was entering into the period that she had feared all her life, that of being alone —alone in not being understood. "This period of vacuum is as close to hell as one can come on earth, the vacuum in which *no one understands*," she later told Lydia.

Forgiving her enemies, but remaining true to the continual petitioning of her people, individually and through the Hawaiian Patriotic League, Liliuokalani was *moi wahine*. She went to the United States to protest against annexation. Annexation would be the final death blow to the Hawaiians. Perhaps she could prevent it. As *moi wahine* (no one ever became *"ex"-moi wahine*), it was her duty to continue to fight on alien ground for her people—perhaps also in alien ways.

In San Francisco she was met by the aging Charles Reed Bishop, a man who despite his wife, Bernice Pauahi, never quite grasped the essential meaning of Old Hawaii. In their youth Bishop and Liliuokalani had not met on mutual ground. In their middle years when Kalakaua was king, Bishop had tried to lead him into *haole* "enlightenment," and had prevented every move Princess Liliuokalani had tried to initiate, either for bank or college, for "high chiefesses" in the new society that grew in the shadow of the Bayonet Constitution. When Liliuokalani became queen, he recommended she be a "constitutional queen"—a figurehead— keeping out of all government activities. Had she followed this suggestion, he and others long insisted, the monarchy would have survived. A casual backward look proves otherwise, even without recalling that Sanford Ballard Dole's compromise-suggestion that Kaiulani be "queen" with a "five-man regency," was dismissed without a moment's consideration.

Charles Bishop had passed through the period of annoyance that the queen had not taken his advice, through the time in which he himself had vilified her, into a moment of exhaustion—or perhaps the spirit of

Bernice had touched him. He had left Hawaii in disgust because of the manner in which the country had been forced to surrender. He was weary of men like Thurston, Serano Bishop, and Gorham Gilham, who struck again and again at a wounded and dying people—struck to the death blow of annexation at any cost, although at one time he himself had helped in delivering the blows.

Charles Reed Bishop, to Liliuokalani's child-like joy, welcomed his sister-in-law in San Francisco. The Spreckels—father and son—and other *haole* families called upon her at the California Hotel. Despite the controversial past in which Claus Spreckels had moved for and against the queen, as the tide seemed to ebb and flow, Liliuokalani was pleased with his "friendship." The press was at first generally kind to her, speaking of the "ex-queen," but somewhat annoyed that she "refused to discuss politics" with the reporters; she consistently refused to refer *by name* to anyone who had "dethroned" her. She referred only to the "missionary party"—and the most was made of this term. Several newspapers gave lavish praise of the first generation missionaries, and not undeserved. The "second generation missionaries," none of them ministers but all businessmen, were as forgotten as the second generation Hawaiian *alii*—from the Princes Liholiho and Lot (Kamehameha IV and V) through Liliuokalani.

Leaving San Francisco, Liliuokalani departed for Boston to visit "her late husband's relatives." Passing through Southern California via the *Sunset Limited,* through New Orleans to the East Coast, Liliuokalani was so impressed by the "rich country" open for "colonization," she could not believe that so "great and powerful a nation" could "covet our little islands of Hawaii Nei."

Liliuokalani made every attempt to avoid "newsgatherers." She wrote, in her *Story,* that the curiosity became so troublesome that the train officials "were obliged to lock the car doors, or close our section, to prevent intrusion."

The growing animosity of the American press was not lost upon Liliuokalani, and she suffered cruelly from its vitriolic attacks. She was deeply grateful to a chance traveller on the *Sunset,* one who fended off many an over-eager journalist for neither her "secretary," Joseph Heleluhe, nor her "maid," Kia Nahaolua, were capable of handling journalists. Parting with this new friend in Washington, D.C., she looked forward, even more hopefully, to arriving in Boston, where she surely would be welcomed by John's relatives.

It was not her relatives, however, who met her at the station, but the man who was to do more for her and ask less than any other man, except perhaps Henry Berger—Julius A. Palmer.

Captain Palmer had first met Liliuokalani when she was a princess in 1873. He was then a young reporter for the *Boston Globe* and *Transcript*, and he was immediately captivated, writing of her dancing that ". . . as she danced . . . it was as if she were in love with every man she danced with."

Palmer escorted her on Christmas Eve, 1896, to her rooms at the Parker House, where she was then greeted by John Dominis' cousins, William and Sara Lee of Lee and Shepherd Publishers. Liliuokalani, family oriented, as Hawaiians are, swept aside Julius Palmer and fell into the bosom of "her family" to forget her distance from "beautiful Hawaii." She was deeply moved that the Lees had made leis from smilax and winter blossoms with which to greet her.[2] It was one of those small gestures of remembering the "little things" that mean so much to a woman.

With her reduced "suite" of Joseph Heleluhe, and Kia Nahaolua, she soon moved to "Stirlingworth Cottage . . . just off Beacon Street, in Brookline" to be near her cousins.

It was then Julius Palmer persuaded Liliuokalani that the pen was mightier than the sword. The sword Liliuokalani had never been able to use. Now there was a "pen." Surely the "hired" journalistic pens of the P.G. and Republic writers had made deep, if not yet fatal, wounds.

For its time, journalism seldom had a better field day than it did in the case for and against the "Queen" or the "ex-Queen"—the "savage" or the "gracious lady"; the "beheader" or "savior of Hawaii blood"; the "primitive" or "the woman who spoke impeccable English"; the "pagan" or the "lady who attended church every Sunday," either St. Andrews or St. Patricks. Scarcely a newspaper or magazine across the country—from San Francisco to New York—did not carry articles on Liliuokalani; whatever else, she was controversially newsworthy.

Julius Palmer interrupted Liliuokalani's social whirl, which Sara Lee had thought would prove to the world that the queen was a lady of breeding, intelligence, education, and charm. She even thought that such proof would be to the ex-queen's advantage. Sara Lee had no concept apparently that to "socialize" with a queen, "ex" or otherwise, was highly desirable; but to support her in any "political" or practical way had nothing to do with partaking of her generosity and hospitality.

Sara had held social events of every sort of which, Liliuokalani wrote, the grandest was a New Year's Eve Party. When she moved to Washington, D.C., to live at the Cairo, two to five hundred people called, ate her food, paid their respects, satisfied their curiosity, and disappeared. She visited President Cleveland, was the guest of Mrs. Cleveland, and even attended the inauguration of President McKinley. All was accomplished through Julius Palmer for the queen's wishes and for the hope of presenting a completely "civilized" woman.

Still, concern in Congress for Hawaii was drifting away, and Julius Palmer, choosing his own mode of expression, insisted she write her "own story."

Liliuokalani preferred a philosophical autobiography that reflected the traditions and customs of Hawaii, while Palmer advised her to give the facts of her own life relative only to the simplest historical events that led to the overthrow.

Liliuokalani's greatest difficulty in telling her own story lay in her nature. She could not be vicious. Angry, furious, bitter to the point of saying J.L. Stevens' daughter's death was punishment from God—yes.[3] But to be vicious as Serano Bishop and her maligners were, she found impossible. In page after page of the typescript of her manuscript, she crossed out passages of venom—with a notation, "not necessary."[4]

Julius Palmer laid aside his personal life; he took a leave of absence from the *Boston Globe* to be her secretary for two years. His own book had been published by Lee and Shepherd, and he convinced her that with the help of editor, Sara Lee, William Lee would publish her book. Both Sara and William agreed on the basis of Palmer's arguments.

Julius Palmer's task continued to be a difficult one. Liliuokalani was easily "pressured" into the social activities, which she was so used to, as well as the invitations to visit Niagara Falls, or any other scenic place. Palmer's writing discipline was hard to impose upon Liliuokalani. While he daily pursued "recollections," she joyously collected her songs to be published to be "given to friends." When it was suggested that a Russian woman wanted to write an opera about her with her cooperation, she fell happily into the plan. She scribbled indiscriminately on envelopes, backs of letters and came up with loose portions of a comic opera.[5]

She conscientiously worked on the translation of the *Kumulipo*— again to be given to a few select friends. Palmer, the literary disciplinarian, daily urged the prosaic work of *Hawaii's Story*, a labor of his love. Liliuokalani never seemed to recognize his sacrifice, for it was *aloha*.

The gallant Palmer, in interviews at which reporters constantly hinted at romance, even headlining articles "Romantic Relations Existing Between Captain Palmer and Ex-queen Liliuokalani"[6] denied not only romance, but stated categorically he was *only* her secretary, helping her with her "literary endeavors."

Liliuokalani did complete her book, *Hawaii's Story by Hawaii's Queen*, with the help of Julius Palmer and the editing of Sara Lee. In no way can the book be said to have been "ghost written." Anyone familiar with the queen's style can find passages she and she alone wrote. A strong editing hand had, however, been placed upon the finished manuscript, as can be seen by comparing her "Bits of History," "Variegated Leaves," "Petals of the Flowers," *Ka Noho Aupuni a Ka, Moi Wahine: Liliuokalani,*[7] to say nothing of her poetry.

The book was to have one slant: how Hawaii had been "illegally" taken over by the United States and why the queen should be restored.

But the essence of the life of the Hawaiian second generation growing out of the Old Hawaii was missing. Differences in culture were deleted. After publication, the book caused some ripple of attention to the "Hawaiian Question."

It was also attacked, but not on the points of whether the United States had acted precipitously, nor whether the queen should be restored; for, in all honesty, most of these viewpoints had already been discussed in the press. Liliuokalani had avoided discussion of all personal relationships, except a few pages relative to her marriage. The first attack came from Thurston, who insisted the queen could not have written the book as it did not compare with the style in her diaries. Secondly, he strongly opposed her allegations against J.L. Stevens, but that was to be expected.

What was unexpected, was that, despite Liliuokalani's gentle hand toward nearly all those who had openly betrayed her, she commented in passing that Judge Widemann, who had been sent at her expense to Washington to present her case, had never given her a report. One can merely speculate on the truth, inasmuch as the judge calmly took a side-trip to England at the time.

The result was a barrage of personal and newspaper letters against her "misinformation" and "defamation of character." Liliuokalani for several months did not bother to answer; then J.O. Carter wrote her that Widemann was an old man "half-crazed with worry and concern," and it would be a kindness for her to reply to him.

Liliuokalani promptly sent a note of apology, saying it was indeed possible she had made an "unintentional mistake," as she herself had been under considerable strain. She did not blame her editor nor anyone else.[8] True to her own character, she apologized in a dignified and queenly manner.

Liliuokalani's equilibrium was further shaken when she received a bill from Lee and Shepherd for the books she had ordered sent out! "J.O. Carter," she wrote upset, hurt, and not a little worried, "said that they should be paying *me*."[9]

❧ 2 ❧

There was another side to Liliuokalani's life between 1896 and August, 1899, while in the United States: the monetary side. Liliuokalani had never understood money as the *haole* did.

Throughout her life she had watched land and land revenues slip away from her without any concept of what was really happening. From the time she lost her *hanai* inheritance in 1848, through Bernice's small apportionment to her, of which she regretted only the loss of her childhood home, Haleakala; through Kalakaua's "taking [her] sister's and [her] lands," to the present, when the P.G.'s and Republic were taking the "crown lands" for their use—she was not fully aware these actions were impoverishing *her*. Both Julius Palmer and J.O. Carter, her agent in Hawaii, tried to explain she should *protest* the taking of the "crown lands," request a compensation for the land, ask for a "pension."[10]

Liliuokalani continued to live on "borrowed monies." The old *alii*-retainer system was strong within her. She could not understand why her "friends" like Sam Damon, Sam Parker, Claus Spreckels and C.R. Bishop would not "lend her monies." They did, but only to a limited extent.

While the money came in, Liliuokalani spent it on lavish receptions and entertainments, which the United States capital has always accepted with aplomb. It was to these the Americans came in droves—some invited, some not. Liliuokalani did not mind; this was *aloha* in Hawaii—all were welcome. But in Hawaii the flow went both ways, not because it was required, but because it was natural. In Boston and Washington receiving was far more blessed than giving.

It was while she was in Washington that Liliuokalani sent for her *hanai* children, from whom she had long been separated, as well as the step-daughter of Joseph Heleluhe, Myra. Kia Nahaolua, at her request, was replaced by Myra's mother. For the first time Liliuokalani became aware of the distinct individualities of her *hanai* children.

Lydia, whom she had seen only infrequently, was completely Ida

Pope indoctrinated: prim, respectful, but above all strangely "independent." Lydia, perhaps more than the boys, had felt "less royal." Ida Pope left no doubt in her mind on this question, and in the previous years, Lydia had taken a step backward from the "princes," because for many years she believed that both Aimoku and Kaipo were John Dominis' sons.[11] This relationship placed them closer to the queen's love in her mind, a love for which she hungered, but felt she didn't deserve. Hers was an example of the psychological trauma the changing *hanai* system was bringing to another generation of Hawaiians.

At fifteen and sixteen, the difference between Aimoku and Kaipo appeared only slight, but the difference was to grow in the next few years. Aimoku was his father's son—helpful in "business matters" to the queen, always referring to her as "the queen."[12] He began resenting Kaipo, whose one interest in life was Kaipo, who was handsome, charming, as personable as David Kalakaua, and as reckless. Kaipo was an accomplished pianist, by nature, not study, and enchanted Queen Liliuokalani with music, song, laughter and gaiety. He was the perfect *hanai* son for her— carefree, always joking, spending money without regard. From birth he had been Liliuokalani's favorite, and still was.

❧ 3 ❧

After *Hawaii's Story by Hawaii's Queen* had been published, Julius Palmer requested permission for a "vacation." He was extremely ill and died in the last month of 1898. He died without recognition of his service to the queen and under the shadow of "romance."

Even before Palmer's death, Liliuokalani had another man come to her "rescue"—a man with as few scruples as Julius Palmer had many. This was Dr. James H. English, who became the queen's personal physician. He was immediately under the illusion that a queen must be wealthy, but if not wealthy, at least noteworthy.

The newspapers had long circulated stories that Liliuokalani was dying of cancer, tuberculosis, pneumonia, or any other popular disease of the time. Liliuokalani, annoyed, wrote in her diary that a woman of sixty might suffer minor inconveniences in her health, but she certainly was not dying. During one of these periods she called upon a Christian Science "healer," Sophie Clarke of Brookline. The stubborn cold she had been plagued with came to an immediate end. Liliuokalani wrote J.O. Carter that she had tried "mental science" and was healed. Carter replied that it was "time [she] gave up doctors and came to realize that the *kahuna* knew far more than the modern doctors."[13] When Liliuokalani told Miss Clarke of this, Miss Clarke gently explained to her that Christian Science[14] was not a "mental science," as she apparently believed it to be. Liliuokalani was confused and left Miss Clarke's care, but not without the Christian Science textbook by Mary Baker Eddy, which later was to bring her great comfort.

Dr. English called on her again to assure her he could cure her of her "cancer," and that her case would be *cause celèbre*. Not only that, but Dr. English also had a cure for leprosy and he was more than pleased to accompany the queen to the Hawaiian Islands, at her expense, and free the lepers from their dreaded disease.

Thus on July 26, 1898, the *SS Gaelic* manifest carried the names of Dr. and Mrs. James English, as well as Queen Liliuokalani's.

❧ 4 ❧

In what Thurston called "missionary luck," the Spanish-American War was brewing. In April, 1898, the United States declared war on Spain to free Cuba. The war moved to the Spanish Philippines in the Pacific. The Hawaiian annexationists couldn't have been happier. For what was more logical now, than to annex the Hawaiian Islands as permanent allies?

The "boys in blue" began arriving in Honolulu.[15] On June 15 the House of Representatives in the United States passed the resolution of annexation 209 to 91. The Senate passed its resolution on July 6, 42 to 21. President McKinley signed the bill for annexation of Hawaii the next day, and a week later the news arrived in Honolulu.

Liliuokalani, who had spent nearly seven months in an attempt to nullify all arguments for Hawaiian annexation, was at this moment sailing for Honolulu, due to arrive on August 2, 1898. The transfer of sovereignty from the Republic to the United States was to take place ten days later—August 12, 1898.

A jubilant annexationist press had poured forth its exulting words on a curiously disinterested populous. The natives were desperately gloomy. Among all was a feeling of holding expressions of either joy or grief in abeyance until Liliuokalani would step off the *Gaelic*.

The *Gaelic* was sighted off Koko Head the night before its arrival, a night described by Mabel Craft as "a perfect moonlit night with natives beginning to gather in small groups near the wharf to await the return of their ex-queen."

Indeed, the Hawaiians gathered to await the ship, completely silent. Kaiulani, who had returned to Hawaii and who had written her aunt that she had never seen her people in worse condition, waited in the same silence with her father and Prince David Kawananakoa in the Cleghorn carriage.

On August 2, 1898, there was room in the heart of both Liliuokalani and Kaiulani for only one emotion—the unbearable grief of the loss of Hawaii forever.

David Kawananakoa went aboard the *Gaelic* to escort Liliuokalani down the gang plank. A small tent-like enclosure had been placed on deck to protect the "ex-queen" from "prying eyes," but there were no "prying eyes" for *moi wahine*. Liliuokalani walked as straight and as proudly as ever down the gang plank, her arm resting lightly on her favorite nephew's. She wore black from her plumed hat to toes that moved straight forward in *Onipaa*.

She paused for a moment and looked down upon the upturned faces of the Hawaiians. Tears flowed uninhibitedly from the eyes of both men and women. There was a total silence, permeated with a love that enveloped the crowd and the queen. Liliuokalani paused, her black eyes looking into individual eyes as they swept the crowd. Then her musical voice rich with emotion broke the silence.

"Aloha."

The answering *aloha* had all the meaning of old *aloha*. One spoke it only from a heart of forgiveness and the recognition of the *mana* of "God-within." A few of the English and American royalists began an abortive cheer; but the silence, that had again fallen, stopped them.

Liliuokalani drove with David through the streets of Honolulu. The carriage was no longer marked *Oni Paa*, but it too went onward. The balconies of Washington Place were festooned with greenery, and torches of the Keawe line flickered in the gardens. Torch bearers, old native men, awaited the queen at the doorway.

While Liliuokalani changed her travelling costumes to a gown of black and lavender and placed a few remaining jewels of diamond pins on her dress, Kaiulani and David waited. Waiting also were throngs of Hawaiians; they stood silent in the court yard near the steps of Washington Place.

Liliuokalani motioned away the refreshments offered her by her retainers and sat down near the doorway, holding out her hands to her people, as Konia had once done, welcoming them. To Konia they had come for supplication; to Liliuokalani they now came to give sustenance. This was the Hawaiian way.

Then the years were swept away and for the first time in nearly a hundred years the native Hawaiian fell on his knees before the *alii,* to creep up the steps of Washington Place veranda, to kiss the hand of *moi wahine.*[16]

Among them was an old blind man, the man for whom Princess Liliuokalani had requested money from Queen Kapiolani in 1886. There was no *kapu* that required these people to give such honor to Liliuokalani. It was not "obeisance" to royalty. It was *aloha* for *moi wahine.*

"Had Liliuokalani remained a queen, she would never have known how much her people loved her," Mabel Craft wrote. As usual, Mabel Craft was wrong, but she never would have understood: Long live *moi wahine!*

HENRY BERGER AND THE ROYAL HAWAIIAN BAND, 1883
Berger stands in front with beard and German military medals.

Courtesy of Don and Leilehua Billam-Walker, and
Compliments of The Friends of the Royal Hawaiian Band.

CHAPTER 2

"Queen Lil"

❦ 1 ❦

During the following ten days hundreds of Hawaiians thronged the yard of Washington Place bringing gifts of every sort. The Hawaiians, broken in spirit, depleted in worldly goods, revived in soul and body to bring their *moi wahine* poi wrapped in ti leaves, live chickens and squealing pigs, fruits of the land, as they had traditionally brought gifts to the *alii*. Now, in what the papers called "final defeat," the ceremony of gift bearing "strangely continued." Not strangely, for *aloha* never dies.

On August 12, 1898, everything ceased. Washington Place was shuttered, as was every other Hawaiian home. No Hawaiian stirred from his own house nor his own thoughts, while the annexationists celebrated. Henry Berger played *Hawaii Ponoi* for the last time, as a free nation's anthem.

The Hawaiian national flag fell like a fatally wounded *oo* bird, no longer snared to give two feathers for a royal cloak and then go free, but shot down in death.

However, American news reports were again to misinterpret what was happening in Hawaii. Thus on January 15, 1899, the *New York Illustrated Magazine* carried an article by J. Martin Miller, who, of course, was not in Hawaii:

> One of the last things ex-queen Liliuokalani did before the American flag was hoisted in August last, was to give a farewell lua [sic] or royal feast, to her former subjects. It was a most elaborate affair.
>
> As a rule a lua is spread out upon the ground, and the natives sit around the spread, dipping poi, a sort of messy paste, from wooden bowls, with a first and second finger of the right hand, several dipping from the same bowl. Poi is made from the taro root, and is the great article of food for the Hawaiians. Besides poi, roast dog, roast pig, raw fish and live shrimps are the chief articles of diet.
>
> A piece of dog meat is passed around from one to another (no

knives or forks are used, only the hands,) and if one refuses to take
a bite he gives offense.

On this occasion the hula dance was given. This dance was made
unlawful by the authorities of the Hawaiian Republic, but it was
practised secretly, . . .

Mr. Miller's report was not only inaccurate, it was insulting. The luau
was not given by the "ex-queen," but *for* the queen. Dog meat had not
been eaten in a royal luau in over a hundred years, and the table service
was complete, if somewhat depleted by the *haole* confiscation, of the best
crystal and dinner ware.

The American commissioners began arriving on the Islands to "investigate" the possibility of complete "territorial status," which had not yet
been determined. The adamant annexationists suddenly feared "too much
Americanism" might be dangerous—it could include the Hawaiian vote.
Natives should be kept from voting: "Irresponsible people should not be
allowed to vote," was the cry of the P.G.-Republic. These "irresponsibles"
included not only the Hawaiians, but surprisingly, the Portuguese, who
had aided the P.G.'s, and of course, the Orientals.

The organ for the Territory of Hawaii was to be drafted primarily by
S.B. Dole and L.A. Thurston, with the help of John T. Morgan, who
more than any other man in the United States Senate, had defended the
Revolution of 1893. It was his report that had attacked not only Blount
but also Willis and supported J.L. Stevens, finding "no one guilty," except the queen. The men of the oligarchy all stood strongly on property
qualifications that would certainly disenfranchise the Hawaiians.

Liliuokalani made a personal attempt to prove that the Hawaiians
were "responsible citizens" by going on an island tour simultaneously
while the commissioners were taking theirs. She had been urged by the
Hawaiian Patriotic League to support their appeal that: 1) Hawaii be
made a legal territory of the United States; 2) that the Hawaiian flag
be retained as the flag of the Territory; 3) that pensions be granted Queen
Liliuokalani, Princess Kaiulani and Dowager Queen Kapiolani, and
4) most important, that male suffrage be made universal with only educational qualification for voters.

When the *Kinau* dropped anchor at Kailua-Kona on the Big Island
of Hawaii, the Summer Palace was opened and a luau prepared. Liliuokalani, now wary, if somewhat too late, of the *haole,* declined the invitation, for the threats of assassination still followed her. Then to the dismay

PRINCESS KAIULANI

of the commissioners, the crowds instantly deserted the Summer Palace, but even more disconcertingly, took the luau with them. The luau was for the queen—and it went on board the *Kinau* for the queen.[1]

A second snub occurred at the Moana Loa crater. If by coincidence or not, the queen's party, arriving moments before the commissioners, were given all the accommodations. The commissioners had to fend for themselves, not an easy thing to do as the accommodations at the time were woefully few.

Liliuokalani quickly saw that these events were a great personal victory for her, but a defeat for her country. Scorned men, no less than scorned women, rival hell in its fury of retaliation. As the situation began to look bad for the Hawaiian Patriotic League's petition, Liliuokalani and Princess Kaiulani began holding a series of social events to which the commissioners came, drank, and were merry—and decided to vote against the requests of the Hawaiian Patriotic League.

Liliuokalani felt she had no choice but to go again to the United States to plead for the rights of the Hawaiian people and for a fair settlement of Hawaiian crown lands. Dr. James English, who had not cured Liliuokalani's "cancer," which she did not have, nor had made any contribution to the leprosy problem, saw the crown lands dance like sugar plums before his eyes. Not until he had come to Hawaii had he been able to catch a glimpse of the fact that the "crown lands" might well belong to the former ruling *sovereign,* not the government.

In November, 1898, Liliuokalani sailed with James Hamilton English and his wife, Joseph Heleluhe and his wife and daughter, Myra, on the *Coptic* for San Francisco. She passed quickly through San Francisco this time and took a central train route straight to Washington, D.C. *Colorado Springs Gazette's* reporters, after being refused an interview with the "ex-queen," used for the first time the hated title of "Queen Lil." Liliuokalani, like Shakespeare, felt such familiarity bred contempt, and the American diminutive of "Lil" infuriated her. After her death, unfortunately, some writers of lesser discernment considered it a term of endearment. It was never so to Liliuokalani, nor to anyone with whom she was closely associated.[2]

The newspaper carried a description of Liliuokalani which seemed to praise even as it intended to damn. ". . . She is not fair but fat and more than 40 according to looks. [She was 61.] Her dark complexion and retrousse nose, while not lending a particularly queenly appearance to the general ensemble, yet they stamp her with an individuality, peculiar to itself."

The description of the queen as being "fat" helped to perpetuate the fallacious idea that "Hawaiian queens" weighed up to 800 pounds! Three hundred was a good average, according to "knowledgeable writers." From Liliuokalani's "measurements" of 1901 diary-addendum, a fair guess would be she was approximately 5' 5" tall and weighed around 160 pounds.

Almost immediately upon arrival in Washington, Liliuokalani sent a protest to the United States Government relative to the crown lands.[3]

Dr. James Hamilton English then began his long and futile correspondence with Senator George Frisbie Hoar of Massachusetts. Senator Hoar had been against annexation and was favorable to Queen Liliuokalani. Dr. English drafted letters to the Senator, which requested a "settlement of $250,000 lump sum to the queen and not be bothered with the relatives." He signed it "Your Humble Servant, Liliuokalani." However Liliuokalani was, by his directions, to recopy it in her "own hand". She rebelled against "not be bothered with the relatives." This phrase she omitted, and in place of "Your Humble Servant, Liliuokalani", she signed it, "James English, for Her Majesty Queen Liliuokalani."[4]

These letters were amended by Dr. English's notations telling her to be "more humble," "use diplomacy," and "forget the relatives." Liliuokalani preferred a different settlement. If she were to lose the crown lands, and if they were to go to her people *for their aid,* she requested a $20,000 pension for herself and $10,000 for Kaiulani. Such, however, would not offer English his "percentage" of the $250,000.[5]

The newspaper took little notice of her except to mention her enjoyment of her new "locomobile," and the fact that she owed "three years rent to the Cairo Hotel in Washington." She had been turned away from the Shoreham, "Hotels in Washington Suddenly Full."[6] The queen's credit in the United States had run out. The Ebbett House was the only one to open its doors to her.

On March 3, 1899, Liliuokalani received notice that her niece Kaiulani had died from a severe cold, turning to pneumonia. She wrote in a letter to Joe Carter that she heard that Kaiulani had been buried from Kawaiahao Church instead of the Executive (Territorial) Building and that David paid for the funeral. ". . . As I write I weep for the last tie I had on earth but she has gone to her rest . . . 'His will be done'."[7]

From 1900 to 1909 Liliuokalani made five more trips to the United States protesting the disposition of the crown lands. It was of little use, for in 1900 Hawaii became a Territory of the United States by Hawaii's Organic Act passed in Congress on June 14, 1900. The Hawaiian Patriotic League won over the annexationists, in "that citizens of the Republic of Hawaii in 1898 would be citizens of the Territory of Hawaii and of the United States." They could vote in all local elections, if male, of age, native born or had a resident requirement. Nothing was said about property qualifications for voters nor candidates.

Orientals were omitted by definition of "citizenship," but by that definition Hawaiians were admitted, and although a defeated dying people, they could still command a majority at the polls. As a result, at the first election neither Republicans or Democrats won, but members of a third party, the Home Rule Party. They won the majority in the Territorial House and the Senate. And they elected their chief spokesman — Robert Wilcox — as Hawaii's delegate to Congress. His election was due, rumors ran, to Liliuokalani's support. Liliuokalani's own public statements and her diary bear no such proof.

A letter to "My very dear Friend" [possibly Hannah Evans] dated March 5, 1901, expresses her usual sentiments:

> Am I happy — yes — I do not trouble myself with affairs of others. Have love of my people but some are Rep. & Dem. & majority Home Rule Independents. I am out of politics . . .
>
> All my property is mortgaged by the overthrow by the "Missionary Party" . . .
>
> My Maker has been good to me — my sleep untroubled — do not lay any weight on the goods of this world — at least not enough to make me worry . . .
>
> Delightful weather so cool & pleasant but from appearances may have a Kona storm, but for it to rain while the sun shines, the old wise ones say that these showers are for strewing the petals of the flowers of our Mt. Apples, preparation to the coming of the fruit — then another shower & the ripening of it. It is very poetical to us — the idea is continuity of life.

It was, however, a typical Wilcox move to have suggested Liliuokalani as "governor" of the territory. Although she must have known she had no chance, she still no doubt felt a glow of appreciation to Wilcox, and he had, as usual, promised his help to her relative to the crown lands.

If asked whom she supported, she may certainly have replied it was he. That was enough for rumors then—and to persist for the next fifty years.

Sanford Ballard Dole was appointed Governor over L.A. Thurston, Liliuokalani and W.O. Smith. It was a wise choice.

The Home Rule Party, unfortunately for the Hawaiians, was an utter disaster. It was much too late to turn back the clock to the Hawaiian language, which the Party insisted on using instead of English, as directed in the Organic Act. They attempted to resurrect as much as possible of the old regime of Kalakaua, and failed—as could have been foreseen.

It became obvious to the Territorial government that the only way to defeat the Home Rule Party at the polls was to choose a royalist native to oppose the "national hero," Robert Wilcox. The Republicans invited Jonah Kuhio Kalanianaole to run against Wilcox in 1902. Kuhio was the nephew of Kapiolani; he had been named by Liliuokalani to succeed his brother, David Kawananakoa, in the event Kaiulani and David should predecease him. Kuhio was elected.

Kuhio had been educated in the United States and England at the expense of his uncle, Kalakaua, and his aunt, Kapiolani, and later by Liliuokalani. He was well liked in both Hawaii and Washington, especially in Washington, as "a good host and guest, a congenial drinking partner and card player."[8] In moments, he was as diplomatic as Kalakaua. The Hawaiians were pleased with their *alii* representative, and Thurston wrote glowingly of "Prince Cupid," who never ceased to greet him in a friendly fashion. He had not yet been so greeted by Liliuokalani, although in his self-justifying *Memoirs* he couldn't understand why—"political enemies" could indeed be friends, couldn't they?

Perhaps it was unfair for Liliuokalani to feel that Kuhio was doing "nothing." She had momentarily had more faith in the fire-brand Wilcox, as incompetent as he was.

Kuhio was attempting to gain a certain amount of "self-rule" on the individual islands and thus get for the Hawaiians larger crumbs that fell from the *haole* business leaders' table. It is true, however, he did little, if anything, for Queen Liliuokalani.

When asked about "crown lands" he hedged nimbly: "he wasn't sure"; "he didn't have first-hand information"; "he hadn't been present during certain transactions."[9]

Liliuokalani finally wrote somewhat bitterly that she "must never ask the prince for anything again."[10] She made her last official plea for reimbursement of the crown lands in November, 1908. She reiterated the historical facts from 1891, when she became lawful "sovereign of the Hawaiian Islands" to the conventions of the three parties in 1900. She included quotes from the records of the Territorial Convention of the Independent Party for Home Rule, August 31, 1908, those of the Republican Platform of September 4, 1908, and the Democratic platform of September 10, 1908. Each had pledged its candidates to secure a lump sum settlement for the "former Queen Liliuokalani." The only mentioned figure was $250,000. The other ambiguous words were "a substantial pecuniary sum commensurate with her former position and dignity."

Liliuokalani listed in her petition that the total crown lands of 911,888 acres, valued at the average of $22.00 per acre, would accrue to approximately $20,000,000. Liliuokalani asked one-half of that sum or ten million dollars.[11]

The problem seemed to be who—if anyone—should recompense the ex-queen—the United States or the Hawaiian Territorial Government. The latter had cavalierly offered all the crown lands to the United States at the time of desired annexation, but now wanted them for themselves.

The official correspondence on this problem from 1893 to 1912 is voluminous, and open to some aspiring attorney to discern fairness, but it is sufficient to say here that in 1912 the Territorial Government began to pay the ex-queen a pension of $12,000 yearly. Kaiulani having passed away, there was no need for compensation to the Cleghorn family. Kaiulani had died without issue. Dowager Queen Kapiolani had also died, leaving not only her estate, but also all of Kalakaua's, to the princes— Kuhio and David. She had not even left money to help carry on the work of the maternity home, Curtis Iaukea wrote in the *Paradise of the Pacific*.[12]

In the meantime, Poverty came to live with Liliuokalani. People who had been willing to lend her money on the hope of a rich inheritance from the government—the United States or the Territory—now began calling in their loans.

Her inherited *alii*[13] lands had never been too clearly defined from the crown lands, and she found herself in constant problems of having injunctions placed against her for "taking sand" from Waikiki.[14] Her agents recommended, time and again, that she foreclose on mortgages she held. But she wouldn't. The land she had set aside, while queen, "free for Hawaiians," she insisted should remain free. No rents should be collected.

To compound her problem many Hawaiians had no concept, even

yet, that the highest *alii* could be impoverished,—she was still *moi wahine*. Consequently, persons from every station of life wished to draw on her almost non-existent resources for everything, from money enough for food to the buying of proper wedding gowns for a some-time "retainer." Liliuokalani's memorandum account books, included in her diaries, constantly juggled her debts of a $1.50 fish bill against that of a gift of $50.00 to someone, a mortgage of $100 paid for someone else, or a horse for Kaipo.[15]

In 1898 in a burst of retrenchment she had ordered J.O. Carter to give "a dollar to Kaipo, Lydia, and Aimoku" for Christmas, but that type of reduction in giving was shortlived.

Liliuokalani had lost her "last blood tie" in Kaiulani's death. There remained now only her *hanai* children. Kapiolani had also died in 1899, and Liliuokalani found herself "coolly treated by the young people"[16]— the two princes and a new princess.

David Kawananakoa, who it was rumored, had been betrothed to Kaiulani (certainly such was Liliuokalani's wish), married Abigail Campbell, daughter of a Hawaiian mother and Scotch-Irish father.

Returning to Honolulu at the end of 1900, Liliuokalani learned that Lydia had been offered a position at Kamehameha Schools, as Miss Pope's secretary. Lydia wrote she was to be "given board and room and twenty dollars a month." Liliuokalani replied saying that if Lydia came "home" she would give her "board and room and twenty dollars a month."

Lydia refused. "I was so independent, so smart. I'll never forgive myself. I didn't know how lonely she was—and I was mad at Myra," she said, some seventy years later.[17]

During the early part of 1900 Aimoku had graduated from St. Albans and had joined the queen on her trips "trying to help her the best I can." Animosity was growing between Aimoku and Kaipo. He wrote to Curtis Iaukea, "I know they don't like me as well as Kaipo. But he has had enough and I shall try to keep him from coming to San Francisco." He couldn't, however. Kaipo happily resigned his governmental clerking position and came to San Francisco.[18]

Both J.O. Carter and Curtis Iaukea wrote disparagingly of Kaipo, to which Liliuokalani replied, "Tell him not to use low language and not to drink. He is not entirely dependent upon me. He has his own land but I don't want him to know it." She also admonished Carter to "talk to him kindly . . . show him wrong . . . tell him what is right and help him . . . Tell him not to associate with low women . . . Think of his future wife . . . Have him play cards with Cleghorn and learn to be in good company."[19]

Somewhere along the line Kaipo over-stepped himself, and Liliuokalani upon a "routine inspection," as ex-queen, visited Kamehameha Schools. There she met the Thompsons, became impressed by the "virtue of working with one's hands," and decided to enroll Kaipo.[20]

❧ 2 ❧

In 1899 Henry Berger married his second wife. It is doubtful the subject of marriage ever passed between Berger and Liliuokalani, but she probably felt a loss, especially as Julius Palmer now was gone from her life, as well. As for James English, upon discovering he could not get his hands on crown-land monies, he sued Liliuokalani for over $700 in "back payment of medical services." J.O. Carter, her agent, paid the bill, and a further disillusioned Liliuokalani returned again in 1904 to Hawaii.

Shuttling back and forth between the United States and Hawaii, in an ever-losing battle not only with governments but with attorneys and agents, Liliuokalani was ready for a respite. She was completely vulnerable when a letter came from Tahiti from Prince Arii Solomon Paea saying that he was actually "engaged from birth to Liliuokalani," and he now wished to make this a fact.

He wrote[21] explaining that in 1849 Princess Ninito Pomare, his aunt, had accompanied her two nieces who were "betrothed" to Prince Moses and Prince Lot. Upon their arrival, however, they discovered that Moses had died in the 1848 measles epidemic and that Prince Lot was abroad with Dr. Judd. It must also have been discovered that early "betrothals" of this time were not necessarily honored, as Lot had just been through his "from birth betrothal" to Bernice Pauahi who in 1849 was married to Charles Bishop. As a result, in a rather fast courtship, the nieces had married the Sumner brothers. Ninito, engaged to Moses and named for her aunt, had married John Sumner, and Mareira, Lot's betrothed, had become the wife of William Sumner. A great deal more was written about genealogy and *hanai,* but the real message was that when Princess Ninito Pomare brought her nieces to Hawaii, she also came to "engage" Prince Arii Solomon Paea (no more than an infant then) to the high chiefess, Kamehameha *hanai* to Konia and Paki, Lydia Kamakaeha.

Liliuokalani was suddenly thrown back into Old Hawaii of *hanai,* and the before birth-betrothals of which she had been influenced by Lunalilo and Victoria. She was vulnerable and willing to return to such

PRINCE ARII
Courtesy, Bishop Museum.

an uncomplicated time. She was also a lonely woman of sixty-eight, looking toward an empty life. On record are only fragments of Prince Arii's letters, except for one copy of hers, so surmise must be made of what she wrote.

She protested the burden she would be to him—an old, sick woman. He replied he did not consider her old, and he would be only so glad to devote his life to serving her and nursing her back to health.

One thing was obvious. Prince Arii did not know Liliuokalani had no money. He asked of her only one "small thing": he explained all his property had been destroyed by a cyclone, and fortunately, only one life was lost, but unfortunately, it was his brother's (Narii). His now being destitute, the small favor he was asking was that the queen outfit a schooner for him to sail into her arms in San Francisco, from where they would sail together to Hawaii.

The one letter from Liliuokalani stated she wished to withdraw her acceptance of marriage because of illness. Again Liliuokalani's diaries show an interest in fortune telling, horoscopes, astrology. But she hardly needed any of these to warn that she should be careful of the "Prince."

On June 19, 1906, Arii Solomon Paea, without schooner, promised to be in San Francisco to meet his "wife": "You can consider yourself my wife from the time you receive this . . . The ceremony and form will be complete when we meet . . . my wife: Arii Paea Vahine, according to the custom of my country."

Liliuokalani had left San Francisco and returned to Hawaii before Prince Arii arrived at his sister's, Mrs. Atwater's.

The prince did not take his rejection with good grace. He instituted a "breach of promise suit" against Liliuokalani, which J.O. Carter paid "for the Prince's expenses"—nearly $1,000.

❦ 3 ❦

From 1901 through 1906 Liliuokalani frequently wrote her diary entries in code—these are the last diaries available for perusal. Someone wrote, "She saw danger in every corner . . . every lawyer deceitful . . . no friend to trust." Perhaps the writer was not too far wrong. The codes prove her reluctance to trust her diaries falling again into the wrong hands, and a concerted effort was made by the Hawaiian repositories to keep the diaries "private" for many years.

Two of her codes were numerical and one was a type of gibberish: part Hawaiian-Tahitian and with possibly made up words. The latter will be of interest to linguists as well the code-breakers. Generally the material dealt with everyday affairs, as did many of her Hawaiian entries. The material was frequently reiterated in English.

The one surprising page of the 1901 coded diary[22] was that of Tuesday, May 14, which when translated from code read as follows:

> We went up to the Royal Mausoleum to deposit Kamehameha in the coffin. Four persons are in the coffin together. Liloa, his bundle is of coconut fibre covered with white tapa which is torn and falling off—at the head of the coffin. Hakau is next—in a lumpy fibre casket with a mouth, wrapped in white tapa, bent in an arch at the head of the coffin with Liloa. Kamehameha himself, not in a braided casket—his bundle is of red and white tapa as is Umi—his bundle is red and white tapa. He was a small man. The middle of Kamehameha's coffin is the bottom of Umi's coffin.[23]

From earliest days to the present the one sacred belief of the Hawaiians was that "only the stars know where the bones of Kamehameha The First rest." It is puzzling then why Liliuokalani, who apparently truly believed the remains she had in her possession were those of Kamehameha The First, recorded the information at all. The only explanation that seems plausible to this author is that already archeological excavations had begun in Hawaii, and now that Hawaii had become a Territory of the United States native Hawaiians felt they would continue and increase despite their protestations.

It was no secret that Kalakaua had made many attempts to find the bones of Kamehameha. His reasons can only be surmised. However, at sometime he revealed the hiding place of what he believed were Kamehameha's remains to Liliuokalani. Despite the thorough ransacking of the Iolani Palace, her homes in Waikiki, and Palama, and even Washington Place, the hiding place had not been found.

It must have been an awesome experience for her and her only trusted friend of the time—David Kawananakoa—to make this early morning journey and carry out the deed.

It must be said that the remains of an unidentified body was found by members of the staff of the Bishop Museum in the designated coffin. It was determined, however, that the remains were those of a woman, and so it is still only the stars that know where lie the bones of Kamehameha the First.

LILIUOKALANI WITH HER HANAI SONS,
KAIPO AEA (left) AND JOHN AIMOKU (right)

CHAPTER 3

A Portrait of an Hawaiian Alii

❧ 1 ❧

In 1910 Liliuokalani returned from her last trip to the United States after her visit with Mrs. Robert Louis Stevenson[1] at Santa Barbara. She had become further disillusioned with Kuhio, who wanted to borrow $1,000 to "push [her] claims." She had come to rely on Aimoku and Curtis Iaukea who had succeeded in securing a loan of $10,000 from Spreckels Company, although it was through a mortgage.

A certain amount of rivalry continued to exist between Aimoku and Kaipo. Aimoku, not unlike his father, kept strict accounts of money which he sent to Curtis Iaukea, who had taken the place of Joseph Aea, Kaipo's father, now becoming infirm and wishing to be relieved of his responsibilities.

Liliuokalani's letters[2] during the past two years to Kaipo had not only reiterated that his life style should be changed, but that his mother Kaheo, whom Joseph had now divorced to marry Helen Kanina, be "given the best room in [Kaipo's] house." Liliuokalani never failed to send love to Kaheo. This was the woman, who with her husband, had threatened the princess with blackmail in 1887. But she *was* Kaipo's mother, and Liliuokalani continued, as she had through the years, to support her and her other children.

Kaipo at the time was living at Washington Place, but wanted the Palama home also, because he was going to marry "one of Miss Pope's girls, upon her return from Seattle."

Eagerly Liliuokalani wrote him Moulaulani would be put into condition for him, but he must "give up carousing . . . making night hideous by receiving low women, singing girls, low people . . . think of your wife to be . . . call on nice people and be seen with them—'my son, if sinners entice thee, consent thou not'." She was happy to think of him "respectable and with respectable friends," and enormously pleased that he was attending the Episcopal Church regularly. "Pray for me as I do for you."

Letters between Curtis Iaukea and Aimoku did not bear out that Kaipo was "respectable." His own letter to Liliuokalani was that he wanted also the property at Waikiki. She wrote in her diary that she, Aimoku and Kaipo had talked of "things as they were," but Kaipo had not been interested. She and Aimoku had cried together.

By the end of 1909 and early in 1910 Liliuokalani began considering wills and trust deeds. She wrote Curtis Iaukea as her "business manager"; Iaukea wiser in the ways of the world requested "power-of-attorney." This power must then be officially removed from Joseph Aea. From May 14, 1909 to March 11, 1910, a series of Liliuokalani's giving power-of-attorney and the retaking of the same, which passed "as agreement" between Joseph Aea and Curtis Iaukea, was to be the basis of bringing a sanity suit against Queen Liliuokalani in 1915 by Kuhio Kalanianaole.[3]

Arriving in Honolulu early in the spring of 1910, Liliuokalani was met at the wharf by *haole, hapa-haole,* and Hawaiians. She stepped off the ship with Curtis Iaukea and was greeted with "Alo-o-oha!"

Liliuokalani stopped, shocked, still. She stood unmoving until the cry melted away as if in chagrin. She looked down upon the crowd. "I greet you", she said in her rich musical voice, "with *aloha. Aloha*—that is the Hawaiian greeting." "Never," she told more than one Hawaiian child, including the adults such as Lydia, "never say *alo-o-oha*. It is a *haole* word. *Aloha* is ours, as is its meaning".[4]

Liliuokalani was home. She was to stay in Hawaii for the next seven years as *moi wahine,* ex-queen, *hanai* to her children and her former retainers and many native Hawaiians. She was to remain the scholar and musician she always had been. She was to become and remain forever the portrait of a Hawaiian *alii.* But from it all she was to fulfill the role of every mystic to triumph over oneself to find Oneself. "He must lose his life to find it," the Christian Master said. "My kingdom is not of this world." And from Sir Edwin Arnold's *Light of Asia,* the Buddhist said, "One must leave the material world to find his Soul."

All these are most dangerous words to utter in any language as one's own truth, because one will be called upon to prove them, as Liliuokalani was.

In many ways Liliuokalani felt alone. Her beloved David Kawananakoa had died June 21, 1908, and his wife "Princess" Abigail Campbell

Kawananakoa was too wise in the ways of the world to understand an old Hawaiian mystic. Her sister, Kamokila Campbell, a student of the old hula, mele, and traditions was closer to understanding the queen, but their contacts were only intermittent.

Liliuokalani took seriously the old requirements of the *alii:* Hostility was the greatest sin; according to Malo[5] then came injustice to the people and lastly inhospitality. Liliuokalani's hospitality continued. She held her receptions and none refused to come. Her doors were open to all. She continued her birthday celebrations of being awakened at 5:00 a.m. by the *mele* singers, the quiet breakfast with close friends, the open afternoon receptions, and the evening luaus. Her retainers were fewer in number, but her faithful Wakeki was back with her.

Kaipo lived at Waikiki; he had not married. Lydia remained with Ida Pope, happily inviting with the "queen's permission" teachers from the Kamehameha School to Waikiki, where Kaipo was a gallant and exciting host. Music, laughter, swimming filled the day, until one day too much of Kaipo's beer sent Lydia away from the "awful place."[6]

Soon after their arrival in Hawaii, Aimoku told Liliuokalani that he wished to marry Sybil McInerny, the young, lovely daughter of a successful Honolulu merchant. It was then Liliuokalani decided that John Dominis Aimoku should become John Aimoku Dominis. She "officially adopted" him under the new name in May of 1910.

On June 27, 1910, Aimoku married Sybil in a "quiet but elegant ceremony" at the McInerny home at Kahala. Liliuokalani, unlike her mother-in-law, attended the ceremony, but then another old mistake was repeated: the young couple, after a San Francisco honeymoon,[7] returned to live at Washington Place.

Liliuokalani had all of her mother-in-law's proprietory interest in her son, and her *hanai* son had all the dedication to "the queen," his father had had to *his* mother. But Sybil had none of the young Liliuokalani's deference to "the queen," nor desire to please-at-all-costs a new mother-in-law. The arrangement was less than blissful.

Then on September 1, 1911, a son was born at Washington Place to Sybil. Liliuokalani waited in her parlor, as she so often had for news—of governmental dissension, revolt, arrest,—now for news of the birth of her grandchild. Moments after the cry of a newborn infant, John Aimoku ran into the room and dropped on his knees before Liliuokalani. Placing his head in her lap, as he had often done as a child, he whispered: "It is a boy—what shall we call him?"

Without a moment's hesitation, the queen replied: "John Owen Dominis." It was the queen's choice, not Sybil's. The highest *alii* in the land had the irrevocable right to name a child—as Kinau had named Liliu Kamakaeha.

A new John Owen Dominis was to live in Hawaii and he was to be the queen's grandson, first and foremost.

❧ 2 ❧

Liliuokalani had for some time planned to have a new tomb for the Kalakaua Dynasty. She had made voluminous notes, tracing genealogies of the Keawe-a-Heulu line. The royal interment was authorized by the Territorial Legislature and completed June 1910.

On June 25, 1910, the *Pacific Commercial Advertiser* gave an exceedingly long account of the "Royal Remains Removed".

> Weird, yet interesting, were the ceremonies attending the removal of the bodies of the members of the Kalakaua Dynasty on the evening of June 24, 1910, from the royal mausoleum in Nuuanu Valley to the vault nearby, chiefs and retainers wearing the ancient feather *ahuulas* of their rank, while participating in one of the most solemn ceremonies that has taken place of late years. In the presence of a throng of Hawaiians who represent today the remnants of a once powerful sovereignty, with the eye of their deposed Queen watching the transfer of each casket, the dead of the last reigning dynasty were consigned to their last resting places in an underground vault, where, sealed in with cement and marble, no other eyes are expected to ever behold them again.
>
> . . . The Queen had taken a deep personal interest in all arrangements, and the manner in which the bodies were to be placed in the crypts was left largely to her selection. The method of arrangement was completed some time previous, subject to one or two changes at the last.
>
> The caskets were each slid down and elevated to their niche in the following order:
>
> Kapaakea, father of King Kalakaua, died November 13, 1866, aged 51 years.
>
> Keohokalole, mother of the King, died April 6, 1869, aged 53 years.
>
> Kaiminiaauao, sister of King Kalakaua and Queen Liliuokalani, died November 10, 1848, aged 3 years.
>
> Governor John O. Dominis, husband of Queen Liliuokalani, died August 27, 1891, aged 60 years.

Leleiohoku (Wm. Pitt), brother of the King, died April 9, 1877, aged 22 years.

Likelike, sister of the King and Queen Liliuokalani, and wife of ex-Governor A. S. Cleghorn, and mother of Princess Kaiulani, died February 2, 1887, aged 36 years.

Kaiulani, niece of King Kalakaua and Queen Liliuokalani, died March 6, 1899, aged 23 years.

Naihe *et al.* Casket containing remains of Kalakaua's grandfather and great-grandfather and Kailimaikai, brother of Kamehameha.

Poomaikalani, sister of Kapiolani, consort of King Kalakaua, died October 22, 1895, aged 57 years.

Kekaulike, sister of Kapiolani and mother of Princes David Kawananakoa and Kuhio Kalanianaole, died January 8, 1884, aged 41 years.

Kawananakoa (David), nephew of King Kalakaua and Queen Liliuokalani, and husband of Princess Abigail Kawananakoa, died June 2, 1908, aged 40 years.

Keliiahonui (Edward), brother of Princes David and Kuhio, died September 21, 1887, aged 18 years.

Kapiolani, consort of King Kalakaua, died June 24, 1899, aged 64 years.

His Majesty King Kalakaua, died January 20, 1891, aged 54 years.

The weather which has often appealed to the superstitions of the Hawaiian race at the burial of a member of the royal family prevailed to the extent of slight rain.

When the casket of Governor Dominis was brought out, the widow did not follow, as she was too feeble to walk out and back again, as it was her duty to remain until the last casket was removed.

. . . During all this time the grounds were illuminated by incandescent lights. These were suddenly turned out, and then amongst the trees appeared torchlights composed of *kukui* nuts and cocoanut fiber, copied after the ancient methods. Eight lined the steps of the mausoleum as the remains of Kapiolani were brought out. The bearers this time wore *ahuulas,* and the scene reminded all of the funerals in the old days.

At this juncture the Queen left the mausoleum supported by Colonel Iaukea and John Sea and entered an automobile which was moved to a position where she could closely watch the transfer.

Last of all came the transfer of the casket of King Kalakaua with its magnificent palls and decorations. The sad ceremony with the torches and darkened grounds prevailed although the moon then pierced the bank of clouds and added to the picturesqueness and solemnity of the scene. Queen Liliuokalani, who was attended by Princess Kawananakoa, leaned forward in the auto, her eyes strained to catch every change in the scene, for to her it meant the last glimpse of all that were dear to her in the past. What thoughts must have crossed her mind as she gazed upon this the second funeral of her royal brother. What memories it must have brought to her of the first funeral ceremony when she was the reigning monarch of the Hawaiian Islands, just then in the first flush of her supreme rule. What memories it must have brought when she compared those days to her present. She presented a pathetic figure, for the glory of the old days has long since departed from her life. . . .

But one casket remained in the mausoleum, not honored by interment in the tomb. This is the casket containing the remains which were once accredited by royal favor with those of Kamehameha the Great. The Casket, however, bore another name.

Much was written about the frailty of the queen and her "withdrawing from society" as well as dissension between her and members of her family. It was true that after the ceremony of the removing of the remains, Liliuokalani did suffer from nervous fatigue. For several weeks she saw no one except a woman companion, Lahilahi Webb (the *hanai* granddaughter of Don Marin). Lahilahi Webb was highly protective of the queen, and erroneous rumors therefore began creeping out from Washington Place.

Thus, despite the accusation of Kuhio during the sanity trial that Liliuokalani broke friendly relations with Kaipo after his father's "dismissal" and death, Liliuokalani actually retained a close relationship with her second *hanai* son.

According to Ulrich Thompson, "The queen was exceedingly proud of Kaipo, and in 1914 when Mrs. Thompson and I were guests in her gracious home, she wanted to know everything about his honors and work. The boy died shortly thereafter . . ."[8]

On September 14, 1914, Ida Pope died and left one financial bequest: $500 to Lydia K. Aholo. Lydia immediately went to Liliuokalani and requested permisson to attend Ida Pope's *alma mater,* Oberlin College in Ohio. Liliuokalani was well pleased with her *hanai* daughter's choice, for it was a college well-known for its excellence in music. She implemented the five hundred dollars and assured her that her education would be paid for—"just send the bills here."[9]

One month after seeing Liliuokalani, Lydia stopped by the old Waikiki residence, where Kaipo lived, to say goodbye to her *hanai* brother. To Lydia's horror she found Kaipo on his knees before Liliuokalani's picture. Tears were rolling down his face and he was crying out *"Hanai, hanai."*

A tearful session ensued in which Kaipo and Lydia shared memories of the past as they had never shared the past together. Kaipo begged her not to leave for he feared he was going to die. He also wanted her to go to Liliuokalani to tell *"Hanai* how much I love her. How wrong I've been and how sorry I am."[10]

The precise, punctual Lydia pointed out she had to be aboard a ship in a short while and told Kaipo to tell *hanai* himself how he felt. Kaipo, however, did not make this self-confession. He died two days later of Bright's disease at the Waikiki home, at the age of thirty-two.

Liliuokalani was too ill to attend the funeral and remained closed in at Washington Place to mourn alone her beloved Joseph Kaiponohea Aea.

❧ 3 ❧

On March 4, 1914, just a few months earlier, Sybil had given birth to a girl, whom she named after herself. But Liliuokalani was satisfied that the baby's middle name was to be Frances, after the sister of Aimoku's father. Her love for young John Owen continued extravagantly.

In a home in which "customs of the Royal Court were carried out in their many details," John Owen ruled as a minor potentate. He reported in an article for the *Paradise of the Pacific*:

> Her Majesty was strong willed and usually had her own way about things. I remember one day when she was going for a ride she put on her hat backwards. It was my delight to go for rides with the Queen but my outing that day was more fun than usual because Her Majesty would not change and wore her hat backwards all the way.
>
> Most of our rides were in the Queen's private carriage which had a high seat in front backing against the higher seat for the coachman. When my mother and I were alone with the Queen we rode in the low back seat with Her Majesty but I had the most fun when someone else was along and I could sit on that high seat and tumble into the Queen's lap whenever we hit a bump. The coachman was in livery and the people used to stand at the curbs and watch us pass.
>
> When the Hawaiian Band came to Washington Place to play for the Queen at breakfast I used to dance for Her Majesty. And in the evenings, after dinner, she used to ask me to dance. It was fun then but I don't think I would enjoy having to do it now.

On special occasions Her Majesty used a State Carriage. This carriage was usually covered with canvas when it was in the stable. I was very fond of this carriage and loved to play in it, although no one other than the Queen was supposed to use it. Many times I slipped out to the stable, crept under the canvas and played in the carriage. Sometimes I took a nap in it. I don't know what would have happened to me if I had been caught.

On her seventy-seventh birthday, September 2, 1915, Liliuokalani decided to give her last public reception. Her hospitality to one and all was to cease, not because *aloha* hospitality ever ceases, but because Liliuokalani was tired of worldly things. This feeling had been growing for some time.

She had forgiven seventy-times-seven, and as many persons, who had betrayed her. She had opened her doors and her heart to all the men of the Provisional Government and the Republic. Although invited, she had never attended one of Sanford Ballard Dole's famous breakfasts, but he had paid his respects at her receptions, and she had received him graciously. They were considered "friends." She had also been present at Territorial "state affairs." She had received members of the Judd family, the Cookes, the Castles and many others in her home. It seemed as if every *haole* now, as much as she, wanted her "friendship."

She, however, had said, in paraphrase, "It shall never *again* be said in Hawaiian *aloha* that the children's teeth are set on edge because the fathers have eaten sour grapes." Although reluctant in 1902 to forgive Charles B. Wilson, by 1914 she had sent his son Johnny Wilson to Stanford University—all expenses paid. In her wills, of which there were many,[11] she left bequests to Robert Wilcox's descendants, even to Willie Kaae's son, Junius.

A few months earlier, on May 18, 1915, Kuhio Kalanianaole held a reception at his Waikiki home, land which had once been Aikanaka's, Liliuokalani's grandfather's. It had come to Kuhio through Kalakaua and Kapiolani.

Liliuokalani sat at the head of the receiving line when Lorrin A. Thurston entered. He wrote: "She extended her hand to me, and said: 'I am very glad to see you here this evening, Mr. Thurston.' Those were the first words she had spoken to me since her deposition, they were the last words she spoke to me. The incident pleased me, for it indicated that she had finally accepted annexation and no longer harbored resentment against me personally."[12] At least Mr. Thurston was correct in his last phrase.

Liliuokalani was coming to peace with herself. There were still Hawaiian groups that had not united with the last line of the monarchy. One of these was the Kaahumanu Society, re-organized in 1905 by Lucy Peabody. Although its first formation had been under Princess Victoria in 1864 and Liliuokalani had been a member, the terrible breach the genealogical trial of 1883 had brought about, caused Liliuokalani not to be invited to join in 1905. There were other Hawaiian factions that had broken off through Robert Wilcox's machinations and a few who unfortunately still held Liliuokalani responsible for the loss of the monarchy. There was nothing she could do about these groups, so she made peace within her own household.

An old Hawaiian proverb was translated by Kalakaua as "Beware when you feel you have gained your own peace, for only I'o brings true peace."

❧ 4 ❧

The blow fell on November 30, 1915, just two months after her "last" reception. Jonah Kuhio Kalanianaole brought suit to break the Trust for the Estate of Liliuokalani on the basis of "incompetency of the queen over a period of six years."

Sensational headlines and stories burst in the press from December, 1915 to March 9, 1916. Charges of coersion were levied against Curtis Iaukea and John Aimoku Dominis. Kuhio presented himself as "next of kin and rightful heir under the law" to the queen's properties and hence, "next of friend." He cited that the queen's "memory was impaired" in that she allowed her known enemies to be her Trustees: Archibald Cleghorn, who had worked to have her deposed in favor of his daughter, Kaiulani; W.O. Smith, Samuel Damon, and Cecil Brown—all of them avowed enemies. They had worked with the P.G.'s and later held offices under the P.G. and Territorial Government. (Cleghorn had died in 1910 but Smith, Damon and Brown were respondents in the court order.)

Kuhio declared that the queen's "mind was so impaired" by the experiences of dethronement and imprisonment that she could not even remember so simple a thing as the service of process upon her, although such service was not unfamiliar. [Her diary entries of 1901-1903 would have proved to the contrary.]

Worry and anxiety over money such as a $70,000 loan from Spreckels [actually $10,000], had caused her to change Power of Attorney from Iaukea to Joseph Aea Sr. seven times from May 4, 1909, to March 11, 1910.

He accused Iaukea of demanding exorbitant monies for being a trustee. Dominis he accused, of "feathering his pockets" by receiving Washington Place, $35,000 in cash and a $6,000 annuity. He further stated that the "accused" persons had kept the queen from her friends "in fear and under absolute domination."

On December 31, 1915, Liliuokalani asked that the action be dismissed as Kuhio had no authority. Then on February 12, 1916, (the day of Kalakaua's coronation 43 years before) the sanity suit was begun against Liliuokalani. The Trust case went to the Supreme Court as well.

On March 9, 1916, the newspapers went wild with headlines: "Discontinuance by Queen in Trust Deed Valid"; "Liliuokalani Bests Kuhio in Big Case"; "W.O. Smith says Queen Sane."

⚓ 5 ⚓

In 1916 Liliuokalani was baptized a Mormon by her old friend and adviser, Abraham Fernandez. She had been interested in the Mormon religion for many years. In 1887, on her way to Queen Victoria's Jubilee, she "stopped for a few hours, meeting not only many prominent elders of the Mormon Church, but quite a few number of our own people who were living there."[13] Shortly after she became queen, she made a special trip to Kahuku at Laie to visit with "residents of the Mormon faith."

She told Lydia that there was an "affinity" between old Hawaiian *aloha* and the practices of the Mormons: "They always take care of their own." Lydia Aholo also joined the Mormon Church.

⚓ 6 ⚓

On September 2, 1916, Liliuokalani had a small reception. She also looked forward to Lydia's return for the Christmas holidays, but Lydia wrote she planned to spend the holidays in Chicago with "friends and relatives of the Popes."

Liliuokalani faced her final betrayal with Kaipo gone, Lydia refusing an invitation to come home, and a decision by Sybil that they were going to move into a "place of their own," despite the fact that Aimoku was to inherit Washington Place. John Owen protested but Liliuokalani remembering the peace Hamohamo gave her away from her Mother Dominis, agreed to "make arrangements as soon as she could make a new will." Sybil and John now had three children. The youngest, Virginia, was one year old, and therefore, Sybil was prevailed upon to wait until "the new will" was to be made.

Defeat and peace seemed to weld as one; then Liliuokalani's greatest victory came.

Unheralded and in what would never have been seen by the *haole* nor tourists, was one of the most picturesque parades ever to be seen in Honolulu. To Liliuokalani it was the final uniting of all Hawaiians. She had not lifted a finger to achieve it—such an act would have been of no avail. For such *aloha* comes not by asking but by being deserving.

The newspaper banners announced:

PARADE MARKS ENDING OF CENTURY OLD CLAN FEUD

REPRESENTATIVES OF VICTORS AND VANQUISHED IN KAMEHAMEHA'S WARS

QUEEN'S INITIATION INTO A HAWAIIAN SOCIETY THE CAUSE

The *Advertiser* of December 17, 1916 carried the story:

> Final testimony to the healing of the sores of a hundred years ago when the island nobility was swept into defeat by the clans under the Great Kamehameha was witnessed yesterday in a unique and pretty parade of the Sons & Daughters of Hawaiian Warriors. The parade was from the Armory to Washington Place, the residence of Queen Liliuokalani. The object was the initiation into the order, the former Queen, hereditary high chiefess of the "victorious clans," of I, Mahi, Palena, Kuahine, Paia.
>
> Queen Liliuokalani, whose own wish it was that she be received as a member into the order, was initiated with simple ceremonies, and the venerable procession went back to the armory where its rites were completed.
>
> It was a Public Display of Friendship.

The fact that the queen was not feeling well enough to attend the meetings of the order made it necessary that it go from its meeting place to her residence and the ceremonial procession thus became what it was,

the first appearance together in public, and on the streets, the representatives of the victorious and defeated clans for the first time, that is, since
the beginning of the past century. "Amity has long privately existed between the two factions, and in fact, one of the objects of the order is to
reestablish it, but the new bonds were never before publicly displayed."

The clans of the "eight islands of the rising sun to the setting sun"
that is the seven inhabited islands of the group were all represented in
their proper order of importance. The so called "defeated" clans represented were: Ihilani, Lace-Kona, Lo-Alii, Loa, Vili, Hiwauli, Poo Uahi,
Paelekulani. The victorious clans were: the I, Mahi, Salena, Lauhine and
Paia.

> It was NOT A STAGED AFFAIR. Each of the representatives
> were dressed according to the order of their rank. Proud kahilis arose
> from the little ranks and a bit of the glamor of Old Hawaii, the
> proud Hawaii shone for a moment. It was not deliberately staged, nor
> was it intended for public show nor for the credit of tourists. It was
> strictly of the Hawaiians concerned with their own matters, sacred
> to themselves, and only the Queen's indisposition, making it necessary
> to go to her residence gave the public an opportunity of witnessing
> it all.
>
> Mrs. Walter Kukailimoku MacFarlane is the premier or kuhina
> nui, of the society, whose purpose is to preserve the ancient tradi-
> tions or kapus of the inner circle of Hawaii's ancient royalty.
>
> The grandfather of Queen Liliuokalani was a warrior with the
> first Kamehameha.

Liliuokalani had not been able to save her physical country from in-
vaders of thought, destroyers of tradition, and seizers of land, but as
Kamehameha the Great had united Hawaii, not only physically but in
spirit, so Liliuokalani, the last queen of Hawaii, had united in love and
spirit all of Hawaii.

These two were "uniters," not destroyers.

❡ 7 ❡

Then unexpectedly, Lydia returned to Hawaii. She confessed to the
queen she was "no musician," could write no *mele*, nor sing, and she had
failed her queen, her *hanai*. Lydia returned to her position as Secretary
with the Kamehameha Girls' Schools, where perhaps, she thought, she
could do the most good. She became a frequent visitor at Washington
Place and Liliuokalani began then to talk to her of *her* times, a "second

generation" of Hawaiian *alii*—royalty. She had shared views of earlier times with Lahilahi Webb, of the mysticism of Mu and Io, which Mrs. Webb revealed in part to Leinani Melville, who later wrote *Children of the Rainbow*.

Mrs. Webb, however, recognized, as Liliuokalani also did, that the true Hawaiian culture had ceased after the missionaries had arrived. She, however, considered that *all* tradition should be of the "early days." In these she remained well versed, but stubbornly rejected the years of the monarchy and Territory from 1820 to 1917.

Liliuokalani knew, however, that nearly one hundred years could not be left out if the Hawaiians were ever to understand the overthrow of their government. It was one thing to "take over" an innocent people and quite another to take over a comparatively highly civilized established monarchy as if it had had no history and no existence, and no struggle among its *alii* against the invading tide of anti-royalty. She knew no portion of the past can dissolve into nothingness and thus connect 1820 with 1917, as if the 97 intervening years had never existed.

So Lydia became Liliuokalani's confidante—Lydia her first born *hanai*, Lydia whom she had lost to *haole* ways through Ida Pope, Lydia the only one left of pure Hawaiian blood whom Liliuokalani felt she could trust. It was to be Lydia's *aloha* to tell Liliuokalani's story of the Hawaiian *alii* from 1838 to her death, which Liliuokalani felt would be soon.

She made strange statements to Lydia, such as, "the overthrow of the government was a small thing; it was a symptom of the disease abroad in the land and thus became inevitable." Not just, not fair, not right, but inevitable.

Liliuokalani spoke enigmatically that "as the morning shadow lies behind one as he faces the sun it is the shadow [the darkness] of the future that comes to rest full upon the person at noon day; then it relentlessly moves on to the shadow of the past—even if it is before one—and is the future."

Despite this "inevitability" her cry, "What have I done that was so wrong that I should lose my country for my people?" showed the paradox of human reason that even when one knows of the slow inevitable move of destruction and even while one still stands firm in right, why does destruction come any way? Job wrestled with this question: "A good and just man," who met disaster after disaster. He was a man who stood firm by his concept of his highest right—his God, as she had done by her concept of *moi wahine*.

Yet in the midst of his inner conviction that he had not sinned, his "friends" insisted he had. So Liliuokalani was tormented until she began to see clearly the slow giant foot steps of the past tread over her generation and their heritage until there was nothing left. "And it will happen again," she prophesied.

(Even in the 1970's Lydia Aholo still did not completely understand her words but she knew "they must be told.")

While Liliuokalani wrestled with a conscience instilled by her missionary Royal School training that was to remain all her life in conflict with her *Aloha* God, who was "too pure eyes to behold evil," who could make scarlet sins white in an instant, her tragic human life went on.

Always seeking for that act of forgiveness, she soon found opportunity for a "public example." No Hawaiian desires "public display" of his *aloha,* but when the material and tangible become overlords of the spiritual and intangible, it appears that the evidence must be seen.

Shortly after the "Hawaiian clans," as the newspapers called them, had brought their *aloha* to Liliuokalani and received her into all the societies, thus displaying the tremendous last step of unity among Hawaiian, the United States declared war on Germany on April 11, 1917.

On April 21, 1917, Liliuokalani, a frail lady of seventy-eight, but straight-backed and firm in resolution walked out the front door of Washington Place and ordered the American flag raised over Washington Place for the first time since her mother-in-law's death a quarter of a century earlier. In 1849 Mrs. Mary Dominis had replaced the Hawaiian flag with the American flag when Anthony TenEyck, American Commissioner, had named the home and declared that there "would always be a piece of America on Hawaiian soil," the *Outlook* reported. In 1891, upon assuming the throne, Liliuokalani had replaced the American with the Hawaiian flag. This gesture, then, "was her final reconciliation to the annexation of her country by the United States . . . that she permitted the American flag to be raised over her home for the first [sic] time. The news that Hawaiians had been killed in the progress of the German submarine campaign was the deciding factor in persuading her to take this step."[14]

Liliuokalani was reported to say, "In the past one hundred years Hawaiians have never shed—nor caused blood to be shed—for their own desires. If now their lives are lost it is to be under a different flag." Whether she said it or not—it was true.

With her final act of forgiving it would seem that life might give her

LILIUOKALANI IN HER LAST YEARS

a respite, but it was not so. Death was again on her doorstep. The test that came to Liliuokalani on July 8, 1917, must have had a finality of earthly loss that only she could understand.

The breach between her and Sybil had grown wider, and when Aimoku became ill in early July and was sent to Queen's Hospital, Liliuokalani sent Lydia to see him; she herself was too ill to leave Washington Place. When Lydia arrived, Sybil refused to allow her to see Aimoku.

Lydia reverted to childhood and returned to the queen: "The queen immediately sent orders that I should be allowed to see him." Standing by Aimoku's bed he called her by the names he had used in letters about her to the queen:[15] "You are her namesake,—'Little sister'—be kind to her."

All the Hawaiian remorse flooded Lydia for the wasted years when her pride had kept her from her *hanai*. Pride, one of the greatest sins of the Old Hawaiian *alii*, had been hers. She had "done her duty," as a good *haole*. She had done her work well in positions she had held. She had cared for her ill sister and loved her sister's children—among them the to-be famous Hawaiian singer—Alfred Apaka.[16] Now, close to forty, she promised she would serve her *hanai* with the *aloha* she deserved.

Aimoku was removed to the McInery home, where he died on July 8, 1917. The *Star Bulletin* and the *Advertiser* carried the news of his death on the inside pages of the papers. In essence they agreed on major points. John Aimoku Dominis was the "ward of the Queen"; his services were to be held at St. Andrews Cathedral. He was thirty-four years old, and died of a "long illness that developed into a hopeless condition. He had received his education first under the care of Mrs. Poakaiulaula Bush, and then at Iolani College, and was a circuit court clerk, assistant to W.O. Smith. Recently he had entered the insurance business. He was leaving a widow and three small children in addition to many dear friends."

The *Advertiser* stated that "Dominis had been considerably in the public eye during the past several years from the fact that he was named by Queen Liliuokalani as one of the Trustees of the Liliuokalani Trust, into which the Queen had placed the greater part of her property and validity of which had been the object during the past two or three years of some sensational litigation which, at one time, threatened to divide the Hawaiian community."

At no time was there a mention that John Owen Dominis, the late husband of the queen, was his father. The *Star* ventured to say that his mother was Mary Pahau, now in her eighties. No mention was made of

Mrs. Lamiki Aimoku, whom Queen Emma had said could be known as "Mrs. Dominis, as in truth, she is . . ."

On July 7, 1917, Sybil McInerny Dominis took her three children and left Washington Place. She made her home temporarily with Rev. and Mrs. Leo Kroll, until she finally moved to the home of her parents in Kahala.

Sybil said the queen was too ill to have three small children around her. Yet the "temporary move" speaks more of a further sudden decision resulting from a break with Liliuokalani. For one who adored children as Liliuokalani did, it is difficult to believe she would have been "disturbed by them."

Lydia came daily, and Lahilahi Webb remained with Liliuokalani—now alone with her greatest struggle. Although she had forgiven and forgiven those who had sinned against her, she had not yet forgiven herself.

"What did I do that was so wrong?" she pleaded again and again with Lydia for an answer, "That I should lose my country for my dear people? Find out for me—and tell them."

Daily she reminisced, struggled for an answer, and studied I Kings, Chapter 21. Herein she read of the strong Ahab, king of Samaria, who desired a small plot of ground owned by Naboth for a garden of herbs. He offered "exchange" or money. Consistently Naboth replied, "The Lord forbid it me, that I should give the inheritance of my fathers unto thee." Then Jezebel, the wife of Ahab, wrote letters in the name of Ahab "and sealed them with his seal." She requested that the sons of Belial bear witness against Naboth, declaring he had blasphemed against God and the King. "And the men of his city, even the elders and the nobles who were the inhabitants of his city, did as Jezebel had sent unto them . . . They proclaimed a fast and set Naboth on high among the people." The children of Belial came, bore witness against him, and stoned him to death.

Ahab now went to take possession of the little vineyard that Naboth had refused to give or sell him. Then Elijah came to tell him the dogs would take precedence over him. When Ahab "humbleth himself," his sins were forgiven but the prophecy remained: "I will not bring evil in his days, but in his sons days will I bring the evil upon his house."

She saw a parallel between herself and the overthrow of her country.

In September Liliuokalani insisted Lydia return to Oberlin. There she could learn how to tell the queen's story as it had been entrusted to her. It was *aloha* and "aloha could be a heavy burden." Lydia carried it with her for fifty-two more years.

While Lydia was at Oberlin Queen Liliuokalani of Hawaii died at Washington Place on November 11, 1917. "I was never with her when she needed me," Lydia said on one of those tearful days almost sixty years later.

Newspapers and magazines the world over carried the news that on November 11, 1917, the Queen of Hawaii died. Exactly one year later Armistice Day was declared—a day that would have been as appropriately declared for her life as it was for World War I. Armistice: "A temporary cessation or suspension of hostilities by mutual consent; a truce." More appropriately to the lexicographer Liliuokalani, perhaps the form *sta*, from which *armistice* comes, would have been important. As her old friend and mentor Abraham Fornander would have known, *"Sta"* has no special cultural value but attests the richness of tradition: "To stand," not sit or lie, but to stand.[18] *Onipaa,* could also mean to stand firm.

The Hawaiian papers gave full reports of the queen's death and funeral, omitting a few details that give the finishing touches to the portrait of Liliuokalani, an Hawaiian *alii*.

Several weeks before Liliuokalani died the red fish appeared in the Hawaiian waters.

> Hawaiians do have their superstitions, as have all other races, but fear of the dead or anything suggestive of the departed are not among their superstitions, which are really traditions based on occurrences of nature that to them portend of some future event to which they look calmly forward with little evidence of fear. So often have Hawaiians predicted coming events that it is difficult for old foreign residents to be skeptical of their prophecies.
>
> As is well known, the more ancient Hawaiians predicted the passing of an *alii*—someone of royal blood—a few months ago, when school after school of little red fish began to come into the island bays from the deep sea. Only on rare occasions does this happen, and Hawaiians always look upon their coming as a sign that an alii is to pass to the great beyond.

Curtis Stewart, a psychic researcher in Hawaii as well as Don Blanding[19] told of the red fish and the natives who said "the Queen shall die," long before the reports hit the newspapers. Liliuokalani, long a good newspaper subject, was now worth several days of speculation, including speculation on her wills of which there seemed to be two.

Lydia Aholo was at Oberlin but her stepmother, Mrs. Aholo, took her place for the funeral arrangements. Lahilahi Webb was by the queen's bedside, and "Poni" lay "on the floor of the great koa bed." Poni was Liliuokalani's dog. "She loved all dogs, but Poni best," said Colonel Iaukea. "The name 'Poni' means coronation. The dog is king." Perhaps Liliuokalani's ironic humor decided the dog was indeed king. It was unlikely she did not remember the story of Naboth.

When the white fish replaced the red fish, by Nature, the queen was dead, and so it was pronounced by her doctor, on November 11, 1917. As was the custom the body of Liliuokalani was removed at midnight "under the fitful gleam of torches, emblematic of the Kalakaua Dynasty" from Washington Place to Kawaiahao Church where it was to lie in state. Liliuokalani was at the time a baptized Mormon;[20] she was a regular attendant at the Episcopal Church, but she was to lie in state at the Missionary Church.

The *Star Bulletin* recorded:

> The hundreds of watchers who had been waiting for this event, some of them for hours, saw first a procession of soldiers from the national guard, who were followed by four torch bearers, men wearing the short yellow and red capes of the chiefs of high order. Next came a group of *kahili* bearers, women in black holokus, and more men wearing the short capes.
>
> After this, immediately preceded and followed by the tabu sticks that marked the limits through which none but the elect could pass, came the slow-moving hearse with its royal burden. More *kahili* bearers followed, and immediately behind them, supported on either side by two strong men, an old, old woman in a white *holoku* dragged her time-tired feet, and chanted in a high, thin treble a '*mele*,' telling of Her Majesty's virtues and the good that had been done by her house.
>
> Long before midnight, in fact as early as 10 o'clock in the evening, the steps of Central Union church were packed full, and the streets approaching Washington Place were lined with people, all quiet, all solemnly waiting, a silence that was almost oppressive, the passing of the last of Hawaii's queens from her last home. Many automobiles held high army officers and their wives, but the crowd was made up of all classes and races.
>
> Just before midnight policemen cleared the streets of cars and people, but after the procession had passed, followed by hundreds of Hawaiian people who seemed really a part of the funeral cortege,

many of the spectators found their way to Kawaiahao Church to witness the entrance into the church.

At the vestibule the *kahilis* were lowered until they almost touched the steps, then were lifted upright, to continue the rhythmic motion that will not cease for a single minute until the body is taken from the church next Saturday night.

The long vigil, which is broken into two-hour watches, is physically very trying, as no word nor smile must pass between the watchers, and no movement is allowed of any part of their body, except the arms, as the *kahilis* are kept in motion. Except for chants or wailing, the silence is never broken.

The crown Liliuokalani had never been allowed to wear in life was placed, at her request, on her head as she lay in state. She was dressed, as was her custom after the overthrow of her country, in black, a holoku of silk brocade.

At the end of the week, after she had lain in state properly embalmed at Kawaiahao Church, her steel casket was carried to Iolani Palace Throne Room. It was placed inside a second casket of koa wood trimmed in the same. The crown was then removed from her head and placed on top of the casket. She had never been "crowned" queen: before such coronation could take place, the P.G.'s had moved quickly to have her dethroned.

Her religious funeral services were conducted in what might be the epitome of ironic "forgiveness," because Rev. Henry Parker, the man who had defamed her name and character, as well as her brother's, from the Kawaiahao Church missionary pulpit from 1886 through 1895, now officiated. He shared honors with her beloved Henry Bond Restarick and Rev. Leopold Kroll of the St. Andrews Cathedral. Military and civilian honors, as well as Hawaiian, attended the queen. From the oldest to the youngest—the children from all the schools she loved so well—all followed the procession that bore the catafalque to the Royal Mausoleum. The newspapers covered eight pages to describe in detail every person and organization that mourned the queen. It is doubtful there was any in all of Hawaii that was not represented.

The Poolas, bearers of the catafalque, were dressed in white and each wore a small cape of red and yellow.

Two long lines of rope bound with black and white ribbon, formed the harness. Just before the coffin was removed from the throne room, the *poolas* formed a double line, each man taking hold of the rope. After the ceremonies at the entrance to the palace were over, they began their steady march to the mausoleum. The catafalque, draped in black and trimmed with narrow lines of white, rolled slowly behind the marchers. A large canopy of black was supported by four posts, and at the four corners, on top, were black plumes. Before the *poolas* moved out of the palace grounds, torches of *kukui* nuts, bound in *ti* leaves, were lighted, a final honor to the royal dead.

The commercial, progressive *haole* were at their posts also.

> Several motion picture cameramen were perched on the small ticket booths which were to have been used for selling tickets to the bleachers. It was decided Saturday night (because of the thorough indignation of the Hawaiians) to abandon the proposed selling of bleacher seats, and the booths were used only for refunding money to early purchasers. An operator from the Jesse Lasky Film Company held the vantage point atop the booth directly opposite the main gate of the capitol grounds, while beside him was another movie camera man. Inside the grounds were two more motion picture operators. These cameramen will ship the films of the funeral cortege to the mainland, where they will be released throughout the United States, an invaluable record of the solemn and historic occasion.

Liliuokalani was now recognized as a part of "historic America" and a part of "Americana."

Although "Aloha Oe" was sung frequently during Liliuokalani's funeral services, it is now known that she requested it never be sung at any funeral service but one.[21] "It is a love song," she said. "Not a funeral dirge." The one funeral at which she had stated it could be sung was Henry Berger's, whom she had presented with a medal in 1916 which was engraved in Greek and read, ambiguously, "To my beloved server." At that time she also gave him the title of "The Father of Hawaiian Music."

The funeral song, because it best symbolized her life, should have been "The Queen's Prayer." But it was not included in the service.

When Liliuokalani's body was moved from Washington Place to Kawaiahao, a whirlwind swept before them. Again when the casket was moved to the Iolani Palace another whirlwind swept the way, several newspapers noted, as "incidental."

Then as the catafalque was guided into the yard of the mausoleum an event occurred that the newspapers of the time ignored, but which two men who were there attested to, as did Lydia Aholo, and later news accounts.

As the catafalque was guided into the yard of the Mausoleum beneath the widespread branches of the monkey pod trees a curious thing happened. Perhaps the carriage lurched, perhaps it was the wind that swept down the Pali, swaying the huge branches, but the Hawaiian crown atop the plumed canopy was struck from its place and rolled in the dust. At this sign a shudder, a frightened whisper swept the long line of mourners:

The Hawaiian rule is at an end. The crown is at the feet of the *haole.*[22]

But some heard a soft whisper of Liliuokalani, the embodiment of an Hawaiian *alii* from 1838-1917, swept on the trade winds: "There will always be a Hawaii as long as there is *aloha* and forgiveness."

Epilogue

In 1887, the beginning of the end for the Hawaiian Monarchy, King David Kalakaua wrote in the Introduction to his *Legends And Myths of Hawaii*:

> In the midst of these evidences of prosperity and advancement it is but too apparent that the natives are steadily decreasing in numbers and gradually losing their hold upon the fair land of their fathers. Within a century they have dwindled from four hundred thousand healthy and happy children of nature, without care and without want, to a little more than a tenth of that number of landless, hopeless victims to the greed and vices of civilization. They are slowly sinking under the restraints and burdens of their surroundings, and will in time succumb to social and political conditions foreign to their natures and poisonous to their blood. Year by year their footprints will grow more dim along the sands of their reef-sheltered shores, and fainter and fainter will come their simple songs from the shadows of the palms, until finally their voices will be heard no more for ever. And then, if not before — and no human effort can shape it otherwise — the Hawaiian Islands, with the echoes of their songs and the sweets of their green fields, will pass into the political, as they are now firmly within the commercial system, of the great American Republic.

In 1917, after Queen Liliuokalani had seen the end of the Hawaiian Monarchy, she said to her *hanai* daughter, Lydia K. Aholo:

> I could not turn back the time for the political change, but there is still time to save our heritage. You must remember never to cease to act because you fear you may fail.
>
> The way to lose any earthly kingdom is to be inflexible, intolerant, and prejudicial. Another way is to be *too* flexible, tolerant of *too* many wrongs, and without judgment at all. It is a razor's edge. It is the width of a blade of pili grass. To gain the kingdom of heaven

is to hear what is not said, to see what cannot be seen, and to know the unknowable—that is *Aloha.* All things in this world are two: in heaven there is but One.

In 1978 Lydia K. Aholo, the queen's *hanai* daughter, and a woman of pure Hawaiian blood and spirit, despaired in her hundredth year.

Hanai could not turn back the clock, but time has sped backward on its own. There is greater provocative nakedness on the beaches today than ever before. The foreign songs have only eroticism, no spiritual meaning. The dances are lascivious; there is no sacred interpretation. The land is ravaged by concrete monsters; neither the sea nor the sky is safe from destruction. There is racism—which our ancestors never knew. And neither the young nor the old can lie down by the wayside in safety as Kamehameha I decreed. There is nothing Hawaiian left; it is all *haole* now.

It is not known that *aloha* spoken with indifference is blasphemy, and *mahalo* in an ungracious mouth is profane.

Until we free our people from misconceptions of Hawaiian heritage, we will continue to be victims of an ignoble past.

In 1983 for the Centennial Jubilee Year of the Kalakaua Dynasty, when as never before the members of the whole world need to know each other, only Susan Marr Spalding's words seem appropriate:

> Two shall be born the whole world apart
> And speak in different tongues and have no thought
> Each of the other's being and no heed.
> And these o'er unknown seas to unknown lands
> Shall cross, escaping wreck, defying death;
> And all unconsciously shape every act
> And bend each wandering step to this one end,
> That one day out of darkness they shall meet
> And read life's meaning in each other's eyes.

Susan Marr Spalding (1841-1908)

Footnotes

This work is based primarily on the queen's diaries, memoirs, and letters; secondarily on historical documents, histories, personal published accounts, newspapers, biographies and personal interviews.

Book titles not cited in full are found in the Bibliography.

Throughout the notes, the author has chosen to use numerous abbreviations for oft-cited references. The abbreviations are as follows:

AH—Public Archives of Hawaii
BPBM—Bernice P. Bishop Museum Library
HHS—Hawaii Historical Society Library
HS—*Hawaii's Story by Hawaii's Queen, Liliuokalani*
HMCS—Hawaiian Mission Children's Society (Library)
L.C.—Library of Congress
L. Diary—Liliuokalani's diary
LKA—Lydia K. Aholo tapes
BPRO—British Public Records Office

Newspapers:
P.C.A.—*Pacific Commercial Advertiser*
D.B.—*Daily Bulletin*
H. Gaz.—*Hawaiian Gazette*
P. of P.—*Paradise of the Pacific*

Private Collections:
D.M.B.—David M. Bray
R.P.M.—Ruth Prosser McLain
H.H.—Hui Hanai (Liliuokalani Children's Center)
L.T.—Liliuokalani Trust
C.S.—Curtis Stewart
D. B-W.—Don and Leilehua Berger Billam-Walker
Stodieck—Betty Dole Stodieck

PART I —

Chapter 1: "Hawaii Nei"

[1] Hawaii *here* spoken by one who was *there.*

[2] Kamehameha had numerous wives. Keopuolani was his "sacred wife," and the children of her body were the designated heirs to the throne.

[3] The Hawaiian language does not form its plural by adding "s," but sometimes through voice inflection (Pukui, *et al, Hawaiian Dictionary*).

[4] Aumakua: family gods; ancestors who had become gods and now gave protection to the family. The aumakua could take the form of an animal, or a plant, or a rock.

[5] Malo, *Hawaiian Antiquities,* pp. 128-29.

[6] Queen Kamamalu, Kamehameha II's half-sister-wife, dramatically boarded the ship for England saying that her chant was a farewell to her country, forever, leaving the people with the strong belief that she was prophesying her own death and that of the king, not an unusual prophecy among the Hawaiians.

[7] Solomon Meleuha, *Famous Songs.* Introduction; also, "Hulilauakea's Explanation": "The Hawaiian singer deals in parables . . . there'is a double meaning in every sentence; often in every word. Each poem is an anagram; highly perfected . . . Mele Hula speaks the unspoken language that only those familiar with the swiftly changing accent, subtle tone of meaning can hope to understand . . . the missionaries had little concept of the nuances of the high chiefs' language . . ."

[8] The missionaries continued to call Hawaii "The Sandwich Islands;" another name was "Owhyee."

[9] The complete story of Nahienaena is found in Sinclair, *Nahi'ena'ena: Sacred Daughter of Hawai'i.*

[10] Fornander, *Collections,* Vol. 6. pp. 438-50.

Chapter 2: "The Infant Alii"

[1] Juliette Cooke wrote: "Today I learned that Lydia [Liliuokalani's Christian name] was born on September 2, 1838, not December 25 . . ." Richards, *School,* 89, 109.

[2] Keohokalole had 10 children (*HS*): only seven are recorded; it is assumed that three died in infancy; two died young, Kaiminaauao and Anna Kaiulani (HMCS). Four came into Hawaiian government (royalty): David Kalakaua, Leleiohoku, Likelike, and Liliuokalani.

[3] The great-grandmother of Liliuokalani, Ululani (18th Cy) was a *haku mele* composer; supposed to have commemorated Kamehameha I's great feat in moving the Naha stone, by which his leadership was established. Newspapers reports re: *Naha Stone.*

[4] There were two levels of usage of the Hawaiian language, the high chief's and the commoner's. "The language stereotyped by the missionaries is the vulgar language of the people and the chiefs spoke a better and more refined language expressing more distinctions and states, which is now dying out and being replaced by a lower one." Henry L. Sheldon, *P.C.A.* to Fornander, editor, of *Polynesian;* Fornander's later studies proved this concept to be true.

[5] The missionaries required the Hawaiians to learn to read and write, *pala-pala,* before they were allowed to "learn" religion or *pule-pule;* many of the high chiefs objected; although they wished to learn to read and write, they did not wish to have it mandatory to become "Christian." It was a clever ploy on the part of the missionaries, for much that is read is believed. See accounts of Kaahumanu; also Judd, Malo and Kamakau, as well as Missionary Journals, (HMCS).

6 L. Diary, January 19, 1891—"No name at all . . . more royal."

7 "Greetings to Mr. Cooke: Here is our thought to you. That you become teacher for our royal children. You are the one to teach wisdom and righteousness. This is our thought to you." (Dated June 1, 1839; signed by the king, but also by Keohokalole, Liliuokalani's mother).

8 The first-born girl child was usually given to the maternal grandmother; the first-born boy child to the paternal grandmother; thereafter, the children were given in *aloha* to other chiefs. The custom existed among the lesser chiefs and commoners as well as among the *alii*.

9 The lands in 1838 belonged primarily to Kamehameha III and to those high chiefs and *haole* who had received land from his father, Kamehameha I, his brother, or himself. Other lands had been given to the missionaries for churches, schools, and homes.

10 In her diary, Liliuokalani wrote of the death of her "beloved" *kahu* who had "tended [her] for many years in [her] youth."

11 The particular "name song" given here is thought by some scholars to have been written later by Liliuokalani's "friends." However, according to custom, and by the spelling of the name, it is much more likely Konia wrote it.

12 Chamberlain's *Journal*, (June 1, 1839).

13 Auhea was better known as Kekualuohi; the Cookes used the name of Auhea. She served as premier for Victoria, who succeeded Kinau, at age two years.

14 *HS*, p. 7.

15 Richards, *School*.

16 Several legends of Hina exist; another one may be found in Kalakaua's *Legends*.

17 Malo, *Antiquities*.

18 c.s., Tape #2:12.

19 LKA, Tape #1:15.

20 John Ii was a teacher, trustee, and adviser of the Royal School; a prominent figure among the missionaries and the royal family. See Introduction of Ii, *Fragments of Hawaiian History*.

21 For a complete report on Laplace incident, see Kuykendall, I, pp. 151-388.

22 What the earlier explorers had heard as "r" became "l," and "t" became "k"—as in *Honoruru* versus *Honolulu* and *Tamehameha, Kamehameha*. Words were frequently "made up," such as *leka* for *letter*.

23 The early chiefs—Kaahumanu and others—were willing to learn *pala-pala*, to read and write; but not contribute to the accuracy or full meaning of the translated language; and the missionaries were not scholars in this sense, but stayed with the basics.

24 Pauahi—The missionaries decreed that the High Chiefs' children should have last names; it was more "civilized." Moses, Lot, Liholiho and Victoria took the last name of Kamehameha. Bernice already had the Hawaiian name of Pauahi, a "family name" of a famous ancestress, from Konia's side. Because the Cookes were not quite sure of Lydia's status under *hanai* (which they did not understand), they chose the term "foster,"—a totally erroneous concept. But as she already had been baptized as "Lydia Paki," she became to them "Lydia Paki, foster sister of Bernice Pauahi."

Chapter 3: "The Royal School"

1 Bernice Pauahi, daughter of Konia (Laura) and Paki (Abner).

2 Emma Rooke, *hanai* daughter of Dr. T.C.B. Rooke.

3 Black and Mellen, *Pauahi Bishop*. Later Charles Cooke, one of the wealthiest men in

Hawaii, refused to lend the "impoverished Queen Liliuokalani" money, and helped in the overthrow of the country.

4 Richards, *School.*

5 *HS,* p. 5.

6 Menehunes were a legendary race of small people who worked at night, building fish ponds, roads, and temples, much like the Irish "Little People."

7 Mrs. Clarence Cooke; Richards, *School;* LKA, Tape #8:43.

8 See Part II, Chapter 2, note 9. However, all teaching was done in English; everything possible was done to "forbid" the Hawaiian language among the royal children; this was, of course, impossible.

9 Richards, *School;* Report to High Chiefs. Lt. Charles Wilkes stated in his United States Expedition report that the Cookes had the true Christian spirit; however he was "not satisfied that the education was proper for princes. The system tends towards Republican forms." (L.C.)

10 Gerrit P. Judd: "The King (Liholiho, now Kamehameha IV) educated by the Mission most of all things dislikes the mission. Having been compelled to be good when a boy, he is determined not to be good as a man. Driven out by morning prayer meeting, Wednesday evening meeting, monthly concert, Sabbath school, long sermons, and daily exhortations, his heart is hardened to a degree unknown to the heathen." (*Polynesian,* February 7, 1852.)

11 Richards, *School.*

12 Newspaper accounts (1871); Richards, *School.*

13 The "romance over the fence" story, popularly told, comes from *HS;* however, actual accounts in Richards, *School,* letters, and Julius Palmer Coll. (Boston) contradict this story.

14 Moses Collection (BPBM).

15 Kaiminaauao, *HS* p. 8.

16 The marriage of Jane Loeau and John Jasper proved to be disastrous and later influenced Konia's and Paki's objections to Bernice Pauahi's marriage to Charles Reed Bishop. Richards *School;* newspaper sources.

17 Ida Pope letter; (August 16, 1889, R.P.M.). "I have never known anyone who is more dedicated to her *hanai* and retainers' children's birthdays than the Princess (Liliuokalani); Lydia tells me that it is because of her own disappointment while at the Royal School when she was only eight or nine . . ."

18 See Introductions to Malo and Kamakau.

19 Mellen, *Heritage.* Kathleen Mellen based her books on personal interviews, but this is an oft-quoted statement, and undoubtedly accepted as valid.

20 Keohokalole was one of the councillors.

21 Rev. William Richards: "The foreign relations of this government must soon be placed on a more substantial basis, or the nation as such must soon cease to exist." Envoys were sent to the United States, Great Britain, and France. (Kuykendall, Vol. I.).

22 Francis Johnson, an American merchant, wrote: ". . . The English and American residents cannot agree at all . . . they cause most of the trouble . . . not the natives . . ." Johnson to Larkin, Bancroft Library, Univ. of Calif., Berkeley.

23 The British foreign office was generally confused, but made so further by correspondence with Daniel Webster, Secretary of State in the United States, who had given the Hawaiians a diffident interview and had expressed only the disinterest of the Tyler Administration to the Hawaiian problem. Unfortunately, the "disinterest" was construed in the British Foreign

Office as a denial by the United States of Hawaiian independence. (Kuykendall, I.)

24 On February 25, 1843, Kamehameha III, said bitterly: "I will give no more. Let them take the Islands," but he added the stipulation that the "Hawaiian government would make every effort to get back its sovereignty." These were tragically prophetic words for Liliuokalani in 1893. The entire Paulet affair is skillfully detailed in Kuykendall, I, pp. 185-302.

25 Through the Ladd Company fiasco Kamehameha III had offered islands to both the United States and Belgium (both had ignored the offer). See Kuykendall, I, pp. 251-55, for a full explanation.

26 Judd, *Informal History*.

27 Judd, *Informal History*.

28 Korn, *Victorian Visitors*, p. 170.

29 Wilkes report: "The royal children were surprisingly well mannered."

30 LKA, Tape #12:36.

31 Liholiho had not left for England until after the death of his mother Keopuolani, as it would have indicated "disrespect" to leave his mother's side for pleasure or desires of his own.

32 Richards, *School*.

PART II —
Chapter 1: "The Young Alii of the Royal School"

1 *HS*; Zambucka, *Ruth*; also letters (AH).

2 Maurice Beckwith followed his two brothers as principal of the Royal School; teacher at Fort Street School; Bancroft Library, UCB; Rep. of Min. of Pub. Inst. 1848-1854.

3 Letters, Archives, Mills College; Keep, *Four Score*; *Mills Quarterly*; James, *Mills*.

4 Letters: (Beckwith), Bancroft Library, UCB.

5 *HS* pp. 11, 17.

6 House Reports, 27 Cong., 3 Sess., #94.

7 Ten Eyck to Buchanan, desp. private and confidential (L.C.).

8 Korn, *Victorian Visitors* is an excellent source for material pertaining to this period: letters of Lady Franklin and Sophia Cracroft.

9 Kent Collection (now at BPBM).

10 Newspaper account *Lunalilo* (AH).

11 *HS*, p. 331.

12 Mellen, *Heritage*, p. 12.

Chapter 2: "Romance in the New Royal Court"

1 Gregg, diary, May 19, 1856 (AH).

2 Julius Palmer, *Memories of Hawaii*.

3 Statement made by Henry Berger (D. B-W.). Newspapers of the time.

4 Kalakaua Coll. (AH).

5 "Dear Brother" (H.H.).

6 *HS*, p. 15.

7 Korn, *Victorian Visitors*.

8 New England Genealogical and Hist. Soc., Boston.

9 *Polynesian*, November 13, 1856.

10 It is unlikely his leg was broken, but no doubt seriously hurt.

Chapter 3: "Problems in the Royal Household"

1 Emma, letters, (AH).

2 Neither the "legal" wives of Kamehameha II or III had any children. It has been thought that Kalama, wife of Kamehameha III, had a child that died at birth.

3 *HS* p. 18.

4 *Ibid.*, p. 19.

5 *Ibid.*

6 Korn, *Victorian Visitors.*

7 The name "Holt" appears as "Hart" in the New England Genealogical and Historical Society records, as "Holt" in Hawaiian records.

PART III —
Chapter 1: "High Chiefess Lydia Paki Marries"

1 John and Liliu letters, (H.H.); quotes not otherwise identified are from *HS.*

2 Dominis-Hart letters (AH).

3 See note 1, this chapter.

4 Kalakaua-Liliu letters (H.H.): Armstrong Journal (AH).

5 Korn, *Victorian Visitors.*

Chapter 2: "Governor Dominis and Lady"

1 James, *Mills;* Keep, *Four Score.*

2 Misc. Letters, Mills College Arch.

3 *Ibid.*

4 Kuykendall. II, pp. 106-14.

5 *Ibid.*, pp. 115-34; *P.C.A.*, July, August, 1864.

6 As there were not sufficient books to go around, the Hawaiians stood around their teachers, and some tried to read upside down. (D. B-W.).

7 Twain, *Letters from Hawaii.*

8 The law of the splintered paddle came from the story that in a conflict a commoner had hit Kamehameha and splintered a paddle. Rather than retaliate, Kamehameha I forgave him, giving the law that the young and old should be able to lie down on the wayside in safety.

9 Malo, *Antiquities;* Mellen, *Heritage,* p. 26.

10 *Ibid.*

11 Unpublished Song Book, (H.H.). Also AH, BPBM.

12 Damon, *Koamalu.*

13 Fornander, *Collections,* "Introduction."

14 Davis, *Fornander.*

15 Korn, *Victorian Visitors.*

16 L. Diaries of 1886 and 1887 (AH, BPBM).

17 Liliuokalani, "Bits of History," (AH).

18 *HS*, p. 32.

19 A different account appears in *HS.* This account is taken from "Bits of History," (AH).

20 Not to be confused with Prince Albert, son of Queen Emma and Kamehameha IV.

21 Later Mrs. Charles B. Wilson.

22 The "grass skirt" was introduced from Tahiti in 1882.

Chapter 3: "Last of the Kamehamehas"

[1] So described in many missionary writings, e.g. Damon, *Koamalu*.

[2] See articles re: Kamehameha V in HHS. Kuykendall, II.

[3] Dominis papers (AH).

[4] The legislative assembly "elected" the king from only the high chiefs.

[5] Kuykendall, II, p. 244.

[6] Schofield and Alexander to Belknap, May 8, 1873, Sen. Ex. Docs., 52 Cong., 2 Sess., #77, pp. 150-54.

[7] Kuykendall, II, p. 256; (Pvt. coll.).

[8] Bishop to Pierce, November 14, 1873, FO Letter Book 52, (AH).

[9] Kuykendall, II, pp. 259-60.

PART IV —
Chapter 1: "The New Royal Line"

[1] Letters (Emma), (AH).

[2] Annual, 1875, Retrospect (BPBM).

[3] Nordhoff, *Northern Calif.*, (preface).

[4] Armstrong, Journal, *Trip Around the World* (AH).

[5] Letters (Emma), (AH).

[6] Kuykendall, III, p. 23.

[7] It was the custom to "read law" with an attorney rather than attend Law School.

[8] Kalakaua Coll., (AH).

[9] Letters, (Emma), (AH).

[10] Kaiulani was baptized in the Episcopalian Church as Victoria Kaiulani Kalaninuiahilakalapa Kawekuii Lunalilo Cleghorn, with Princess Ruth as her god-mother. Ruth at that time presented the land of Ainahou to Kaiulani.

Chapter 2: "Birth of Princess Liliuokalani"

[1] L. Diary, January 19, 1891.

[2] Letters, "Dear Hannah" (Hannah Evans), (Pvt. Coll.).

[3] *HS*, p. 58.

[4] "Bits of History." (H.H.); also Iaukea, *P. of P.*, "Land to Kapiolani," June, 1926.

[5] Mills' doctor; Keep, *Four Score*.

[6] Tennyson's poem of Kapiolani.

[7] "Notes," Mills College Arch.

[8] Thrum's *Annual*, 1880-1881.

[9] Ralph S. Kuykendall attempts to explain the confused situation in the three volumes of *The Hawaiian Kingdom*.

[10] In *HS*, Liliuokalani implies Ruth was not there. Zambucka quotes the newspapers supporting and denying ("suppressing") Ruth's activities.

[11] *HS*, p. 91.

[12] Letters (Emma), (AH).

[13] See newspapers for varying accounts of Mary Hale Pahau, Mary Purdy Pahau, Mrs. Mary (John) Lamiki Aimoku, and Mary Purdy.

[14] Trouseau Letter, Bancroft Library, U.C.B.; Tisdale, Mills Arch.

[15] D. B-W.

[16] Letter, Lyman Lby., Hilo.

Chapter 3: "Coronation & Trial"

The material on the coronation in this chapter is taken from newspapers of the time.

[1] Newspapers: *Ko Hawaii Pae'aina; Ku'oku'a* (May 15-November 10, 1883); *Elele; Po'akula* (Translated by Dorothy Barrere).

[2] Ii, John, *Fragments.*

[3] Kapukauinamoku (Hawaii historian), (*P.C.A.*), December 11, 1955: Song of Eternity series. Other sources from pvt. coll.

[4] Gibson, diaries.

[5] *P.C.A.*, September 3, 1886.

[6] Bella Lyman to Liliu, Lyman Lby., Hilo; Liliu's diaries, 1885, 1886, 1887, (AH, BPBM).

[7] See Kuykendall for full explanation, vol. III.

[8] L. Diary, 1886.

[9] *HS*, p. 107.

[10] L. Diaries, 1886-87, (AH, BPBM).

[11] Kamehameha I: "Increase their needs, not their wants."

[12] L. Diary, October 16, 1884.

[13] LKA, Tape #8:268.

[14] Black and Mellen, *Bishop.*

[15] Korn, *Victorian Visitors*, "Intro."

[16] L. Diary, October 16, 1888.

Chapter 4: "Grief and Joy"

The material in this chapter is taken largely from Liliuokalani's 1886 diary (BPBM), from Henry Berger's diaries and journals in the Hawaii State Archives, and private collection of Leilehua and Donald Billam-Walker (Leilehua Berger Billam-Walker is the daughter of Henry Berger).

[1] LKA, Tape #18:619.

[2] L. Diary, June 18, 1886, (BPBM).

[3] Bella Lyman to L., September 10, 1886 (Kalanianaole.-Coll.-BPBM); Lyman House Museum, Hilo; L. Diary, February 26, 1886, May 3, 1886 (BPBM).

[4] D. B-W.

[5] Davis, *Fornander*, pp. 265-67.

[6] *HS*. Kitty Townsend Wilson had been brought up in her home. Blount Report, p. 368.

[7] Armstrong, microfilm, Mich. Univ.

[8] Palmer, *Memories*, pp. 7-8.

[9] *Nua Lehua* and *Nua Aupuni* have had a variety of translations, but all indicate a "love relationship," "sweetheart," according to Hawaiian language scholars. The diaries, including the 1886 one, were taken from her home in 1895 at the time of her imprisonment, and supposedly not recovered until 1945. However, Lorrin Thurston refers to passages in other diaries when he wrote his book in 1936. It is highly possible the archivist to whom the diaries were given in 1946 erased portions felt "injurious to the Queen."

10 The *Hooponopono* (simplified from Lynette Paglinawan) was a family council having eleven steps to the solution of a problem: 1) Statement of problem and "gathering of emotional and spiritual forces" to help; 2) prayer—not that God solves the problem— but that wisdom is attained to solve it; 3) the injurer and the injured are bound together by doing and ' blaming"; 4) the "grudge" or "fault" must be released from the one holding it; 5) a period of silence and reflection; a quieting; 6) both injurer and injured must be released for each feels the pains of the other; 7) the "layers" of the trouble are talked about from all points of view; 8) forgiveness takes place after confession and repentance; 9) *Kala-kala*, "I unbind you from the wrong and thus I may also be unbound from it"—release of all parties; 10) the wrong is separated from the person; 11) a prayer or act of completion.

11 LKA, Tape #34:110.

12 Liliuokalani Coll., German notebooks, (AH).

13 Newspapers of 1893-1898 (see later chapters).

14 Astrology, mental-sciences, seances, spiritual searches were all rampant in both Europe and America, from Rasputin in Russia, to respectable religious organizations of Ellery Channing and Mary Baker Eddy. All Hawaiian life had a deep underlying spiritual basis, sometimes confused with psychic or mental phenomenon.

Chapter 5: "Queen's Invitation"

1 Elizabeth Longford, *Queen Victoria: Born to Succeed* (New York, 1964).

2 L. Diary, January 15-16, 1886 (BPBM).

3 Letters, (H.H.)

4 Kalama's *hanai* son; illegitimate son of Kamehameha III.

5 L. Diary, February 3, 1887, (AH).

6 Newspaper notice, *P.C.A.*, February 16, 1887.

7 LKA, Tape #1:68.

8 Korn, *Victorian Visitors.*

9 L. Diary, March, 1887, (AH).

10 LKA, Tape #4:109: "I think the Queen also found it was hard to live among royalty and not be royal."

11 L. Diary, April 11, 1887, (AH).

12 "She [Queen Liliuokalani] was fond of quoting poets," Palmer to E.P. Gould, Boston Pub. Lby. See "Variegated Leaves," a typescript of *HS* partially edited, (AH).

13 LKA, Tape #12:50.

14 *HS* and "Variegated Leaves," (AH).

15 *HS.*

16 LKA, Tape #18:31.

17 *HS*, p. 129; L. Diary, 1887, (AH).

18 *Ibid.*, p. 133; *Ibid.*

Chapter 6: "A Queen's Jubilee"

Much of the material in this chapter is based on Liliuokalani's two accounts: her diary of 1887 and her *Hawaii's Story*, pages 128-176, coupled with her reminiscences to her *hanai* daughter, Lydia K. Aholo, on Tape #16.

1 *HS*, p. 136.

2 *Ibid.*, p. 137; LKA, Tape #16:81.

[3] *HS*, p. 142.

[4] *Ibid.*, p. 143.

[5] Letters, June 14, 1887, (AH).

[6] *HS*, p. 153.

[7] *Ibid.*, pp. 162-63; (L. Diary).

[8] Fornander to Dominis, February 3, 1886; April 5, 1886, Kalanianaole Coll., (BPBM). Fornander had pleaded with Dominis for a personal meeting, sending him his exact schedule. Dominis managed to get to Lahaina when Fornander was sure to be absent.

[9] Letters from Dominis to Kamehameha V, n.d., (AH).

[10] *HS*, p. 169.

[11] *Ibid.*, p. 155. The reference is to the sun shining on Kalakaua and Kapiolani at their coronation.

[12] *Ibid.*, p. 126.

[13] *Ibid.*, p. 172.

[14] L. Diary, July 23, 1887, (AH).

[15] *San Francisco Chronicle*, later summation, September 5, 1887.

[16] LKA. Tape #10:23-52.

Chapter 7: "Life Under the Bayonet Constitution"

[1] Kuykendall-Day, p. 151.

[2] It was told that Kalakaua sold the opium license twice; T. Aki, it was purported, had bought the opium license from Kalakaua for $71,000, but another Chinese gentleman had out-bid him and had been given the license. The $71,000 had never been returned. Although Junius Kaae was accused of the action, with or without the consent of the king, Kalakaua accepted the blame and the debt. (Hawaii *Gaz.*, May 17, 1887.)

[3] Robertson; LKA, Tape #6:04-28. Also see later diary references.

[4] Kuykendall-Day, p. 171; interview with Gibson's grandniece; Bailey, *Royal . . . Minister*.

[5] "As for himself, he thought the constitution (1887) was a good one . . . [of the new cabinet] . . . They are safe, conservative men . . . The kingdom will prosper under their guidance." *San Francisco Chronicle*, August 7, 1887.

[6] RPM; Ida Pope ("A review of the times") in a letter of March 8, 1910; Bailey, *Royal . . . Minister*.

[7] L. Diary, November 4, 1887, (AH).

[8] *Ibid.*, November 20, 1887.

[9] *Ibid.*, December 12, 1887.

[10] *Ibid.*, December 26, 1887.

[11] LKA, Tape #8: 406.

[12] See documents re: Thurston, (AH), L.C., and Maine Hist. Soc., Portland, re: J.L. Stevens.

[13] U.S. Commissioned in Hawaii in 1853. The Hawaiian Patriotic League pretending to want a new constitution, actually wanted a Republic. (Kuykendall, III, pp. 421-528.)

[14] L. Diary, January 14, 1888.

[15] *Ibid.*, January 21, 1888.

[16] *Ibid.*, January 15, 1887.

[17] *Ibid.*, February 4, 1885.

[18] *Ibid.*, February 4, 1888.

[19] LKA, Tape #1:10-21.

[20] BPBM: 1878, 1885-86, 1892, 1898, 1901-03, 1906; AH: 1887, 1889, 1894.

[21] LKA, Tape #29:8; New England Hist. and Geneol. Soc. (Jones).

[22] L. Diary, February 12, 1887.

[23] Wodehouse to F.O., #11, 13, 14; September 27, Oct. 25, 29, 1889; BPRO, F.O. 58/242.

[24] *Friend*, December, 1889.

[25] Carter to D.K. Confidential, November 9, 1889, (AH).

[26] For complete explanation, see Kuykendall, III, pp. 466-67.

[27] The following is paraphrased directly from LKA, Tape #5:10-87.

[28] *P.C.A., D.B., Friend;* January 29, February 12, 1891; *San Francisco Chronicle,* January 28, 1891, with Mrs. Dr. Buli-King.

Chapter 8: "A King is Dead; A Queen is Born"

[1] *HS*, p. 209.

[2] "Dear Lois . . . ," (RPM).

[3] LKA, Tape #20:24.

[4] "Song Book," (AH).

[5] *HS*, pp. 213-19.

[6] Letters (Stevens), Maine Hist. Soc. Lby. (Portland).

PART V —

Chapter 1: "The New Queen"

[1] Kuykendall, III, p. 480. *Scribners Mag., V:* 634. Girls were sent to St. Anthony's Priory as well as Kawaiahao Seminary at her expense.

[2] Fornander, notes by Liliuokalani, (AH).

[3] Letters of Liliuokalani to Bernice Cook (1898-1904). Courtesy of P. Kawanakoa.

[4] Translated by Liliuokalani; there are later translations.

[5] Malo, Kamakau, John Ii.

[6] Moses explained a similar situation in the Bible.

[7] Ii; Kamakau; Malo.

[8] *HS*, p. 206.

[9] Letters: Liliuokalani from Ashford (AH).

[10] *HS*, pp. 206-07.

[11] Letters to Queen Liliuokalani, (AH; BPBM, 1891).

[12] USDS Dipl. Hawaii, Vol. xxv, #20.

[13] House Ex. Docs. 53 Cong., 2nd Sess., #48, p. 78.

[14] Trouseau: Blount Report, p. 1218.

[15] Charles Reed Bishop letters, (BPBM).

[16] Ida Pope to "Dear Popes," letter May 3, 1891, (RPM).

[17] *H. Gaz:* and other newspaper clippings, courtesy of "Cleghorn Scrapbook," T.A.K. Cleghorn.

[18] *HS*, pp. 220-23.

[19] Johnny Wilson, an unpublished ms.

[20] S.B. Dole letters to "Dear George," May 10, 1891, courtesy of Betty Dole Stodeick.

[21] *Ka Leo O Ka Lahui,* HHS Library, newspaper file (726:18).

[22] Wilson later retracted the statement, saying it was he who had suggested smashing the presses. A.S. Cleghorn Coll., (AH).

[23] LKA, Tape #28:419.

[24] Liliuokalani Coll. (letters), (AH).

[25] Wilson to J.O. Carter, Eleanor Porter Gould.

[26] Newspapers: *P.C.A., H. Gaz.,* & others.

27 *HS*, p. 225.

28 Diary entries: 1886, 1888, (AH), (BPBM).

29 Liliuokalani Coll., (BPBM).

30 L. Diary, 1906, (BPBM).

31 Letters to Kaiulani, Cleghorn Coll., (AH).

32 *P.C.A.*, September 9, 1891, p. 2, col. 1.

33 Notes of Thrum's *Annual*.

34 *Annual*, (BPBM).

35 Mott-Smith to Parker, December 30, 1891, Treaty Doc., (AH).

Chapter 2: "Year of the Longest Legislature"

1 L. Diary, February 17, 1892, (BPBM).

2 *P.C.A.*, March 23, 1935, (E.A. Taylor).

3 L. Diary, January 15, 1892, (BPBM).

4 *Ibid.*, January-February, 1892, (BPBM).

5 Albertine Loomis, "Longest Legislature," (HHS), 71st Annual Report, 1962.

6 *HS*, p. 231.

7 Letter to Kaiulani, Cleghorn Coll., April, 1892. (AH).

8 *P. of P.*, June, 1892, (AH).

9 Kuykendall, III, p. 532. Thurston gave the date as July, but as the interview was held in June, Kuykendall is probably correct in assuming it was January.

10 L. Diary, February 17, 1892, (BPBM).

11 *P. of P.*, June, 1892, (AH).

12 Thurston, *Memoirs*, p. 232.

13 Loomis, "Longest Legislature;" also see Loomis, *Stars*.

14 L. Diary, July 29, 1892, (BPBM).

15 Loomis, among others.

16 *P.C.A.*, June 2, 1892.

17 L. Diary, July 10, 1892, (BPBM).

18 *P. of P.*, June, 1892.

19 L. Diary, July 19, 1892, (BPBM).

20 From correspondence in the Hawaiian State Archives. A detailed article appeared in *The Hawaiian Journal of History*, Vol. 10, 1976.

21 Liliuokalani Coll., letter, (AH).

22 *Ibid.*

23 *San Francisco Examiner*, 1898.

24 The cabinet should be chosen by the opposition.

25 James Robertson, "Some Historical Truths," (HHS).

26 Harvard Univ.

27 *P.C.A.*. October 18, 1892.

28 S. Bishop to G. Gilman, October 19, 1892, (BPBM).

29 Wodehouse to Rosebery, (BPRO), Dispatch #21.

30 *Ibid.*, Dispatch #301.

31 *Ibid.*, Dispatch #20, November 9, 1892.

32 L. Diary, July, 1892, (BPBM).

33 *D.B.*, December 29-31, 1892.

34 Robertson; Kuykendall, III, p. 576.

Chapter 3: "Three Days of Revolution"

1 Testimony of January, 1894 (Senate Reports 53; Vol. I, pp. 325-525).

2 Special Dispatch: *San Francisco Examiner,* January 4, 1893.

3 L. Diary, August 2, 1892, (BPBM).

4 *HS*, p. 279.

5 S.B.D. to "Dear George," January 12, 1893 (Stodieck).

6 L. Diary.

7 Blount Report, p. 487.

8 LKA, Tape #12:17.

9 Kuykendall, III, p. 585.

10 Newspapers: *P.C.A., D.B., Ka Leo O Ka Lahui.*

11 *Ibid.*

12 A day or two later Glade and Wilcox were replaced by Ed Suhr, a German, and John Emmeluth, an American.

13 Alexander, *Later Years.*

14 Thurston to Foster, February 21, 1893, USDS Hawaiian Legation, Vol. IV; Blount, p. 496.

15 Thurston to Foster (preceding note).

16 Blount, pp. 1029, 1031, 1035, 1037.

17 *P.C.A.,* January 17, 1893.

18 Senate Reports, 53 Cong., 2 Sess., No. 227, Vol. I, pp. 540-73.

19 Blount, pp. 118, 590.

20 Newspapers: see note 10 above.

21 *D.B.,* January 17, 1893.

22 Blount, pp. 57-58; Morgan Report, pp. 546-47.

23 Foreign Relations, 1894, II, 538.

24 Letter to Kaiulani, (AH).

25 LKA, Tape #24:38.

26 Kuykendall, III, p. 597.

27 Dole Coll., (AH); Morgan Report, pp. 547-49; Blount, pp. 439-40, (L.C.).

28 Morgan, pp. 624-25, (L.C.).

29 Blount, p. 477; Morgan Report, pp. 546-47, (L.C.).

30 *P.C.A., D.B.,* 1893, (BPBM).

31 L. Diary, January 18, 1893, (AH).

Chapter 4: "The Provisional Government"

Material for this chapter has been taken from voluminous correspondence and reports found in the Library of Congress in Washington, D.C., and the British Public Records Office in London and from newspapers across the United States. In general the account is also supported by Kuykendall, Vol. III.

1 C.R. Bishop to W.D. Alexander, November 9, December 26, 1893, Alexander Coll., (HMCS), and other places.

2 L. Diary, 1893, (AH).

3 Kuykendall, III, p. 617; also foregoing p. 605-17.

4 Newspapers; Kuykendall, Vol. I, II, III.

5 Congressional Record; newspapers of U.S. and Hawaii.

6 Letters between Wodehouse and Davies, (BPRO).

7 Stenographic Report of Interview with Foster, February 21, 1893; usds Hawaii.

8 Davies, "Some Bits of History," (*P.C.A.*), April 6, 1896.

9 Letter (Pope), "Dear Lois," (rpm).

10 The following account is from the unpublished papers of Daddy Bray (dmb Coll.). *Also,* L. Diary, previously quoted.

11 L. Diary, entries February 5-7, 1893, (ah).

12 Cong. Rec., 52 Cong., 2 Sess., pp. 1207-08.

13 Mrs. Walter Lamar, *Biography of Blount,* (1936).

14 Kuykendall, iii, p. 625.

15 Dr. Hyde had previously engaged in such defamation of character of Father Damien that he had roused the anger and violent newspaper exchanges with Robert Louis Stevenson. In 1890 Stevenson published "Father Damien: An open letter to the Rev. Hyde."

16 L. Diary, April 27, 1893, (ah). Some of this attitude appeared also in the *Examiner.*

17 L. Diary, July 15, 1893, (ah).

18 See Blount Report, (l.c.).

19 Kuykendall, iii, p. 630.

20 Material on this interview has been taken from Willis' later reports, the queen's diary entries of the same day, and *HS.*

21 Sister Theresa "confidential" to "Dear Friend," Episcopal Church Arch.; (Pvt. coll.).

22 Kuykendall, iii, p. 646.

Chapter 5: "Mrs. Dominis vs. the Queen"

1 Lyon papers, ms. gr. 38 acc. 77.55 (Hilo-Lyman Lby. Also l.c.).

2 *Ibid.,* ms. gr. 37.28. (Also l.c.).

3 Letters (Dole), "Dear George," February 3, 1894, courtesy Betty Dole Stodieck.

4 Thompson, "Memoirs," courtesy of Mrs. Clarence Cook.

5 L. Diary, May 7, 1894, (ah).

6 Daws, *Shoal of Time,* p. 281.

7 New York *Sun,* February 26, 1894.

8 Dole Coll., (Stodieck). She never received a reply (lka).

9 Stevens' Coll., Maine Hist. Soc., Portland.

10 State doc. #1318; 1384.

11 Letter from "Willie," (hhs).

12 *P. of P.,* 1926.

13 L. Diary, July 13, 1894, (ah).

14 Dole Coll., (Stodieck), July 26, 1894.

Chapter 6: "The Queen is Arrested"

1 Thrum's *Annual*; *P.C.A., D.B.*

2 Loomis, Cooke, Judd, and others.

3 See earlier chapters.

4 Cleghorn, Bishop, others.

5 See Loomis, *For Whom Are the Stars,* pp. 103-86, for a lengthy detailed account of the counter-revolution.

6 Dole Coll., "Dear George," (Stodieck).

7 Thurston, *Memoirs,* p. 273: "I cannot but believe that it [the overthrow] was the result of fate, foreordained from the beginning of things."

8 Letters (Dole), "Dear George," September 30, 1895, (Stodieck).

9 *HS*, pp. 267-72.

10 Many accounts of Lot Lane: Loomis, Daws, Mellen, newspapers.

11 Loomis, *Stars*, p. 183.

12 "Rebellion of 1895" by Ed Towse, *Hawaiian Star*, 1895, 2nd ed., (HHS).

Chapter 7: "On Trial"

Voluminous legal documents can be found in the court records and some material reprinted in the Hawaiian Historical Society regarding the trial. Many interpretations have been placed upon the decisions by the differing attorneys. The following is merely a factual report based on the above documents of what happened during the trials of the "rebels" against the Republic, with emphasis on Liliuokalani.

1 Fed. Ct. P.O. Law #3612; re: Kalanianaole.

2 Towse, "Rebellion," (AH).

3 L. Diary, December 28, 1894, (AH).

4 Winthrop and Greenleaf, "On Evidence," (BPBM).

5 Towse, "Rebellion."

6 These diaries were seized by L.A. Thurston on January 16, 1895, and in 1946 were placed in the Archives of Hawaii, catalogued as part of "Liliuokalani's Tin Box."

Chapter 8: "A Queen Imprisoned"

1 Daws, *Shoal*, p. 283.

2 Letters (Dole), "Dear George," March 20, 1896, (Stodieck).

3 Daws, *Shoal*, p. 290-91.

4 Damon, *Dole*.

5 Dole Letters, November 21, 1896.

6 Thurston, *Memoirs*, pp. 517-63.

7 L. Diary, January 2, 1887, (AH).

8 See pages on regency, herein.

9 L. Coll., (AH).

10 *Independent*, (Honolulu).

11 *HS*, p. 292.

12 *HS;* Mellen; Damon; LKA, Tape #15:8-24.

13 Fragments of each of the mentioned writings can be found in the AH, BPBM, HMCS, H.H., under "Liliuokalani Collection."

14 D. B-W.

15 Liliuokalani Trust papers (HH).

16 This translation is taken from AH, as are others in this book.

17 The *Hui Hanai Song Book*, soon to be published, will have differing translations and interpretations. It is not the primary function of this book to delve deeply into the song material.

18 Letters (Hannah Evans), Liliuokalani Trust (HH).

19 *Memoirs*, Johnny Wilson, courtesy Poomaikalani Kawananakoa; LKA, Tape #20:26.

20 LKA, Tape #6: "She was an extremely religious woman. In prison she began to wonder if . . ."

21 Fragrance of the royal chief: Paoakalani was the name of the queen's home near the street with that name in Waikiki.

22 Sung every Sunday in the Kawaiahao Church.

23 *HS*, pp. 293-94.

24 Episcopal Church Records, Honolulu.

PART VI —
Chapter 1: "The 'Ex-Queen' Becomes an Author"

1 *HS*, p. 307.

2 Boston *Globe*, December 26, 1896.

3 L. Diary, March 25, 1893, (AH).

4 Letters (H.H.), (AH).

5 Opera, *Honolulu Magazine*, 1977.

6 *Independent*, Honolulu, December 29, 1897.

7 Howard Lby., Harvard Univ.; Boston Lby., Rare Book Room Coll.

8 Letters, Kalanianaole Coll., (BPBM).

9 Diary, 1898, (BPBM); Letters, (H.H.).

10 J.O. Carter Letters (H.H.). (D. B-W.).

11 LKA, Tape #1:20.

12 Letters, to Iaukea, Liliuokalani Trust (HH).

13 Letters (H.H.), (D. B-W).

14 The Clarke family were prominent Christian Science practitioners and were careful that no misrepresentation should be made (*C.S. Journal*, 1893). Christian Science textbook is by Mary Baker Eddy, *Science and Health with Key to the Scriptures*.

15 Letters (Pope), "Dear Lois," May 26, 1898, RPM.

16 Webb, *Kaiulani*.

Chapter 2: "Queen Lil"

1 Webb, *Kaiulani;* also newspapers.

2 LKA, Tape #18:26-38.

3 Liliuokalani Coll. #17, (H.H.), December 19, 1898; (AH).

4 Letters (AH).

5 L. Diary, December 25, 1901, (BPBM).

6 *Ibid.*, October 20, 1901.

7 Letters (H.H.), March 24, 1899.

8 Washington papers; Daws, *Shoal.*

9 *World Today*, July-December, Vol. 3, 1902, p. 1950.

10 L. Diary, 1901 (BPBM).

11 Petition to President-elect Taft; L.C.; H. Fed. Cts., LKC 933a.

12 *P. of P.*, Iaukea, (re: Kapiolani).

13 Aikanaka lands.

14 L. Diary, February 1, 5, 1901, (BPBM).

15 L. Diary memoranda (AH), (BPBM).

16 L. Diary, August 12, 1902, (BPBM).

17 LKA, Tape #31:84.

18 Liliuokalani Letters, (H.H.)

19 Kaipo Letters: Liliuokalani Trust; (D. B-W.).

20 Thompson, "Memoirs."

21 Letter Collection: Liliuokalani (AH).

22 1901: May 14, (BPBM). The code was broken by Don Britton, Honolulu, and Roberta Sprague, Honolulu. Copies exist in AH and BPBM.

23 Dorothy Barrere, (BPBM).

Chapter 3: "Portrait of a Hawaiian Alii"

1 Letters: Liliuokalani Trust (HH).

2 (D. B-W.) (HH).

3 Circuit Court Records: Probate #5122.

4 LKA, Tape #34:21; Inez Ashdown, interview.

5 See Bibliography, herein.

6 LKA, Tape #16:12.

7 San Francisco *Examiner*, July 6, 1910.

8 Thompson, "Memoirs."

9 LKA, Tape #10:36.

10 *Ibid.*, #16:24.

11 Circuit Court Records, 1900-21, No. 5322-5324, Equity 1748.

12 Thurston, *Memoirs*.

13 *HS*, p. 119.

14 *The Outlook*, November 21, 1917.

15 Letters: Liliuokalani, 1902 (HH).

16 Alfred Apaka's son, Alfred Apaka II, was to be known worldwide as a Hawaiian singer. His son, Jeff Apaka, carries on the tradition.

18 *American Heritage Dictionary*, Appendix.

19 Blanding, *Hula Moons*, p. 266; Stewart, Curtis, unpublished papers.

20 Certificate of Baptism, ms. cl. 4277, Salt Lake City, Utah.

21 LKA, Tape #8:56; Berger files, (D. B-W.).

22 Blanding, *Hula Moons*, p. 266; Stewart, Curtis, unpublished papers.

Bibliography

In addition to the following reference works, the author obtained considerable information from several collections in private hands. Though their locations are not given, out of respect for the wishes of those parties, they are cited in the notes when used.

Adler, Jacob. *Claus Spreckels*. Honolulu: 1969.

Alexander, Dr. William D. *History of Later Years of the Hawaiian Monarchy and the Revolution of 1893*. Honolulu: 1896.

Armstrong, W.N. *Around the World with a King*. New York: 1904.

Bailey, Paul. *Hawaii's Royal Prime Minister: The Life and Times of Walter Murray Gibson*. New York: 1980.

Bingham, Hiram. *A Residence of Twenty-one Years in the Sandwich Islands*. New York: 1848.

Black, Cobey, and Kathleen Dickenson Mellen. *Princess Pauahi Bishop and Her Legacy*. Honolulu: 1965.

Blanding, Don. *Hula Moons*. New York: 1930.

Bryan, Edwin H., Jr. *Ancient Hawaiian Life*. Honolulu: 1938.

Craft, Mabel. *Hawaii Nei*. San Francisco: 1899.

Damon, Ethel M. *Sanford Ballard Dole and His Hawaii*. Palo Alto: 1957.

———. *Koamalu*. Honolulu: 1931.

Davis, Eleanor Harmon. *Abraham Fornander: A Biography*. Honolulu: 1979.

Daws, Gavan. *Shoal of Time*. Honolulu: 1974.

Dole, Sanford Ballard. *Memoirs of the Hawaiian Revolution*. Honolulu: 1936.

Emerson, Nathaniel B. *Unwritten Literature: The Sacred Songs of the Hula*. First published in *Bulletin of Bur. of Am. Thenology*, 38, Washington, D.C.: 1909. (Reprint by Tuttle.)

Fornander, Abraham. *Collection of Hawaiian Antiquities and Folklore.* 1887. *Memoirs of the Bernice P. Bishop Museum,* Vol. 6 (1919).

Fuchs, Lawrence H. *Hawaii: Pono.* New York: 1961.

Furnase, J.C. *Anatomy of Paradise.* New York: 1947.

Ii, John Papa. *Fragments of Hawaiian History.* (Trans. by Mary Kawena Pukui, ed. by Dorothy Barrere.) Honolulu: 1963, 1973.

James, Elias Olan. *The Story of Cyrus and Susan Mills.* Stanford, Ca.: 1953.

Judd, Gerrit P., IV. *Hawaii: An Informal History.* New York: 1961.

Kalakaua, David. *The Legends and Myths of Hawaii.* New York: 1888. (Reprint by Tuttle, 1972.)

Kamakau, S.M. *Ruling Chiefs of Hawaii.* Honolulu: 1964.

Keep, Rosalind A. *Four Score and Ten Years.* Oakland, Ca.: 1946.

Korn, Alfons. *The Victorian Visitors.* Honolulu: 1958.

————. *News from Molokai.* Honolulu: 1976.

Krout, Mary H. *Memoirs of Hon. Bernice Pauahi Bishop.* New York: 1908. (Reprint by Kamehameha Schools Press, 1958.)

Kuykendall, Ralph S. *The Hawaiian Kingdom.* 3 vols. Honolulu: 1938, 1953, 1967.

Liliuokalani. *Hawaii's Story by Hawaii's Queen.* Boston: 1898.

Loomis, Albertine. *For Whom Are the Stars?* Honolulu: 1976.

Malo, David. *Hawaiian Antiquities.* (Trans. by Dr. Nathaniel B. Emerson.) Honolulu: 1951, 1971.

Meleuha, Solomon. *Famous Songs.* Honolulu: 1914.

Mellen, Kathleen Dickenson. *Hawaiian Heritage.* New York: 1963.

————. *An Island Kingdom Passes.* New York: 1958.

Melville, Leinani. *Children of the Rainbow.* Wheaton, Ill.: 1969.

Nordhoff, Charles. *Northern California, Oregon and the Sandwich Islands.* New York: 1874.

Palmer, Julius A. *Memories of Hawaii.* Boston: 1897.

Pukui, Mary K., and Samuel Elbert. *Hawaiian Dictionary.* Honolulu: 1977.

————, and E.S. Craighill Handy. *The Polynesian Family System in Ka'u, Hawaii.* Rutland, Vt.: 1972.

————, E.W. Haertig, M.D., and Catherine Lee. *Nana I Ke Kumu*. 2 vols. Honolulu: 1972.

Richards, Mary Atherton, ed. *The Chief's Childrens' School*. Honolulu: 1937. (Reprint by Tuttle.)

Sinclair, Marjorie. *Nahi'ena'ena: Sacred Daughter of Hawaii*. Honolulu: 1976.

Stewart, Charles. *A Residence in the Sandwich Islands*. Boston: 1839.

Thompson, Ulrich. "Memoirs of Hawaii." Unpublished manuscript in the private collection of Mrs. Clarence Cooke.

Thrum, Thomas G. *Hawaiian Almanac and Annual*. Honolulu: 1874-1917.

Thurston, Lorrin A. *Memoirs of the Hawaiian Revolution*. Honolulu: 1936.

Towse, E. *The Rebellion of 1895*. Honolulu: 1895.

Tregaskis, Richard. *The Warrior King*. New York: 1973.

Twain, Mark. *Mark Twain's Letters From Hawaii*. (Grove Day, ed.) New York, 1966.

Webb, Nancy and Jean Francis. *Kaiulani: Crown Princess of Hawaii*. New York: 1963.

Zambucka, Kristin. *Princess Kaiulani: The Last Hope of Hawaii's Monarchy*. Honolulu: 1976.

————. *The High Chiefess Ruth Keelikolani*. Honolulu: 1976.

Index